Wesley, Wesleyans, and Reading Bible as Scripture

Wesley, Wesleyans, and Reading Bible as Scripture

edited by

Joel B. Green
David F. Watson

BAYLOR UNIVERSITY PRESS

© 2012 by Baylor University Press
Waco, Texas 76798-7363

All Rights Reserved. No part of this publication may be reproduced, stored in a retrieval system, or transmitted, in any form or by any means, electronic, mechanical, photocopying, recording, or otherwise, without the prior permission in writing of Baylor University Press.

Cover Design by Nita Ybarra
Cover image ©Shutterstock/Compos Sui

Library of Congress Cataloging-in-Publication Data

Wesley, Wesleyans, and reading Bible as Scripture / Joel B. Green and David F. Watson, editors.
  p. cm.
 Includes index.
 ISBN 978-1-60258-627-7 (pbk. : alk. paper)
 1. Wesley, John, 1703-1791. 2. Bible—Hermeneutics. 3. Wesleyan Church—Doctrines. I. Green, Joel B., 1956- II. Watson, David F., 1970-
 BX8495.W5W53 2012
 220.088'287—dc23
                        2012007963

CONTENTS

List of Abbreviations   vii

Introduction   xi

PART I: Wesley on Scripture

1. John Wesley—"A Man of One Book"   3
   Randy L. Maddox

2. Scripture as a Means of Grace   19
   Kenneth J. Collins

3. Reading Scripture, the Literal Sense, and the Analogy of Faith   33
   Robert W. Wall

4. Wesley as Interpreter of Scripture and the Emergence of "History" in Biblical Interpretation   47
   Joel B. Green

PART II: The Nature and Authority of Scripture among Wesleyans

5. Scripture among African American Methodists   65
   Reginald Broadnax

6	Scripture among Hispanic Methodists *Justo L. González*	81
7	Scripture among Korean Methodists *Meesaeng Lee Choi and Hunn Choi*	99
8	Scripture and Divine Revelation *William J. Abraham*	117
9	A Wesleyan Understanding of the Authority of Scripture *Douglas M. Koskela*	133
10	The Holiness of Scripture *Jason E. Vickers*	147
11	Scripture as Canon *David F. Watson*	161

PART III: Wesleyans Working with Scripture

12	Scripture and Social Ethics *D. Brent Laytham*	179
13	Can We Speak of a Wesleyan Theological Hermeneutic of Scripture Today? *Steven J. Koskie*	195
14	Reading Scripture for Christian Formation *Elaine A. Heath*	211
15	The Place of Scripture in Worship *Karen B. Westerfield Tucker*	227
16	The Place of Scripture in Preaching *Michael Pasquarello III*	245
17	Scripture and Evangelism *Laceye Warner*	263

Notes	277
List of Contributors	325
Index of Names	327
Subject Index	334

LIST OF ABBREVIATIONS

General Abbreviations

AV	Authorized Version
cf.	*confer*, compare
ch(s).	chapter(s)
ed(s).	edition(s); edited by
e.g.	*exempli gratia*, for example
esp.	especially
i.e.	*id est*, that is
KJV	King James Version
n.p.	no pagination
NRSV	New Revised Standard Version
NT	New Testament
OT	Old Testament
St.	Saint
v(v).	verse(s)
viz.	*videlicet*, "namely," "that is"
vol(s).	volume(s)

Modern Literature

IDB	*Interpreter's Dictionary of the Bible*. Edited by George A. Buttrick. 4 vols. Nashville: Abingdon, 1962.
KB	Kingswood Books

Letters (Telford)   *The Letters of the Rev. John Wesley, A.M.* Edited by John Telford. 8 vols. London: Epworth, 1931.
NIB   *New Interpreter's Bible.* Edited by Leander E. Keck. 12 vols. Nashville: Abingdon, 2003.
OTL   Old Testament Library
TDNT   *Theological Dictionary of the New Testament.* Edited by Gerhard Kittel and Gerhard Friederich. 10 vols. Grand Rapids: Eerdmans, 1964–1976.
Works   *The Bicentennial Edition of the Works of John Wesley.* Nashville: Abingdon, 1980–.
Works (Jackson)   *The Works of John Wesley.* Edited by Thomas Jackson. 14 vols. Grand Rapids: Zondervan, 1958.

Biblical Literature, including the Apocrypha

Gen	Genesis	Amos	Amos
Exod	Exodus	Obad	Obadiah
Lev	Leviticus	Jonah	Jonah
Num	Numbers	Mic	Micah
Deut	Deuteronomy	Nah	Nahum
Josh	Joshua	Hab	Habakkuk
Judg	Judges	Zeph	Zephaniah
Ruth	Ruth	Hag	Haggai
1–2 Sam	1–2 Samuel	Zech	Zechariah
1–2 Kgs	1–2 Kings	Mal	Malachi
1–2 Chr	1–2 Chronicles		
Ezra	Ezra	Add Esth	Additions to Esther
Neh	Nehemiah	Bar	Baruch
Esth	Esther	Bel	Bel and the Dragon
Job	Job	1–2 Esdr	1–2 Esdras
Ps(s)	Psalm(s)	4 Ezra	4 Ezra
Prov	Proverbs	Jdt	Judith
Eccl	Ecclesiastes	Ep Jer	Epistle of Jeremiah
Song	Song of Songs	1–4 Macc	1–4 Maccabees
Isa	Isaiah	Pr Azar	Prayer of Azariah
Jer	Jeremiah	Pr Man	Prayer of Manasseh
Lam	Lamentations	Sir	Sirach (Ecclesiasticus)
Ezek	Ezekiel	Sus	Susannah
Dan	Daniel	Tob	Tobit
Hos	Hosea	Wis	Wisdom of Solomon
Joel	Joel		

Matt	Matthew	1–2 Thess	1–2 Thessalonians
Mark	Mark	1–2 Tim	1–2 Timothy
Luke	Luke	Titus	Titus
John	John	Phlm	Philemon
Acts	Acts	Heb	Hebrews
Rom	Romans	Jas	James
1–2 Cor	1–2 Corinthians	1–2 Pet	1–2 Peter
Gal	Galatians	1–3 John	1–3 John
Eph	Ephesians	Jude	Jude
Phil	Philippians	Rev	Revelation
Col	Colossians		

INTRODUCTION

Everyone would agree that Scripture was central to John Wesley's life and thought. Beyond general statements like this, though, consensus would be more difficult to reach. What was his doctrine of Scripture? In what sense for Wesley was the Bible authoritative? What was the status of Scripture in relation to other theological sources and norms? What interpretive approaches influenced his reading of Scripture? Wesley never discoursed on the doctrine of Scripture, at least not in print. Nor did he follow in the path of some in his day, who wrote handbooks for the practice of biblical interpretation; this is true even if we find in more than one place in his writings what might have been the précis of a Wesleyan handbook of this nature. Whether in his view of things or in that of those who opposed his theological emphases or both, the theological and ethical fault lines were apparently to be found elsewhere. He wrote extensively, therefore, on a host of theological and ethical questions—predestination, economics, Christian perfection, and slavery, for example—but not on the nature and interpretation of the Bible. With regard to Wesley's understanding and use of Scripture, then, students of Wesley might engage in the work of recovery, making plain what was implicit in Wesley's practices and assessing his commentaries, sermons, hymns, letters, and the like for their assumptions about the nature and role of Scripture in faith and life.

As interesting and important as this kind of spadework might be, it does not address our most central questions. True, some will approach Wesley like modern archeologists seeking to find a defense of their own approach to Scripture. Likewise, others will assess Wesley by today's late modern or postmodern standards and, finding him lacking, dismiss his ongoing significance. For such persons, the potential for learning from Wesley will have been cut short prematurely. For others—indeed, for us—the issues are not so straightforward. We want to know what it means to stand in the Wesleyan stream. We want to know what it means to work and live out our theology as heirs to a Wesleyan legacy. We want to know what informs and shapes his theology of Scripture and his interpretive practices. We want to explore how Wesley engaged in theological interpretation of Scripture. But we do so because we know that these teach us something about what it means to be Wesleyan.

If this is a ressourcement, though, it is a critical one. As the essays gathered here demonstrate easily enough, sometimes we embrace Wesley and at other times we question him. This is not surprising, since we map our ecclesial and theological frontiers with different lines and colors than Wesley would have used to chart his time and place. Even so, integral to our need for reformulations and new assessments is a deeper need for allegiance to the very tradition we seek to extend. We return to Wesley not so that we can learn better how to march lockstep to his cadence or match his gait with our own. Rather, we identify ourselves within ecclesial communities whose theological and social character has been formed by Wesley and in which the Wesleyan theological tradition is embodied and even now continues to develop. We seek to be Wesleyan in the sense that our work is shaped by the assumptions and practices that comprise Wesley's theological craft. We learn from Wesley how certain beliefs about the nature of Scripture and how certain commitments regarding the overall message of Scripture might shape our own serious, engaged reading of the Bible as Wesleyans. And so we learn how we might exhibit in our interpretive practices and beliefs the distinctive marks of our Wesleyan/Methodist heritage.

This examination of Wesleyan perspectives on Scripture is composed of three interrelated sections. The essays in Part I "Wesley on Scripture" share a historical focus, examining Wesley's use of Scripture within his own eighteenth-century context. Even if those in the

Wesleyan tradition cannot simply mimic the perspectives and interpretive practices of their forebear, their theologies and uses of Scripture should be organically related to Wesley's. Part II "The Nature and Authority of Scripture among Wesleyans" takes as its starting point pivotal issues regarding Scripture at the turn of the twenty-first century and asks how we in the Wesleyan tradition might address those theological issues. Sometimes those theological issues are heard in a different key when they arise within particular communities of our tradition. In this section, then, we address some of the standard loci of a doctrine of Scripture, such as inspiration and authority, but we also recognize how some of these issues play out among African American Methodists, Hispanic Methodists, and Korean and Korean American Methodists. Contributors to Part III "Wesleyans Working with Scripture" show how working within the Wesleyan tradition shapes one's approach to Scripture in relation to the life of the church.

The Wesleyan movement is complex and varied. It has taken many different forms and generated and encompassed a considerable range of theological perspectives throughout the years. Whatever else it is, however, Wesleyanism at its core is a movement meant to bring about holiness. It is about the work of God in the everyday circumstances of human existence, changing us from the inside out into the people God calls us to be. Scripture, along with prayer and the sacraments, is among the primary means through which God works within us. In the preface to his *Explanatory Notes upon the Old Testament*, Wesley writes that one's reading of Scripture should be closed with prayer, "that what we read may be written on our hearts."[1] Through the Bible, God changes us; we become more Christlike people. The essays in this volume explore some of the myriad ways in which Wesleyans have thought, and continue to think, about God's redeeming work within us through Scripture.

PART I

Wesley on Scripture

1

JOHN WESLEY—"A MAN OF ONE BOOK"

Randy L. Maddox

Engaging Scripture, as a witness to and setting of divine revelation, was central to John Wesley's Christian life and to the spiritual communities that he helped gather and lead. The elderly Wesley stressed this point when reflecting on the early movement at Oxford University:

> From the very beginning, from the time that four young men united together, each of them was *homo unius libri*—a man of one book. God taught them all to make his "Word a lantern unto their feet, and a light in all their paths." They had one, and only one rule of judgment in regard to all their tempers, words, and actions, namely, the oracles of God.[1]

It is characteristic that Wesley's primary focus in this quotation is on the Bible as the rule or guide for Christian practice—and a central means of grace evoking and sustaining that practice.[2] But he also valued it as the rule of Christian belief, insisting that he regulated his theological convictions by Scripture.[3] This role is a bit more prominent in the often-quoted passage from Wesley's preface to the first volume of his *Sermons*, which begins:

> I want to know one thing, the way to heaven—how to land safe on that happy shore. God himself has condescended to teach the way: for this very end he came from heaven. He hath written it down in a book. O give me that book! . . . Let me be *homo unius libri*. Here

then I am, far from the busy ways of men. I sit down alone: only God is here. In his presence I open, I read his Book; for this end, to find the way to heaven.[4]

"A Man of One Book"—and a Thousand Books!

Read in isolation, these quotations might suggest that Wesley relied solely on Scripture (and solely on his private reading of Scripture) in seeking spiritual nurture or considering theological issues. But elsewhere he responded to the claim of some of his lay preachers, "I read only the Bible," with strong words: "This is rank enthusiasm. If you need no book but the Bible, you are got above St. Paul. He wanted others too."[5] That Wesley did not put himself above St. Paul in this way is clear from the books that he owned, read, or consulted through his life.[6] They number well over a thousand volumes and cover the full range of topics in his day—from the history of early Christianity, to medicine, politics, poetry, and more. Significantly, Wesley assigned the same range of reading to his pastoral assistants and to both men and women participating in his Methodist movement.[7]

As Wesley described his practice more carefully in *Plain Account of Christian Perfection*, to be *homo unius libri* is to be one who regards no book *comparatively* but the Bible.[8] This more precise formulation affirms the primacy of authority assigned to Scripture, without setting other books aside. It also hints at Wesley's deep conviction that Scripture is understood most helpfully and faithfully when it is read *comparatively* and *in conference*. The purpose of this essay is to demonstrate this conviction by sketching several aspects of Wesley's practice of reading the Bible. As readers consider this practice, I hope that they will recognize not only Wesley's formative impact on the traditions descended from his ministry but also some elements of wisdom from his example for our present life and vocation. That is, the header for each section describing how Wesley *read* the Bible can also be taken as a suggestion for how to *read* it today.

Read the One Book *Comparatively* in Its Many Embodiments

Consider first the question of the identity of the One Book to be read as Scripture. A clear possible answer for Wesley was the currently "authorized" English translation (commonly called the King James

Version [KJV]). He deeply appreciated this translation, quoting it throughout his life. But he did not confine himself to this embodiment of the One Book. Like his brother Charles, John Wesley studied other English translations as well as translations in German and French. This can be demonstrated most fully for Charles because we have catalog lists of Charles' personal library around 1765.[9] In addition to the KJV (1611), these lists include the New Testament in the English translation of Miles Coverdale, which was the first English version of the Bible authorized for the Church of England by Henry VIII in 1539 (often called the "Great Bible"). Charles also owned an English rendering of Theodore Beza's translation of the New Testament into German (in 1556), along with a German New Testament and the "Geneva Bible" (1560) in French. While much of John Wesley's personal library has been lost, his copy of Luther's German translation of the Bible survives at Wesley's house in London.[10]

Going a step further, the Wesley brothers valued the Bible in its original languages over all later translations. They inherited this emphasis from their father, who once described comparing different translations with the original languages as "the best commentary in the world," and encouraged pastors to use a polyglot Bible that included texts in Hebrew, Greek, Chaldean Aramaic, Syriac, Samaritan, Arabic, Ethiopic, and Persian.[11] While there is little evidence of facility with the other languages, John and Charles were both proficient in Greek and Hebrew. They frequently appealed to these languages in suggesting alternatives to current English renderings of biblical words or phrases. And they equipped themselves to read in this comparative manner. Consulting again the more complete records in Charles' case, his personal library included a Hebrew Testament, two Hebrew Psalters, a copy of the Septuagint (the OT in Greek), and four different Greek versions of the New Testament.

We can identify at least four versions of the Greek NT that John Wesley owned as well.[12] This is particularly significant because John (who tutored Greek as part of his role as a fellow of Lincoln College) was aware that there is no pristine Greek text handed down from the earliest church. Rather, we have multiple manuscripts, with numerous variant readings, which must be read comparatively in seeking the most reliable text. Among the versions that Wesley owned was John Mill's two-volume set, which gathered in footnotes the most complete list at the time of variant readings in these manuscripts.[13]

The Greek NT that John Wesley favored was that of Johann Albrecht Bengel (1734), which is agreed to be the best critical Greek text of his day. Bengel's text corrected the Textus Receptus (the Greek text used for the translation of the KJV) at numerous points. These corrections and other issues had led to a growing number of calls for a new English translation of the Bible and scattered attempts to undertake this task. John Wesley owned a copy of one of the most thorough defenses of the need for a new English translation.[14] This may have encouraged him to venture out when preparing *Explanatory Notes upon the New Testament* in the 1750s. Drawing on his range of resources, Wesley offered his own translation of the Greek text that varies from the KJV in over twelve thousand instances.[15] Most of the variants were modernizations of the English or minor in nature, but some reflect text-critical decisions that remain standard in biblical scholarship. Wesley's translation as a whole reflects the fruit of a lifetime of reading the One Book *comparatively* in its many embodiments.

READ THE ONE BOOK *COMPARATIVELY* WITH SCHOLARLY TOOLS

To study the Bible in its original languages, one needs more than just copies of both Testaments in these languages. Some scholarly tools are also essential. Thus we find Wesley citing or commending standard tools like Johann Buxtorf's Hebrew grammar (1609) and lexicon (1613), and Richard Busby's similar resources for Greek (1663). He even published abridged versions of these for use in the school for children that he started at Kingswood.[16]

Wesley's endorsement of these standard works is significant because it took place in the midst of a debate over Hebrew language materials in particular. The earliest texts of the Hebrew Testament spell words using only their consonants (in part to save space). The oral rendering of the text (with the vowels) was passed down by tradition. During the medieval period, these vowels were inserted into the written text as small marks (vowel points) under the consonant letters. Early in the eighteenth century, John Hutchinson launched a vigorous attack on use of these vowel points. His reasons were largely idiosyncratic, with little historical consideration or justification. In effect, he turned the Hebrew Testament into a "code book" of the secrets of the universe by rendering the consonant stems into often fanciful words and meanings. While Hutchinson's views were broadly challenged by biblical scholars, they gathered influential supporters among a few fellows at Oxford University of High Church persuasion—mainly because these fellows appreciated how Hutchinson used his approach to combat Isaac Newton's philosophy, with its apparent deistic implications.[17] John Wesley was acquainted with several Hutchinsonians, so he had to consider the debate. His conclusion was that Hutchinson's "whole hypothesis, philosophical and theological, is unsupported by any solid proof," and prone to encourage folk to read whatever they please into Scripture.[18]

Put in other terms, Wesley's concern was to avoid idiosyncratic reading of Scripture by reading it *comparatively* with the standards accepted in the community of scholarship on biblical languages. So he relied mainly on long-standard sources, though he was also happy to obtain newly published tools that advanced careful study of Hebrew grammar.[19]

If Wesley stood within the mainstream of his day in debates over linguistic and textual criticism of the Bible, what was his stance regarding the early forms of historical criticism that surfaced in the second half of the seventeenth century? Writers like Thomas Hobbes, Jean Le Clerc, Richard Simon, and Benedict Spinoza began to apply forms of critical analysis used on other literary texts to the various books of the Bible, calling into question traditional assumptions about the authorship of some books, challenging the historical accuracy of certain biblical accounts, and highlighting human dynamics in the long process of canonization. Some advocates of this agenda appeared to reduce the Bible to a mere collection of antiquated human texts.

The response of the vast majority of eighteenth-century Anglican scholars and clergy to these developments was defensive, insisting on the historical uniqueness and accuracy of the biblical accounts.[20] John Wesley generally reflected this response. At the same time, he found that some studies of the customs of the ancient Israelites and the early Christians enriched his reading of the Bible—so much so that he published an abridgment of one study for his lay preachers.[21] This suggests a rudimentary appreciation for insights that can be gained from reading the Bible *comparatively* with its historical and cultural context.[22] That said, the comments that Wesley provides in his *Explanatory Notes* on the OT and NT almost never focus on clarifying the meaning of a text in its original historical context. Rather, as he describes his goal, his comments are intended to give the "direct, literal meaning" and keep the reader's eye "fixed on the naked Bible."²³

Read *Comparatively* the Many Books in the One Book

This might suggest that the meaning of any particular text in the "naked Bible" will always be clear to the faithful reader. As one who had been reading the One Book all of his life, Wesley knew that this is not the case. Returning to the preface for his first volume of *Sermons*:

> I sit down alone: only God is here. In his presence I open, I read his Book; for this end, to find the way to heaven. Is there a doubt concerning the meaning of what I read? Does anything appear dark or intricate? . . . I then search after and consider parallel passages of Scripture, "comparing spiritual things with spiritual." I meditate thereon, with all the attention and earnestness of which my mind is capable.²⁴

Biblical passages are often ambiguous or unclear, and readers must labor to understand many passages. Wesley assumed that this laboring should include reading them *comparatively* with other passages. Those who follow his example will quickly confront the reality that the One Book is a collection of many books. They will likely also become aware that many Christians ignore, deprecate, or even reject certain books within the Book—reducing the range of any comparative reading that they do. What was Wesley's practice in this regard?

The first point to make concerns the scope of the canon, or official list of books that belong in the One Book. The KJV, as published through Wesley's lifetime, included the sixteen books commonly called the Apocrypha. Article VI of the Anglican Articles of Religion affirmed these works as worthy to read "for example of life and instruction of manners," though not as authorities for doctrine. Wesley's father specifically encouraged reading the apocryphal books as aids for understanding the more authoritative books in the canon.²⁵ Thus, it is not surprising to find scattered citations from or allusions to the Apocrypha in Wesley's writings.²⁶ In keeping with the Articles, these are never presented as warrant in doctrinal debate; they typically support appropriate Christian manners, such as the exhortation in his *Journal* for Christians to "honor the physician, for God hath appointed him" (Sir 38:1-2).[27] More significantly, Wesley eventually adopted a more stridently Protestant stance on the Apocrypha than that of his father or his Anglican standards. This was stated most sharply in 1779: "We cannot but reject them. We dare not receive them as part of the Holy Scriptures."[28] Five years later, when he abridged the Anglican Articles of Religion to provide doctrinal standards for the Methodist Episcopal Church that was organizing in the newly formed United States of America, Wesley deleted all reference to the Apocrypha from the Article on Scripture.

Whatever difference he may have had concerning the Apocrypha, Wesley clearly shared, and had been deeply shaped by, the Anglican commitment to reading the *whole* Bible. The *Book of Common Prayer* prescribed a pattern of daily readings that covered the Old Testament once and the New Testament (except Revelation) three times a year. Wesley passed this expectation on to his Methodist followers, encouraging them to read a portion of *both* Testaments each morning and evening.[29] Lest children avoid the Old Testament, because of its size, Wesley prepared a special abridgment for them.[30]

Wesley's pastoral practice reflects his commitment to the theological and spiritual value of the whole Bible. For example, he left behind records of his biblical texts for sermons through much of his ministry. These demonstrate extensive preaching in both Testaments. Indeed, we can document Wesley preaching on texts from every book in the Protestant canon except Esther, Song of Songs, Obadiah, Nahum, Zephaniah, Philemon, and the third Epistle of John.[31]

Among the significant features embedded in Wesley's pastoral practice is a firm rejection of the tendency for Christians (tracing back at least to Marcion in the early church) to ignore or even excise the Old Testament.[32] Most specifically, Wesley refused any suggestion that the emphasis on grace and forgiveness in the New Testament should be posed against the emphasis on living by God's law in the Old Testament.[33] Rather, as Wesley liked to put it, every moral command in *both* Testaments should be read as a "covered promise"—a promise both that the basic intent of the law is our well-being and that God will graciously enable our obedience.[34] This conviction allowed him to read the Old Testament as an authoritative unfolding of *Christian* truth, while affirming the New Testament as the *final standard* of Christian faith and practice.[35]

In short, for Wesley an adequate understanding of any particular passage of Scripture should include *comparative* reading with other relevant texts throughout the Protestant canon.

Read *Comparatively* in Light of God's Central Purpose

Wesley was equally concerned to read the entire canon with attention to those themes and emphases that emerge repeatedly:

> Every truth which is revealed in the oracles of God is undoubtedly of great importance. Yet it may be allowed that some of those which are revealed therein are of greater importance than others as being more immediately conducive to the grand end of all, the eternal salvation of [humanity]. And we may judge of their importance even from this circumstance, that they are not mentioned only once in the sacred writings, but are repeated over and over.[36]

Notice Wesley's identification of the grand end of God's revelatory work in Scripture as the eternal salvation of humanity. We will see below that he came to recognize that God's saving concern reached beyond humanity to embrace the whole creation. The key in this passage is that Wesley focused the purpose and truthfulness of Scripture around its function as a witness to and means of God's saving concern. This point comes through as well in the elderly Wesley's "Thoughts upon Methodism":

> What is their fundamental doctrine? That the Bible is the whole and sole rule both of Christian faith and practice. Hence they learned: (1). That religion is an inward principle; that it is no other than the mind that was in Christ; or in other words, the renewal of the soul after the image of God, in righteousness and true holiness. (2). That this can never be wrought in us but by the power of the Holy Ghost. (3). That we receive this and every other blessing merely for the sake of Christ; and, (4), that whosoever hath the mind that was in Christ, the same is our brother, and sister, and mother.[37]

Wesley is following here the lead of 2 Tim 3:16-17, where the inspiration of Scripture is related to its role of instructing in Christian belief and training in lives of righteousness. He frequently cites this text in teaching sermons, affirming the Bible as "infallibly true" on these matters.[38] In scattered other settings Wesley insists that there are no "errors" in Scripture.[39] Some interpreters have taken these quotations to indicate that Wesley would align with the modern model of biblical inerrancy, which insists that the Bible is accurate in every detail, including historical allusions and descriptions of the natural world. I believe that consideration of the range of his comments on Scripture and his central theological convictions places him instead within the long tradition of Christian interpreters who focus the authority of Scripture in matters of faith and practice.[40]

If Wesley stands within this long tradition, he is also a striking example of distinctive emphases within the tradition. While Christians share the same Bible, from the beginning we have found ourselves gathering into various traditions within the broader family. Several factors have contributed to this. One crucial factor is differing judgments about which aspects within the rich tapestry of Scripture provide the dominant motif in light of which to appreciate the other aspects. Christian history makes clear that, as finite creatures, readers of Scripture soon adopt a "working canon," a group of texts to which they appeal most often, as presenting most clearly the dominant motif in light of which to read the rest of Scripture. Wesley was aware of this fact: "We know, 'All Scripture is given by inspiration of God,' and is therefore true and right concerning all things. But we know likewise that there are some Scriptures which more immediately commend themselves to every [person's] conscience."[41]

So what was Wesley's working canon? In the quotation just given he went on to say, "In this rank we may place the passage before us," namely, 1 Corinthians 13. He also highly prized the Sermon on the Mount in Matthew 5–7. But the biblical book that Wesley prized most highly was the first Epistle of John. He referred to this epistle as "the deepest part of Scripture" and a "compendium of all the Holy Scriptures."[42] Most tellingly, he used the first Epistle of John for his sermon text and alluded to it within sermons much more frequently (relative to the number of verses in the book) than any other biblical book.[43]

Wesley privileged the first Epistle of John because of some of its key emphases: that our love for God is a *response* to knowing God's pardoning love for us (4:19), that the goal of God's pardoning love is to *heal* and *transform* our lives, and that God's goal is to make us *perfect in love* both of God and neighbor (4:7-18). When we add to these the insistence that God's love is *universal*, offering pardon and healing to all who will respond (which Wesley most frequently affirmed invoking

Ps 145:9, "His mercy is over all his works," BCP Psalter), we have the most central motif about God's saving purpose that Wesley was convinced ran through the whole of Scripture. His privileging of the first Epistle of John was a reflection of his commitment to reading all of Scripture *comparatively*, in light of this motif of God's universal prevenient transforming love.

READ THE ONE BOOK IN *CONFERENCE* (OR *CON-SPIRACY*) WITH THE HOLY SPIRIT

While more could be said about Wesley's concern to read the One Book *comparatively*, it is essential to consider as well his related—and equally deep—concern that individual readers engage Scripture *in conference*. The place to start in developing this concern is the section elided in the middle of the second extract above from Wesley's preface to *Sermons*. This section contains one of Wesley's deepest convictions about Christian life in general and study of Scripture in particular. Here is the extract with the missing material:

> Is there a doubt concerning the meaning of what I read? Does anything appear dark or intricate? I lift up my heart to the Father of lights: "Lord, is it not thy Word, 'If any man lack wisdom, let him ask of God'? Thou 'givest liberally and upbraidest not.' Thou has said, 'If any be willing to do thy will, he shall know.' I am willing to do, let me know, thy will." I then search after and consider parallel passages.[44]

Wesley's emphasis on the role of the "inspiration of the Spirit" in all of Christian life is reflected here. His typical use of this phrase is broader than considerations of the production of the Bible. In the *Complete English Dictionary* (1753) that Wesley published to help his followers read Scripture and other writings, he defined "inspiration" as the influence of the Holy Spirit that enables persons to love and serve God. This broad use of the word trades on the meaning of the Latin original, *inspirare*: to breathe into, animate, excite, or inflame. The broader understanding is evident even when Wesley uses "inspiration" in relation to the Bible, as in his comments in *Explanatory Notes upon the New Testament* on 2 Tim 3:16. He affirms God's guidance of the original authors, but his focal emphasis is encouraging current readers to seek the Spirit's inspiring assistance in reading Scripture. As he put it elsewhere (quoting Thomas à Kempis), "we need the same Spirit to *understand* the Scripture which enabled the holy men of old to *write* it."[45]

While Wesley clearly was encouraging readers to confer with the Spirit for guidance in understanding Scripture, his fundamental concern was personal *embrace* of the saving truth in Scripture. He recognized that such embrace, such "true, living Christian faith . . . is not only an assent, an act of the understanding, but a disposition which *God hath wrought* in the heart."[46] So he laid particular stress on the Spirit's *inspiring* presence that enables this embrace, inviting us to "breathe back" (or con-spire) what is graciously offered.[47]

READ THE ONE BOOK IN *CONFERENCE* WITH OTHER READERS

Bearing in mind this foundational dependence on the Spirit's empowering and guiding presence, let me draw attention once more to Wesley's preface to *Sermons*. After encouraging his readers to pray for help and stressing the need to compare Scripture with Scripture, Wesley continues, "If any doubt still remains, I consult those who are experienced in the things of God, and then the writings whereby, being dead, they yet speak."[48] The crucial concern to note in this concluding line is not just that an individual might turn to other books to help understand the One Book, but that we as individuals need to read the Bible in conference with other readers.

Several dimensions of this need deserve highlighting. Note first that Wesley identifies consulting particularly those "more experienced in the things of God." His focal concern is not scholarly expertise (though he is not dismissing this) but the contribution of mature Christian character and discernment to interpreting the Bible. Where does one find such folk whose lives and understanding are less distorted by sin? One of Wesley's most central convictions was that authentic Christian character and discernment are the fruit of the Spirit, nurtured within the witness, worship, support, and accountability of Christian community. This is the point of his often (mis)quoted line that there is "no holiness but social holiness." As he later clarified, "I mean not only that [holiness] cannot subsist so well, but that it cannot subsist at all without society, without living and conversing with [other people]."[49] While the class and band meetings that Wesley designed to embody this principle were not devoted primarily to Bible study, they helped form persons who were more inclined to read Scripture and to read it in keeping with its central purposes.

I hasten to add, secondly, that Wesley's emphasis on the value of reading the Bible in conference with others was not limited to considerations of relative Christian maturity. It was grounded in his recognition of the limits of *all* human understanding, even that of spiritually mature persons. He was convinced that, as finite creatures, our human understandings of our experience, of Christian precedent, and of Scripture itself are "opinions" or interpretations of their subject matter.[50] God may know these things with absolute clarity; we see them "through a glass darkly." Wesley underlined the implication of this in his sermon on a "Catholic Spirit."

> Although every man necessarily believes that every particular opinion which he holds is true (for to believe any opinion is not true, is the same thing as not to hold it); yet can no man be assured that all his own opinions, taken together, are true. Nay, every thinking man is assured they are not, seeing *humanum est errare et nescire*: "To be ignorant of many things, and to mistake in some, is the necessary condition of humanity."[51]

Wesley went on in the sermon to commend a spirit of openness in conferring with others, where we are clear in our commitment to the main branches of Christian doctrine, while always ready to hear and weigh whatever can be offered against our current understanding of matters of belief or practice (or the meaning of a particular text). His goal for this commended conferring is clear: to seek together *more adequate* understandings of the topic being considered.

The final dimension to highlight about Wesley's call for reading the Bible in conference with others should be obvious: it is vital that we do not limit our conferring to those who are most like us or those with whom we already agree. We should remain open to, and at times seek out, those who hold differing understandings. Otherwise, we are not likely to identify places where our understanding of something in Scripture (usually shared with those closest to us) might be wrong. That is why Wesley specifically invited any who believed that he presented mistaken readings of the Bible in his first volume of *Sermons* to be in touch, so that they could confer together over Scripture.[52]

Read the One Book in *Conference* with Christian Tradition

Among those outside of his circle of associates and followers whom Wesley was committed to including in conference over the meaning of Scripture were Christians of earlier generations. As he noted, our primary means of hearing their voice is through their writings.

It is widely recognized that John Wesley valued the writings of the first three centuries of the church. He specifically defended consulting early Christian authors in a published letter to Conyers Middleton. Middleton had argued that such consultation was not necessary because Scripture is both complete and clear in its teachings. Wesley responded, "The Scriptures are a complete rule of faith and practice; and they are clear in all necessary points. And yet their clearness does not prove that they need not be explained, nor their completeness that they need not be enforced.[53] He went on to insist that consultation with early Christian writings had helped many avoid dangerous errors in their interpretation of Scripture, while the neglect of these writings would surely leave one captive to current reigning misunderstandings.

One specific conviction that early Christian writers emphasized was the need to read unclear or ambiguous passages in the Bible in light of the "rule of faith." This term referred to what was most central and unifying in Christian faith, as found in the "more open parts of Scripture" and early baptismal creeds and related catechetical materials.[54] The topic of the "rule of faith" became a battleground during the Reformation. Some teachings and practices had been advanced on the authority of the church through the medieval period that the Reformers judged lacking in biblical support or contrary to clear biblical teaching. In response they championed "Scripture alone" as the rule of faith. But for most Protestants, this did not mean rejecting the value of consulting some communally shared sense of the central and unifying themes in Scripture when trying to interpret particular passages. They changed the name for this shared sense to the "analogy of faith" but typically defended under this label the practice of consulting at least the Apostles' Creed when seeking to interpret Scripture correctly.

Wesley inherited through his Anglican standards this Protestant commitment to Scripture as the rule of faith, interpreted in light of the analogy of faith.[55] His specific commitment to reading the Bible in light of the Trinitarian (and other) themes affirmed in the Apostles' Creed is embodied in his advice: "In order to be well acquainted with the doctrines of Christianity you need but one book [besides the NT]—Bishop Pearson *On the Creed*."[56] John Pearson's volume was an exposition of the Apostles' Creed, which had been commended to Wesley by both of his parents and was used as a text during his study at Christ Church in Oxford. It was the theological text that Wesley himself most often assigned to his assistants and recommended to his correspondents.

READ THE BOOK OF SCRIPTURE IN *CONFERENCE* WITH THE BOOK OF NATURE

Another commitment that Wesley imbibed through his Anglican upbringing was a stronger emphasis than in most Protestant circles on the value of studying God's revelation in the natural world (the "book of nature") alongside of studying the book of Scripture. Thus, in the midst of publishing *Explanatory Notes* on the NT (1755) and the OT (1765) for his followers, Wesley took time to provide them as well with his *Survey of the Wisdom of God in Creation* (1st ed., 1763).

Wesley's *Survey*, which grew to five volumes in length, is devoted to an overview of the natural world—beginning with the human body; moving to other animals; then to plants, fossils, and the physical elements of earth, fire, and water; and finally turning toward the heavens, considering air, meteors, and cosmology.[57] It distills some standard works in natural philosophy (what we now would call the natural sciences) of his day. Wesley interlaced the description with periodic theological reflections (again, often drawn from others) on the significance of what we see in the natural world.

Comparison of *Survey* with the sources that Wesley read and used makes clear that he carefully resisted three alternative tendencies. First, he removed from his extracts of other writers their reflection of the growing Enlightenment agenda of basing religious teachings solely on universal, empirically based observation, an agenda that effectively shifted authority from the book of Scripture to the book of nature. Second, while he was aware of prominent "concordist" writers, like Thomas Burnet, who tried to explain scriptural accounts of creation, the flood, and the future cataclysm in terms of current science, Wesley brought no such accounts into *Survey*.[58] Third, as noted earlier, Wesley rejected Hutchinson's "reverse-concordist" claim that the Bible taught (when properly read without the Hebrew vowel points) its own physics, biology, and the like—with the implication that any alternative in current science should be rejected.

These moves on Wesley's part are consistent with his sense of the focus of Scripture's authority in matters of faith and practice. They also evidence that his primary concern for bringing the book of Scripture into conference with the book of nature was not to *prove* the reliability of Scripture or provide a *foundation* for belief in God. He understood that authentic faith is born of the Spirit, through the Word. At the same time, if God the creator is evident in some way through the creation, as Scripture affirms, then consideration of the creation might appropriately serve to *strengthen* the faith, reverence, and love awakened by the Spirit. This was Wesley's primary purpose in distilling recent treatises in natural philosophy for his followers.

Wesley's Precedent of "Honoring Conference" in Reading Scripture

Wesley's engagement with current studies of the natural world also proved helpful in reconsidering some of his inherited interpretations of Scripture. We are able to consider only one example, which can be introduced by returning one last time to the preface of the first volume of *Sermons*.

In that preface Wesley opined, "I want to know one thing, the way to heaven—how to land safe on that happy shore." This way of expressing his longing reflects a long development in Christian history. Although Scripture speaks of God's ultimate goal in salvation as the "new heavens and earth," a variety of influences led Christians through the first millennium to assume increasingly that our final state is "heaven above." The latter was seen as a realm where human spirits, dwelling in ethereal bodies, join eternally with all other spiritual beings (a category that did not include animals) in continuous worship of God. By contrast, they assumed that the physical universe, which we abandon at death, would eventually be annihilated. Wesley imbibed this understanding of our final state in his upbringing, and through much of his ministry it was presented as obvious and unproblematic.

This makes it all the more striking when, in the last decade of his life, Wesley reclaimed boldly the biblical imagery of God's renewal of the whole universe, specifically championing the notion that animals participate in final salvation.[59] A major factor in this change was the study he undertook, in his sixties, of some current works in natural philosophy that utilized the model of the "chain of beings." Central to this model is the assumption that the loss of any type of "being" in creation would call into question the perfection of the Creator. Prodded by this emphasis in the study of nature, Wesley began to reconsider his long-standing interpretation of Scripture, taking more seriously the biblical insistence that God desires to redeem the whole creation.[60]

This example hints at the dynamic of "honoring conference" that characterized Wesley's theological reflection at its best. Confronted by an apparent conflict between current human accounts of the natural world and his current (human) understanding of Scripture, Wesley did not simply debate which was more authoritative. He reconsidered his interpretations of *each*, seeking an understanding that *honored both*. In this way he upheld the authority of the One Book, while embracing the contribution of broad conferencing to understanding that Book.

2

SCRIPTURE AS A MEANS OF GRACE

Kenneth J. Collins

Communicating the presence of God in the Methodist societies laced throughout eighteenth-century Britain was ever the concern of John Wesley. Indeed, beyond the first two precepts of natural law of (1) doing no harm and (2) doing good as found in the *General Rules of the United Societies*, Wesley wisely added a third rule, namely, "attending upon all the ordinances of God,"[1] in order to foster an awareness of the Holy Spirit in Methodist life. In addressing this need, and also in responding to the strains of quietism that had erupted at the joint Methodist/Moravian society meeting at Fetter Lane in London, Wesley composed the sermon "The Means of Grace" in 1746, taking Mal 3:7 as his text.[2] In this sermon, Wesley defined the means of grace as "outward signs, words, or actions, ordained of God, and appointed for this end, to be the ordinary channels whereby he might convey to men preventing, justifying, or sanctifying grace."[3] In this definition not only does Wesley reveal his largely sacramental approach to life, whereby signs, words, and actions hold theophanic or numinous power, but he also indicates his broad understanding of the means of grace that can be conveyed via a variety of conduits.

THE VARIETY OF THE MEANS OF GRACE

Ever careful not to champion ideas that would fail to make proper allowance for divine freedom and initiative, Wesley explored the *ordinary* channels (God is free to use extraordinary ones as well) of grace along three major lines: (1) the *general means of grace*, which would include such virtues as "universal obedience; keeping all the commandments; denying ourselves, and taking up our cross daily";[4] (2) the *instituted means*, chief of which are "prayer, whether in secret or with the great congregation; searching the Scriptures; (which implies reading, hearing, and meditating thereon); and receiving the Lord's supper, eating bread and drinking wine in remembrance of Him"[5] (fasting and Christian conference were added to these in the *Minutes of Several Conversations*[6]); and (3) the *prudential means of grace*, which embraced "arts of holy living,"[7] suggested by reason in light of the telos, or goal, of Scripture and which are conducive to the life of God in the soul, such as visiting the sick, attending class and band meetings, and reading devotional literature.[8]

So generous was Wesley's understanding of the means of grace, of those channels that could mediate both the favor and power of the Spirit of God, that he maintained the Methodist covenant service itself held at the beginning of the new year was a "scriptural means of grace which is now almost everywhere forgotten except among the Methodists."[9] Moreover, like his brother Charles, John Wesley also lifted up human suffering as a "quicker means . . . [that] sinks us deeper into the abyss of love."[10] Beyond these numerous works of piety just noted, Wesley pointed out in two key sermons that doing good to one's neighbor, or works of mercy as he chose to call them, are genuine means of grace. For example, in his sermon, "On Visiting the Sick," written in 1786, Wesley asked, "Are there no other means then these [works of piety], whereby God is pleased, frequently, yea, ordinarily, to convey his grace to them that either love or fear him?" And he replied, "Surely there are works of mercy, as well as works of piety, which are real means of grace. They are more especially such to those that perform them with a single eye."[11] In addition, in his sermon "On Zeal," published a few years earlier in 1781, Wesley pointed out that by works of mercy, such as feeding and clothing the poor, "we exercise all holy tempers, by these we continually improve them, so that all these are real means of grace, although this is not commonly adverted to."[12] The undertaking of such works with a single eye, as Wesley put it, surely entailed the wisdom and insights, the very goal, of religion, highlighted so ably in Scripture. In other words, works of piety and works of mercy were ever connected.

Scripture as a Means of Grace

Growing up in an Anglican rectory during the eighteenth century, informed by rich Protestant traditions, John Wesley along with his siblings had numerous opportunities to be shaped by the pages of the Bible. Indeed, the family practice was to read psalms as well as a few chapters from the Old and New Testaments each morning, "the household being filled with the Word, the very sounds of redemption."[13] Samuel Wesley, who considered himself to be something of a biblical scholar, not only produced a *History of the Old and New Testaments* but a *Life of Christ* as well.[14] Shortly before his death, the elderly Samuel asked his son John to deliver a copy of his magnum opus, a commentary on the book of Job in verse, to the Queen. Susanna Wesley, for her part, composed "manuals of biblical instruction"[15] for her children, beyond her practice of meeting with each child for spiritual instruction on a particular day of the week. With such a background in place, it is little wonder that the writings of both John and Charles Wesley are replete with the language, the very idioms, of the Bible.

With a few exceptions, John Wesley often read the King James Version of the Bible, though his *Explanatory Notes upon the New Testament* reveal that he made several corrections to this text in his own translation. Moreover, as the Apocrypha did not have the same status as the Bible within Anglicanism and was suggested simply for edification, John Wesley insisted that this body of literature was not to be read as sacred Scripture. In his *Roman Catechism and Reply*, for example, Wesley observes with respect to the status of the apocryphal writings: "We cannot but reject them. We dare not receive them as part of the Holy Scriptures. For none of these books were received as such by the Jewish Church (to whom 'were committed the oracles of God')."[16] In his own devotional life, Wesley continued the practice of his Epworth upbringing and read from both Testaments on a daily basis. To be sure, he cautioned against the heedless practice, evident in some corners of the church, of "making light of the Old Testament," a body of writings that constituted in his judgment nothing less than "one half of the oracles of God!"[17] Wesley's extensive knowledge of the Old Testament is revealed in an observation made by Matthew Schlimm, who points out, "In the 151 sermons by Wesley in the critical edition of *Wesley's Works*, Wesley quotes, cites, or alludes to the Old Testament 2,455 times (an average of

16 citations per sermon), omitting no book from the Old Testament except Ruth and Obadiah."[18]

When Wesley lists Scripture among the instituted means of grace, as for example in the *Minutes of Several Conversations* or in his sermon "The Means of Grace," he invariably places it second behind prayer, both private and public.[19] Moreover, as the late Ole Borgen observed, "In sixty-eight places, where [Wesley] lists *two or more* of these means, prayer heads the list, being mentioned sixty-one times; . . . the Word (read, heard, preached, meditated upon) fifty-four times."[20] Such an ordering, however, is not indicative of the relative worth of any particular instituted means of grace but simply represents a flow, a sequencing, that Wesley believed to be descriptive of the devotional life of serious Christians.

Word and Spirit

In his own day, Wesley recognized the uncanny, God-breathed nature of the Bible as a key means of grace, that reading this book repeatedly resulted in the transformation of lives in a way that no other writings, however celebrated, could ever accomplish. And though one of Wesley's basic arguments for the inspiration of the Bible, its Spirit-infused nature, is flat footed and not even sound,[21] he nevertheless thought better of the whole matter and made a broad appeal to the *Testimonium Spiritus Sancti* in affirming the inspiration of the Bible.[22] For one thing, Wesley clearly did not intend "a mechanical theory of inspiration,"[23] as is offered in some fundamentalist circles today. And the mere assent to the divine inspiration of Scripture as a propositional truth is "no more than the 'faith of a devil.'"[24]

In light of these observations, Gayle C. Felton is surely correct when she notes that by the inspiration of Scripture Wesley actually had in mind a twofold, not a singular, process; that is, to use Wesley's own words, "The Spirit of God not only once inspired those who wrote it, but continually inspires, supernaturally assists, those that read it with earnest prayer."[25] Again, in a letter to the Bishop of Gloucester published in 1763, Wesley opined, "We need the same Spirit to understand the Scripture which enabled the holy men of old to *write* it."[26] Enlightened by the Spirit and empowered by what Wesley referred to as supernatural assistance, readers within the Methodist infrastructure undertook what looks like a *lectio divina*. In other words, the Bible was read in a prayerful way and with a sense of expectancy by being open to the Spirit's presence through the many words that mediate that presence, a genuine *universalia in re*.

That the Bible as an instituted means of grace is inspired by the Holy Spirit suggests something of the significant role it must play in the community of believers—and Wesley made this connection explicit. Commenting on 2 Tim 3:16, for example, he maintained that since Scripture is so infused with the Spirit's presence, it is therefore profitable for doctrine, instruction, reproof, correction, and training in righteousness. These further roles for sacred Scripture, indicative of its authority, are of immense value for the Christian community and underscore not only the Bible's preeminent and abiding soteriological role (rather than a large epistemological one) but also why Wesley referred to himself on one occasion as *homo unius libri*.[27] Put another way, since the Bible so clearly shows the way to heaven, "how to land safe on that happy shore," Wesley could only exclaim, "O give me that book! At any price give me the Book of God!"[28] Here then is a means of grace of inordinate value.

The authority of Scripture in the context of a diversity of means of grace (general, instituted, and prudential) suggests something of the Bible's normative role in terms of both a "source of truth and as [a] norm of truth."[29] That is, the illumination and clarity that the Word of God brings to the ongoing Christian life must surely be considered a part of what is meant by a means of grace, since the truth so communicated and emblazoned on the human heart can only be brought about through the enlightening powers of the Spirit of Truth. Thus, in defining the faith of Protestants, Wesley observed that it "embraces only those truths necessary to salvation which are clearly revealed in the oracles of God. . . . They believe neither more nor less than what is manifestly contained in, and provable by, the Holy Scriptures."[30] Affirming that the illuminating power of the Spirit is associated with the Bible in an unparalleled way, Wesley clearly rejects the notion that the church fathers or even the early councils of the church could ever fill such a role. To illustrate, in his *Advantage of the Members of the Church of England*, drafted in 1753, Wesley observed, "As to the Fathers and Councils, we cannot but observe that in an hundred instances they contradict one another."[31] And to clarify his meaning further, Wesley reasoned, "Consequently, [the Fathers and Councils] can no more be a rule of faith to us than the Papal decrees, which are not grounded on Scriptures."[32] Put another way, the Holy Spirit is by no means associated with the writings of the church fathers in the same way as Scripture. Here, then, marks a *categorical* difference.[33]

Beyond this, Wesley affirmed that "the Christian rule of right and wrong is the word of God."[34] And in adjudicating disputes within the church Wesley's approach was remarkably straightforward: "Bring me plain, scriptural proof for your assertion, or I cannot allow it."[35] Well aware of the human teachings that had accrued over time in the form of various traditions, some of which helped to render the gospel opaque, Wesley made it abundantly clear and in a way that those steeped in the genius of the Reformation would surely appreciate that "the Church is to be judged by Scripture, not Scripture by the Church."[36] Earlier in 1756 Wesley touched on this same theme in a letter to William Dodd in which he declared, "I try every Church and every doctrine by the Bible."[37] Again, in the preface to his *Explanatory Notes upon the New Testament*, published a short time earlier, Wesley remarked that the Bible is "the fountain of heavenly wisdom, which they who are able to taste, prefer to all writings of men, however wise, or learned, or holy."[38] Indeed, one of Wesley's favorite ways of referring to Scripture was as the *touchstone* of the faith, indicating that this body of literature is not just any means of grace. In a letter drafted earlier around 1747 he exclaimed, "The Scriptures are the touchstone whereby Christians examine all, real or supposed, revelations."[39] On this issue Wesley was willing to take an emphatic stand: "My ground is the Bible. Yea, I am a Bible-bigot. I follow it in all things, both great and small."[40]

Law and Grace

The distinctiveness of Scripture among the instituted means of grace, such as prayer and receiving the Lord's Supper, is that the Bible is not only a rich means of grace, a channel though which the gracious presence of the Holy Spirit is so ably mediated, but it also contains within it (and in this latter instance is unlike the other means) the wherewithal through which any grace of God—whether prevenient, justifying, or sanctifying—is to be rightly comprehended and embraced. In other words, the Bible brings forth a clear articulation of the moral law, the holy law of love, which is expressed in an Old Testament context in the form of the Ten Commandments and in the New Testament setting in the form of Jesus' Sermon on the Mount. For Wesley, the mediating power of the moral law is considerable not only in that this holy law of love constitutes the express will of God in a flush of illumination, but also in that it communicates the divine presence so wonderfully in the community of faith. To illustrate, Wesley observes in a key sermon on this topic that the moral law is all of the following: (1) "an incorruptible picture of the high and holy one that inhabiteth eternity," (2) "the face of God unveiled," (3) "the heart of God disclosed to humanity," (4) "divine virtue and wisdom assuming a visible form," and (5) "a copy of the eternal mind."[41] Furthermore, and in a way that draws a relation between the moral law and christological attributes, Wesley observes, "we may apply to this law what the Apostle says of his Son: it is 'the streaming forth or out-beaming of his glory, the express image of his person.'"[42] Elsewhere in this same sermon, Wesley describes the moral law as "the fairest offspring of the everlasting Father, the brightest efflux of his essential wisdom, the visible beauty of the Most High."[43]

In light of the preceding, Scripture is indeed a distinct means of grace and evidences a balanced conjunction that Wesley was in earnest to reflect in the *style* of his own practical theology,[44] specifically in terms of the mediation of grace *and* the norms, in the form of the moral law, through which that grace must be properly understood. Interestingly enough, Wesley himself noted the failure of many of his contemporaries to come to this balanced understanding, especially as they considered the operations of the third use of the moral law which played such an important illuminating, prescriptive role as the ongoing grace of God was received by believers. He wrote, "The third use of the law is, to keep us alive. It is the *grand means* whereby the blessed Spirit prepares the believer for larger communications of the life of God. I am afraid this great and important truth is little understood, not only by the world, but even by many whom God hath taken out of the world, who are real children of God by faith."[45] Simply put, Scripture as an instituted means of grace clearly evidences one of the most important conjunctions of Wesley's practical theology, namely, law *and* grace. That is, the Bible is a vital means of grace, and yet it also contains within its pages the norm, the moral law, *through which that grace is to be understood.*

The Bible as Sacred Scripture

Reading the Bible is always a function of at least two poles of attention: a text and a reader. Even in his own eighteenth-century setting, Wesley was well aware that the biblical narrative could be read in various ways depending on the presuppositions, worldviews, social and cultural environment, and even the basic metaphysics of the reader. Significant shifts in terms of how readers approached the biblical text were evident in the works of Thomas Hobbes (1588–1679) and Benedict Spinoza (1632–1677) in the seventeenth century, and in those of Jean Astruc (1684–1766) and Johann Gottfried Eichhorn (1752–1827) in the eighteenth. The rationalism of these centuries, coupled with the rise and eventual success of an empirical methodology so favored by science, meant that some readers brought to the text an interpretive approach that could never be fully embraced by Wesley, for it suppressed an understanding of the Bible precisely as a means of grace.

As a body of literature penned by flesh-and-blood authors over a great stretch of time, the Bible is an artifact that on one level should be read as any other book. Nevertheless, attention to other levels (inspiration for example) indicates why such an approach must not become the only suit in the deck, so to speak. Additional developments in the area of biblical criticism beyond the age of Wesley have issued in the notion that "'good' biblical interpretation is primarily about acquiring background knowledge,"[46] with the result that readers are in many respects placed at the center of the interpretive process whereby all that falls under their vision is simply deemed an object. In other words, such readers are not open to the various ways that the biblical text can result in the transformation of readers themselves in a process that is wonderfully (or disturbingly, depending on one's perspective) de-centering. All such "subjective" possibilities have been shunted aside in an Enlightenment metanarrative of objectivity. In fact, as Joel Green points out, some scholars today, Michael Fox among them, insist that "faith-based study of the Bible is not scholarship."[47] In light of this judgment, Fox advocates bracketing out faith at every turn. "The best thing for Bible appreciation," he writes, "is [a] secular, academic, religiously-neutral hermeneutic."[48] Such a perspective, however, is hardly neutral. In his attempt to lend credibility to his particular methodology, whose first principles remain unexamined, Fox has actually ended up privileging unbelief.

Underscoring what it means to read the Bible *as* Scripture, as a genuine means of grace, Green denies the possibility of interpretive neutrality and maintains that the ecclesial location of the reader is after all important.[49] Put another way, to make the claim that "the Bible is Scripture,"[50] entails both a theological statement and a distinct vision that appear to be appropriate in terms of the kind of literature the Bible actually is. To illustrate, John Wesley and the early Methodists in their own day were a part of a rich interpretive community whose vision, unlike "objective" modernistic projects, allowed for the kind of personal transformation that is one of the more salutary consequences of Bible reading. Indeed, the Bible will hardly function as a significant means of grace if the presuppositions of the reader methodologically exclude the possibilities of faith at the outset. Green's work is so important, then, because it reminds us that the interpretive community in which Wesleyans participate not only embraces the ways particular passages of the Bible are understood (Romans 7, for example) in what can be called a Wesleyan interpretive tradition, but it also calls attention to the theological vision and openness that renders Scripture reading a dynamic, multivalent phenomenon, one that engages not simply a cogitating intellect but the entire *person*.

In offering the Bible as a suitable means of grace, Wesley of course was mindful of his own Anglican tradition, which had for the most part placed a premium on "standing under" the Word of God, thereby allowing the Holy Spirit to transform the tempers and dispositions of the heart in ways that oriented these holy affections to a transcendent God. In the eighteenth century, however, the Church of England was challenged by both rationalists and deists, and, in *response* to such threats, some Anglican leaders failed to emphasize properly the vital role of the Holy Spirit in Christian life. When these same clergy looked in Wesley's direction, they often saw an "enthusiast" or what today would be called a fanatic. "Sir, the pretending to extraordinary revelations, and gifts of the Holy Ghost is a horrid thing—a very horrid thing," Bishop Joseph Butler intoned.[51] For his part, the Vicar of Furneaux, the Rev. Charles Wheatly, denounced the Methodists from his pulpit in St. Paul's Cathedral in 1739 as "rapturous enthusiasts,"[52] and George Lavington, the Bishop of Exeter, weighed in during 1749 and sent *The Enthusiasm of Methodists and Papists Compared* off to the press. Such tension between Wesley and his peers within the Church of England may suggest a difference not only in assessing the Spirit's role in the interpretation of and meditation on the Bible but also in terms of a broader theological vision.

John Wesley's Basic Reading Strategy

Clues as to how Wesley carried out his own counsel of reading, hearing, and meditating on Scripture as a means of grace can be found in the preface to his *Explanatory Notes upon the Old Testament*.[53] Such an approach presupposes the community of faith as the proper context, the appropriate social location. Taking into account the wisdom of the great biblical commentator Matthew Henry (1662–1714), Wesley advised the Methodists to be disciplined enough to set aside a time, morning and evening, for this very purpose.[54] Having learned to employ time as a steward, a trait that he had acquired from perusing the writings of Jeremy Taylor (1613–1667), Wesley understood that the day should be ordered in terms of Scripture reading itself. In other words, such reading and reflection is not an incidental activity but one that defines the very fabric of the life of the serious Christian. Moreover, knowing that Jesus the Messiah could not be properly embraced unless one understood the old covenant, Wesley urged those who looked to his leadership to read from both the Old and the New Testaments on a daily basis.

Wesley revealed his general rule for interpreting Scripture in a letter to Samuel Furly in 1755 in which he maintained that "the literal sense of every text is to be taken, if it be not contrary to some other texts."[55] The following decade, in his *Plain Account of Christian Perfection*, published in 1766, Wesley tied the "plain, literal meaning of any text" with fending off the danger posed by fanaticism, with its highly imaginative and at times preposterous interpretations of the Bible.[56] Despite this basic hermeneutical posture, Wesley was a good enough exegete to realize and to admit quite frankly that not every passage of the Bible can, after all, be taken literally.[57] Knowledgeable with regard to the different genres evidenced in Scripture, Wesley cautioned in one of his later sermons, "On the Church," published in 1785, that "it is a stated rule in interpreting Scripture, never to depart from the plain, literal sense, *unless it implies an absurdity*.[58] Though what is deemed beyond the range of possible interpretations will no doubt be informed, at least to some degree, by the light of reason, Wesley never laid out in any great detail just how such judgments are made and what body of evidence is in effect considered informative.

While the grammatical and historical contexts of biblical passages were clearly important to Wesley in his emphasis on the literal sense, his interest did not stop there. Ever mindful of the purpose for which Scripture was written, Wesley recommended that readers should have a single eye in this endeavor in order that they might rightly discern the will of God.[59] One of the difficulties of placing the Bible in the hands of laypeople, even if they are a part of a *community* of faith, is that a diversity of interpretations of sacred Scripture may emerge which in the worst instances will quickly become an exercise in confusion and self-will. In order to prevent this malaise, Wesley advised that any passage of the Bible is to be read with an eye to the *analogy of faith*.[60] In other words, the basic doctrines of the Christian faith, which are deeply rooted in Scripture and which have been articulated by the church, must guide any interpretation. Such teachings include "Original Sin, Justification by Faith, the New Birth, Inward and Outward Holiness."[61] The basic idea of the analogy of faith so championed by the Protestant Reformers, Luther in particular,[62] is that Scripture forms a blessed unity or harmony that cannot and should not be disrupted by an idiosyncratic interpretation. Though interpreters may contradict each other, the Bible cannot contradict itself.

With an emphasis on the operations of the Holy Spirit as the Bible is read by the faithful, Wesley clearly developed a second sense of interpretation beyond the literal, namely, the spiritual sense. In his *Address to the Clergy*, for example, penned in 1756, he questioned his fellow servants of the gospel along the following lines: "Do I know the grammatical construction of the four Gospels; of the Acts, of the Epistles; and am I master of the *spiritual sense* (as well as the literal) of what I read?"[63] In fact, Wesley contended that "the plain and obvious meaning" of the words of the Spirit of God (the literal sense) may be foolishness to the person in the natural state because "they are perceivable by that spiritual sense which in him was never yet awakened."[64] Remarkably enough, it is possible that Wesley actually discerned a connection between the literal and spiritual senses of the Bible and the natural and spiritual senses of readers that mark their being. In his *Earnest Appeal to Men of Reason and Religion*, written in 1743, he argued:

> You know, likewise, that before it is possible for you to form a true judgment of [true conclusions], it is absolutely necessary that you have a clear apprehension of the things of God [which surely must include Scripture], and that your ideas thereof be all fixed, distinct, and determinate. And seeing our ideas are not innate, but must all

originally come from our senses, it is certainly necessary that you have senses capable of discerning objects of this kind: Not those only which are called *natural senses,* which in this respect profit nothing, as being altogether incapable of discerning objects of a spiritual kind; but *spiritual senses,* exercised to discern spiritual good and evil.[65]

In order to be properly understood, then, the plain meaning of the words of the Spirit of God, which is another way of referring to the literal sense of Scripture, may require an awakening, whereby spiritual senses are quickened, lest the fruits of any such reading be rejected as foolishness. In other words, the spiritual senses of interpreters are necessary not only in terms of the spiritual sense of the Bible but also in terms of its literal meaning as well. Because of the distinct kind of literature that sacred Scripture is, as inspired by God, it cannot be properly read, in Wesley's judgment, apart from a consideration of the spiritual condition of the reader. Simply put, reading the Bible is a dynamic enterprise that entails both text and person, in which both are understood in a full-orbed way.

So then, in contrast to some of the reading strategies championed during the Enlightenment that have made their way into academic circles, Wesley maintained that readers must approach the text in a participatory and engaging way (not as an " object" to be mastered by an autonomous self). Consequently, reading should occur in a meditative attitude, one that is both preceded and followed by prayer. Here, of course, the discernment of the *presence* of the Holy Spirit is once again vital. "Scripture can only be understood thro' the same Spirit whereby 'it was given,'" Wesley affirmed, a point noted earlier.[66] Not surprisingly, Wesley by and large rejected any reading of the Bible that left the self, the Thou that has been created in the image and likeness of God, unaddressed. This diminishment of readers, evidencing a deficient anthropology, took place by bracketing out any serious consideration of the subjectivity and transformative possibilities of *persons* due to a methodological preference for universality and objectivity. In rejecting this utterly "objective" approach, Methodists could avoid any study of Scripture that was little more than the outworking of a practical agnosticism or even atheism.

Wesley's last counsel in looking to the Bible as a suitable means of grace involves the willingness on the part of readers to be open to both instruction and correction "with regard to our hearts, and lives."

Such an examination may issue in praise, in terms of what conformity to the will of God is already in place, or in humiliation (though Wesley likely means "humility" in this context) and prayer with respect to those things "where we were conscious of having fallen short." With an emphasis on the consequences of this Spirit-infused activity, the Father of Methodism advised that those who have undertaken such an examination should employ "whatever light you then receive . . . to the uttermost, and that immediately. Let there be no delay."[67]

THE GOAL OF SCRIPTURE AS A MEANS OF GRACE

Though Wesley fought against the stillness championed by Molther and Bray at Fetter Lane in London in 1740, a quietism that had underestimated the value of the means of grace (as noted at the outset of this chapter), he nevertheless demonstrated great balance in this area, so typical of his conjunctive theology, by contending that the means of grace may yet be overestimated as well. To illustrate, in November 1739 Wesley noted in his journal that "a man might both be harmless, use the means of grace, and do much good, and yet have no true religion at all."[68] Earlier, on February 1, 1738, as the ship *The Samuel* was pulling into Deal Harbor, Wesley exclaimed, "But does all this . . . make me acceptable to God? Does all I ever did or can know, say, give, do, or suffer, justify me in his sight? Yea, or the constant use of all the means of grace? . . . By no means."[69] A decade later Wesley lifted up the same three rules (do good, avoid evil, and use the means of grace) that had become a part of the *General Rules of the United Societies*, but now he referred to them as constituting "the religion of the world."[70] Moreover, in a letter to the Bishop of Gloucester, William Warburton (1698–1779), drafted in November 1762, Wesley once again concluded as he had done back in 1739 (the continuity is striking) that "a man might both be harmless, use the means of grace [reading, hearing and meditating on Scripture, for example], and do much good, and yet have no true religion at all."[71]

Affirming that "it is God *alone* who is the Giver of every good gift," Wesley maintained that "all outward means whatever, if separate from the Spirit of God, cannot profit at all."[72] Beyond this, he repeatedly cautioned the Methodists that true religion does not consist in "externals only,"[73] that outward fruits must proceed from an inward principle, and that it would be the bane of the Methodist people if they simply had "the form of godliness without the power."[74] All of this pointed counsel highlights the basic truth for Wesley that the means of grace in general, and Scripture in particular, point beyond themselves to what is the goal, the telos, the suitable end of the proper Christian faith, namely, holy love. Indeed, Wesley's enduring hope as expressed in a letter to "John Smith," was that "God would first, by [the] inspiration of his Spirit, have wrought in our hearts that holy love without which none can enter into glory."[75] Put another way, the use of Scripture as a means of grace must ever be conducive to "the knowledge and love of God."[76] Those who mistake the means for the end (and in terms of Scripture commit bibliolatry) forget, as Wesley points out, that "the end of every 'commandment is love, out of a pure heart', with 'faith unfeigned,' the loving the Lord their God with all their heart, and their neighbor as themselves."[77] There is nothing higher than this.

So then, Scripture itself, as a means of grace, is properly conceived only in terms of a means/end relation that looks toward the inculcation of holy love through the *presence* of the Holy Spirit in the community of believers as the proper goal of the Christian faith. Put another way, the Bible is a suitable means to such a blessed end which so clearly expresses the purpose of the church as it ministers to a hurting world. Such an understanding, ever championed by Wesley, also suggests a basic hermeneutic as displayed, for example, in the earlier writings of Augustine, specifically in terms of his *De Doctrina Christiana*: "Whoever, therefore, thinks that he understands the divine Scriptures or any part of them so that it does not build the double love of God and of our neighbor does not understand it at all."[78]

3

READING SCRIPTURE, THE LITERAL SENSE, AND THE ANALOGY OF FAITH

Robert W. Wall

INTRODUCTION
Wesley's Doctrine of Scripture

The three topics combined in this chapter cannot be understood apart from Wesley's theology of Scripture. Even though rarely considered anymore as a condition of its interpretation, what the interpreter believes about the Bible influences how the Bible is interpreted and practiced. For the sake of clarity, then, I want to begin with a brief reflection on the question, what is Wesley's conception of Scripture?[1]

For many Wesley scholars, the opening of any discussion of his theology of Scripture is not doctrinal or methodological but deeply personal. Wesley famously called himself *homo unius libri*, "a man of one book." What he meant by this self-appellation is that the Bible was always the one book he kept close at hand, an indispensable auxiliary of the Spirit's formative work throughout his life and gospel ministry. Wesley never wrote an essay nor preached a sermon on the doctrine of Scripture, an omission that probably reflects a former day when the Bible's authority was simply assumed, even among the nonreligious. While he certainly was shaped by England's reception of the Enlightenment and insisted on "clear and plain reason" when reading Scripture, the skepticism initiated by David Hume during Wesley's lifetime only later emerged during the nineteenth century as a Kantian import from the Continent. The biblical criticism of early modern England was more interested in the modest critical tasks of discerning genuine from embellished texts and orthodox from spurious interpretations according to the criteria established by the ancient church and reaffirmed more recently during the Magisterial Reformation. Accordingly, Wesley believed that "the whole of Scripture is not merely God's address to the believer; it is inspired by the Holy Spirit who in turn inspires the believer's understanding."[2] The dogmatic soil into which he roots this more functional conception of Scripture, then, belongs to the Reformation's principle of *sola Scriptura*, which makes its various roles in a congregation's worship and catechesis indispensable in the formation of faithful readers.

Wesley's various Bible practices in the cultivation of Christian existence, especially worked out in his canonical sermons, are apropos of this core belief.[3] The principal genre of his biblical commentary was the sermon. Even though the long eighteenth century was a time of unprecedented intellectual and theological ferment and fuss, Wesley's use of the sermon to speak Scripture into life must be viewed as an unmitigated ecclesial practice. Scripture is performed and paraded for the church, whether in missionary preaching or in the priestly care of saints. In fact, Wesley's practice of Bible preaching follows from the importance he placed on the Church of England's *Books of Homilies*, which played a significant role in his own theological instruction. Preaching was his way of speaking God's word directly, plainly, and practically to an audience whom God had targeted for holy ends, whether that audience gathered together as a Christian congregation or in a field filled with curious God-seekers. Although Wesley vested his sermons with the theological commitments of a covenantal Arminian redaction of the English Reformation, his theology of preaching is from Luther, for whom the sermon was not only an agent of reform but an essential means by which God's Spirit could communicate God's word to faithful auditors as an auxiliary of the risen Lord in drawing his disciples to himself for instruction and encouragement.[4] Luther believed that preached Scripture, when received by a faithful audience as a means of God's empowering grace, became nothing less than the *viva vox Dei*—the very words of God that informed and so formed and reformed a people into conformity with God's redemptive purpose.

To be sure, the bare bones of a doctrine of Scripture that secures Wesley's complete trust in the church's "speaking book" may be reasonably excavated and put back together again from the two integral prefaces to his *Explanatory Notes* on the NT (1754) and OT (1765). What is most essential for us to glean from his exposition is that for Wesley the nature of Scripture "may be observed (as) the word of the living God . . . which remaineth forever." Scripture is not the epistemic depository of timeless truth claims to be asserted in dogmatic debate but a "fountain of heavenly wisdom" to be "tasted as good" because it provides holy space for a reader's hearing of the words of a living God.[5] This wisdom is hardly arcane, since God's words are "of inexhaustible virtue." The human language of Scripture's various authors "sink nothing before it [since] God speaks not as man, but as God." Scripture is, quoting Luther, "a grammar of the language of the Holy Ghost."[6] In this sense, then, Scripture proceeds from God by the action of the inspiring Spirit who enables the community of readers and auditors to receive it as divine teaching and so as a means of grace. As such, the reception of Scripture's teaching must give "the direct, literal meaning of every verse, of every sentence, and as far as I am able of every word in the oracles of God."[7] Wesley's Scripture was a revelatory text, then, inspired by the same Holy Spirit who continues to guide all serious readers and auditors who receive it in faith as the *viva vox Dei* for the love of God.[8]

Still, the quest of Wesley's biblical hermeneutics is full of uncertainty of one kind or another. Most Wesley scholars avoid the topic, because they are embarrassed either by Wesley's uncritical biblicism (when judged by contemporary standards) or by the doctrine of Scripture itself, which seems unimportant to many when compared to his doctrine of salvation or his heroic ministry as a pioneering evangelical revivalist and leader of the Methodist movement. The present interest of this chapter is not to adjudicate Wesley's talent as a biblical exegete; others have done this work for us and very well.[9] Rather, in response to the general neglect of this topic, Wesley is put forward as an exemplar of theological interpretation whose Bible practices actively participate in a people's ongoing struggle to live holy lives before a God who is light and love.

READING SCRIPTURE

There is no clearer expression of Wesley's aim for Scripture's faithful reader than that found in this added prefatory sentence that gives instructions "To The Reader" of his edited version of Cranmer's *Homilies*: "He that desires to more perfectly understand these great doctrines of Christianity (i.e., salvation, faith and good works) ought diligently to read the Holy Scriptures, especially St. Paul's Epistles to the Romans and the Galatians."[10] While this sentiment is widely shared by Protestants even today, Wesley reads Scripture from and for a particular social location at a pivotal moment and in a crucial place in the history of the Christian Bible—in eighteenth-century England when the study of Scripture, forged in the fires of the Magisterial Reformation, was reshaped by England's reception of the Enlightenment. Wesley's Bible practices were steeped in both the Protestant principle of *sola Scriptura* and the epistemology of scientific humanism, which prompted him to practice the earliest tools of modern biblical criticism in service of the church to the glory of God.

Against those who accuse him of an unsophisticated biblicism, Wesley employed an impressive range of interpretive strategies available to him in the eighteenth century. He was thoroughly alert to the emerging tools of biblical criticism and employed them all, even if with caution and modestly so. Not only did he have an appetite for biblical languages, he was especially interested in textual criticism, which was the primary critical method of his day. On occasion he offered corrections to the Textus Receptus, used in the KJV translation—a dangerous activity in those days, since the transmission of the biblical text was linked by church confession to its revelatory role.[11]

Whether in the teahouses of London or the classrooms of Oxbridge, England's reception of the Enlightenment concerned human nature and the nature of divine revelation. Central to the hard intellectual battles occasioned by this interplay of the human (esp. free will) and divine (esp. transcendent) was the rejection of *mere* religious tradition, insisting that any claim for revealed truth must be held accountable to human reason and experience. Wesley agreed and worked hard to construct firm supports for his theology. He selectively admired the work of John Locke, whose empiricism stipulated that any person could and should apply scientific reasoning to what we learn from experience.[12] Close observation of life is foundational for understanding human nature and divine revelation. Even the conservative apologetics of Grotius (and all those who rode his wake) considered competent human testimony, such as retrieved from the plain portions of Scripture (e.g., the Gospels), as necessary evidence in securing a belief in the very miracles and fulfilled prophecy that validated Scripture's special revelation.

Wesley's spiritual reawakening at Aldersgate was a defining moment of his intellectual journey. His religious experience challenged Locke's suspicion of the individual's inward senses and led him to extend his empiricism to include the spiritual senses—that is, the sensory experiences of God's grace that forge a more expansive understanding of the real world to include the spiritual world occupied by a transcendent God and marked out by the work and witness of God's Spirit. We learn God not only by the media of special revelation, such as Scripture, but by our inward and manifest experiences of God, which confirm and are confirmed by the church's creed and canon.

Wesley received and studied both canon and creed, along with the traditions and histories that attended each, with gratitude and scrupulous attention.[13] He was no dissenter or latitudinarian. He embraced the Reformation's emphasis on the individual believer's freedom to interpret the Bible, and was well schooled in Renaissance humanism with its keen interest in the Bible's original sources. Wesley came from the Enlightenment projects and so embraced the critical methods of his day, including a lifelong interest in textual criticism and the importance of reading sacred texts in their linguistic and historical contexts. While he firmly rejected Hume's skepticism, he famously claimed to those who accused him of uncritical "enthusiasm" that "to renounce reason is to renounce religion . . . and . . . all irrational religion is false religion."[14]

The concerns of the Enlightenment for individual progress also shaped Wesley's interpretive interests, some might say too much.[15] Consider, for instance, that prior to the Enlightenment, happiness was understood to be the province of the virtuous and aristocratic few. But Locke famously announced that "the business of every man is to be happy in the world," and Wesley baptizes that sort of optimism in the transforming power of divine love that cooperates with our obedience in reforming believers according to the likeness of God. Yet this optimism in an individual's potential for life, liberty, and happiness was chastened by the Evangelical Revival of the 1730s and its reminder of a person's inability to flourish in the face of persistent sin without a radical intervention of divine grace. While David Bebbington reminds us that this great Revival, in which Wesley played a significant role, carried a theological freight keenly influenced by the optimistic tempers of England's Enlightenment,[16] Aldersgate taught him that the way forward toward human flourishing is predicated on an "optimism of grace." Reading Scripture without doubt and in firm confidence of God's good company is an essential marker of Wesley's hermeneutics, whether applied to his morning office or in sermon preparation for his congregation.

In fact, Wesley's congregation included many rank-and-file converts who, even though unschooled, were deeply interested in Scripture's teaching, and most were able to detect obscure biblical allusions in current popular literature. Biblical commentaries topped the list of books borrowed from the public libraries, and purchases of inexpensive Bible study aids exceeded the sales of any other kind of publication by a factor of four.[17] Wesley himself contributed to this robust market of ordinary readers by publishing his best-selling *Explanatory Notes*. Wesley's interpretation of Scripture was not only responsive to a widespread cultural interest in Bible study, then, but was also engaged with a particular reading audience and what it required of him as their spiritual director. Perhaps for this reason, he rarely mentions the contemporary controversies of the educated elites, not because he thought them impious or unimportant, but for fear that to "inflame the hearts of Christians against each other" might distract his readers from learning "at the feet of our common Master, to hear his word, to imbibe his Spirit, and to transcribe his life in our own!"[18]

Most Wesley sermons include long strings of different Bible verses cobbled together, one glossing the other to express Scripture's sense in Scripture's phrase. Wesley writes to John Newton, "The Bible is my standard of language as well as sentiment. I endeavor not only to think but *to speak* as the oracles of God."[19] Wesley sometimes expresses concern for a preacher's orthodoxy when hearing a sermon that did not contain much quoted Scripture. This concern is not rhetorical but theologically adduced: quoting Scripture is a matter of trusting Scripture. If the very nature of Scripture is holy and its effect produces salvation, then its words read aloud are able to disclose God without need of the preacher's pretentious adornments.

Finally, the authority Wesley granted the spiritually mature reader of Scripture should not be minimized in this discussion. Although modernity soon came to value a reader's suspicion of the biblical text and to question its capacity to disclose God's truth about the world, Wesley did not. Quite apart from following the standard rules that guide biblical interpretation, as an heir to the importance the Reformation placed on "inner religion," he emphasizes the formation of a reader's holy dispositions by the means of grace. Grace is a countervailing force to suspicion and rather forms faithful readers more receptive to the Spirit's guidance, thereby more knowing of and responsive to the Scripture way of salvation.

Literal Sense

In his influential "An Address to the Clergy" (1756), Wesley speaks of the importance of "acquired endowments," those skills, independent of the Spirit's gifting, which enable and mark out a competent clergy. Surely reflecting his "enlightened" age, Wesley claims that knowledge is first among these endowments; he then goes on to catalog different kinds of knowledge and know-how that clergy must learn. Most important is the minister's knowledge "of all the Scriptures"—*all* the Scriptures since "one part fixes the sense of another." Wesley claims that "none can be a good Divine who is not a good textuary. None else can be mighty in the Scriptures, able both to instruct and to stop the mouths of gainsayers,"[20] which surely are the two essential tasks of clergy by his definition.

In explaining what kind of biblical knowledge clergy must acquire, Wesley asks this critical question: "Ought he not to know the literal meaning of every word, verse, and chapter, without which there can be no firm foundation on which the spiritual can be built?"[21] Two observations based on his sentiment frame this discussion of Wesley's definition of Scripture's literal sense. First, his interpretive strategy is text centered. While the "Address" describes an expansive array of sources that supply what the cleric must know, including Scripture's "original tongues," they are all concentrated on "the literal meaning" of Scripture's every word. No task is more important than the sacred text's address of its faithful, careful reader; it stipulates the reader's "firm foundation." Second, a "good textuary" is expected to seek after "the spiritual." That is, to hold every word of Scripture captive allows the reader to gain a sense of the text's theological meaning and practical application.

Wesley has in mind a familiar protocol of biblical interpretation that begins with text-centered exegesis that provides the "firm foundation" for a theological reading of Scripture, guided by the analogy of faith, which makes "a suitable application to the consciences of his hearers." This movement from Scripture's literal sense to its theological meaning orders the flow of Wesley's sermons and helps locate biblical interpretation in and for the church. Gaining first a clear sense of every word of Scripture literally (or, better, literarily) requires the interpreter to engage in a linguistic analysis of a biblical text similar to any other literary text.

To some extent, Wesley's search for the text's literal sense reflects the Reformation's worry that allegorical readings of Scripture are sometimes employed to secure Rome's theological beliefs or are unnecessary to understand a text's plain teaching of God's salvation. What he means by literalism is a preference for what the text plainly reveals to be true on evidence both grammatical and theological. Wesley's seamless move from literal to spiritual suggests that the literal always points us to God's intended purpose.

S. E. Fowl has recently distinguished between ancient and modern definitions of literal sense.[22] His study compares Aquinas, who is exemplary of premodern biblical interpretation, with modern criticism's different conception of literal sense. Whereas modern criticism locates a text's literal sense in a single, normative meaning, which is typically linked to the human author's communicative intentions, Aquinas' reflection on the text's reception by the church's sainted teachers—Origen, Ambrose, Irenaeus, Augustine—and his own experience with the text convinced him that each biblical text has a *multivalent* (rather than singular) literal sense that interpreters seek to retrieve and apply to their own situation under the aegis of the Spirit.[23] Not only does this square with the nature of a *living* God whose self-communication is not static and timeless but dynamic and occasional, but Scripture is also part of a living tradition that changes and expands with each communion of saints.

Following this ancient model, the literal sense is not fixed by a single, normative meaning, defined by the human author's intention and discerned by linguistic and historical analysis. Rather, the literal sense of a biblical text is ever changing and defined by the divine author's intentions, understood in cooperation with the Spirit and discerned by rigorous application of the analogy of faith (see below pp. 42–45). Viewed from this angle, Scripture's literal sense for any faithful interpreter is "not an end in itself, but a central way in which God draws us into ever deeper friendship."[24]

The contrast Fowl makes has not so much to do with competing methodological interests in discerning the literal meaning of a biblical text: modern teachers of the academy are as interested in the text's literal sense as premodern teachers of the church were. The primary difference between them is epistemological: whether the text's literal sense should be considered "true." B. S. Childs points out that modern criticism reconstructs the literal sense as a matter of historical fact and typically in terms of the author's intended (i.e., a particular) meaning. The Reformers, followed by Wesley, meant something different from the modern usage: the literal sense regards the text's *Christian* meaning. It was the sense ordinary believers made of what they heard or read in the words of Scripture, not the sense made of a replacement storyline proffered by scholars.[25] If so, then it is reasonable to assume Fowl's discussion of Aquinas as roughly in agreement with the Reformers. The single sense apprehended by particular readers of Scripture at their location, for their day, in response to their spiritual needs and so to cultivate their friendship with God may very well have differed from the single sense apprehended by other readers. This "multifaceted literal sense" is characteristic of Scripture's reception during the Reformation and by its tradents during the long eighteenth century.[26]

This current elaboration of Scripture's literal sense is offered here to contextualize what Wesley calls "the naked Bible," a rubric that trades on the importance the Reformers placed on the biblical text qua text. Influenced by Newton's science of critical observation, Wesley demands that the interpreter pay close attention to what the text plainly says. This is not anti-intellectualism or critical naïveté but a commitment to the meaning of words and phrases rooted in his core belief that those words and phrases are revelatory of God.[27] At the same time, however, he ridiculed "abstract reasoning" that isolated a careful analysis of the text from its implication for real life.

In his canonical but neglected sermon, "The Nature of Enthusiasm," Wesley reflects on how one makes inquiries into the will of God. Although a radical response to the more individualistic and inward "enthusiasm" of his day, as we would expect, Wesley advises one to consult "the oracles of God." One finds God's heart in the text. But his practical concern is not where to locate God's will but, "how shall I know what is the will of God in a particular case?"[28] His answer is quite extraordinary and not often included in the various lists of Wesley's hermeneutical rules. It does not concern a textual strategy but an existential outcome. He contends that if God's will in every case is sanctification—"that we should be inwardly and outwardly holy"—then "experience tells [the interpreter] what advantages he has in his present state, either for being or doing good; and reason is to show what he certainly or probably will have in the state proposed."[29] That is, one knows whether a biblical interpretation is a right one by considering whether its actual performance produces a result that accords with holiness. This discernment is not based on one's critical orthodoxy or even the theological orthodoxy of one's interpretation; it is a measurement of what an interpretation produces in life, whether it contributes to inward or outward holiness and so draws the reader into closer communion with a holy God. Simply put, Wesley's search for the literal or "Christian" sense of a text targets a meaning that makes a *particular* communion of readers wise for sanctification.[30]

THE ANALOGY OF FAITH

The concluding summation of the prior discussion of Scripture's literal sense is elaborated by Wesley's explanatory note on Rom 12:6, which defines the "analogy of faith" as an interpretive principle:

> Having then gifts differing according to the grace which is given us—Gifts are various: grace is one. Whether it be prophecy—This, considered as an extraordinary gift, is that whereby heavenly mysteries are declared to men, or things to come foretold. But it seems here to mean the ordinary gift of expounding scripture. "Let us prophesy according to the analogy of faith"—St. Peter expresses it, "as the oracles of God," according to the general tenor of them,[31] according to that grand scheme of doctrine which is delivered therein, touching original sin, justification by faith, and present, inward salvation. There is a wonderful analogy between all these; and a close and intimate connexion between the chief heads of that faith "which was once delivered to the saints." Every article therefore concerning which there is any question should be determined by this rule; every doubtful scripture interpreted according to the grand truths which run through the whole.[32]

Significantly, Wesley does not take the prophetic gift in its "extraordinary" sense—to declare divine revelation or foretell the future—but in its more mundane sense to "expound Scripture." Perhaps Wesley rightly senses here Paul's exhortation for humility and solidarity. In any case, prophecy is the only charism Paul links to "the faith" (*hē pistis*): the proper exercise of prophecy—or "expounding Scripture" in Wesley's reading—is "according to the analogy of faith." Although the phrase has puzzled scholars, Wesley takes it as a reference to the apostolic tradition—that is, "the chief heads of the faith 'which was once delivered to the saints.'"

The articular "the faith" recalls the earlier phrase, "measure of the faith" (v. 3), which stipulates a standard of self-criticism. Almost certainly Paul does not mean that every believer is given a different "measure" or amount of faith by God but rather that the quotient of Christian faith is equally measured for all believers by the core beliefs of Paul's gospel set out in the letter. As N. T. Wright nicely puts it, "The 'measure' here is not a kind of measuring-jug containing different amounts of faith, apportioned to different people, but a measuring-rod, the same for all, called 'faith.'"[33] The use of "faith" in verse 6 carries a similar theological freight. The prophet's exposition of Scripture, as Wesley understands the gift, should agree with the Christian faith in both content and effect.

Although the word translated "analogy" (*analogia*) occurs only here in the NT, its basic meaning is well known from its wider use by schools of philosophy. An analogy relates two subjects in right proportion with each other. For Wesley, Paul's phrase, "analogy of the faith" (12:6; *kata tēn analogian tēs pisteōs*), stipulates an interpretive principle, or "rule of faith," that every use of Scripture must exist in right proportion to the core beliefs of the Christian faith.

Maddox observes, "there were British voices in Wesley's century, like John Locke, who criticized allowing the Apostles' Creed or any authoritative 'analogy of faith' to shape one's interpretation of Scripture. They argued that this contradicted the role of Scripture as itself the 'rule of faith.'"[34] However, not only did the apostolic rule of faith come prior to the formation of the biblical canon rather than originating from it, but this ecclesial rule subsequently functioned during the formation of Scripture as *norma normans* ("a rule that rules") to confirm the apostolicity of all its parts, which self-evidently does not concern their apostolic authorship but rather the content and consequence of their instruction. In this sense, both creed and canon are *norma normata* ("a rule that is ruled").

A hermeneutical circle is thus forged for every faith communion of the apostolic tradition that insures a right handling of the word of truth. This same apostolic rule that was first used in Christ's absence by his Spirit to guide the theological formation of his disciples later supplied the canonization of Scripture with its hermeneutic that continues to guide its reception and ongoing interpretation within today's church under the Spirit's direction—in Tertullian's apt phrase, of *gubernaculum interpretationis* or "governor for interpretation."

What, then, are the theological agreements that make up this apostolic grammar? Wesley charts a "grand scheme of doctrine" that narrates God's way of salvation that includes "original sin, justification by faith, and present, inward salvation." In its various articulations from antiquity forward, the apostolic rule of faith retains its narrative shape, its Trinitarian substance, and relates together the core beliefs of Christian discipleship in a way that allows believers to confess and communicate their faith in a coherent way to one another—as a mark of their oneness—and to outsiders—as a mark of their holiness or distinctive "otherness." Accordingly, knowledge of God is inseparable from knowledge of God's Son and Spirit, and such knowledge is impossible apart from its revelation in the events of or actions within history: inaugurated by God's creation of all things, testified to by the prophets, climaxed in and by the life and work of the risen Jesus and the Pentecost of his Spirit, whose work continues in the transformed life and transforming ministry of the one holy catholic and apostolic church and will be consummated by the Creator's coming triumph at the *parousia* of the Lord Christ. The catholic and apostolic church's confession and transforming experience of this narrative of God's gospel, deeply rooted in and confirmed by its collective memory, supplies the rule's raw material. The results of biblical interpretation must ever conform to this confession and experience.

The communion of Methodists speaks with glad hearts of Wesley's *via salutis*—his "way of salvation." This is his "grand scheme of doctrine" that unifies Scripture and both regulates and animates a Wesleyan reading of Scripture. No part of this grand scheme departs from the doctrinal loci of the church's ecumenical creeds, especially articulated by Anglicanism's Articles of Religion. Yet no part is more strategic to Wesley's soteriology than the doctrine of new birth; no reading of Scripture can escape its impress. The believer's regeneration is the lynchpin that holds justification by faith and one's "present, inward salvation" together.

In his sermon "Great Privilege" Wesley explains that while justification occurs when the sinner trusts God to pardon him from the guilt of inherited and past sins, regeneration occurs when that new believer is released from sin's captive power to begin a new life under the direction of the Spirit. New birth involves a *supernatural* change in human nature. If God's justifying grace puts to rights a sinner's personal relationship with God, God's regenerating grace transforms the senses of her inmost soul. She becomes a child of God, reborn with God's image with new capacities for a participatory partnership with God. As Wesley put it, new birth occasions a "vast, inward change."[35] All the resources necessary to live a holy life are given by God *at our new birth*, in the twinkling of God's eye: "as soon as he is born of God there is a total change in all his particulars—he sees the light of the world, he hears the voice of God, he feels the love of God shed abroad in his heart by God's Spirit. And now he may properly be said to live."[36]

When Scripture's testimony to God's saving grace is understood Wesley's way, regeneration marks a gateway into the body of Christ where still other operations of divine grace begin the hard work of sanctification. Precisely because regeneration changes the will, the believer need not willfully sin. Precisely because regeneration transforms the senses, it is now possible to resist evil tempers and thoughts. Precisely because regeneration restores the image of a loving, truth-telling God within the believer, the believer is now assured of God's love and confident of participating in God's coming victory. Precisely because regeneration purifies the human spirit, God's Spirit can bear witness in our spirit, which in Wesley's understanding paves the path for a robust cooperation between God's people and God's Spirit as broker of God's sanctifying graces.

Central to Wesley's radical conception of Christian perfection is this dynamic cooperation between the divine and human spirits that marks out the believer's new birth as God's child (cf. Rom 8). While new birth is a supernatural event that changes our nature, sanctification envisages a working arrangement between God and the believer who is sanctified by grace in proportion to the amount and quality of grace received. The various practices of Christian discipleship—works of piety and mercy—when complemented by the ordinary means of grace ordained by the church, occasion a profuse outpouring of God's salvation-creating grace that transforms the believer into a conspicuous saint. Every meaning and performance of Scripture at its ecclesial location is analogous to this conception of salvation.

Conclusion

In his famous comment about Scripture's importance in the preface to his published sermons, Wesley writes, "I want to know one thing, the way to heaven: how to land safe on that happy shore. God Himself has condescended to teach the way; for this very end He came from heaven. He hath written it down in a book! O give me that book! At any price, give me the Book of God! I have it: here is knowledge enough for me."[37] While sometimes this is taken at face value either to promote Wesley as exemplary of a fundamentalist reading of Scripture or to demonize him for the same, doing so misses the point. For Wesley, Scripture's importance for the church is understood in its capacity to reveal God's instruction of "the way to heaven." This in no way shortchanges the cooperation of the competent interpreter, since God's inspired instruction is not magically given or received. For our own day, Wesley stands as our mentor and exemplar in this regard. Scripture is the Spirit's auxiliary for growing the church's wisdom, but such is received only by faithful readers who study the sacred text carefully in expectation of hearing a sanctifying word from the Lord God Almighty.

4

WESLEY AS INTERPRETER OF SCRIPTURE AND THE EMERGENCE OF "HISTORY" IN BIBLICAL INTERPRETATION

Joel B. Green

Modern assessment of John Wesley as a reader of the Bible has tended to relegate his work to the category of the "uncritical,"[1] often drawing attention to Wesley's lack of a genuinely historical consciousness and his concomitant failure to allow concerns with historical reconstruction and historical context their determinative roles in assessing the meaning of biblical texts. In this essay, I examine this charge, first, by demonstrating its anachronism; and second, by commenting on ways in which Wesley demonstrated historical interests appropriate to mid-eighteenth-century biblical interpretation. Along the way I hope to show how, in any case, his commitment to read the Bible within and for the church would have mitigated any wholesale embrace of the protocols of historical criticism, as these were developed toward the end of his career and in the centuries after him. Consequently, I will urge both that this charge against Wesley is only partially sustainable, and that those who follow in Wesley's theological footsteps would do well to restrain their capitulation to modernism's historical-critical enterprise.

THE "UNCRITICAL" MR. WESLEY

What would it mean today to label as "uncritical" John Wesley's work with the Bible? Prior to the last three decades, which have seen a number of innovations in what counts as academic biblical studies, it could only mean that Wesley's engagement with the Bible was not constrained by the assumptions and protocols of historical criticism.

Critical Study as Historical Criticism

Even if historical criticism no longer occupies the same place of taken-for-granted privilege that it did as recently as the 1980s, John Barton can still proclaim, as he did in 2007, that "the preferred description of biblical criticism [is] the 'historical-critical method.'"[2] The stage was set for Barton's evaluation toward the end of the eighteenth century, when Johann Philipp Gabler (1753–1826) distinguished methodologically between dogmatic theology and biblical theology in his 1787 inaugural address at the University of Altdorf: "There is truly a biblical theology, of historical origin, conveying what the holy writers felt about divine matters; on the other hand there is a dogmatic theology of didactic origin, teaching what each theologian philosophises rationally about divine things, according to the measure of his ability or the times, age, place, sect, school, and other similar factors."[3] Gabler went on to sketch a three-stage process by which one might move from historical analysis of the biblical texts to this "biblical theology": (1) careful linguistic and historical analysis; (2) engagement in a synthetic task, the purpose of which was to identify those ideas common among the biblical writers; and (3) arrival at the transcendent (timeless and universal) principles of the Bible. If one were to engage in dogmatic theology, one would begin with these transcendent ideas, adapting them to particular contexts. Biblical studies thus enters the picture as the (sole) foundation on which theology might be constructed.

Krister Stendahl's more recent, widely celebrated distinction between "what it meant" and "what it means" is not exactly Gabler's proposal *redivivus*, but the similarity is obvious, and Stendahl's phrasing now defines for many the discrete work of biblical studies.[4] Heikki Räisänen insists that Gabler was right in his programmatic distinction between the historical and religious tasks, for example, just as Peter Balla affirms in his reassessment of the field that the task of New Testament theology is distinct from systematic theology; for Balla, the New Testament is viewed as "source" for theology and is not itself "faith seeking understanding."[5] Indeed, the modern flourishing of biblical studies as a discipline has traded on this pivotal distinction between the descriptive task (of biblical scholars) and the constructive task (of theologians), with the descriptive task understood chiefly in historical-critical terms. As Stendahl represented the work of biblical studies: "Our only concern is to find out what these words meant when uttered or written by the prophet, the priest, the evangelist, or the apostle—and regardless of their meaning in later stages of religious history, our own included."[6]

In an essay first published in 2004, John J. Collins sketches a contemporary understanding of historical-critical scholarship.[7] Recognizing that "historical criticism" refers to a family of methods, he claims that historical criticism is characterized by its ideal of objectivity (though recognizing that this ideal is never realized) and its non-negotiable emphasis on interpreting biblical texts in terms of their historical contexts. Biblical texts must be read in terms of the literary and cultural conventions of their time: "Time is of the essence, and anachronism is a deadly sin."[8] Underlying these commitments are three key assumptions, which Collins borrows from the classic discussion of the historical method by Ernst Troeltsch (1865–1923) as it was reformulated by Van Harvey (1926–).[9] The *autonomy* of the historian—that is, the historian's "freedom from tradition"—is the first principle of historical criticism, a principle Collins derives from Harvey rather than from Troeltsch, even if one might argue that it was latent already in Troeltsch's work. "As Harvey has well described it, autonomy represented a change in what may be called the morality of knowledge. Where medieval culture had celebrated belief as a virtue and regarded doubt as sin, the modern critical mentality regards doubt as a necessary step in the testing of knowledge and the will to believe as a threat to rational thought."[10] That is, faith is catalogued as a hindrance to knowledge, with the result that, for Collins, "historical criticism, consistently understood, is not compatible with a confessional theology that is committed to specific doctrines on the basis of faith."[11] Having established this *sine qua non* of critical scholarship, Collins goes on more briefly to posit two further principles: *analogy* ("We can assess what is plausible in an ancient situation because we know what human beings are capable of") and *criticism* ("Scholarship is an ongoing process; its results are always provisional and never final").[12]

Allow me to summarize some of the corollaries of this critical approach as these have been realized in modern biblical studies:

1. Even if meaning, for some historical critics, is not exhausted by history, meaning is determined by its original context (often articulated

as the human author or redactor's original intent). Hence, the biblical materials were not written "for us."

2. Biblical texts must each be understood in terms of its singularity—that is, the historical situation within which each book or even each source was written or redacted—with the consequent loss of the singular voice of the Bible when read as a whole. (On a given issue, therefore, even within the Pauline corpus, Romans might say one thing, Philippians quite another, and the traditional "Hymn to Christ" cited in Phil 2:6-11 something else still.) Historical criticism dismisses any claims regarding the literary simultaneity of the Bible—that is, the assumption that all biblical voices speak at the same time, with the same voice, and of the same reality.[13]

3. Historical criticism thus eventuates in an emphasis on the diversity of Scripture at the expense of its (potential) unity.

4. A collection of biblical books, such as the New Testament, bears witness to a theological judgment rather than a historical one; since its concern is with understanding the nature of early Christianity, then, historical criticism accords no necessary privilege either to the New Testament books or to the New Testament itself.

5. Critical biblical studies can speak to how people in ancient times might have spoken about god or the gods, or faithfulness to god; however, if God is to have a voice in the present, that voice will be heard not through the work of biblical studies but through the work of theologians, ethicists, or homileticians—and then only after history has first spoken.

6. With respect to credal or confessional influence, critical study allows no quarter. The results of biblical studies may have ramifications for the church, but traffic from one to the other is decidedly one way.

Before departing this discussion of biblical criticism, I should underscore Collins' recognition that "historical criticism" itself is a slippery phrase, so much so that it is no longer unusual to find references to historical criticisms (in the plural) and, more important, that it is useful to acknowledge different and not necessarily related critical practices associated with the phrase. Three such practices are primary: (1) the reconstruction of historical events in order to narrate the past (i.e., historical criticism proper), (2) excavation of traditional material in order to explain the process led to their textualization in the biblical writings (including such historical criticisms as tradition criticism, form criticism, source criticism, and redaction criticism), and (3) study of the socio-historical situation within which the biblical materials were written.[14]

Wesley and Eighteenth-Century Biblical Criticism

Was Wesley "uncritical"? Although an unmitigatedly affirmative answer would seem to follow from our discussion thus far, this characterization of Wesley would prove too hasty on at least two interrelated grounds. First, the term "uncritical" itself is here a dismissive anachronism grounded in the arrogance of a form of presentism that has it that the only legitimate reading of a biblical text is one oriented toward historical-critical concerns. Subjecting the historical-critical enterprise itself to historical analysis reveals that the critical tradition is far more inclusive than the modern hegemony of historical criticism might allow. Some readings are mimetic in theoretical orientation, others pragmatic, others expressive, and still others objective. Each finds the locus of meaning in its own place—for example, in "the universe," in "the work," in "the artist," or in "the audience"—and so each in its own way is "critical" insofar as it is concerned with adjudicating among competing interpretations.[15] From this vantage point, it would make more sense to label Wesley as a premodern, rather than uncritical or precritical, interpreter. Second, this label overlooks the degree to which Wesley himself participated in the emergence of modern biblical studies—and, indeed, in the Enlightenment project, insofar as he accorded significance in his theological enterprise to reason, for example, or evaluated various readings of Scripture in relation to the findings of the New Science emerging from the seventeenth century. From this vantage point, it becomes difficult simply to place Wesley in the category of premodern interpreters and makes more sense to recognize the degree to which, with respect to his engagement with the biblical materials, he occupied the interstices between premodern and modern eras. This is an important point since, arguably, ours is an analogous age, characterized by the overlapping of modernist and postmodernist impulses in study of the Bible.

Werner Kümmel summarizes the turn of the era like this: "About the turn of the seventeenth to the eighteenth century ideas fundamental to a consideration of the New Testament emerged in two areas— ideas that prepared the way for the first attempts at a strictly historical view of the New Testament—in the field of textual criticism and in the critical attitude toward religion by English Deism."[16] On the one hand, Kümmel's synopsis understates the importance of the historical concerns that emerged in the 1600s and 1700s. On the other, though, his observations reveal why modern attempts to label Wesley's work as uncritical would have to be dismissed as anachronistic. Wesley developed his interpretive habits prior to the emergence of what would become known as the historical science of biblical studies.

Let me refer to two exemplars of exegetical practice, one of which was certainly influential on Wesley, the other of which may have been. In the first instance, I refer to Johann Albrecht Bengel (1687–1752), whose *Gnomon Novi Testamenti* (1742) provided the basis for much of Wesley's own *Explanatory Notes upon the New Testament*.[17] Bengel devoted much of his energy to textual criticism. His edition of the NT text (*Novum Testamentum Graecum*), published in 1734, inaugurated "a new stage in the history of the textual criticism of the New Testament"; in fact, text-critical work today proceeds in part on the basis of principles Bengel identified.[18] Establishing the text was the first step in exegesis, to be followed by philological and linguistic work, as well as attention to the literary context of a text and the purpose of the biblical writer—though these should be understood in relation to the whole of Scripture, "the full and comprehensive force of Scripture in its whole connection." "Separate thoughts of each writer must be determined as to their sense according to grammatical and historical laws, but this in constant reference to the totality of the faith, and to revelation as a whole." In presenting his *Gnomon Novi Testamenti* for publication, Bengel indicated his desire "to indicate what lies within the compass of the sacred text; for Scripture is its own best and safest interpreter"; that is, his notes were to be understood as programmatic rather than exhaustive, as his attempt to guide readers into their own research. His interpretive work prioritized historical matters ("the *bones*") as well as spiritual ("the muscles, blood-vessels, and nerves"). "As the *bones* are necessary to the human system, so Scripture *must* have its *historical* matters. The expositor who nullifies the *historical* ground-work of Scripture for the sake of finding only spiritual truths everywhere, brings death on all correct interpretation. Those expositions are the safest which keep closest to the text."[19]

The second is Augustus Herman Francke (1663–1727), whose religious work was known to Wesley, even if it is not clear that Wesley was familiar with Francke's exegetical handbook, *Manuductio ad lectionem scripturae sacral* (1693; translated as *A Guide to the Reading and Study of the Holy Scriptures*).[20] Francke's guide is divided into two major sections: "Of Reading as It Respects the Letter of the Scriptures" and "Of Reading as It Respects the Spirit of the Word." "All Reading . . . respects either the LETTER or the SPIRIT of the Inspired Writings. Separate from the latter, the former is empty and inconsistent; but when both are united, the study of Divinity is rendered complete."[21]

Study of the letter of the Scriptures concerns itself first with grammatical reading—study of the Bible in its original languages; understanding issues of etymology, syntax, signification, and idiom; and familiarity with the Aramaic Targumim and the rabbinical writings (though students are advised not to fill their minds with "Judaical absurdities" but rather with "divine truths" and "divine pleasures").[22] Moving on to historical reading, Francke referred, first and foremost, to the student's knowledge of the content of the Old and New Testaments and then to a knowledge of their authors, the occasion of each of the writings, their scope, and the nature of their arguments. Moreover, he referred to "the seats of subjects"—that is, a working knowledge of where in Scripture each of the loci of the Christian faith is discussed, a kind of working index of theological subjects. A historical reading must also account for such external circumstances as those taken up by textual criticism and the preparation of critical editions of the Bible. Reading for the letter of Scripture also involves an analytical reading; here Francke concerns himself with what we might call literary forms, rhetorical and stylistic devices, structure, and interpretive issues that proceed from genre analysis.

The second main section of Francke's handbook focuses on the spiritual meaning of the Scriptures. First, interpreters concern themselves with an "expository reading" of the Scriptures—that is, with Scripture's "literal sense" (not to be confused with the "sense of the letter," above). This literal sense given Scripture by the Holy Spirit is available to the converted only; after all, the literal sense surpasses mere theoretical and historical knowledge. Scripture cannot be read as one might read Aristotle, as though we might be satisfied with what natural reason teaches us. Help for those seeking Scripture's literal sense includes reading Scripture in light of Scripture (including reading parallel texts in relation to teach other, since the biblical voices are harmonious) and the analogy of faith (i.e., the church's doctrines, which exemplify Scripture's unity). Second, Francke discussed "doctrinal reading," namely, "that by which we so apprehend the truths contained in Scripture, as to derive thence a just and saving acquaintance with the nature and will of God."[23] The third and fourth aspects of spiritual reading—inferential reading and practical reading—are closely related in that they emphasize the need to draw out the sense of the text for contemporary life. These processes are based in a principle of analogy but one of a very different sort than was set forth by Troeltsch and rearticulated by Collins. For them, "analogy" refers to the laws of nature. The laws that we observe today are no different than those operative in the times to which the biblical materials bear witness; hence, whatever claims would be dismissed on the basis of the laws of nature today ought also to be dismissed when they are made in the biblical texts. For Francke, though, the theological and spiritual witness of Scripture and its role in the formation of a person's "affections" (i.e., his or her deeply rooted dispositions) was immediately relevant to contemporary readers, who are needful of the same instruction, encouragement, challenge, and formation. Here is an "analogy and harmony of things sacred."[24]

We see from these two examples, Bengel and Francke, the importance historical issues have begun to play but also the relatively limited role allocated to historical considerations.[25] Interpreters should engage in historical reading in order to make plain foreign habits of thought and expression, to fill in the blanks, as it were, so as to make the text accessible. Attention to history might serve as a prophylactic against uncontrolled mysticism or spiritualizing. But historical inquiry does not call into question the basic unity of Scripture, it does not counter either the capacity of Scripture to speak with one voice or the expectation that it will do so, and it does not undermine the role of the analogy of faith in scriptural interpretation. In contrast to the historical-critical paradigm that would begin to take shape in the late eighteenth century, in these formulations truth was not a correlate of historical veracity; historical inquiry did not eventuate in wholesale renarration of Israel's past, Jesus' life, or the church's emergence; and the immediate relevance of Scripture for contemporary readers was a working assumption.

Wesley as Biblical Interpreter and History

Although Wesley did not follow in the footsteps of those authors, like Francke, who penned student handbooks or exegetical guides, his writings do sometimes evince his reflections on reading and interpreting Scripture. These, together with the interpretive practices on display in his *Explanatory Notes upon the New Testament,* locate him squarely on the trajectory we have sketched with reference to Bengel and Francke.

Consider, for example, the counsel he provided at the conclusion of the preface to his *Explanatory Notes upon the Old Testament*: "If you desire to read the Scriptures in such a manner as may most effectually answer this end, would it not be advisable . . . to read this with a single eye, to know the whole will of God, and a fixed resolution to do it? In order to know his will, you should . . . have a constant eye to the analogy of faith, the connexion and harmony there is between those grand, fundamental doctrines, original sin, justification by faith, the new birth, inward and outward holiness. . . ."[26] Again, consider the report he gave of his own approach, found in the preface to his *Sermons on Several Occasions*. "Does anything appear dark or intricate?" he inquired. For practitioners of the historical-critical paradigm, the key to making sense of difficult passages in the Bible is further inquiry into history. Wesley took a different path:

> Does anything appear dark or intricate? I lift up my heart to the Father of lights: "Lord, is it not your Word, 'If any lack wisdom, let them ask of God'? You 'give generously and ungrudgingly.' You have said, 'If any be willing to do your will, they shall know.' I am willing to do, let me know, your will." I then search after and consider parallel passages of Scripture, "comparing spiritual things with spiritual." I meditate thereon, with all the attention and earnestness of which my mind is capable. If any doubt still remains, I consult those who are experienced in the things of God, and then the writings whereby, being dead, they yet speak. And what I thus learn, that I teach.[27]

Wesley did not thus eschew the sort of historical data he might glean from further research but locates this kind of study *after* seeking divine help, comparing Scripture with Scripture, and consulting with the spiritually mature and theologically well formed. In a telling reversal of the historical criticism characteristic of the modern era, Wesley seems to assume that the chief chasm separating readers from their understanding of Scripture would be spanned less through the acquisition of more historical detail and more through knowing better God and God's ways.

At the same time, Wesley took seriously the text-critical work of such forebears as Bengel and insisted on learning the biblical languages—both staples of the historical inquiry of his day. Moreover, he sometimes brought the findings of natural science to bear on his interpretive work. For example, in his comments on Jesus' commission to the disciples, that they should "cast out devils" (Matt 10:8), Wesley observed that someone had said that diseases ascribed to the devil in the Gospels "have the very same symptoms with the natural diseases of lunacy, epilepsy, or convulsions," leading to the conclusion "that the devil had no hand in them." Wesley continued:

> But it were well to stop and consider a little. Suppose God should suffer an evil spirit to usurp the same power over a man's body as the man himself has naturally, and suppose him actually to exercise that power, could we conclude the devil had no hand therein, because his body was bent in the very same manner wherein the man himself bent it naturally?
>
> And suppose God gives an evil spirit a greater power to affect immediately the origin of the nerves in the brain, by irritating them to produce violent motions, or so relaxing them that they can produce little or no motion, still the symptoms will be those of over-tense nerves, as in madness, epilepsies, convulsions, or of relaxed nerves, as in paralytic cases. But could we conclude thence, that the devil had no hand in them?[28]

In fact, Wesley had made something of an avocation of familiarizing himself with study of the central nervous system, a science that was not yet a century old, thus indicating his willingness to take seriously the importance of science for biblical interpretation and for Christian mission. In terms of biblical interpretation, here his solution is openness to the truth of both faith and science; rather than deny the truth of stories of demonized persons in the Gospels or of scientific explanations, he allows that both could be true.

Wesley's work often puts on display the results of historical research. He provides brief introductions to the cities to which Paul's letters are addressed. Sometimes his comments suggest familiarity with classical literature (he was, after all, schooled in the classics) and with some postbiblical Jewish literature (including the Maccabean literature, Josephus, and Philo). Indeed, in "An Address to the Clergy," Wesley sketched a series of questions regarding the preparation of true ministers of Christ, himself included, and a number of these questions have to do with one's abilities as a reader of Scripture. He asked whether clergy have a critical understanding of Greek and Hebrew, background in Greek and Roman antiquity as well as ancient Jewish customs, knowledge of the sciences (including "natural philosophy"), an acquaintance with patristics, and so on.[29] Such knowledge is necessary in addition to "a full and clear view of the analogy of faith," which guides the interpreter through Scripture, as well as an intimate familiarity with the whole Bible, both Old Testament and New Testament. Wesley's list of expectations shadows the earlier teaching of Francke:

> Upon the mention of any text, do I know the context, and the parallel places? Have I that point at least of a good textuary? Do I know the grammatical construction of the four Gospels; of the Acts; of the Epistles; and am I a master of the spiritual sense (as well as the literal) of what I read? Do I understand the scope of each book, and how every part of it tends thereto? Have I skill to draw the natural inferences deducible from each text?[30]

Clearly, Wesley expected clergy to be close readers of the biblical text and schooled in a wide range of ancillary disciplines, knowledge of which should be brought to bear on one's study.

What of so-called critical issues in biblical study? With regard to relationships among the Gospels—which emerged as a key issue for New Testament criticism in the late eighteenth and nineteenth centuries—Wesley observed, "St. Mark in his Gospel presupposes that of St. Matthew, and supplies what is omitted therein. St. Luke supplies what is omitted by both the former; St. John, what is omitted by all the three."[31] On the authorship of Hebrews, he observed the ancient tradition that Paul had written Hebrews, a judgment with which he agrees; after all, "St. Paul's method and style are easily observed therein."[32] He does not question the traditional authorship of the New Testament Gospels and letters.

More pervasive in Wesley than engagement with what would become standard critical issues in Old Testament and New Testament introductions are those places in his *Explanatory Notes* where he provides background information not readily available in the text itself.[33] Consider this sampling from his notes on the Gospel of Luke.

1. According to 1:5, Zechariah belongs to the priestly order of Abijah. Wesley explained that priests were divided into twenty-four orders, that Abijah's was the eighth (1 Chr 24:10), and that each order served the temple for seven days with the role of each priest determined by lot.[34] Here and at other points as well, Wesley's comments suggest dependence on the Jewish Mishnah, a codification of oral interpretation of Torah.
2. At 1:27, Luke tells us that Mary "was espoused" to Joseph. Translations today sometimes oversimplify by reporting that Mary "was engaged" to Joseph (so the NRSV), but Wesley commented that "it was customary among the Jews for persons that married to contract before witnesses some time before."[35] This helpfully locates Mary in the in-between state of "betrothal"—contractually committed to marry Joseph but not yet married.
3. At 10:30, Luke's account of Jesus' parable of the good Samaritan begins, "A certain man went down from Jerusalem to Jericho." Wesley wrote, "The road from Jerusalem to Jericho (about eighteen miles from it) lay through the desert and rocky places: so many robberies and murders were committed therein, that it was called 'the bloody way.'"[36] Wesley thus gives his readers an insider's perspective on what presumably everyone knew in the first century.
4. At 22:38, one of Jesus' disciples volunteers two swords in response to Jesus' directive that anyone "who has no sword must sell his cloak and buy one." Wesley noted, "Many of Galilee carried them when they traveled, to defend themselves against robbers and assassins, who much infested the roads." Then he added, "But did the apostles need to seek such defense?" before observing that Jesus "did not mean literally that every one . . . must have a sword."[37] Why Wesley provided this note is unclear. Was it to identify these swords as defensive (rather than offensive) weapons? Was he thinking of the traveling conditions in eighteenth-century Britain? In any case, he does not allow this historical conjecture to overshadow the point that Jesus' words of reply, "It is enough," are words of exasperation at the dullness of his followers.

Wesley's notes are often of this kind and were a means for providing details that might aid his "plain" or "ordinary" readers. They are sometimes historical, sometimes geographical, and sometimes related to ancient customs, though mostly his notes are concerned with the meaning of words or phrases. Sometimes they help to draw out the sense of a passage on its own terms and sometimes they treat a passage as though it were written for people in eighteenth-century Britain; it is unclear whether Wesley's historical consciousness was sufficiently developed to make a distinction between these two options, since his primary concern was to make Scripture plain.

Wesley's work with Scripture, then, manifests a family resemblance with that of Francke and Bengel, as well as others of the period. For William Baird, this is due especially to their shared conviction regarding the role of religious experience in the writing and reading of the Bible. For these interpreters,

> the Bible is viewed not as a collection of data and doctrine but as a witness to a normative religious experience. Since this normative experience took place in history—in the lives of the people of the Bible—the historical character of the biblical revelation is affirmed. To reconstruct this history, scholars like Francke, Bengel, and Wesley were dedicated to discerning the plain, literal meaning of the text. . . . Thus, they dedicated themselves to textual, linguistic, grammatical, and historical interpretation.[38]

Baird's summary indicates the degree to which Wesley moved in the direction of scientific scholarship, which would emerge in Germany during the waning years of his life as a more thoroughgoing historical method. Baird's comments in this regard are significantly mitigated, though, by his and our recognition that Wesley's ecclesial and theological commitments are everywhere on display in his interpretive work, not least with regard to his ongoing appeal to the analogy of faith and the way his notes steer his readers away from a predestinarian reading of the Old and New Testaments.[39]

WESLEY, WESLEYANS, AND HISTORY

The charge against Wesley, that he was uncritical in his approach to Scripture, is only partially sustainable, and in any case such a charge would be undermined by his concern specifically to read Scripture within and for the church. Of course, the charge might still be made, but it would fail to take seriously that Wesley's aims with Scripture, and therefore his practices, do not align well with the historical-critical paradigm whose birth pangs were evident in his own lifetime. By way of concluding this essay, let me indicate four ways in which Wesley's work fails to participate in scientific exegesis.

First, Wesley's historical consciousness was underdeveloped such that he was unable to see that his interests in the histories of the people addressed in the Bible ought to have pulled the rug out from under his commitment to what I have called Scripture's literary simultaneity. He did not take seriously enough, for example, that Paul's words to the Corinthians were shaped by the shared story of Paul and the Corinthian Christians and by Paul's grasp of the historical contingencies of the Corinthian experience. He did not take seriously enough that Paul's words to the Philippians arose in a different context and, therefore, ought not to be thrown too quickly into the melting pot of religious experience as Wesley understood it. The unity Wesley found in Scripture came at a heavy price: namely, the silencing of voices in favor of a soteriology articulated in the key of Paul (justification by faith) and John (new birth). If biblical studies in the modern period has taught us anything, it is that we cannot read Scripture faithfully if we ignore the diversity of its voices. (Whether diversity has the last word, as scientific exegesis tends to assume, is an altogether different issue, of course.) We would do well to press beyond Wesley in our historical consciousness.

Second, Wesley's interest in history was limited in another sense. Earlier, I observed that historical criticism has promoted three species of practices: (1) the reconstruction of historical events in order to narrate the past, (2) the excavation of traditional material in order to explain the process that led to the final composition of biblical texts, and (3) the study of the socio-historical realities within which these texts were written and, then, which help to give these texts meaning. We find in Wesley's interpretive work the beginnings of this third practice of historical criticism but no inklings of the first two. Even if these practices of reconstruction and excavation were well developed in Wesley's day, it is not clear that he would have embraced them. This is because of his commitment to making plain the literal sense of Scripture in the service of the church and its mission. Reconstruction and excavation are by nature antitextual (i.e., less concerned with the text per se, more concerned with what lies behind the biblical text) and thus would run counter to Wesley's interests. In this regard, interestingly, Wesley's premodern understanding of biblical texts, a view that assumes that texts and the past are coterminous, has much in common with postmodern historiography, which prioritizes the text as a narrative representation of the past; both premodern and postmodern views tend to prioritize the text, then, and this contrasts sharply with the modernist segregation of the past from the text, with priority given to the past. Although naive in its own way, Wesley's focus on reading texts as witnesses to God's engagement with his creatures remains important for theological interpreters.

Third, Wesley did little to anticipate the historical-critical principle of autonomy. Nor, for that matter, did he anticipate the naturalistic reductionism of historical criticism. Instead, he assumed God at work in and through history, granted the veracity of biblical reports of miracles, and interpreted Scripture in conversation with the analogy of faith. This is not to say that he regarded the analogy of faith as a thing separate from Scripture since for him and many others in the post-Reformation era, the analogy of faith was thought to cohere with Scripture. In these respects, Wesley's work identifies key issues for contemporary theological interpretation of Scripture, namely, God's participation in the world and the status of the analogy of faith in engagement with Scripture.

Fourth, in contrast to the dispassionate neutrality of historical criticism, we find in Wesley a well-developed expectation regarding the immediate relevance of Scripture. From the perspective of later biblical studies, Wesley simply failed to seek or maintain the appropriate critical distance. Instead, he read Scripture and taught others to do so as a spiritually and theologically formative exercise. If this perspective seems out of step with modernity, it is surprisingly how prescient it would be of current initiatives in the recovery of theological interpretation of Scripture, for which the aim of engagement with Scripture is first and foremost to know God.

Wesley lived in the dawning years of the modern period while we occupy its waning years. We ought not to imagine that we can simply turn back the clock, as though the intervening years, during which the light of the historical-critical method had shown so brightly, did not happen or were not important. We might admit, though, that the brilliance of the historical-critical light blinded students of the Bible to other approaches and interests and that the dimming of that light in recent years has allowed us to see again and recover what had for too long been hidden in the shadows. I refer to the ramifications of a theological exegesis able to appreciate socio-historical interests without reducing the meaning of a biblical text to its context of origin, to acknowledge the role of theological commitments in the reading of the church's Scriptures, or to recognize the formative role of Scripture in life of the church and in the lives of God's people. Even if we might struggle with one another as we identify how best to revisit Wesley's view of Scripture and his interpretive practices—at what points to set them aside, engage them critically, or embrace them wholeheartedly—it remains the case that Wesley's work serves as an exemplar from which we might learn something of the road ahead, those of us interested in the ongoing role of Scripture in the life of the church.

PART II

The Nature and Authority of Scripture among Wesleyans

5

SCRIPTURE AMONG AFRICAN AMERICAN METHODISTS

Reginald Broadnax

Bishop Joseph A. Johnson of the Christian Methodist Episcopal Church states:[1]

> The *Bible* for the Black preacher is the greatest book that has ever been written. In it God Himself speaks to men. It is a book of divine instruction. It offers comfort in sorrow, guidance in perplexity, advice for our problems, rebuke for our sins, and daily inspiration for our every need. The *Bible* is not simply one book. It is an entire library of books covering the whole range of literature. It includes history, poetry, drama, biography, prophecy, philosophy, science, and inspirational reading.
>
> The Black preacher believes the *Bible* alone truly answers the greatest questions that men of all ages have asked: "Where have I come from?" "Where am I going?" "Why am I here?" "How can I know the truth?" For the Bible alone reveals the truth about God, explains the age-old problem of sin and suffering.[2]

Some may see this passage as hyperbolic, but it is an expression of the high esteem in which the African American community holds the Bible. Now, I must admit that the African American community is very diverse, including many different religious and nonreligious traditions. For Christians within the community, however, the Bible is a source of "life, health, and strength."[3] Through the words of the Bible, we learn the story of God's compassion and concern for all human beings, and God's purpose for our lives is revealed. "So when we say that the Bible is God's Holy Word, we mean that God has spoken and continues to speak through the persons, events, and teachings written about in the Bible."[4]

Many African Americans first experienced the Bible during slavery where it was used to justify the slave system and to keep slaves docile, obedient, and not given towards rebellion.[5] Yet, even within this system, many slaves were able to first accept Christ as Savior then express their freedom in the words of the Bible. One such person was Richard Allen.

Allen, born a slave in Philadelphia in 1760, writes of his conversion: "I cried unto Him who delighteth to hear the prayers of a poor sinner, and all of a sudden my dungeon shook, my chains flew off, and, glory to God, I cried. My soul was filled. I cried, enough for me—the Saviour died. Now my confidence was strengthened that the Lord, for Christ's sake, had heard my prayers and pardoned all my sins."[6] Allen's language of his dungeon shaking and his chains falling off is an allusion to Acts 12:7. But Allen may not have first encountered these images from Scripture itself, but rather through a Methodist hymn. Dennis C. Dickerson argues that the language Allen uses is from Charles Wesley's hymn of 1738, "And Can It Be That I Should Gain an Interest in the Savior's Blood!" The crucial third stanza, which drew from this scriptural passage, declared:

> Long my imprisoned spirit lay,
> Fast bound in sin and nature's night:
> Thine eye diffused a quickening ray,
> I woke; the dungeon flamed with light;
> My chains fell off, my heart was free,
> I rose, went forth, and followed thee.[7]

Dickerson argues that it was in the hymns of Methodism that many African Americans first encountered the Scriptures, and it was the language of these hymns that provided the framework for expressing their salvation, but it also provided the framework to express their liberation from slavery.

> The apostle was restricted to a jail cell and Allen was confined to slavery. Divine intervention, however, set both men free. The angel liberated Peter from prison and a Wesleyan evangelist set Allen free

from sin and inspired his release from slavery. Wesley, in his hymn, drew upon the metaphor of imprisonment to represent the bondage that evil and sin imposed upon humankind. God, however, through the agency of angels, both celestial and clerical, could set people free. When that happened, chains flew off and hearts were free![8]

Many African Americans during slavery, because of the prohibitions against literacy, learned the Bible through hymns and other songs (Negro spirituals), as well as through stories told to them from the Bible. Primary in the role of transmitting stories was the African American preacher: "slaves became increasingly familiar with the Bible through black preachers who would interpret Scripture through the dramatization of the biblical story and its application to African American life. This use and interpretation of the Bible eventually became the slaves' primary means of adapting Christianity."[9] Thus, Harry V. Richardson says that the slaves loved the Bible. The stories they heard from the Bible helped them to frame a narrative of a God "who was both good and just, who would reward righteousness and punish evil, and who, in his own good time, would destroy slavery and elevate the slaves."[10]

While slaves loved the Bible and held the Bible in high esteem, not all of the Bible was viewed equally; in fact, they openly rejected parts of the Bible that did not affirm their humanity and equality before God.

> Patience in the face of earthly trial and obedience to earthly masters loomed large in the slaveholders' message, but slaves found other themes more to their liking. Theologically, they had little truck with the doctrines of Paul and, instead, maintained the egalitarianism of the eighteenth-century revivals, emphasizing the equality of mankind before God and the irrelevance of earthly status to one's chance for eternal life. They identified particularly with the people of the Old Testament and their heroic exodus from bondage. The message of the fundamental equality of all in the eyes of God and—when the master was out of range—in the eyes of man remained a central tenet of African-American Christianity long after it had ceased to echo in the slaveholder's church.[11]

Slaves felt free to reject parts of the Bible that did not affirm their experience as human beings and instead framed a narrative that not only affirmed their humanity but also gave them hope—hope in a day when the wicked would be punished and slavery would be destroyed.

It is my argument that African Americans have always felt the freedom to reject parts of the Bible that did not affirm their experience of humanity. The question I now raise is whether, within the Wesleyan/Methodist tradition, a hermeneutical practice can be found that gives credence to the long-held practice of African Americans. In this essay I shall (1) review the recent discussion of scriptural authority, the quadrilateral, and Wesley's method of interpretation, (2) examine Wesley's use of Scripture with respect to the issue of slavery, and (3) with Wesley as a guide, attempt to frame an African American Methodist hermeneutic.

The Primacy of Scripture

For John Wesley, the most basic authority for Christian life and faith was the Holy Scriptures. Wesley says that as Methodists, "We believe the written word of God to be the only and sufficient rule both in Christian faith and practice."[12] However, as Randy Maddox points out, the word *only* or the Protestant mantra of *sola Scriptura* should not be taken too literally. According to Maddox, "In reality, Wesley interpreted the Protestant *sola Scriptura* (in good Anglican fashion) to mean that Scripture is the primary, rather than exclusive, Christian authority."[13] But what do we mean by "primary authority"? This debate has gone on for several years, with regard to both the authority of Scripture as well as the place of Scripture in relation to other authorities. This debate has had particular significance within The United Methodist Church as it has grappled with the concept of the Wesleyan quadrilateral.

Ted Campbell points out that the quadrilateral was "foreshadowed" in Colin Williams' book, *John Wesley's Theology Today*.[14] In his book, Williams divided the discussion of "Authority and Experience" into five subcategories—the first two dealing with the authority of Scripture, followed by experience, reason, and tradition. These subcategories were incorporated into an interim report in 1970 of The United Methodist Theological Study Commission on Doctrine and Doctrinal Standards. This Commission was authorized by the uniting General Conference of 1968 to report to the 1972 General Conference on the church's doctrinal statements. The interim report's discussion of "The Wesleyan Concept of Authority" was an accounting of John Wesley's views on religious authority, as understood within both the Methodist and Evangelical United Brethren churches. The report states, "In this quadrilateral of 'standards,' Scripture stands foremost without a rival." Thus, within the interim report, "final authority of Scripture, consistent with John Wesley's own views, was unambiguously asserted."[15]

However, the statement adopted by the 1972 General Conference changed this understanding of scriptural authority. First, the quadrilateral was not attributed to Wesley or given within a discussion of John Wesley's understanding of scriptural authority. Rather it was stated as doctrinal guidelines for theological reflection within the church. Albert Outler, in an introduction to the statement, said that the Commission's concern was with "guidelines," which could be used in any creed or statement that would have authority in the United Methodist Church, or by United Methodist people.[16] Outler believed that the report was faithful to the best "traditions of the Wesleys, of Albright, and Otterbein, not by replication, but by re-presentation and re-interpretation." Thus, in the report, "instead of presuming to tell our people what to think, theologically, we have tried to offer basic guidance as to how we may all do theology together, faithful to our rich and yet very diverse heritage, and yet also relevant to our present ideological confusion."[17]

Second, the 1972 statement was criticized for presenting less a "quadrilateral" and more an "equilateral," in which the four categories held equal authority. A critical pair of sentences states, "There is a primacy that goes with Scripture, as the constitutive witness to the biblical wellsprings of our faith. In practice, however, theological reflection may find its point of departure in tradition, 'experience,' or rational analysis."[18] While the first sentence seems to uphold scriptural authority, the "however" lent credence to the criticism that the second sentence seriously weakened or qualified the first.

After much discussion on the issue of authority and the primacy of Scripture and even the validity of the quadrilateral itself, the 1988 General Conference adopted a revised statement meant to clarify the previous statement of 1972. This statement asserts that "scripture is the primary source and criterion for Christian doctrine."[19] The statement also asserts that tradition, experience, and reason are integral to the study of Scripture without displacing the primacy of scriptural authority for faith and practice.[20] However, even after this clarification by the 1988 General Conference, discussion continues concerning the primacy of Scripture within the church. One person who has taken up the issue is Randy Maddox. While Maddox acknowledges that Wesley never himself used the term "quadrilateral," he states that it is reflective of Wesley's "standards of doctrine" and the criteria by which he interpreted Scripture. Thus, it is warranted to focus on these four categories to discuss Wesley's process of judgment. "The issue then becomes how Wesley construed these elements and how he drew upon them as criteria in his theological activity."[21]

With respect to the question of Wesley's judgment, interpretation of Scripture, and the criteria he used for that interpretation, Scott Jones points out that the categories of the quadrilateral have been misinterpreted. The term "tradition" has a negative connotation for Wesley in its association with Roman Catholicism and can never be vested with authority in religious matters.[22] Jones, instead, suggests that Wesley understood two distinct periods within the broader Christian tradition as authoritative: Christian antiquity and the doctrines of the Church of England. Thus, for Jones, there are actually five components of interpretation: Scripture, reason, experience, Christian antiquity, and the Church of England. Within this structure, Scripture still maintains primacy over the other components; however, for Wesley, the elements are defined in such a way that they constitute one locus of authority with five aspects. Christian faith and practice are governed by Scripture, which is reasonable in its claims, exemplified in antiquity, vivified in personal experience, and most fully institutionalized in the Church of England.

Jones continues his argument by showing that, within this locus of authority, Wesley also used the "analogy of faith," which shows that Scripture is a unitary whole, consistent in all its parts, with respect to the essential doctrines of salvation. While the analogy of faith is an important element in understanding how Wesley both viewed and interpreted Scripture, I wish to return to Jones' discussion of reason, for it will prove to be important for our further considerations.

According to Jones, reason has two important functions in interpreting Scripture. First, reason assists us in understanding Scripture. Second, reason helps us to determine when there is an absurdity in Scripture. Wesley believed in the clarity of Scripture and that the literal sense of a text or passage could be maintained unless that text either contradicted another Scripture (a contradiction arises when two or more Scriptures say mutually exclusive things[23]), or that it leads to an absurdity. How then do we determine whether something is absurd? Jones writes that the ability of reason to identify an absurdity in

Scripture is limited to two specific areas. First, matters of fact to which experience and natural science testify can supersede the literal sense of Scripture. Second, where Scripture appears to contradict itself, reason recognizes the conflict and determines that it must be resolved.[24]

In sermon 144 "The Love of God" Wesley writes, "'Tis true, if the literal sense of these Scriptures were absurd, and apparently contrary to reason, then we should be obliged not to interpret them according to the letter, but to look out for a looser meaning."[25] Wesley appears to use the word "absurd" to mean something contradictory to reason and common experience. What is important to understand here is that Wesley understands that while a literal sense or a literal interpretation of Scripture can be derived in most instances, there are some Scriptures from which a literal interpretation would be absurd. In sermon 139 "On the Sabbath" Wesley states, "We have no pretence to interpret any Scripture figuratively but when an absurdity follows a proper interpretation."[26] And in those cases, we are not obliged to interpret them literally. This is an important consideration in light of our discussion of scriptural primacy. I believe that one such issue where a literal interpretation of Scripture cannot be derived—that, in fact, leads to an absurdity that releases us from the obligation to interpret the Scripture literally—concerns the issue of slavery.

Wesley on Slavery

Our understanding of the primacy of Scripture should lead us to Wesley's interpretation of the Bible, to what the Bible teaches concerning slavery. Key to our examination will be Wesley's *Explanatory Notes upon the New Testament*.[27] With respect to biblical passages concerning slavery, three texts are instructive for our study: Eph 6:5; Col 3:22; and 1 Pet 2:18. All three give essentially the same instruction: "Slaves, obey your earthly masters" (Eph 6:5; Col 3:22 NRSV); "Slaves, accept the authority of your masters" (1 Pet 2:18 NRSV).

The Authorized Version (AV) was the standard translation of the day, and this translation served as Wesley's base, though in his translation Wesley made numerous alterations.[28] Wesley was "committed to the idea that establishing the best text is important, and he knows that the texts used by the translators of the AV could be improved upon." While often criticized for his diligent study of the biblical languages, this knowledge served him well in the translation of the New Testament. Wesley also benefited from improvements in the study of

Greek syntax since the original translation of the AV. Therefore, "it can be said that the translation of John Wesley was a highly successful one for his day, based on the soundest learning at his disposal. While there are a few mistakes and some visible influences of his theology, his revision as a whole can be verified from the text itself."[29]

One thing that stands out in our three passages is that in each, the word "servant" is used instead of the word "slave." This is the standard rendering of the AV, and Wesley maintains the AV's rendering of "servants." The Greek word translated here is *douloi*, "slaves." Although "servants" is a possible translation, *doulos* and its cognates "describe the status of a slave or an attitude corresponding to that of a slave"; indeed, "the meaning is so unequivocal and self-contained that it is superfluous to give examples of the individual terms or to trace the history of the group."[30] It is difficult to know today why the AV uses "servant" rather than "slave." Bishop Alfred G. Dunston of the African Methodist Episcopal Zion Church,[31] suggests that the AV was influenced at this point by the fact that, at the time, England was heavily involved in the slave trade, with the result that the translators obscured the meaning of the text in their translation.[32] I am not suggesting that Wesley did the same thing in his translation; however, by following the AV, he falls victim to the same criticism, namely, obscuring the meaning of the text in the translation.

Clearly at this time, slavery was an issue about which Wesley was concerned. In his note on 1 Tim 1:10, he writes, "Mansteaalers—The worst of all thieves, in comparison of whom, highwaymen and housebreakers are innocent. What then are most traders in negroes, procurers of servants for America, and all who list soldiers by lies, tricks, or enticements?"[33] Here too Wesley uses the word "servant," which I suggest is the standard rendering of the time but could obscure the meaning; yet, he uses it in the context of slavery, so clearly he is concerned with the issue (even referring to those who trade in Negroes as "mansteaalers," the worst of all thieves).

Turning to an examination of our three passages, at Eph 6:5 Wesley writes: "*Your masters according to the flesh*—According to the present state of things: afterward the servant is free from his master. *With fear and trembling*—A proverbial expression, implying the utmost care and diligence. *In singleness of heart*—With a single eye to the providence of the will of God."[34] Wesley ignores the clause, "servants [i.e., slaves], obey" and only picks up the verse with "your masters according to the flesh." "According to the present state of things" could be suggestive of a temporary state to which the slaves were to be complicit because afterward they would be free. This is a tacit condoning of the practice.

At Col 3:22 Wesley, writes: "*Eyeservice*—Being more diligent under their eye than at other times. *Singleness of heart*—A simple intention of *doing right*, without looking any farther. *Fearing God*—That is, acting from this principle."[35] Again, Wesley picks up the verse without comment on the command to obey; this is curious because in verse 18 he directly comments on the admonition, "Wives, submit yourselves to your own husbands." Wesley writes, "*Wives, submit*—Or be subject *to*. It is properly a military term, alluding to that entire submission that soldiers pay to their general."[36] So the fact that Wesley does not address the command of slaves to obey their masters is curious. However, he does say that slaves should fear God, which is to act on the principle of *doing right*. Doing right is to obey one's master, both with the heart, and in fear of God.

In 1 Pet 2:18 Wesley writes: "*Servants*—Literally, *household* servants. *With all fear*—Of offending them or God. *Not only to the good*—Tender, kind. *And gentle*—Mild, easily forgiving."[37] The text refers to *oiketai*, or "house slaves," but this certainly is not the practice of slavery Wesley witnessed in South Carolina and Virginia. However, a question can be raised as to the meaning of obedience "with all fear." Does this refer to the conduct of the slave in relationship to his master; or "does the expression refer to an individual's relationship to God? In that case, the passage has picked up the image of Christians as 'free persons' who live as 'slaves of God' from verse 16."[38] In saying, "Of offending them or God," Wesley seems to have both meanings in mind. But why should slaves be fearful of offending their masters? Is this again not a tacit condoning of the practice?

At the time of the publication of his *Explanatory Notes*, Wesley was firmly against slavery and had stated his opposition in other places. The General Rules of 1743 forbid the buying and selling of persons for the intention of enslaving them. In his journal entry for April 27, 1737, Wesley writes concerning the practice of slavery: "O how hath God stretched over this place 'the lines of confusion, and the stones of emptiness!' Alas for those whose lives were here vilely cast away, through oppression, through divers plagues and troubles! O earth! how long wilt thou hide their blood? How long wilt thou cover they slain?"[39] Not only do the General Rules and this journal entry show his opposition to the practice, but in another passage within the *Notes* (at 1 Tim 1:10, cited above), Wesley states his opposition to slavery. Yet, in our passages concerning the practice of slavery, Wesley does not address the issue at all. In fact, Wesley's comments can actually be read as an accommodation to the practice. This is unfortunate because a reading of these passages alone could give one the false understanding of Wesley as supportive of or indifferent to the practice of slavery.

However, what can be understood from the three passages we examined is that, clearly, Wesley is not interpreting the Scripture according to its literal sense. Here we clearly read, "Slaves, obey your earthly masters" (Eph 6:5; Col 3:22, NRSV), and "Slaves, accept the authority of your maters" (1 Pet 2:18, NRSV). So if a literal interpretation is not in operation here, then we must ask whether this is an instance where Wesley, using reason, has found that these passages are either contradictory or absurd. One way of determining this is to examine another text where Wesley discusses the issue of slavery. One such text is Wesley's *Thoughts upon Slavery*.

Wesley's strongest condemnation of slavery is his *Thoughts upon Slavery*, published in 1774.[40] In this essay, Wesley attacks the practice of slavery as morally indefensible and inconsistent with both justice and mercy. Wesley's work was influenced by Anthony Benezet's *Historical Account of Guinea*, and some have suggested that Wesley's *Thoughts upon Slavery* was an abridgement of Benezet's work;[41] however, Warren Smith states that Wesley used about 30 percent of the work in his *Thoughts upon Slavery*.[42] This being stated, Wesley puts together a well-organized and systematic argument against slavery, appealing to both English and natural law.[43]

The work is divided into five sections. In section 1, Wesley gives an introduction to his argument, stating that slavery is "an obligation of perpetual service, an obligation which only the consent of the master can dissolve."[44] This service passes through parents to children, from generation to generation. The practice "prevailed" among the Jews, Greeks, Romans, and ancient Germans but, after the rise of Christianity, fell into decline until revived by Spain at the end of the eighth century and continued until the middle of the fourteenth, at which time it fell "nearly extinct" until the sixteenth century with the discovery of America and the need for Negro labor.

In section 2, Wesley takes up the argument of supporters of slavery, that they are in fact rescuing Negroes from a land or country that is "horrid, dreary, and barren."[45] Wesley, most likely drawing from Benezet's study of Guinea and other works,[46] explains that the region of West Africa from which the Negroes came, far from being horrid and dreary, is actually "exceeding fruitful and pleasant, producing vast quantities of rice and other grain, plenty of fruit and roots, palm wine and oil, and fish in great abundance, with much tame and wild cattle."[47] Wesley next inquires into what sort of persons the Negros are; what of their manner and behavior? Wesley notes that they are well governed in their respective villages, that many are "Mahometans" (i.e., Muslims), and that they will drink nothing stronger than water. Being Mahometans, they have daily prayer, "and it is surprising to see the modesty, attention, and reverence which they observe during their worship."[48] Wesley concludes by saying that, far from being the stupid, brutish, lazy barbarians they are made out to be, they are sensible, industrious to the highest degree, fair, and just in all their dealings.[49]

In section 3, Wesley turns to the question of how Negroes are procured. They are captured in battle or stolen out of their cottages or from the fields, or roads—all by their own kinsmen—and sold to slaveholders. When brought either to the Caribbean or to the colonies; they are held in perpetual servitude by law for life. In section 4, Wesley inquires "whether these things can be defended, on the principles of even heathen honesty; whether they can be reconciled (setting the Bible out of the question) with any degree of either justice or mercy."[50] On the question of mercy, Wesley says that slave holding is so utterly inconsistent that it needs no other proof. To the question of justice, Wesley asks,

> Where is the justice of inflicting the severest evils on those that have done us no wrong? Of depriving those that never injured us in word or deed, of every comfort of life? Of tearing them from their native country, and depriving them of liberty itself, to which an Angolan had the same natural right as an Englishman, and on which he sets as high a value? Yea, where is the justice of taking away the lives of innocent, inoffensive men; murdering thousands of them in their own land, by the hands of their own countrymen; many thousands, year after year, on shipboard, and then casting them like dung into the sea; and tens of thousands in that cruel slavery to which they are so unjustly reduced?[51]

Thus for Wesley, "all slavery is as irreconcilable to justice as to mercy."[52]

In section 5, Wesley appeals to the captains, merchants, and planters who perpetuate slavery. All of them are guilty in Wesley's eyes, guilty of a grave injustice, that of depriving human beings of their liberty. "Liberty is the right of every human creature, as soon as he breathes the vital air; and no human law can deprive him of that right which he derives from the law of nature."[53] Liberty was part of the image of God; hence, slavery must be wrong.[54] "If, therefore, you have any regard to justice, (to say nothing of mercy, nor the revealed law of God,) render unto all their due. Give liberty to whom liberty is due, that is, to every child of man, to every partaker of human nature. Let none serve you but by his own act and deed, by his own voluntary choice."[55] With this appeal to liberty, Wesley concludes his *Thoughts upon Slavery*.

In reading *Thoughts upon Slavery*, two observations stand out: first, we do not find a direct appeal to Scripture in Wesley's argument; that is, Wesley never condemns slavery on the basis of a particular biblical text. This is striking, considering our previous discussion of the primacy of Scripture for Wesley. As Maddox points out, not only did Wesley appeal to Scripture for doctrinal issues, but for moral issues as well.[56] There could be no greater moral issue in his day than the issue slavery and the slave trade, yet Scripture does not play a major role in Wesley's argument. And, in his important study of Wesley's encounter with the practice and the development of his thought on the issue, Smith does not refer to Scripture as a warrant for Wesley's condemnation of slavery. Instead, as Jason Vickers points out, Wesley's appeal is not to Scripture, but to natural law.[57] In the absence of an appeal to Scripture, though, Wesley does appeal to God, but this appeal is a condemnation. "Is there a God? You know there is. Is he a just God? Then there must be a state of retribution; a state wherein the just God will reward every man according to his works. Then what reward will he render to you? O think betimes! Before you drop into eternity! This now, 'He shall have judgment without mercy that showed no mercy.'"[58]

Second, not only does Wesley not appeal to Scripture, but he in fact sets it aside. Considering the question of whether slavery can be reconciled to either justice or mercy, Wesley asks "whether they can be reconciled (*setting the Bible out of the question*) with any degree of either justice or mercy."[59] The phrase "setting the Bible out of the question" must be questioned, particularly in light of the three passages we examined where the Bible condones the practice of slavery, texts concerning which Wesley's own notes can be interpreted as a tacit acceptance of the practice. We must conclude, therefore, that Wesley sets the Bible "out of the question" because he believed either that it contradicted another passage or that at this point the literal sense was absurd. The reason we must come to this conclusion is because of Wesley's strong condemnation of slavery in the other works we have previously cited. Here we apply the test of Scripture previously cited in Jones, that "matters of fact to which experience and natural science testify can supersede the literal sense of Scripture."[60] Clearly, both Wesley's experience with slavery in Virginia and in South Carolina and Wesley's own understanding of natural law (science) brought him to the conclusion that the literal sense of the Bible can be superseded, or set out of the question. The fact that Wesley, who believed in the primacy of Scripture, can set aside the Bible on such an important moral issue as slavery can be instructive for African Americans as we address theological issues concerning the authority of Scripture.

Framing an African American Methodist Hermeneutic

While African Americans have always held a high regard for the Bible, African Americans have also been painfully aware of how the Bible has been used against their community and personhood. Historically, the Bible has been used not as an instrument of freedom and liberation, but rather as an instrument of oppression against African Americans. Against such oppressive hermeneutics, African Americans have championed a variety of interpretive responses.

One response to these oppressive hermeneutics was to reject Christianity altogether. As a Christian theologian I reject this option, yet I acknowledge that this option is operative both historically and even today among many within the African American community. This is most expressly seen in the Nation of Islam, but it can also been seen in the writings of Anthony B. Pinn, who has rejected a traditional Christian hermeneutic in favor of a more humanistic approach to oppression and suffering.[61]

Another response to oppressive hermeneutics was to reject them in favor of a hermeneutic that supported and inspired the African American quest for freedom and liberation. James Evans states that, in the face of the biblical mandate for slaves to obey their masters, slaves, and the African American community in general, have recognized that the slave mandate exemplified neither the gospel nor the central thrust of the biblical message, which they believed was a message of freedom and liberation. Thus, an oppressive hermeneutic was rejected in favor of a hermeneutic that supported the African American quest for freedom.[62]

Another response has been to judge Scripture by one's own culture and experience. Christian Methodist Episcopal Bishop Thomas Hoyt Jr. identifies such a hermeneutic within the African American community of Scripture and culture.[63] In this hermeneutic, culture gives authority to Scripture. In much the same way that stories functioned in the ancient Near East to give interpretation to the community of *their world*, African Americans find in the story(ies) of the Bible an affirmation of their own story, their struggle against oppression and depersonalization. "In black culture 'the story' is that which establishes the authority of the Bible, for in its story, blacks find the essence of their story in modern life":[64]

> For blacks the Bible attains its authority as that authority conforms to the black story through experience and culture. The biblical stories make sense to blacks because these have inspired blacks with a retrospective view of their own history, have given them a confession that tells of what God has done in the history of another people, have evoked a telling of what God has done in their own history, and have provided a perspective of faith and hope with regard to what God will do for their freedom. In this respect, the Bible is one of the chief components of the black experience; it enables myth to function coherently in the lives of blacks.[65]

Framing the African American story within the story of the Bible has (1) allowed the Bible to speak both critically and constructively to each new situation, (2) given African Americans confidence of God's presence in their struggle for political and social justice, (3) solidified theological grounds for opposing racism and injustice, and (4) established the authority of the Bible on grounds of their experience.[66] This interpretative framing of the African American story within the story of the Bible necessarily contradicts both the story of our oppression and even certain passages within the Bible itself. In each case, African Americans have rejected the story of oppression and have reframed the story in favor of an interpretive story of value that upholds the dignity and humanity of the community.

From the beginnings of Methodist preaching in America, African Americans have been attracted to Methodism's bold stance against both slavery and human oppression.[67] From Wesley to Coke to Asbury and all of the itinerant preachers who succeeded them, Methodist preachers abhorred the practice of slavery in the strongest of terms and proclaimed a God of liberation, both from sin and from human oppression. Admittedly, often this message has waned, but this has been the historical thrust of Methodism.

Yet this proclamation of a liberating God has been based on Scripture in a way that contradicts other scriptural texts that advance the practice of slavery. As we have seen, in such cases, Wesley (and Methodists who followed him) either rejected biblical passages that condone slavery in favor of a more liberating, analogous view of the Bible (an analogy of faith), one that incorporates the whole of the biblical message and not just one particular passage, or rejected those passages according to reason, experience, and natural science. In this sense we can say that Wesley had a progressive view of Scripture in that he understood that, in some cases, a literal interpretation of Scripture cannot be maintained. Thus, in some cases, the literal sense (and the passage itself) must be rejected in favor of an interpretation of the biblical message consistent with the revelation of Jesus as Christ. As Jones stated, some passages are either contradictory or found to be absurd, and, in such cases, the literal sense of the passage can be superseded on the basis of experience.

This type of analogous reading of the Bible, a rejection of some passages in favor of an interpretation more representative of the liberating message of the Bible and the struggle for liberation against oppression and depersonalization, has been the operative hermeneutical lens through which African Americans have read the Bible.[68] Clearly, African Americans have viewed the Bible as primary authority for doctrine, Christian faith, and practice. At the same time, the community has also recognized the absurdity of certain passages and how those passages can and have been used as a means of oppression. Thus, in these instances, when asked whether the Bible in its entirety (i.e., every passage contained therein) must be given primacy of authority, the African American community must answer, *No!*

In these instances, the experience of the community in its relationship with a God known as deliverer who struggles with them against oppression must be given primacy of authority over such passages that oppress and dehumanize. In such cases, those passages must be judged in light of a God who not only came in the person of Jesus as Christ to seek and to save those who were lost but also came to set at liberty those who are oppressed. It is to this witness that the primacy of authority must be given.

6

SCRIPTURE AMONG HISPANIC METHODISTS

Justo L. González

Some Preliminary Issues

As one broaches the theme of Scripture among Hispanic Methodists, several points need clarification. The first of these is the very definition of "Hispanic."[1] While this term is usually employed to refer to people of Hispanic culture and traditions living in the United States, for the purpose of this article that definition may be too narrow. Indeed, the connections between Hispanic Methodists in the United States and Methodists in Latin America have such a long history and are so frequent that much of the manner in which Hispanics in the United States read Scripture is in dialogue with and reflects what others are doing beyond the confines of this country. When Methodist work among Hispanics began in the Southwest, this was considered of one piece with work in Mexico. This was true not only in the understanding of the mission itself, but also in its structuring, so that agencies and judicatories often worked on both sides of the border.[2] Eventually Methodist work in Mexico was separated administratively from work among Mexican Americans, resulting over time in such different bodies as the Methodist Church of Mexico and the Rio Grande Conference of the (now United) Methodist Church. But even then, constant border crossing continued. To this day, many of the United Methodist pastors in the American Southwest—and increasingly in the Midwest and other regions—were born south of the border, mostly in Mexico but also in

Central America. Many of them were already in ordained ministry before coming to the United States, and thus their biblical interpretation reflects much of what they learned in Mexico or Central America. Accordingly, while in this essay I shall be focusing my attention on the work that takes place in the United States, readers will note that much of this is similar to what takes place south of the border.

Similarly, a high proportion of United Methodist pastors in the Northeast—and increasingly in other regions of the country—are of Puerto Rican origin.[3] Most of them received their theological education in the Evangelical Seminary of Puerto Rico, an institution where dialogue with the rest of Latin America is active and constant. So, once again, it is difficult to distinguish between the theological perspectives and hermeneutical practices of Puerto Rican pastors and leaders in the United States and those on the island. In more recent times, there has been an influx of pastors from the Iglesia Evangélica Dominicana—a church that resulted from an unprecedented ecumenical missionary venture of the churches in Puerto Rico—many of whom were trained and ordained in the Dominican Republic or in Puerto Rico. Finally, although for political reasons contacts have been curtailed in recent decades, there was always a close connection between Cuban Methodism and Methodism in Florida. Indeed, the first Methodist churches in Cuba were not founded by missionaries from the United States, but by Cuban exiles who had become Methodist—some having attended seminary and been ordained—in the United States, who returned to the island as possibilities there improved.[4] When there was a Latin District in the Florida Conference, the background of most of its leadership was Cuban. Until the time of the Cuban Revolution, the bishop of Florida presided over the Cuban Annual Conference. And when, after the revolution, Methodist Hispanic work in south Florida was revived, once again most of its leadership proceeded from Cuba. For all these reasons, it is obvious that one must not speak of a "Hispanic" use of Scripture as if this were entirely different and disconnected from the use of Scripture in Mexico, Puerto Rico, the Dominican Republic, or the rest of Latin America.

Second, the term "Methodist" needs to be clarified. By a wide margin, most Hispanic Wesleyans are not United Methodist—neither in the United States nor in Latin America. Thus, to speak of "Methodists" as if they were the sole—or even the principal—heirs of Wesleyanism is to ignore the reality of the enormous impact of the Wesleyan tradition far beyond the borders of what today we call Methodism. While in a given city in the United States there may be two or three United Methodist Hispanic churches, there are probably at least the same number representing the holiness tradition and several dozen representing the Pentecostal tradition that emerged from it.[5] All of these are heirs of Wesleyanism and, even though there may be wide differences among them, there are also linkages that must not be ignored. Hispanic Wesleyans reading Scripture are not all part of "the people called Methodists," but they are Wesleyans nevertheless.

Third, it is important to note that most Hispanic Methodists do not identify themselves primarily as Methodist, but as Protestant or *"evangélicos"*—which is not exactly the same as "evangelical."[6] While a number of United Methodist Hispanics descend from generations of Methodists, this is not the case with the majority of Hispanic Methodists. Many of them are converts from Roman Catholicism, others have joined The United Methodist Church from other Protestant bodies, and others were previously unchurched. As a result, when asked what in their use of the Bible is typically Methodist or Wesleyan, most Methodist Hispanics—including most pastors—have no clear answer. Many are Methodist because of historical or social circumstances rather than for theological reasons. Indeed, a large number of United Methodist Hispanic pastors were previously members—and even pastors—in other denominations. Of these, many joined The United Methodist Church because they were invited by a district superintendent to serve as local pastors or because they disliked the arbitrariness that prevailed in their previous churches. Among those who cite theological reasons for joining The United Methodist Church, the most frequent answer is that they were attracted by the United Methodist concern for and involvement in social issues—although there are also many who say that the one thing they dislike about United Methodism is its progressive social policies and statements. For our purposes in this essay, this means that there is not always a clear-cut line between Hispanic Methodist use of Scripture and that of other Hispanics.

Finally, it is important to remember that, as is the case in any population group, there are wide theological and social differences among Hispanic Methodists. Many use the Bible as mostly a repetition of what they were taught by the larger church or by those who first brought them to the church. The full spectrum of interpretation that is found in the church at large—from fundamentalism to radicalism—is also found among Hispanic Methodists.

For all of these reasons, here I shall not attempt to describe the entire gamut of uses and interpretations of the Bible found among Hispanic Methodists. This would be very similar to what is found in the great variety of perspectives encompassed under the wide umbrella of United Methodism. Rather, what I shall try to do is to show those elements in the Hispanic Methodist use of Scripture that may make a contribution to the church at large and to its own use of Scripture.

Sources

Given the wide variety of theological positions among Hispanic Methodists, the sources reflecting their use of Scripture are equally varied. Most are oral, coming from reports on discussions in Bible study groups, sermons, theological debates, and the like. Again, among such daily discussions and acts of interpretation, the vast majority reflect little that is particularly Hispanic and therefore will not be employed in the present article. But they also include fascinating reports of moments of insight that will certainly be taken into account in the present reflections.

In addition, some written sources reflect Hispanic Methodist use of Scripture. Of these, the most significant is the Sunday-school magazine *Lecciones cristianas*, which has been published in various formats from 1939 to present. This is an invaluable source for the development of Methodist hermeneutics—one which requires further study and which would provide a fertile field of research for scholars interested in the development of Methodist Hispanic theology. During its first decades, all the authors in *Lecciones cristianas* were Methodist. As one reads those early issues of the magazine, traits can be noted that are typically Methodist but not particularly Hispanic—the joining of faith and action, of learning and piety, and of concern for the spiritual life of individuals and for the well-being of society at large.[7] Beginning in the 1970s, one can discern a growing consciousness that, while much is to be learned from traditional Methodist interpretations of Scripture, a specifically Hispanic series of experiences, concerns, and issues must also be reflected in biblical interpretation. It is at this point that some of the paradigms that I discuss below begin to emerge. One must note, however, that it was also at this time that the authorship of the magazine began to expand to include authors of other denominations—particularly Presbyterians, Disciples, and American Baptists. It was also at that time that an agreement was made with the American Baptists that they would also publish *Lecciones*, with some adjustments, under the title of *Fe y vida*. Thus, as one researches the development of Hispanic Methodist use of Scripture as reflected in *Lecciones cristianas*, it is important to remember not all the more recent authors in that magazine are Methodist.

Another significant source for the study of Hispanic Methodist use of Scripture is the journal *Apuntes*, published since 1981 through a collaborative agreement between the United Methodist Publishing House and the Mexican American program at Perkins School of Theology. While not all articles in that journal deal with the use of the Bible and not all are written by Methodists, many clearly set out to provide new readings of Scripture from a Hispanic perspective.[8] Other journals include occasional articles on the subject.[9]

Then, a number of Bible commentaries and studies of particular books illustrate Methodist Hispanic interpretations of particular books or sections of the Bible—for example, Jorge A. González, *Daniel: A Tract for Troubled Times*; Aquiles E. Martínez, *Después de Damasco: El apóstol Pablo desde una perspectiva latina*; as well as three texts by Justo L. González: *For the Healing of the Nations: The Book of Revelation in an Age of Cultural Conflict, Acts: The Gospel of the Spirit*, and *Luke*.[10]

Finally, one must take into account the project of the Mexican American Program at Perkins School of Theology, which in 1992 began a series of discussions on Hispanic use of Scripture and four years later published a report on that discussion.[11]

The Authority of Scripture

It almost goes without saying that Hispanic Methodists lay great store on the authority of Scripture. In this, they stand with the vast majority of Christian tradition. But this authority is experienced and understood in ways that result from the historical use of the Bible among *evangélicos*, which thus presents its own particular nuances. When the Bible was first used by *evangélicos*, both in Latin America and within Hispanic communities in the United States, it was a source of support for otherwise unpopular and even suspect ideas. Early *evangélicos* lived in a context in which few of their neighbors knew anything about Protestantism beyond the view that it was a heresy. This was true from the beginnings of Latino Protestantism early in the nineteenth century to at least the middle of the twentieth century—and in some areas of Latin America even today. *Evangélicos* were surrounded by neighbors who were convinced that this new religion was what exactly what their very conservative priests—and nuns in schools—told them. I still remember conversations that I had with my classmates early in the 1950s, trying to convince them that, even as an *evangélico*, I believed in the divinity of Jesus, and that this was also the faith of the entire church I attended. Other *evangélicos* and I constantly found ourselves pitted against the authority of much-respected priests and of nuns who had taught our neighbors that Protestants did not believe in Jesus, or at least that we were misguided zealots who did not understand what Christianity was all about.

In that context, the Bible came to our rescue. Here was an authority that our neighbors had been told they must respect and follow. In those days before the Second Vatican Council, many of those neighbors had rarely seen—much less read—a Bible. But they knew this was an authoritative book. And we came to them with the open Book in our hands. We knew the Book in ways they did not. Thus, in the many debates I had with my classmates, the Bible became my ally. Here was an authority beyond that of priests and the entire hierarchy of the church, an authority that even that hierarchy acknowledged to be supreme. And we could show the connection between what we said and did and what the Bible said.

It is difficult for people in the United States, and in the twenty-first century, to understand that context and the profound influence it had on Hispanic Protestantism. It was a context of frank and open hostility between Catholics and Protestants. It was a context in which the social structure and the entire cultural tradition favored the former against us *evangélicos*. It was therefore an unequal context. But in that context we had a great ally: the Bible. Thus, on any given Sunday evening one could recognize *evangélicos* by the Bibles they carried to church.

It was in that background that much of the *evangélico* reading of Scripture took place. We read the Bible, yes, as guidance for our lives, but we also read it as an arsenal of weapons and arguments against our detractors. We read it looking for passages that contradicted common Catholic religiosity or even the declared doctrine of the Roman Catholic Church.

Things have changed much since those days. On the one hand, particularly after Vatican II, Roman Catholicism has begun to lay more stress on the reading and study of Scripture. Back in the fifties, the vast majority of Bibles sold in Spanish were Protestant, and Catholic Bibles were mostly expensive pieces of typographical art—all of them translated from the Latin Vulgate, not directly from the original languages. Today this has changed radically, with thousands of Catholic groups gathering all over Latin America and in the United States to study the Bible. On the other hand, we have all changed, coming to see the commonalities we all have as Christians, and dwelling less on the differences that sixty years ago seemed so crucial.

One must acknowledge that old habits take a long time to change. Even now, half a century after Vatican II, echoes of those earlier days resound. Many *evangélicos* speak of their joining Protestantism as "when I became a Christian," and there are Catholic bishops who, on the Day of Prayer for Christian Unity, speak about the far-away Eastern Orthodox while ignoring their Protestant neighbors. Thus, a significant number of *evangélicos* still read and employ the Bible exactly as my friends and I did sixty years ago.

However, in the United States our older emphasis on the authority of the Bible has taken a new dimension. In Cuba, where I grew up, I was a minority because of my religion, and as a minority I learned to employ the authority of Scripture against those who would call us heretics—an authority particularly valuable because it was accepted also by our foes. Now, in the United States, we *evangélicos* are still a minority, although not now for reasons of religion but rather for reasons of race and culture. And in this new context Hispanics once again find that Scripture is an important ally in their struggle for recognition both in church and in society. In the particular case of Methodists, but also in most other denominations, we find in Scripture an authority that is recognized by those of the dominant culture and therefore a valuable ally in our struggle to make our presence felt in the church and to have the church take its mission among Hispanics more seriously.

In brief, Hispanic Methodists—as well as others—read Scripture both as guidance for our own lives and as support for our struggles. Scripture is thus an authority, not only for us, but also for the church at large.

Fundamentalism?

Given this emphasis on the authority of Scripture, many in the dominant culture see their Hispanic *evangélico* brothers and sisters as fundamentalists. There is a measure of truth in this, for many Hispanics—including some Methodist Hispanics—allow themselves to be embroiled in the debates that currently engage many in the dominant culture—creationism versus evolution, prayer in public schools, and the like. But the truth is that most *evangélicos* are not fundamentalists but what one might well call "naïve readers" of Scripture. This is an important distinction. Historically, fundamentalism developed as a reaction against modernism. The famous "five fundamentals" of the Niagara Falls meeting were not a list of basic biblical teachings but rather five points selected in order to serve as touchstones to determine who should be considered a true Christian and who should be rejected as a liberal modernist. Such reactionary movements usually bear the imprint of that against which they react, and fundamentalism bears the imprint of the very modernity against which it reacted.

In practical terms, this means that, while many Hispanic readings of Scripture are as literal as those proposed by fundamentalists, they are usually not the result of a desire to reject views considered wrong or heretical but simply the result of a precritical reading of the text—a reading that is often not aware of the modern challenges to traditional interpretations of the text. It also means that too often believers of the dominant culture, on hearing Hispanics comment on Scripture and use it, dismiss them as fundamentalists who are unwilling to be convinced of the possibilities of different readings.

It further means that it is quite possible to move such Hispanics from their precritical readings of Scripture but that it is often difficult to do this by simply pointing out the conflicts between modern critical attitudes—or modern science—and the Bible. If, instead, one uses the Bible itself to invite Hispanics to new understandings and interpretations of a particular text, they are not as resistant as typical fundamentalists would be. Their interest is not in upholding a particular understanding of the Bible but rather in what the Bible itself may be saying to them today. (At the same time, one must point out that this leaves many Hispanic believers vulnerable to novel interpretations based on the "discovery" of hidden meanings in the text or on numerological schemes. Hence we face the greater pastoral need to develop in Hispanic believers a neocritical attitude that will allow them to distinguish between what is properly grounded in the text and what is simply a matter of personal fantasy or baseless speculation.)

Particular Paradigms

As indicated above, the purpose of this essay is not so much to present a full picture of all the existing Hispanic ways of interpreting and using Scripture but rather to point out what may be some of the Hispanic contributions to the reading of Scripture by the church at large. On this score, the contribution of Hispanic Methodists—as well as of other Hispanics—is significant.

The best way to understand such contributions is in terms of certain basic paradigms of interpretation that are practiced by many Hispanic Methodists and which result in novel interpretations that often are quite relevant to the conditions in which Hispanics live in the United States. These paradigms are not principles of interpretation conceived in the abstract but rather elements in the Hispanic experience itself, which then flow out into patterns of interpretations—sometimes consciously, and sometimes not.

Mestizaje and Mulatez

The paradigm most often found in Hispanic Methodist interpretations of Scripture is a sense of in-betweenness that is often expressed in the terms *mestizaje* and *mulatez*. The notion of *mestizaje* as a hermeneutical paradigm came to the foreground in 1925, when Mexican scholar José Vasconcelos published his much debated book, *La raza cósmica*. While Vasconcelos has repeatedly been faulted for his uncritical affirmation of the Mexican *mestizo* race, there is no doubt that his book gave voice to the deep-seated feeling among Mexicans and other Latin Americans that the Eurocentric view of culture that prevailed in much of Latin America must be overcome. This theme was then affirmed by Mexican American Roman Catholic priest Virgilio Elizondo, whom many credit with being the founder of consciously Hispanic theology in the United States. In his doctoral dissertation for the Institut Catholique in Paris, and later in a number of publications,[12] Elizondo argued that the notion of *mestizaje* provides significant insight into biblical interpretation. The word *mestizo*, meaning "of mixed blood," had long been employed in Latin America to refer to a person of both Spanish and Indian descent. As used by whites, it assumed a pejorative connotation, meaning that the *mestizo* was not quite up to the level of those of pure European descent. (This view was reflected in the common phrase, that *mestizos* were simply "better dressed Indians"—*indios con levitas.*) As a reaction to that, Vasconcelos affirmed the value of the encounter between cultures and races and therefore of *mestizaje* as a source of creativity—which led him to speak of the *mestizo* Mexican race as *la raza cósmica*, the "cosmic race." Without going to such extremes, Elizondo took the "them" of *mestizaje* as a source of creativity and as a sign of the future, and he applied it to biblical hermeneutics and to theological methodology.

Elizondo points out that the *mestizo* is a person belonging to two races and therefore to none. Whites tend to view *mestizos* as almost Indian, while Indians consider them almost white. This was very much the case with Galilee, which Romans considered Jewish, while people from the center of Judea considered it almost Gentile. As a Galilean, Jesus was rejected both by the Romans and by the Judeans, and both groups eventually worked together for his death. And yet, Jesus pointed the way to a new future both for Jews and for Gentiles. As a Mexican American living in Texas, Elizondo was commonly classified as Mexican; but when he visited Mexico, he found that he was seen as a Texan. Likewise, the Hispanic population in the United States is a *mestizo* population, not only in the sense that it includes people of various races, but also in the sense that it is both North American and Latin American and yet neither of the two.

Elizondo's proposal of *mestizaje* as a paradigm for biblical interpretation resonated with what many other Hispanics in the United States were experiencing. A common way of expressing that experience was by referring to "life at the hyphen" connecting (and separating) two elements of Hispanic identity—as in Mexican-American, Cuban-American, and so on. Later some have suggested the Nahuatl word *napantla*—"the land between"—as a way of expressing the connection between the psychological and cultural dimensions of *mestizaje* on the one hand and the geographical realities of the borderlands on the other.[13] Along similar lines, some are exploring the theme of *mulatez*—derived from *mulato*, or the person of mixed European and African descent—as parallel to *mestizaje*.[14]

The common theme underlying all these expressions—*mestizaje*, life at the hyphen, *nepantla*, *mulatez*—is in-betweenness. The Hispanic experience in the United States is one of belonging to two different worlds and yet to neither of them.

Many concrete examples illustrate how this impacts biblical interpretation—beyond the paradigmatic example already given of Jesus as a Galilean. Moses is the son of Pharaoh who is not quite an Egyptian. Esther is seen as a person living in between her role as queen and her personal identity as a Hebrew. The two names of Saul/Paul point to his double identity as a Jew and a citizen of Tarsus and of Rome—just as so many Hispanics today are María Luisa/Mary Lou, Jesús/Jesse, and the like.

Aliens, Exiles, and Migrants

A second paradigm that appears repeatedly in Hispanic biblical interpretation centers on the identity and experience of being aliens and exiles in the land, of not being permanent residents. Although this theme has been part of Latino theology for a half century, the current debate on the theme of immigration into the United States has brought it to the foreground. Since much of what is said in that debate has ethnocentric and even racist undertones, even those Hispanics who are not immigrants feel that they too are objects of the debate. Indeed, Hispanics in the Southwest whose ancestors lived in the land before it became part of the United States are made to feel as aliens even in the land of those ancestors. Alongside them is also the large number who are indeed immigrants and who therefore have good reason to feel as aliens in the land.

An important element in the experience of immigration is often forgotten in the present debate. This is that immigrants into the United States are also emigrants from the land of their birth—that in a sense they are exiles. The Mexican and the Salvadoran who now live at the margins of society have memories of a village or a neighborhood where they were at home—and where they would rather live. But they also know of circumstances—economic oppression and exploitation, violence, political corruption, lack of education for their children, ever-narrowing possibilities for the future—that led them to leave that home in order to be marginalized immigrants and aliens in another land. Thus, while from the perspective of the dominant society these immigrants have come to the United States in order to benefit from its economy and its opportunities, from their own perspective they are people who, given equal circumstances, would much rather live in the land of their birth and among their friends and family.

Another element that is equally forgotten is the enterprising spirit of the immigrant population—particularly those who are commonly dubbed "illegal aliens." In our national lore we admire the rugged individuals who carved out a place to live on the frontier. And yet we underestimate the courage and determination of people who are willing to leave their homeland, cross deserts, and live in constant fear of deportation, all in order to carve out a place to live for themselves and their families.

Being an alien—or at least been considered one—is a common experience among Hispanics in the United States. Therefore, it is also a basic paradigm for biblical interpretation. Thus, while many of our Latin American brothers and sisters read the story of Exodus focusing on God's mighty act liberating Israel from the yoke of Egypt, Hispanics in the United States tend to focus on the story of Israel as an alien people in the midst of Egypt. Joseph went to Egypt in involuntary exile. In Egypt, he was nothing but a slave until his unique gifts were discovered and he was able to save Egypt from famine. His family followed as refugees from famine. But when their descendants became too numerous, history was rewritten, Joseph's contribution was forgotten, and his descendants found themselves once again in slavery. This story resonates with the experience of Hispanics who know of the role that people of their culture played in the founding of this nation and yet see that role forgotten both by history and by society at large.

Needless to say, the story of the exile in Babylon is also paradigmatic for Hispanic readings of Scripture. While the usual reading of that story focuses on the people being forced into exile finally being allowed to return to their homeland, Hispanic readings tend to be much more nuanced. Life in exile is not merely a parenthesis until return becomes possible. Life in exile is an ambiguous situation in which the people continue dreaming of their lost homeland and yet also engage in building houses and planting vineyards. Life in exile is life between memory and hope on the one hand and present reality on the other. This is an ambivalence seldom seen by those who say, "why don't they integrate?" or by those who say, "why don't they go home?" The exile wants to integrate yet also wants to return home. And neither of the two is really possible.

Furthermore, the experience of exile is often confused by ironic turns of history. Mexican immigrants in California do not need to be reminded that their ancestors made an important contribution to that land. All they need to do is look at the names of places and cities: Los Ángeles, San Francisco, Sacramento. Commenting on that situation, a Hispanic Methodist wrote:

How the world turns! The descendants of Eli, who was Yahweh's priest at Shiloh, were expelled from Jerusalem and forced to live in Anatoth. . . . Now Jeremiah, a descendant of Abiathar, the priest whom Solomon deported, returns to the very temple from which his family had been expelled, and it is precisely in that place that he proclaims his message.[15]

Although he does not say so in this writing, the author of these words was himself a Methodist Cuban exile, some of whose ancestors had fled to Cuba as exiles from Apalachicola when Florida became British. Thus, his words reflect not just a historical reading of Jeremiah but also a reading from the point of view of his own family and personal history—a reading and a history that show that exile and migration are not as unambiguous as many would imagine.

Similar themes of exile and alienness appear repeatedly in Hispanic Methodist use and interpretation of Scripture. The very first article in *Apuntes*, whose purpose was to set the tone for the new journal, uses the story of Amos, a prophet from another kingdom who dares to preach in the king's sanctuary, and whom the king's servants then attempt to silence and to banish as a foreigner.[16] Adam and Eve are exiles from Eden; Jacob is exile from the land of his father; Moses is exiled from Egypt. And, above all, Jesus himself grows up as an exile in Egypt.

Marginality

A third paradigm or central theme in Hispanic Methodist biblical interpretation is marginality. This marginality has to do both with culture and with power. Although sheer numbers are bringing about significant changes in this regard, Hispanics constantly experience marginality in terms of culture. While mostly imposed by the surrounding culture, to a degree this marginality is also self-imposed. From outside the Hispanic community come all sorts of messages, both subliminal and direct, to the effect that Hispanic culture is somehow inferior. For years, high school students who had to meet a foreign language requirement but did not really want to work at it would take Spanish. The reasoning was that Spanish is much easier than French or German—though it is not, if taught well. The reality was that those who took French or German were expected to learn them well, while those who took Spanish learned that their knowledge of the language was measured by much lower standards. Then, as Hispanics and other cultural groups increased in numbers, "bilingual education" came to the foreground. But this education was not really bilingual in the sense of promoting bilingualism; in truth it was remedial, a temporary measure until such time as students who spoke other languages could be mainstreamed into the monolingual curriculum. Today much of this has begun to change, but its imprint will still be felt for some time.

Then, Hispanics also find themselves culturally marginalized by other Hispanics. Those who did not have the opportunity for a solid education in their lands of origin are often considered ignorant by other Hispanics whose language is closer to standard, cultured Spanish. Hispanics from one country of origin criticize the way others speak—forgetting that, after all, the best Spanish is mostly a very poorly spoken Latin.

Besides these imposed forms of cultural marginalization, there is also a self-imposed form. Exiles and aliens find it important to keep their identity—to eat the foods that their grandmothers cooked, to sing nostalgic songs about their own land, to remember old times, to speak the language of their cradles, to pass along jokes that only they can understand. Thus, even while they seek to become integrated into the general culture of the surrounding society, Hispanics also seek ways to keep their own traditions—an attitude that the surrounding society often interprets as rejection and refusal to join the mainstream.

Then, marginalization also has to do with power. Until fairly recent times, there were few Hispanic leaders in business, politics, and church. While this is beginning to change, such changes have to do mostly with a very narrow band within the Hispanic community. There may now be a Hispanic sitting in the Supreme Court, but still many Hispanics shiver when they have to appear before traffic court. The number of Latino-owned businesses may be growing, but still most Hispanics mow lawns, wash dishes, and clean offices. Something similar happens in the life of the church. In The United Methodist Church, for instance, there are now Hispanic bishops, district superintendents, general agency executives, and seminary professors. Even while rejoicing in all of this, it is still true that the very structures of the church are organized in such a way that the average Hispanic Methodist does not feel very much connected to the church at large. The entire church is organized in terms of a middle-class, relatively affluent membership, and therefore those who do not belong to that class, particularly Hispanic congregations—most of whose members are poor, recent immigrants—do not feel that they are really part of it. Hispanics are welcome to positions of leadership in Annual Conferences but only if they shift their focus from their Hispanic, poor congregations to typical United Methodist ones.

The paradigm of marginalization is quite visible in the manner in which Hispanic Methodists read Scripture. The references to the Galilean experience given above illustrate this., but in many other passages this comes to the foreground.[17] In Acts 1, Peter gives a speech proposing that someone be named to fill the vacancy left by Judas. Most readers find the passage strange and clearly feel that positions in the church should not be filled by drawing lots. But many Hispanics see other dimensions in the passage. Peter suggests that the person elected should have some qualifications: it should be "one of the men who have accompanied us during all the time . . . beginning from the baptism of John until the day when he was taken up from us" (Acts 1:21-22). It is interesting that Peter sets standards that most of the twelve do not meet: not all were with Jesus from the beginning, and at the end only John remained with him. To many United Methodist Hispanics who have appeared before Boards of Ordained Ministry, this is a familiar experience: some of those who are already "in" argue for "higher" standards that in effect keep the new ones "out." Some of those who argue for "higher" standards were admitted under other, perhaps "lower," standards. Significantly, in making his proposal, Peter is not following the commandment of Jesus, which was to go to Jerusalem and wait for the gift of the Spirit. For Peter in this passage, structure and requirements must be dealt with even while the disciples wait for the Spirit. There is no need to explain why; for many Hispanics the same happens in the church today.

With reference to cultural marginalization, the story of Pentecost in the next chapters of Acts provides significant insights. The story is so familiar that many read it as if it had nothing new to tell. We marvel at the extraordinary signs, particularly at the miracle of communication, and we let it go at that. What we seldom notice is that the miracle of communication is also an affirmation of the culturally marginalized. If the purpose of the Spirit was that the Gospel be communicated to all the various people then residing in Jerusalem, the Spirit had two options. One was to make it possible for all those present to understand the language of the disciples; the other was to make them all understand, each in his or her own tongue. In terms of mere communication, the result would be the same: people would hear the message of the disciples. But in terms of the place of various cultures in the life of the church, the differences would be enormous. Had the Spirit chosen to have all hear in the language of the disciples, that tongue would forever have remained the language of the church. Other languages might have been employed, but only as ancillary to the true language of revelation, the Aramaic with a Galilean accent that the disciples spoke. Had the Spirit chosen the first option, the center of the church would have remained forever among those who spoke the language of the first disciples. (In a way, this is what happens in Islam, where the only proper language for the Koran and for worship is Arabic, for this was the original language of revelation.) But the Spirit chose the second option, to have all hear, each in their various tongues. From that point on, the language of a Cappadocian or of a Phrygian can be a vehicle of revelation and an instrument for the service of God, just as much as the original language of the disciples. Furthermore, this has connotations for the system of government and of authority in the church. Presumably, no matter what happened at Pentecost—and as a result of Pentecost itself—there would now be churches that the disciples would not be able to control. (Imagine Peter walking into a church in which worship and business were taking place in another language. Would he be able to control it in the same manner in which he could control a church in Joppa?) Hispanic Methodists see the difference between these two approaches to multicultural ministries, and are also aware of their implications for the actual life and governance of the church.

On the issue of being at the center of power or at its margins, Hispanic Methodists can also note another point that should be quite clear in the early chapters of Acts but which is often ignored by commentators. In those chapters, "the people" are generally in favor of the followers of Jesus, and it is the social and religious elite that oppose and persecute them—the captain of the temple, the Sadducees, the rulers, elders, scribes, and the high priest. Thus, the early chapters in Acts paint a picture of struggle that goes far beyond the purely religious or doctrinal terms in which we often read them.

But those conflicts do not take place only outside the church. By the time we come to Acts 6, we are told of difficulties and disagreements between the Hebrews and the Hellenists within the church. Again, the twelve decide on a structure in which they would keep the task of preaching, while seven Hellenists would manage the resources of the church—which had been the source of friction between Hebrews and Hellenists. Significantly, this is a much more liberal arrangement than most major denominations make today to accommodate minority groups. But even so, this is not enough for the Spirit, with the result that Stephen, who is not supposed to be preaching, preaches the longest sermon in the book of Acts, and after his death Acts turns to the preaching and teaching of another of the seven, Philip.

A Clearly Plural "We"

In contrast with English, Spanish still retains the difference between the singular and the plural "you"—in earlier times, "thou" and "ye." Thus, while the most common readings of Scripture in English take "you" to be a direct address to the reader individually, Spanish readers soon see that the Word is not addressed only to them individually, but also to the community—to that "ye" that is the entire people of God. This has many consequences, which it is not possible to spell out here. For our purposes here, suffice it to say that this is the reason why, at the beginning of this essay, I said that my interest was in exploring what contributions Hispanic Methodists might make to the reading and use of Scripture by the church at large. We are not interested only in the Word *to me*, to the individual. We are also interested in the Word of God *to us*, to the entire community of the people of God. Therefore, it is not just as an exploration of quaint or different readings of Scripture that this essay has been written. It has been written in the hope that the Spirit of God will somehow take our Hispanic insights and use them to speak to the church at large. So be it!

7

SCRIPTURE AMONG KOREAN METHODISTS

Meesaeng Lee Choi and Hunn Choi

From the beginning of Korean Christianity, the Bible has been accepted without question as the sacred text of the Christian faith. In fact, "Bible" in Korean is *sung-gyung*, "holy sacred book." This essay will, first, briefly trace the history of Korean Hangul Bible in Korean Christianity. Then, we will examine how Scripture has functioned authoritatively among Korean Methodists and Wesleyans within the social context of a marginalized group looking for upward mobility. We will discuss then an approach to Scripture that addresses the fact that the immigrant community stands at a liminal point.

The Korean Hangul Bible in Korean Christianity

Korea had three dominant religions throughout its history—Animism or Shamanism, Buddhism, and Confucianism—until the twentieth century when Christianity became the largest religion in the country. Korea's first contact with Christianity goes back to as early as the sixteenth century.[1] From the end of "The Catholic Century" (1784–1886),[2] the Bible was made available in hangul (the Korean native alphabet). The translation of the Bible into hangul was launched in 1872, and the first entire Bible, *The Korean Bible*, was published in 1911. According to Samuel Hugh Moffett, "The Protestants had landed with [a hangul] Bible in hand [from 1882] and an enthusiasm of evangelism that was destined to change Korea in a way that few could have imagined during the hundred years of terror so recently ended."[3] As missionaries visited Korean villages, many "had already come to Christian faith through the reading of the Scripture and . . . about 600 people were candidates for baptism and about a thousand families were reading the Bible every day in their family devotions."[4] In the 1890s, the same number of Bibles was distributed in ten years in Korea as had been distributed in China in fifty years.[5] During the period of 1908–1940, the British and Foreign Bible Society distributed in Korea 85 percent of all the Bibles they sold.[6] In Asia, "people in no other country more welcome the Bibles . . . than people in Korea."[7] Thus Korean Christianity has been known as "Bible Christianity" or "a Bible-loving community."[8] A missionary leader even exclaimed: "I wonder that there would be any Christian in the world who knows the Bible better than the Korean Christians!"[9] The love of the Bible and the tradition of the Bible studies were hallmarks of early Korean Christianity.[10] Furthermore, as William Blair and Bruce Hunt reported, the Bible has shown to be the single most important contributor to the birth and growth of the Korean Christianity.[11] As a result, now Korea has become the second largest missionary sending nation in the world.[12]

Such a phenomenal growth of Christianity is seen not only in Korea but also in the Korean American community in North America. The growth of the Korean American church, from its beginning in 1902 to the present, is both a social and spiritual phenomenon. Korean American immigrants are "one of the most 'churched' of all ethnic groups in the United States."[13] They are known as "the champion church builders."[14] A little over a century after the first two churches were founded—one on October 14, 1902, in San Francisco and the other on January 13, 1903, in Hawaii (after the arrival of the first Korean immigration, which brought 101 Koreans to work on Hawaii's sugar and pineapple plantations)—their followers and descendants have established 4,100 churches across the 50 states, about one church for every 500 members of their community.[15] As R. Stephen Warner rightly comments, "Overwhelmingly Christian, for the most part evangelically inclined Protestants, Korean immigrants are avid churchgoers."[16] When Koreans migrate to America, they find a new world and context and churches for multiple purposes, as places of worship, social gathering places, employment centers, travel agencies, and centers of local and transnational politics.[17] Away from their homeland, these churches provide them with an important means of negotiating the circumstances of life. For many Korean American Christians, Christianity informs the dilemma of their racial status in the U.S. For them, religious life through church involvement is a source of acceptance and community. The confluence of faith and race helps them engage the complexities and contradictions of their experiences in the U.S.[18] Religious practices like reading the Bible and rituals like worship services infuse imaginations, comfort souls, and provide meaning for Korean American immigrants.

Korean Methodists and Wesleyans in America alike hold to the centrality of the Bible. In fact, Korean American Methodists and Wesleyans hold a very high view of the Bible as the Word of God and are committed to the full authority of the Bible, just as John Wesley viewed the Bible as the highest and final authority in all doctrinal matters. The reading of Scripture for Korean American Methodists and Wesleyans is a reading "with a constant eye to what Wesley called 'the Scripture way of salvation' . . . toward the ongoing formation of people of God in holiness."[19] For them, reading the Bible takes seriously both the aim of Scripture (to show the way to heaven) and its consequences (to find the way to heaven). It is to transform their lives, because through Scripture, God can grab their attention, help them, and shower them with grace.[20] Another purpose of reading Scripture is to develop an understanding of and appreciation for God's missionary activity, the *missio dei*, in the Bible. Given their own unique history and social location, Korean American Methodists and Wesleyans engage the Bible in ways that will allow them to be faithful to the Bible and relevant to their particular context, to bring forth the Bible's transformative power in their lives.

Undoubtedly, the social location of Korean Americans matters to their reading of the Bible. The way we locate ourselves as people of faith and as Bible readers has much to do with the meaning we construct in our engagement with the biblical texts.[21] For much of the history of the Korean people, their social location has been one of marginalization. In their own homeland, they were oppressed by foreign powers and internal despots. As immigrants in America, they faced the difficulties of being a minority group. These experiences have led to a unique approach to reading the Bible, one that emphasizes the promise of liberation, increasing social status, and blessings (both spiritual and material). While this approach to Scripture is deeply embedded in Korean and Korean American history and still reflects the marginalized status of the Korean American community, we propose that a new way of approaching Scripture is needed. As Steve Kang writes, Korean Americans must find a new reading that will enable them to "see themselves as God's people who are in the process of moving from the margins of society to the center of God's kingdom."[22]

READING AT THE MARGINS

From early on Korean Christians read and interpreted the Bible in relation to their own historical situations. During the period of Japanese colonialism (1910–1945), Korean Christians read Scripture in the context of their suffering under imperialism. To these readers, the biblical stories were not simply ancient stories but rather a reflection of their own experiences. When they read about the Israelites' captivity in Egypt, they saw their own political oppression. When they read the exodus story, they saw the hope of their liberation from the Japanese colonial regime. When they read Jesus' proclamation to the powerless and the poor, they identified themselves as the deprived who would be set free by the chosen one. They would read and understand the biblical stories as they engaged in the way they imagined their lives and in the hearing of old stories from their parents or grandparents. In short, the Bible was viewed as a guide not only to personal salvation from sin but also to national salvation from a foreign oppressor. During this period, the two most popular books of the Bible were Exodus and Revelation, the former with its emphasis on freedom from bondage and the latter with its emphasis on the defeat of the oppressive enemy and the promise of a liberated future.[23]

The status of the Bible as the national symbol of hope and freedom was solidified in 1948, when Syngman Rhee, the first president of the nation after it gained independence from Japan, took his oath office with his hand on the Bible.[24] In the eyes of Korean Christians, the Bible became the new nation's symbol of a new beginning, in light of a new faith. The Bible became a symbol of God's loving presence with the nation, a symbol of God's liberation and freedom.

A reading of the Bible that emphasized freedom from oppression rose again during the presidency of Chunghee Park (1961–1979). Park clamped down on personal rights and freedoms under the provisions of a state of emergency and employed the Korean CIA to curtail the constitutional rights of freedom of speech and the press. This led to the development of *minjung* theology, in which the Bible was read from the perspective of the suffering of the oppressed, the *minjung*, and interpreted in the context of the human struggle for liberation against the use of the Bible to legitimize participation in oppression.[25] *Minjung* theologians connected the liberating and saving stories of the Bible with the *minjung* who had been politically and socially oppressed by utilizing the social reality of the *minjung*, not the Bible, as the starting point—sharing their struggles, pains, sufferings, aspirations, success, and failures, and envisioning hope for a new heaven and earth. Hence, the sources for *minjung* theology are not limited to the Bible but include the *minjung*'s life story, tradition, and history. In the end, the Bible is not the norm, but rather a reference, of *minjung* theology. The Bible is used only to seek the meaning of *minjung*'s life and struggle as well as the answer to their suffering. *Minjung* theology contributed to the Korean church and society through its rediscovery of the gospel of liberation and justice.[26] It was intended to uplift the poor, like the gospel of holistic blessing, which we will discuss below.

Reading Scripture as Immigrants

Korean Americans read the Scriptures from their social location as immigrants, a context that led to an emphasis on a number of themes: a hyphenated existence, marginality, and upward mobility. Let us first consider "hyphenated space." Korean American immigrants live on the "hyphen" between their Korean origins and the American culture in which they live. Within this situation, they try to find a sense of a hybrid identity, being American yet holding onto the Korean heritage.[27] Their hyphenated existence is one of "both-and" in which one cannot exist "without the other, without being incomplete. As such, the hyphen signifies that two separate entities are now joined and belong together."[28]

For this reason, Korean Americans often turn to biblical depictions of a hyphenated existence. Some of the best examples in the Bible are Joseph living in Egypt and the prophet Daniel living in Babylon. For Korean American Christians, these two figures are exemplars of how to live in the hyphenated world. Just as they lived in a hyphenated life, as worshippers of Yahweh living in a foreign land, so Korean American Christians may also be called to live lives in which they negotiate competing sets of loyalties and responsibilities, finding "new ways to be all three: Koreans, Americans, Christians."[29]

The second element that informs Korean American approaches to the Bible is marginality. Most Korean Americans, when speaking of their own experience and predicament in the U.S., identify with the image of marginality. For one thing, as Nadia Kim articulates in her book *Imperial Citizens*, marginality means that Korean Americans are marginalized by their relative social and political invisibility in the American public imagination.[30] Korean Americans have long been the so-called perpetual foreigners, or forever guests. She pays careful attention to both the invisible dimensions of foreignness as well as immigrants' everyday struggles with being visibly foreign. In an eloquent way, she explains how Korean Americans are marginalized:

> Korean Americans encounter and resist racial discrimination against their group as visible foreigners, typically as "foreign model minorities." Again, the depth and consistency of their resistance speaks volumes about their willingness to scrutinize their pro-Americanism and face contradictions ("How could they discriminate . . . while . . . they were most superior citizens?") They must wrestle with the seeming "contradiction" between the *model minority* and persistent foreigner, one that, below the surface, betrays a circular relationship. This circularity explains why Asian American groups' "success" has not lifted them out of their foreigner status and into the ranks of American authenticity.[31]

In addition, marginality plainly means that Korean Americans experience a social and cultural displacement or uprootedness on their arrival in the U.S. They are no longer in their home country, yet they are not really part of their newly adopted country. Jung Young Lee describes his experience as a Korean American as being on the margins, being "in-both" as well as in between his Korean and American cultures. He defines marginality—no longer as defined by the center—as the intersection of all of his experiences.[32]

Sang Hyun Lee, explaining his plightful experience as an immigrant in America, appropriates the story of Abraham as the story of a pilgrim through whom Korean American immigrant Christians should not only articulate their identity and vocation but also read and interpret the Bible. Korean Americans left behind the security of home in pursuit of God's promise in a foreign land. In this light, Korean Americans live in a new situation in which they do not simply find themselves in a new land but are called to discover a mission as they recognize their own situation in the biblical narratives.[33] As a result, they have "a perspective from which to judge the theological, social, and cultural imperfections of the society in which they find themselves and to join with other marginalized people to create a more just society."[34]

When they read the Bible, Korean immigrant Christians consider many of the biblical themes in light of their immigrant and marginalized situation. First, the Bible relates many important frameworks of migration: Abraham migrating from Haran to Canaan, Jacob and his family migrating to Egypt, the Israelites exiting from Egypt and migrating to and possessing Canaan, Israel's moving out and returning because of exile and recovery, Jesus' descending into history (incarnation) and his itinerant ministry, the believers' scattering from Jerusalem to Gentile lands, and Paul and other church leaders' moving around the world for mission.[35] The prominence and frequency of these biblical themes allow Korean Americans to identify their immigrant life with these biblical figures who experienced migration or immigration and marginalization in their new social contexts. As Kang comments, "All Christians are called to be marginalized people who seek God's will and obey it, as God's instrument in the world in order to accomplish his will."[36]

Jesus of Nazareth, hyphenated Jesus-Christ because he is always Jesus *and* Christ—like Korean-Americans, always Korean *and* American—was the marginal person par excellence.[37] Jesus was a stranger to his own people. They did not accept him (John 1:11). He was rejected by the dominant groups—both religious leaders and Romans—and became a friend of marginalized people—tax collectors, outcasts, women, the poor and oppressed, "sinners," and Gentiles. In other words, Jesus related abnormally well to those people and was accepted by them, because he was himself an outcast, a homeless person (Matt 8:20) living in two worlds (human and divine) without fully belonging to either.[38]

Korean Americans have experienced that, through the reading of the biblical stories, God is especially present at the margins of society. God stands for individuals and communities who are set apart from mainstream society on the basis of position, wealth, health, and so forth. A reversal of the social order is anticipated as an essential aspect to the coming of God's reign. God's incarnation in Jesus of Nazareth affirms that the margins of society are in fact at the core where the Spirit of God is working on reconciliation and transformation.

Kibock Sinang—A Gospel of Holistic Blessing

Because both Korean and Korean American Christians find their identity in the margins of society, both groups have traditionally viewed the Bible not only as a promise of freedom but also as a promise of blessing and upward mobility. A prominent manifestation of this perspective is a gospel of holistic blessing (known as *kibock sinang*, "blessing seeking faith," or "faith of seeking blessings"), based on "the three-fold blessing" of spiritual, material, and physical well-being.[39] Ig-Jin Kim, in her seminal work, *History and Theology of Korean Pentecostalism*, points out that *kibock sinang* is based on 3 John 2 as a key verse for reading and interpreting the Scriptures in support of the view that God's holistic salvation given through Christ's redemption may be materialized in the present.[40]

Historically, Korean Christians wanted to receive not only the spiritual blessings of repentance and forgiveness but also material and physical blessings, so much so that they met as groups on prayer mountains for prayer and fasting.[41] It seemed that the message of the expected blessings for those who seek prevailed. As Sebastian Kim points out, "While conservative theology may meet the need of spiritual fulfillment and eschatological hope, *kibock sinang* has harnessed the people's desire for dream-fulfillment in the present context. In Korean religiosity, the desire for something better, both spiritual and material, is expressed as seeking blessings. It is the humble desire of those who have not experienced fullness of life and who are constantly facing despair and poverty."[42]

This gospel of holistic blessing was good news to the poor in the Korean context, especially after the Korean War, when most Koreans were destitute. Korea has "a remarkable story of human triumph over adversity."[43] Many Korean Christians view their faith as a contributing factor in their dramatic national economic growth in spite of various national tragedies—Japanese occupation, the Korean War, and political oppression—believing that their personal and national success and prosperity are indications of God's blessing. According to them, Christianity has played a major role in Korea's economic success.

Though often criticized, *kibock sinang* is not without its emphasis on the suffering of Christ and the cross: "It may be appropriate to preach on suffering, the Cross, inner spirituality and future hope to those who are experiencing material blessing, but the poor are suffering and carrying a cross."[44] Indeed, a Christian message of deliverance and liberation from poverty and suffering and the promise of God's blessing in the here and now is not improper but part of the Christian gospel—often expressed as *shalom*, the peace and well-being of God's people.[45] In the context of postwar Korea, *kibock sinang* was an appropriate Christian response to the socio-political issues of the period.

Historically speaking, Korean Americans, relative latecomers to America, first came to the U.S. with the mind-set that it was a land "flowing with milk and honey," where they could obtain their goals of immigration—material blessing and status. Though highly educated, many first-generation immigrant Koreans took on low-skilled, low-paying jobs because of language and structural barriers, with the hope that their children would be able to achieve the American dream. As Sharon Kim correctly observes, "Many immigrant parents have experienced downward mobility in the United States and hence have had to defer their hopes and dreams for upward mobility to their second-generation children."[46] Within this social location, Korean Americans have looked to the Bible as a promise that the material blessings and upward mobility to which they aspire will be delivered as a part of divine blessings. It is also true, though, that many Korean American Christians have used the Bible as a series of proof texts to support their desire for material blessings.[47]

While this way of approaching the Bible has deep roots in the Korean and Korean American experience, our proposal is that Korean American Christians need to move beyond an approach to the Bible that strongly emphasizes personal blessing. What is needed is a recognition of the centrality of the Bible's call for both the individual Christian and the corporate church to fulfill its role in the *missio dei*. This is not to suggest that Korean Americans, as immigrants, have somehow escaped society's margins. Korean American communities remain marginalized in several significant ways, all of which are unique to the Korean American experience.

A Need for New Ways of Reading from the Margins

Even though, when compared to the past, the experience of Korean Americans is not that of coercive liminality, it is naïve to suppose that this expression no longer applies to them. That would be an unwarranted assumption. Korean Americans still linger at the margins, though no longer owing explicitly to racist laws or explicit attitudes. The liminal experiences of the first Korean Americans may be different from those of subsequent generations. Whereas the former may experience uprootedness from their homeland and social structures, the latter experience high educational achievement and upward mobility. Yet, second- and subsequent-generation Korean Americans, though fluent in English language and culturally assimilated into American culture, still live in liminality; that is, they live in the hyphenated or hybrid space as Korean Americans. As a result, "they may in some contexts be accepted as neither Korean nor American, both Korean and American, not American but Korean, or not Korean but American."[48]

Even as a marginalized group, however, it is of the utmost importance that we Korean Americans move beyond a reading of Scripture that focuses only on the possibility of upward mobility away from margin. There are a number of reasons why this transition needs to be made.

First, a gospel focused on prosperity exhibits a variety of deficits. James Sunghoon Myung, a Korean scholar who has carefully examined *kibock sinang*, suggests that it is too weak on sanctification, sacrifice, and self-denial, and, without such emphasis, it can end up as "another typical health and wealth gospel contributing to self-centered dreams."[49] Hwa Yung is right when he says that, given the fact that the socio-economic situation has changed completely, with Korea now in the ranks of the developed nations, the theology of *kibock sinang* "needs much more restating today. Otherwise, it will end up essentially encouraging Korean Christians to go after the American dream, or its Korean equivalent, and end up leading covetous and materialistic lives where God is increasingly pushed aside."[50] Soong-Chan Rah also criticizes the Korean immigrant church's inability to provide a spiritual and theological corrective to the materialist narrative of American culture prevalent in the second-generation ideology.[51] The American dream—prosperity, wealth, and individualism—has become conflated with scriptural Christianity.

For this reason, a Wesleyan reading of the Bible is now especially urgent because of our society's tendency to reduce human existence to commodity. For Korean American Methodists and Wesleyans, "the way to accomplish social sanctification is to transform the individual."⁵² Korean American Christians should seek a changed society through changed hearts, through salvation and sanctification. As Wesley asserted, "you have nothing to do but save souls"⁵³—and the converted would press on toward that holiness; personal holiness must always result in "social holiness." Korean American Christians must not lose the missionary goal of the gospel, as well as its sanctification emphasis.

True prosperity, as Wesley once expressed in "The Use of Money," is to live simply and to give so much to others during one's life that, upon death, one would have successfully given it all away.⁵⁴ He spent his life ministering to the poor. Regarding wealth, he told Methodists, "Gain all you can," "save all you can," and "give all you can." He continued to exhort:

> The fault does not lie in money, but in them that use it. It may be used ill: and what may not? But it may likewise be used well. . . . In the hands of His children, it is food for the hungry, drink for the thirsty, raiment for the naked: it gives to the traveler and the stranger where to lay his head. By it we . . . may be a defense for the oppressed. . . . It is, therefore, of the highest concern, that all who fear God know how to employ this valuable talent: that they be instructed how it may answer these glorious ends, and in the highest degree.⁵⁵

Korean American Christians must align themselves with Wesley's prophetic voice, pursue universal justice through personal piety and holiness, and transform the global consumer culture by adopting a kingdom ethic: loving God and neighbor is living a life of "responsible grace."⁵⁶

There is a second, and perhaps more important, reason that the Korean American community needs to adopt a new approach to reading Scripture. True, Korean Americans, as an immigrant community, find themselves on the margin of society. And yet, this social location can be a point of calling and blessing, rather than simply a state of suffering from which one needs salvation. As Steve Ybarrola rightly states,

> While liminality may at times be psychologically stressful and limiting (a person being neither/nor), it can also be used to develop the ability to "make connections across borders" (both/and). In a globalized world, having intercultural competency can be a great advantage for the furtherance of the Kingdom, and those

experiencing liminality as immigrants in a new land may have a greater opportunity to develop this competency than those in the host society that have not experienced such in-betweenness.[57]

The Old Testament patriarchs and matriarchs, the children of Israel, the disciples, and Jesus himself lived lives of marginality; therefore, to be followers of Christ, the church needs to see itself as being in a liminal state—in-between and marginalized. For Korean American Christians, it is their devotion to God, their sincere faith in the midst of various difficulties, and their desire to learn God's word and obey him that place them in the center of God's kingdom. It is human nature to want to move away from the margins to be part of the center of the dominant society. However, in the person of Jesus, we see a marginalized person, who lived a marginalized life and died a marginalized death. Being at the margins enables the marginalized to share the experience of Jesus' marginalization and adds meaning to their own multiple aspects of marginalization. Being on the margins can drive and empower the Korean Americans to live in the center of God's kingdom and will for their lives.

One of the biblical stories Korean American Christians so dearly love is the story of the Canaanite woman in the Gospel of Matthew. As Daniel S. Schipani rightly observes, this text "suggests and calls for several kinds of stretching. Geographic, ethnic, gender, religious, theological, socio-cultural, moral, and political dimensions are involved." For Korean Americans now living in the global world, such stretching is a commonplace experience. In the story, this marginal Canaanite woman occupies and "emerges as the center of the story! In fact, the story is primarily her story." Korean American Christians discover a pleasant, surprising, transforming reversal in the story, when her great faith was demonstrated through a persistent demand for inclusion and an unwavering challenge to the gender, ethnic, religious, political, and economic barriers. Korean Americans desire to be "boundary walkers and boundary breakers" like both the woman and Jesus,[58] and to be a prophetic voice to American society at large.

> By eventually choosing to relate and minister "out of place," Jesus and the woman pointed the way to God's utopia. "Utopia" means literally "no place," not in the sense of never-never land, illusion or fantasy, but the stuff of prophetic dreams. From a biblical perspective, utopias are places that are not yet, not because they are

mere ideals beyond reach, but because evil and sinful structures and behaviors resist and contradict God's will for ethnic and racial justice and reconciliation.[59]

For Korean American Christians, the story of the Canaanite woman helped "undermine and even dismantle chosenness as ideology, as justification for excluding and discriminating against the other, the stranger, the foreigner." In addition, as this story must have aided the early readers of Matthew to understand their new place and role in the God's plan and reign and "also have helped them free from the ideology of chosenness so that they could be transformed into a more liberating and inclusive faith community," so the stories of Korean American Christians can be used as God's instrument of transformation and renewal in American society. They can be used to strive for a new community where there is no longer Jew or Greek, slave or free, male and female, for all are one in Christ (Gal 3:28), where diversity is embraced, celebrated, and fully integrated, and where all are called "to celebrate, embody, and be an agent of the coming reign of God, the future in which God is making all things news."[60]

Korean Americans must see a new possibility, that the margins of a society can become, as Sinyil Kim rightly observed, a place of God's calling (Gen 28:10-20; Exod 3:1-12; Judg 10:2-3), a place of God's training (Dan 1:9-17; Jonah 2:1-10; Matt 4:1-11), a place for a new beginning (1 Kgs 19:1-18; Acts 8:26; 1 Tim 3:16), and a place for a new ministry of *shalom*, God's original plan for harmony, right relationship with God and others, and the proper functions of all elements in the world. Suddenly, then, a new task of bringing *shalom* into all aspects of life ethnically (Jonah 1:11-13; Rom 10:12), culturally (Dan 1:3-21), and spiritually (John 3:16; Acts 16:30-34) arises in the new context of their hyphenated American life.[61] In Wesley's words, Korean American Christians believe that God has raised the "people called (Korean American) Methodists (and Wesleyans)" "to reform the nation, particularly the church, and to spread scriptural holiness over the land."[62]

How Should Korean American Methodists and Wesleyans Read?

The hybrid Korean American context can create for Korean American Christians a new space for hermeneutical creativity—reading from the margins for the marginalized. Rather than unceasingly pursuing the materialistic American dream, Korean American Christians should read the Scriptures asking what their Christian faith has to do with their identity and their life as marginalized and liminal people in America and in the world. In *From a Liminal Place: An Asian American Theology*, Sang Hyun Lee includes an interesting reading of Hebrews 11 from an Asian American perspective. He suggests a challenging goal for Korean Americans: to continually live in America as strangers and foreigners but work to build a better America, whose architect and builder is God. Taking the term "heavenly" (Heb 11:16) as something other than a reference to an otherworldly place, he argues that Abraham and his descendants understood themselves as strangers and foreigners in the land of Canaan and saw the "better country" not as some place beyond history but as an actual place that he and his descendants could work for as a concrete historical reality. He proposes that Abraham's story can be particularly pertinent for Korean American Christians who may be wondering what the meaning of their existence in America can be. "Abraham's story can be interpreted as saying that now that the [Korean] immigrants have left home and are here in America, it is an opportunity to take up the pilgrimage toward 'a better country' and work to make America a country that is more according to God's will. Their situation can be seen as a calling to live as the creative minority in America."[63]

Adapting words from the *Epistle of Diognetus*, we can say that Korean American Christians dwell in the U.S., but only as sojourners; they bear their share of all responsibilities as citizens, and they endure all hardships as strangers. Every foreign country is a homeland to them, and every homeland is foreign. Their existence is on earth, but their citizenship is in heaven (5.5-9). America is a temporary home away from home (both Korea and heaven). Though the marginality of Korean Americans has become less coercive, America is still a liminal place for many who are daily struggling with marginality. Korean American Christians can make their homes and communities venues for the marginalized, that is, culturally and socially disenfranchised or even culturally and socially less-privileged people, to have shared experiences, shared meanings, and shared identities, and also see their own transformative potential in a marginalized position.

In this vein, Bible reading among Korean American Christians must be missional to reflect God's character in, for, and to the world.

As Brian Russell states, they must engage in what is called a missional hermeneutic, which is to approach "Scripture through the lens of mission."[64] Our faithful reading of the biblical text (hermeneutics) should enable readers to hear what God is saying to his people (God's address), that is, "hermeneutics and God's address are two sides of the same coin."[65] Mission is central to a faithful hermeneutic. At the end of their reading, Korean Americans must come to know the specific *missio dei* for them. They must read the Bible for the world on behalf of "every nation, tribe, people and language" (Rev 7:9). Korean American Christians must use their liminal status to build bridges between the Korean and American communities for the furtherance of the gospel, using what has been referred to as "reverse mission," actively engaging in a global evangelical discourse within which "the world is my parish" in order "to spread scriptural holiness" throughout the world. Korean American Christians can serve as a catalyst for spiritual revival not only in America but also globally, desiring Korean American churches to become not merely a compensatory institution but an empowering one.[66]

Korean American Christians, being, if not becoming, people who overcome marginality without ceasing to be marginal,[67] must reach out to the marginalized in the world, employing the hermeneutics of hospitality. They need "to be more ecumenical than in their home context."[68] Affected by their own liminal experiences, they can better understand those in similar situations, such as refugees and other immigrants, both legal and illegal, and reach out to them with "radical hospitality, compassion, and justice," extending "material, legal, and social support," and "proclaiming the gospel in a context of relationships of mutuality and engagement."[69] The Bible clearly shows that hospitality begins with God. God, as a God of hospitality, creates a space for hospitality, extending the invitation for creation to dwell with him, "in a majestic display of cosmic hospitality. From the hand of divine hospitality, human culture is born and asked to extend divine hospitality."[70] What Korean American churches and Christians should do is to read Scripture in ways that can inform and help them exercise a twofold, incarnational hospitality: border crossing into other people's worlds and welcoming others into our world.

As Su Yon Pak and other Korean American Christians testify, first-generation Korean American Christians read the story of Abraham's hospitality to strangers (Gen 18:3-8) with a strong sense of affinity, because they know the meaning of hospitality from their experiences of being strangers and living liminally and culturally alienated in a strange world. In America, Korean churches function as "ricing" communities. Treating "ricing" as an active verb of "rice" to denote hospitality as one of the fundamental components of the church life is originally and purely Korean. For Korean American Christians, "the practice of feeding and feasting is to extend hospitality and to strengthen the ricing community,"[71] but they must go beyond. Given their context of marginalization, Korean Americans must not only "attend to their experience of alienation and isolation" but also "attend to the strangers who come along the way,"[72] regardless of their racial, ethnic, or religious identity.

In addition, in the face of growing globalization, one of the greater challenges for Korean American churches is to engage more in incarnational hospitality by reaching out to those living on the margins and welcoming them into our churches as hosts who anticipate the hospitality of God's kingdom. As Soong-Chan Rah suggests, we also "move from hospitality to a whole new level of connection: the household and family of God."[73] The fullness of the encounter God offers in Scripture is partnership with him (Genesis 2–3). "Merely practicing hospitality is just the beginning." Korean American churches, as communities of liminal and marginalized people "who have the God of unconditional acceptance and love through the transforming experience of *communitas* with Jesus in the power of the Holy Spirit,"[74] can make room for other ethnic groups and help them form independent worshipping congregations in their own language by sharing space mutually and becoming multicongregational churches. We can do this, not through mere accommodation, but through mutual partnership, transitioning from an ownership model to a stewardship mentality to foster mutual partnership, even equal ownership. Korean American churches must continue to align with the eschatological vision of the everlasting city of God in which God's people will be gathered "before the throne and before the Lamb," "from every nation, from all tribes and peoples and languages" (Rev 7:9).

Conclusion

As Walter Brueggemann observes, it was during times of exile, when the community of faith was marginalized, that Israel became "an intensely textual community."[75] Living as strangers in a strange land,

Israel's very identity as a people was threatened, so they read and listened to stories to remind themselves who they were, where they were, and where their true home was. In much the same way, the spiritual identity of the Korean American community can and should be solidified in its "exiled" state on the margins of American society. Korean American churches must become storied communities, or textual communities, where Korean American Christians will find their identity by the stories they will share. This means "returning again and again to the biblical stories and the reflections on them, and to live *into* them and *from* them. These *stories* and the practice they generate—living life living [*sic*] reflectively, prayerfully, sacramentally[,] communally, hopefully, faithfully—are the vehicle of the gospel."[76] The timeless stories of Scripture have the power to connect or reconnect people with and participate in the reality of God's grace in Jesus Christ. Our desire is that every Korean American Methodist and Wesleyan can say, "It is now becoming clearer that the scriptural story is our home in exile. . . . Now that the world no longer provides such an accommodating home for the scriptural community, Scripture has become our home."[77]

Furthermore, "scriptural holiness" entails more than personal piety and personal blessings. The love of God must be always linked with love of neighbors, which is "the sum of Christian perfection,"[78] and a passion for justice and renewal in every corner of the world. Reading from the margin in a new way, then, should move the Korean American community to rethink its previous reading, focused as it has been on personal blessing, and adopt a missional reading, so that it can live out its identity as the people of God, living by the unvarying truth that "the world is my parish," or the amended truth that "the world is in my parish."[79]

8

SCRIPTURE AND DIVINE REVELATION

William J. Abraham

Treating scripture straightforwardly as divine revelation represents a vision of scripture and a vision of divine revelation that should long ago have been consigned to the ash bin of history.[1] The conventional move to identify scripture as divine revelation causes untold pastoral and ecumenical problems: it corrupts our understanding of scripture as we actually have it in the church; it involves a network of conceptual errors with respect to revelation, inspiration, and other related concepts; and it inhibits the development of good work in the epistemology of theology. The problems run so deep in Wesley and the Wesleyan tradition that the best one can offer is that of the voice of one crying in the wilderness. There are indeed extremely important insights buried in Wesley and the tradition he spawned, but it is far from easy to separate the wheat from the chaff. In this paper I shall seek to do precisely this en route to delineating a positive account of the relation between divine revelation and scripture.

Begin with these two simple observations. Scripture in and of itself is a deflationary concept; it means simply "writings." "Revelation" is a rich epistemic concept. It signifies that something hidden has now been made known. If we identify scripture with divine revelation, we have immediately moved to a theological vision of scripture that places it firmly in the field of epistemology. We have moved to think of scripture as a criterion of truth in theology. This move has a long pedigree, reaching right back into the Jewish tradition.[2] Wesley stood firmly in this tradition, as a wealth of primary and secondary sources make clear. There is no need to repeat the evidence here; it will suffice to provide a meaty summary.[3]

"Revelation" is a beautiful epistemic concept. As noted, it means that something hidden has been disclosed. Applied to scripture Wesley spelled this out initially in terms of a story of divine speaking, divine dictation, divine inspiration, divine illumination, and divine authorship. These action predicates captured the truth about the origination of the Bible. Constituted as "canon," the Bible is both the source and norm of Christian theology. Given his account of the divine action involved in the origination of scripture, it is not in the least surprising that he considered scripture inerrant and infallible. Yet the subject matter of scripture is circumscribed by it is soteriological aims. To speak of scripture as divine revelation was to claim that God disclosed his plan of salvation for the world in a book. Even then, it was to be interpreted literally, except when reading the text this way rendered it absurd: its central message of salvation was clear; unclear passages were to be interpreted by parallel passages and the "analogy of faith," that is, the sense of scripture as a whole. In the interpretation of scripture, one consulted reason, Christian experience, the tradition of the first three centuries, and materials from the Church of England. However, these are privileged not epistemically but hermeneutically. They are normative for interpretation of scripture; they are not normative as an independent source and norm of truth in theology. Even though Wesley developed a fascinating vision of perception of the divine along the lines of the spiritual senses tradition, the appeal to perception had itself to be validated by an appeal to scripture. It would be anachronistic to think of Wesley as a classical foundationalist, given that this term was invented in the late twentieth century to deal with earlier texts in another context; however, his vision of the epistemology of theology is one that is riddled with epistemic anxiety and that seeks out a foundation for theology that will be infallible and inerrant.

There is no quick fix for this aberrant and spiritually debilitating network of commitments. To be sure, Wesley found a personal security and a spiritual self-confidence in his preaching that is admirable and attractive. So too did the initial generations of theologians after him who valiantly sought to develop full-scale schemes of Methodist dogmatics.⁴ However, the security enjoyed, as deeply psychological as it was, was an illusion, and it is no surprise that by the late nineteenth century the best Methodist theologians were fooled into reaching for alternative sources of epistemic security that proved equally ephemeral over time. If we are to develop an apt and accurate account of the relation between revelation and scripture, it cannot be executed by another round of slogans or half-baked measures. It will require sustained attention to scripture as it is and to its primary purpose, it will require careful conceptual work on the concept of revelation, and it will require serious work both in the epistemology of theology and in discerning the place of such work in the life of the church as a whole. Happily, we can combine both these ventures without abandoning the Wesleyan heritage at its best. On the contrary, they can liberate us to reappropriate, for example, Wesley's canonical sermons with renewed enthusiasm.

Scripture as It Is

Taking scripture seriously, as it is before us, means that our disposition in reading it should be radically inductive rather than deductive in spirit.⁵ Scripture stands over against us; we do not know in advance of reading it what it says, whether its contents harmonize, how we should apply it to our lives, and the like. To approach scripture deductively is to read it with a prior theological theory that constrains what it can say to us. The Reformation alerted us to this temptation, in that it insisted on the relative clarity of scripture in issues related to salvation. To be sure, their claims on the perspicacity have to be severely qualified, for the Reformers failed at times to execute their best intentions by insisting that their theologies be read into the text; some went so far as to use the organs of state to enforce their own interpretation on the public at large. Wesley himself stood firmly in the Anglican tradition on all these fronts. As he makes clear in his famous preface to his *Sermons on Several Occasions*, he was determined to immerse himself in the letter and content of scripture, no matter what the results.⁶ As many have noted, he also availed himself of the best tools of his day.⁷ It is less often noted that he was a debtor to the confessional church, universities, and state, who had their own way of imposing their account of the content of scripture as a critical condition of public service. The primary concern, however, was to read scripture for what it said rather than for what we want it to say.

We can take this one step further and help ourselves to the information furnished by the varied forms of historical investigation. Given that the texts come to us from diverse ancient contexts, we utterly depend on expert judgments about language, literary form, historical context, and authorship. It is crucial to know what sources may have been deployed, how important concepts and themes were received and changed over time, how the final form of the text may have been constructed, and how the material has been interpreted when repeated within scripture itself and when received in the long history of interpretation. The aim is to discover what scripture really says over against what we want it to say today. The proper place to begin such work is the work of historical investigation.

The standard way to state this move in the modern period is to insist on the propriety of historical criticism in the interpretation of scripture. I prefer the more modest term historical investigation. Our object of inquiry is the action of past human agents, and the ordinary term we use to understand past human actions is historical investigation. Such work is not done without a host of presuppositions. Moreover, approaching the past in an inductive spirit does not at all involve some kind of naïve realism about our investigation of the past. Unfortunately, as applied to scripture, when historical investigation assumed the name of historical criticism, it became laden with all sorts of metaphysical and causal assumptions that begged relevant epistemological questions and operated imperialistically in its construal of its conclusions. In some ways the shift to postmodernism has exposed the hidden agendas in much modern historical criticism, even as it has imported its own ideological agendas into the readings of texts without apology. The crucial points to register here are two. First, historical investigation involves both person-relative and non-person-relative assumptions that can readily be exposed by good philosophical inquiry. Second, it is simply silly to assume that the only proper way to read scripture is as functional atheists. We are entitled to deploy the best theological insights we can muster in reading a sacred text; we are not reading mathematical material or merely great literature.

Recent interventions in the debate about reading scripture have emphasized the importance of social location and communal experience in hermeneutics.[8] White racists, it will rightly be said, read scripture differently from oppressed minorities; patriarchal men read scripture differently from liberated feminists. However, as Ellen

Charry has perceptively noted, this can readily lead to the creation of networks of victims who claim unique access to the truth about God. Reductionist and vague generalizations about experience in time become the political tools for "advancing the agenda of special interest groups who rewrite the Christian map along sociological, cultural, and bioethnic lines."[9] Read epistemically, these appeals bear all the hallmarks of the classical foundationalist appeal to self-evidence and incorrigibility. They are presented in a way that protects the speaker from radical criticism; they operate to insulate the various groups of readers from obvious and often devastating objections, even as they balkanize the church into various factions at odds with each other.

However, there is a crucial insight dormant in this development that Wesleyans should harvest from this discussion. Personal and communal experience can indeed lead us to read texts more accurately: they can alert us to alternative possibilities all too often overlooked by standard interpretations. What is at issue here is not yet the appeal to experience per se as a ground for theology but as an important hermeneutical asset for reading texts. Even then, it is crucial to return to the text and make sure we are not engaged in eisegesis. At this point there is a thin line between appealing to experience as essential to the logic of discovery over against appealing to experience as essential to the logic of justification for this or that reading of scripture. The practice of justification must return again and again to close reading of the text.

Wesleyans can exploit the force of these observations by noting that the tradition from Wesley on (and before that in Pietism) rightly saw features of the claims of scripture that can be readily missed. We can cite several examples. Wesley's reflections on the experience of new birth and sanctification bring him into line with more recent readings of Paul that attend to the place of law in Jewish and Christian identity. One enters the life of the people of God by grace but one sustains that life by works. His own and others' experience of assurance led him to develop a fresh interpretation of Romans 8 on the inner witness of the Holy Spirit. This is much more compelling than what we find generally in the Reformed tradition. His experience with the poor and derelict nourished a better reading of those texts that deal with the danger of money. However, we should keep our nerve as we proceed and avoid eisegesis. These appeals to experience better fit a rich account of the psychology of discovery than the logic of justification. In the end, as Wesley insisted, we must return to the text and double-check our interpretations.

Wesleyans should also heed Wesley's general orientation in the reading of scripture. He read scripture in order to find the way to heaven. He insisted that the proper scope and subject matter of scripture is salvation.[10] On his own terms, this claim would have to be tested against the data and claims of scripture; otherwise, we run the risk of setting prior constraints on the meaning of scripture typical of deductive approaches to the text. It is better to see the soteriological approach to the content of scripture and accept it for what it is, namely, the beginning of a theology of scripture that should be articulated and defended on its own terms within the wider arena of systematic theology. This venture would relocate scripture within the doctrine of the church as a critical means of grace or within the doctrine of sanctification as an endless source for fostering spiritual wisdom. This is precisely the direction our work on the theology of scripture should take in the future.

We can expect that many in the Wesleyan tradition will accept this but insist on a stronger vision of scripture as divine revelation. They may well become alarmed if we do not, as Wesley did, locate our soteriological interests within a vision of scripture as divine revelation. However, we cannot develop a better option than that embraced by Wesley unless we clear that air conceptually.

Conceptual Considerations

It astonishes me how readily theologians and philosophers confuse the concepts of divine speaking, divine dictation, divine inspiration, divine revelation, divine illumination, divine authorship, and the like as applied to scripture. Unless we gain clarity at this level, all is lost when it comes to thinking through the relationship between divine revelation and scripture. Two simple aphorisms, one positive and one negative, may help in sorting through the confusion. First, in making sense of specific action predicates as applied to God, we should before all else look to relevant analogies drawn from the same specific action predicates as applied to human agents. Second, in understanding particular action predicates as applied to God, we should not treat distinct action predicates as identical. Once we take these aphorisms seriously, we can then move to a robust vision of divine speaking, divine revelation, and divine inspiration.

No one seeking to understand the concept of divine creation would naturally turn, say, to the concept of divine forgiveness to understand its meaning. We should instead reach for our everyday conception of "create" as predicated of human agents and then make the necessary qualifications. We think of God creating, but creating ex nihilo. Consider another example. No one seeking to understand the concept of God as "Father" would turn to the concept of God as "Mother" to understand the claim in hand. We naturally turn to fatherhood as applied to human agents and make the necessary qualifications. We think of God exercising the tender care of a loving, gracious father with his children. Yet we all too readily forget this when we think, say, of divine revelation and inspiration as applied to God. We learn these concepts first as applied to human agents and then make the move to their usage as predicated of God; or so we should. Moreover, just as we would find it odd to confuse revelation and inspiration as applied to human agents, we should also find it radically odd to confuse revelation and inspiration as applied to God. Yet we readily do so again and again in debates about divine revelation and divine inspiration.

Consider now the following observation. The concepts of revelation and inspiration are polymorphous; we reveal ourselves and we inspire others in and through other acts we perform. Hence it is rare to find these verbs in the imperative mood. We reveal ourselves through what we say and what we do; we inspire other agents by performing this or that act through which we motivate and breathe new life into the actions and lives of others. In rare circumstances we may order someone to reveal, say, their true intentions. The proper response will be, say, declaring cleanly and clearly what we are doing and the motives for what we are doing. It is though the relevant speech acts that we reveal our true intentions. Similar considerations apply to the concept of inspiration. We may hear someone say, "I am off to inspire another generation of scholars." What we expect to happen is that they will engage in specific actions of lecturing, answering questions, grading papers, encouraging intellectual virtues, and the like, and that through these acts they hope to light a fire in their students to become serious scholars. In other words, the activity inspiration supervenes on other actions agents perform. They provide a richer redescription of those actions, delineating that they disclose various features of the agent in question (revelation) or that they indicate that the agents in question ignite and breathe life into those impacted by their actions (inspiration).

Once we deploy these conceptual considerations, we can readily develop our doctrines of divine revelation and inspiration. God reveals himself in his actions in creation, conscience, Israel, in Jesus Christ, and in our own lives today. Within this network of actions, some are more revelatory than others. As the epistle to the Hebrews notes, the full and final revelation of God is given in the actions in his Son, Jesus Christ. "In many and varied ways God spoke of old to our fathers by the prophets; but in these last days he has spoken to us in a Son, whom he appointed heir of all things, through whom he also created the world. He reflects the glory of his nature, upholding the universe by the power of his word" (1:1-3). This crucial revelatory role is sometimes captured by saying that Jesus is the Word of God. This makes sense because, by analogy with human revelatory activity, we often say that it is our word that discloses who we really are, what we really think, and what we are really doing. *Mutatis mutandis*, divine inspiration takes place as God interacts with us in a host of actions (beginning with his revelatory acts) to breathe new life into us, to take us to a higher level of thinking and acting. Such activity is not confined to scripture, even as it is illustrated magnificently by the inspiration of scripture. Thus through his encounter with the Risen Lord, through God's word to him as a prophet, through inner illumination of the Holy Spirit, and through myriad providential activity, God inspires the apostle Paul to write, say, the epistle to the Romans. In time God inspires the church to gather this material into various canonical collections. Inspiration construed in these terms applies to the life of the whole church, her missionary work, her worship, her ruminations on the gospel, and the like.

The relation between revelation and scripture now falls nicely into place. Scripture should not be identified with divine revelation, nor should divine revelation be identified with scripture. Scripture mediates special divine revelation given in Israel, in Jesus Christ, and in Paul. General revelation in nature and conscience exists outside these parameters, as does person-relative special revelation given to individuals and to Christian communities. Divided into Old and New Testaments, but both together mediate the Word of God to his people.[11] It is common, therefore, to speak of the scriptures as the Word of God. Given its complex contents and origination, it would be better to consider the whole of scripture as the Wisdom of God. Doing so would avoid falling into the trap of thinking of scripture as analogous to the incarnation;[12] it would also steer us clear of the trap of thinking of scripture as authored, written, and even dictated by God. Once we head down these roads, we have substituted other divine actions (incarnation, divine authoring, and divine dictation) for the primary divine action related to the origination of scripture, namely, that of inspiration.

The Epistemology of Theology

Claims about divine revelation are not just first-order claims about what God has done; they also provide appropriate norms for adjudicating the truth and falsehood of other theological claims. One reason for construing scripture as divine revelation was precisely to privilege its position as the *norma non normans* (the norm that is not normed) of theology. This dovetails with the interpretation of scripture as canon, where "canon" is taken as a criterion. Wesley at this level shared the conventional tradition that he inherited from the Reformation. He was wonderfully clear in following up the consequences of that inheritance. In order for scripture to be canon in this sense, one needed to know the exact boundaries of the canon, so he rejected the Apocrypha. He developed a short and easy way to establish the inspiration of scripture, for without this he would have no way of deciding in favor of Christian scripture rather than, say, Muslim scripture. He worried that admitting one mistake would undermine any and every appeal to scripture, as indeed it would if it was really the kind of norm he thought it was. He was panicked into thinking that if we gave up this vision of scripture then all we could have was a free-for-all in theology, for he in part accepted the conventional tradition because it relieved his epistemic anxiety in a way other epistemic options did not. These sentiments are alive and well inside and outside the Wesleyan tradition; abandoning them can evoke astonishing agony of soul and mind.

Yet outside these deliberations, Wesley was astonishingly astute in deploying other epistemic ruminations in his account of the justification of Christian belief. Like many of his successors, he had little faith in natural theology construed in terms of proofs for the existence of God. However, he articulates in his own inimitable way arguments from perception of the divine, arguments from the fulfillment of divine promise, and arguments from conspicuous sanctity. Moreover, I think his insistence that these arguments be lodged in a wider vision of divine revelation shows that in an inchoate way he realized that once one thinks of justification in diachronic rather than simply synchronic terms, the revelation is not just one more epistemic resource; it involves the crossing of a threshold where all our epistemology may have to be refigured in the light of divine revelation. In my judgment Wesley informally captured a range of epistemic considerations that are salient and weighty, and they do indeed underwrite the justification of Christian doctrine.[13] Like all arguments that crop up generally in epistemology, they are contested, but this is as it should be in this arena.

Methodists since the days of Wesley have readily engaged in efforts to provide backing for their theological claims; these in turn have led to efforts to provide a deeper epistemological horizon within which these backings make sense. Too often they have missed the full range of fascinating epistemic suggestions that show up in Wesley himself. To be sure, Wesley does not provide an integrated epistemological vision, nor does he reconcile the tension between his panic about the loss the authority of scripture as he conceives it and his exceptionally positive deployment of cogent arguments that arise outside his appeal to scripture construed as special divine revelation. However, anyone who takes Wesley seriously must engage with the full round of epistemological material he makes available. There is much more in his writings than his conventional ideas about biblical revelation.

Decisions will have to be made at some stage of the discussion about what to retain as fruitful and illuminating and about what to set aside as a dead end for future work. In this respect the very meaning of what it is to be Wesleyan or what it means to inhabit a Wesleyan perspective will be essentially contested. We can imagine a vision of the Wesleyan tradition that privileges his conventional identification of divine revelation with scripture, but we can also envisage a vision of the Wesleyan tradition that prefers the broader network of proposals that take up, say, perception of the divine as essential to a well-rounded epistemology of theology. We can think of these options as important research agendas in the epistemology. As such, these research programs will need to accommodate the virtues of its rival. My own preference is to take the second route. In turn, that will require an appropriate account of special divine revelation as it relates to scripture. The health of the tradition is best served if both of these options are explored to their limits with rigor and in a spirit of friendly rivalry.

The Status of Epistemological Claims

Decisions will also have to be made at two other forks in the road at this point. First, within the church as a whole, what status do we ascribe to any epistemological proposals we develop? And, second, should we continue to think of canon as a criterion?

On the first of these issues, I think it best for Christian communities to refrain from adopting any particular epistemology as canonical. Consider in this regard the recent dense and subtle proposals of John Paul II. Echoing the claim of Pius XII, he insists that "the Church has no philosophy of her own nor does she canonize any one philosophy in preference to others."[14] More fulsomely, John Paul II argues for great caution in dealing with philosophical claims:

> It is neither the task nor the competence of the Magisterium to intervene in order to make good the lacuna of philosophical discourse. Rather it is the Magisterium's duty to respond clearly and strongly when controversial opinions threaten right understanding of what has been revealed, and when false and partial theories which sow the seeds of serious error, confusing the pure and simple faith of the People of God, begin to spread more widely.[15]

At first blush, this is a very promising first move on stating the status of philosophical proposals in the life of the church. However, the question before us is not the status of philosophical proposals in general but the status of epistemological proposals in particular. Even on the more general claim, *Fides et Ratio* clearly favors a Thomistic philosophical perspective, however that perspective is to be parsed in detail. The Magisterium "has repeatedly acclaimed the merits of St. Thomas' thought and made it the guide and model for theological studies."[16] On the status of particular epistemological claims, it is clear that the Roman Catholic Church has not hesitated to canonize various elements of an epistemology of theology, even as it leaves open the possibilities of further insight and development. The working of the Magisterium itself constitutes a privileged epistemic site within the system as a whole. So too does the Pope of Rome, as the relevant canons on papal infallibility make abundantly clear. These claims are not simply doxological, nor are they secondary. They are epistemic, and they are constitutive of Roman Catholicism. In this respect these claims mirror those Western Protestant counterparts who canonize, say, a vision of scripture as divine revelation, or, say, a joint appeal to scripture, tradition, and reason as the appropriate ground of proper theological claims.[17]

There are three obvious problems in this stance. First, if we follow this trajectory, then the church will have to commit itself officially on complex epistemological proposals. To do this, she cannot avoid taking sides on speculative philosophical issues and thus cannot avoid alienating those members who cannot for professional or other reasons agree with her canonical decisions. It is best to avoid this development. Second, like it or not, such epistemological commitments readily become foundational in a way that marginalizes the gospel, the deep theological truths of the faith, the canonical practices of the church, and the like. We are offered recipes along with the meal, and too many end up becoming obsessed with the recipe rather than the meal. Third, if we canonize our varied epistemologies, then the likelihood of deeper and deeper divisions in the church is inevitable. This surely is an outcome we can avoid by eschewing canonical commitments in the epistemology of theology and leaving even the best work in this domain in the bosom of the church. Indeed, such a policy might encourage the kind of rich exploration of the epistemology of theology that we sorely need.

As to the question whether we should continue to think of canon as a criterion, I can be brief by urging the following resolutions. First, at one level there is nothing amiss with thinking of canon as a criterion. This usage has a long history, and there is nothing intrinsically wrong in continuing it, but only so long as we know what we are doing. We are appropriating and developing one line of thought in the epistemology of theology. Thus we can envisage a vision of scripture as mediating special divine revelation that would allow us to still think of canon as a criterion, using the appeal to scripture as shorthand for an appeal to special revelation. The crunch comes when we insist that this was the only ancient way of understanding canon and as the only way to think of scripture. So, second, I favor a more deflationary reading of canon as list, insisting that the primary meaning of canon is that of the list of doctrines adopted by the church (the canon of truth) or the list of scriptures to be read week in and week out in the liturgy. This usage fits snugly with ancient claims about canon law, a canon of saints, a canon of bishops, and the like. Once we do this, we can see how scripture fits in a wider canonical heritage designed to enable the church to operate optimally in bringing salvation to the world through the agency of the Holy Spirit. Third, following the earlier move to think of scripture soteriologically, I think we should do the same for other phenomena that we designate as canonical. Thus, canon law, to take but one example, should be thought of not just in juridical terms (which, of course, it should) but also in soteriological terms. By this I mean that the application of canon law in the church should be exercised with the help of the Holy Spirit to minister to the souls of those who are rightly brought under its jurisdiction.[18]

The Retrieval of Wesley for Today

The vision I am developing here involves both discontinuity and continuity with Wesley's own teaching on the relation between revelation and scripture. As I indicated at the outset, I do not think we can simply repeat what Wesley held on this topic in his day. There is no shirking the discontinuity at this point. However, there is also continuity in that I have sought to retrieve neglected aspects of his legacy as manifest in his important epistemological insights and in his insisting that we read scripture soteriologically, that is, as a book whose primary purpose is to make us wise unto salvation and show us the way to heaven. Some will balk at this because they are convinced that it is precisely Wesley's vision of scripture as spoken or authored by God that should be retained; without these we will not find our way to heaven. Others will balk at this selective retrieval of Wesley because they would prefer to develop Wesley's vision of divine revelation in a Barthian direction or because they would prefer to develop his soteriological vision in a radically emancipatory direction. It is the mark of a fecund theological tradition that these kinds of diverse developments are natural and inescapable. What matters at this point is ruthless honesty about the selective retrieval that is being canvassed and rigorous development of the favored epistemic trajectory.

We have now entered into a new dimension of our inquiry. How should we construe such retrieval and how should we deploy the vast array of materials and practices given to us from the past by Wesley?

One way to proceed is to settle for a strongly if not purely historical attitude to Wesley. Whatever the secondary interests involved, the primary interest is to understand Wesley as accurately as possible. This approach was especially prominent in the middle of the twentieth century in the fierce reaction against triumphalist and hagiographical readings of Wesley. This was an important corrective; the fruit of this reaction is a first-rate edition of his writings. No serious engagement with Wesley can ignore this great gift of scholarship. As with scripture, we must read Wesley as he is, in his context, using all the historical tools that apply. The hallmark of a good historical work is to get the history as straight as we can and initially to leave the normative appropriation of Wesley as a totally open question. Maybe he does or maybe he does not help us in the normative issues we face in the current scene. What we need is first-rate historical investigation. Applied to the publication of Wesley's sermons, this result is a selection that arranges them chronologically so that we can see how his ideas develop over time.[19]

A second way to proceed is to move beyond historical investigation and begin to piece together a fulsome systematic theology, drawing on the entire Wesley corpus but reading it in such a way as to answer our own systematic theological concerns in the present. Consider the efforts to read Wesley as a proto-Liberation theologian or as a practical theologian focused on the theme of responsible grace.[20] In these instances Wesley can be seen as a folk theologian whose proposals need to be expanded and updated with contemporary insights that fill in the gaps in his epistemological and theological commitments. It is a tribute to both the lacuna in his work and the fecundity of his thought that radically diverse ways of appropriating Wesley are available in the Wesleyan tradition across the centuries.

My own approach takes issue with both these options. I begin certainly with a rigorous historical disposition to read Wesley accurately in terms of his eighteenth-century context. The distance separating us from Wesley is real and cannot be glossed over, as if we can simply operate on the model of a microwave. My fundamental historical judgment is that Wesley is neither a folk theologian who should be beefed up into a systematic theologian, nor a systematic theologian of significance. His great gifts lie in the arena of ascetic theology. He is first and foremost a theologian of the Christian life. Hence, it is a scandal that his canonical sermons are not used today for the making of disciples in the United Methodist tradition. However we draw the boundaries of those sermons, they are arranged as a manual of Christian teaching for new believers.[21] Thus they move naturally from how to become a Christian, to being a Christian, to remaining a Christian. The chronological arranging and reading of his sermons, while important, say, in a historical seminar on Wesley, cannot capture this dimension of his work. This ordering completely misses the catechetical dimension of his activity as an evangelist.

Once we accept the judgment that Wesley is first and foremost an ascetic theologian, we can relax when it comes to Wesley's insight into the various themes of systematic theology. We can move in and out of the extraordinary corpus of material and use it as best fits our own overall vision of systematic theology. This work in systematic theology will have to be articulated and defended in its own right. Once we realize this, there is no pressure to press Wesley's insights into service beyond what they are able to bear. His legacy on the contested question of the relation between revelation and scripture is a case in point. We honor him best by discarding his errors and by developing his insights in ways that best serve the truth of the gospel and the glory of God in the salvation of souls today.

The tragedy of Methodism in the twentieth century is that for the most part Methodists have been caught in the two-party system that came to dominate church life in the wake of the early twentieth-century divide between modernists and fundamentalists. Its shadow lingers on in the polemical battles between progressives and conservatives, between extremists and centrists, between Pietists and social activists, and now between modernists and postmodernists. Given that the pluralism officially adopted in the 1970s is both internally incoherent and unworkable, this map making remains virtually ineradicable. Its most recent incarnation is the invidious contrast between mainline and evangelical Christianity, where we are corralled into opting either for a progressive form of Christianity that eventually self-destructs or for a narrow version of fundamentalist evangelicalism that is archaic and ineptly aggressive in the public arena.[22]

When it comes to our options on the relation between scripture and revelation, we are doomed to two standard possibilities in this scenario. We can either accept the findings of historical criticism with its Enlightenment dismissal of direct divine action in history and in our lives or stick to a defensive conservatism that identifies scripture straightforwardly with special divine revelation. As I have found across the years in teaching seminary students and local church members, it is thought impossible to combine a critically informed account of scripture with a thoroughly robust appropriation of canonical Christian doctrine. One must either dump divine revelation, pretending that this can be done without shedding theological tears, or swallow whole a vision of scripture as divine speaking that even a cursory reading of the biblical material undermines.[23] The former leaves us thoroughly impoverished spiritually and intellectually; the latter leaves us with an unrealistic ultrasupernaturalism. The former paves the way for our children and grandchildren to walk out of Christianity into the wastelands of secularism; the latter sets us at odds with a proper harvesting of the results of science and history. The former provides succor for stultifying forms of secular imperialism in the political arena; the latter leads to a strident inability to cope with the complex demands of our current political context.

The Christian tradition cannot flourish without massive immersion and deployment of the resources given to it in its scriptures. It cannot survive on a diet that fails to plumb the depths of the Bible as we actually have it. Equally, it cannot intellectually defend itself against criticism without a serious commitment to special divine revelation. It cannot make good its claim to truth merely by recourse to natural theology and religious experience, and even less so on a menu of fideistic appeals to communal perspective or social location. Scripture mediates an indispensable Word from God. In that Word we have reliable access to the truth about God that is indispensable for our salvation and for defending the credibility of Christianity. We need both the scriptures in all their glorious diversity and a vigorous apologetic that speaks forthrightly and humbly about special divine revelation; Wesley sought to develop both these insights with flair in his day. We need equally forthright accounts of the indispensability of scripture and of special divine revelation today.

9

A WESLEYAN UNDERSTANDING OF THE AUTHORITY OF SCRIPTURE

Douglas M. Koskela

It is relatively commonplace for Christian communities from across the ecclesial spectrum to affirm, in one sense or another, the authority of Scripture. When they begin to flesh out precisely what such authority entails, however, they move quickly into contested territory. Indeed, the very contexts in which Scripture's authority is generally invoked—hot-button ethical issues, for example—tend toward the polemical. In the course of such conversations, it often becomes abundantly clear that differing and even competing notions of biblical authority are on display.[1] Given this situation, it is worth clarifying what is meant by affirming Scripture as authoritative. In the context of the present volume, my particular aim is to explore biblical authority in a Wesleyan key.

Late in his life, while reflecting on the identity of the earliest Methodists, John Wesley wrote, "They were one and all determined to be *Bible-Christians*. They were continually reproached for this very thing; some terming them in derision *Bible-bigots*; others *Bible-moths*—feeding, they said, upon the Bible, as moths do upon cloth. And indeed unto this day it is their constant endeavour to think and speak as the oracles of God."[2] We can likely agree that the image of moths feeding on cloth lacks elegance, as might be expected of a phrase intended as an epithet. Yet Wesley's willingness to embrace this derisive term as a mark of honor is illuminating. The very idea that his early critics saw as so distasteful—of feeding on Scripture, of drawing sustenance and nourishment from it—is precisely what Wesley lifted up as commendable. Whatever else Wesley had to say about the Bible (and to be sure, he had plenty), he was adamant that it was life giving and capable of shaping one's thought and speech. The passionate drive of those early Methodists to devour the Scriptures was clearly something Wesley celebrated.

I would suggest, furthermore, that the image of feeding on Scripture can orient a Wesleyan account of biblical authority. As I will argue, a Wesleyan vision of Scripture need not and indeed should not uncritically embrace the entirety of Wesley's approach to the Bible.[3] Yet his apprehension of Scripture as nourishing, formative, and salvific continues to serve his heirs well in the early twenty-first century. In that light, I aim in what follows to develop a vision of Scripture's authority that emphasizes our relationship to Scripture, namely, that we stand under God's word as a transformative means of grace. The *ground* of biblical authority is the salvific work of the triune God. The *telos* of biblical authority is soteriological and formative. Elsewhere, I have reflected on the ecclesial conditions that need to be in place for Scripture's authority to obtain.[4] While my primary focus in the present essay lies elsewhere, the role of the church's rule of faith, its teaching office, and its immersion in worship and the means of grace remain important to receiving God's word faithfully. Throughout the present discussion, as with my earlier piece, the epistemological categories that often dominate reflection on Scriptural authority are subordinated to formative categories. While knowledge of God and God's purposes is doubtless involved in the formation of faithful Christians, such knowledge is not itself the ultimate aim of God's salvific work. In a similar vein, while the Scriptures are used by God to make us "wise unto salvation" (2 Tim 3:15 KJV), the role of Scripture in the economy of salvation is much greater than merely imparting knowledge. Thus an account of biblical authority that is limited to affirming the Bible's veracity or epistemic reliability will inevitably fall short from a Wesleyan perspective. What is needed is a fuller vision of the multifaceted function of Scripture within the life of the church and, more broadly, within God's salvific purposes. To set the stage for such a task, it is worth considering the notion of "authority" itself.

THE CONCEPTUAL CONTOURS OF AUTHORITY

Situated as we appear to be in the evening of modernity, a note of ambivalence can be detected in the broader culture regarding the idea of authority. At least since the coming of age of the baby boomer generation, there is a certain romantic appeal to the call to question authority—a call whose deeper roots lie in the soil of Enlightenment sensibilities. A related dynamic can be recognized in the deep suspicion of institutions that is prevalent in the contemporary setting.[5] To the degree that an institution has power in a given sphere, that suspicion tends to intensify. At the same time, in a number of settings authority bears a positive resonance. On the evening news, an anchor might engage with an "authority" on Keynesian economics (or Victorian literature or international terrorism) in a posture of deference and respect. A patient with agonizing back pain is not generally inclined to question the authority of the physician standing before him interpreting his x-ray. Indeed, while patients and patient advocates are perhaps increasingly willing to ask difficult questions of care providers, the practice of medicine is one sphere where a positive sense of authority remains largely intact in contemporary culture.

Part of the ambivalence reflected in the foregoing examples, of course, can be attributed to shifting uses of the term "authority." To say that the Supreme Court has judicial authority and to say that someone is an authority on American jurisprudence are obviously two different things. At first glance, it is interesting that the uses of the term that tend to be regarded favorably appear to be those that emphasize a deep or unique *knowledge*, while those that tend to garner suspicion emphasize *power*. To take a colloquial example, we are rarely surprised when hecklers interrupt a town hall meeting hosted by an elected official, but we would be quite surprised if the same thing were to happen at a plenary session of a biochemistry conference.[6] We can likely recognize in this phenomenon the epistemic privileging of reason and (most especially) empirical knowledge, the lineage of which can be traced to the Enlightenment. Such an observation may help us understand why accounts of biblical authority that focus on Scripture's historical or scientific reliability have proven so tempting in the last two centuries. For the purposes of this discussion, however, two things should be kept in mind. First, our concern is not primarily what expressions of authority are culturally appealing in this or any particular context. Rather, our aim is to gain some clarity on what actually constitutes authority proper. Second, despite the apparent cultural preference for authority-as-knowledge over authority-as-power, knowledge and power are more closely connected than such a simple dichotomy would suggest. Not only is it difficult even to conceive of knowledge that holds no potential for influencing action, but the grasp of such knowledge would hardly constitute "authority." I would argue, in fact, that authority proper implies some power or ability to effect change. Just as with a police officer or a state governor, the authority associated with a physician or a biologist is connected to the capacity to influence lives.

At this point, we are in a position to identify the essential conceptual elements of authority. I suggest that someone or something holds authority when three such elements are in place: (1) power (on the part of the one holding authority), (2) legitimation of that power (with reference to a transcendent moral order), and (3) reception or recognition (on the part of those under authority). As indicated above, some form of power is involved in any meaningful instance of authority. Authority can be held by an agent or institution,[7] or it can be vested in a document or object.[8] In the case of the former, power generally implies the ability to influence by persuasion or force. In the case of the latter, power refers both to the fittingness of the object to its task and to the power of the agent or institution who has vested the document or object with authority as an auxiliary. Let me offer two examples to flesh out what I mean by "fittingness of the object to its task." If someone has committed a traffic violation and is handed a citation by a police officer, we could rightly say that the citation has a particular power or authority. For the citation to be authoritative, it certainly needs the backing of the local police jurisdiction—a citation written by a street vendor would have neither power nor authority. But the power of that citation also depends on the clarity of instructions within it. A traffic ticket that contains nothing but a series of letters and numbers in no discernable pattern has no power because one does not know how to respond appropriately to it—it is not fitting to its task. Or, as a second example, players involved in a heated board game may appeal to the authoritative rules of the game to settle a dispute. The authority of the rulebook depends on the authority of the institution lying behind the document; in this case, it is reasonable that the manufacturer of the game has an appropriate claim to determine the official rules. But if the rulebook does not address the issue under dispute, its authority at that point immediately is nullified. Again, it is not fitting to the task.

The power to effect change is a necessary condition for authority, but it is not a sufficient condition. A key distinction between authority and bare power is that the former implies that power is held and exercised legitimately. A TSA agent and an armed robber both have the power to make a person take off his or her shoes, but only the former is generally regarded as having the authority to do so. The legitimacy of power is thus a second essential component of authority. When we ask what *constitutes* legitimacy in this discussion, however, we raise a rather thorny question. The answer will depend to some degree on context, as can be illustrated by a number of examples. The legitimacy of a parent's authority, for instance, seems at least initially connected to the biological relationship between the mother or father and the child. Parents have the authority to set rules and levy consequences for their own children, but of course they do not hold the same authority with other children. However, parental authority can be ceded to someone else (in the case of adoption) or lost (in the case of a child removed from an abusive home by a child welfare agency), in which case legitimacy would be rendered in other ways as stipulated by the particular legal environment. The natural authority of the parent is thus subject to a deeper standard of justice.

To take another example, the power of a referee in a professional football game is deemed legitimate by the league office. The endorsement of the league office depends on extensive training and ongoing performance review. But suppose a journalist were to uncover a scandal in which referees had been instructed by the league office to call games so as to favor the teams that draw the highest television ratings. The legitimacy of both the power of the league office and the power vested in the referees—that is, their authority—would immediately be undermined. The ethical transgression would presumably invalidate the social arrangement by which the league office deems the power of referees legitimate.

Turning to the political realm for a final example, suppose a rebel alliance takes control of a capital city and declares that a new government has been established. While power is clearly in the hands of the rebel leaders, the legitimacy of that power is generally acknowledged by formal recognition of the new government by other states. Such recognition is often a delicate and contested matter, and the international community does not always respond in unison. In extreme cases, a new government may be deemed illegitimate by an alliance of other nations and removed by force.

The main point to be drawn from the foregoing exercise is this: while various kinds of social agreements or juridical stipulations are in place to recognize power as legitimate, in each case such arrangements are held accountable to a higher standard of morality, justice, and/or truth. From a theological perspective, then, it is entirely appropriate to insist that the legitimacy of power involves more than juridical or social contract. Authority requires some intrinsic connection to the moral order, and for Christians the best access to the moral order is that which God has given in both general and special revelation.[9]

A third essential element of authority is reception on the part of those under authority. Without reception, authority gives way to mere coercion (in the case of an agent or institution) or ineffectuality (in the case of an object or document). It should be said that reception in this sense does not imply total compliance. Rather, it involves the recognition of the legitimacy of the power that is held (though as we noted above, such legitimacy is usually *established* by other means). So, for example, a teenager may choose to miss curfew and accept the consequences, all the while recognizing the authority of the parents to enforce those consequences. When such reception is not in place, power might be maintained, but it would be difficult to say that authority has been maintained.[10] Joseph T. Lienhard makes this point by means of the category of freedom: "Authority operates within the ambit of freedom, at least in a minimal sense: the response to authority always includes some residue of human freedom. Once the last vestige of freedom is suppressed, authority is supplanted by brute power."[11] In the case of an auxiliary authority such as a document, the absence of recognition renders that document ineffective in that context.[12] Let us return to the example of a heated dispute among the players of a board game. Suppose that one couple appeals to the rulebook that came with the box to support their contention that they made a legal move. In response, the other couple accesses an updated version of the official rules on the manufacturer's website that supports their contention that the other couple's move was illegal. *Both* sets of rules are backed by the endorsement of the game's manufacturer, and both sets of rules are sufficiently clear to be fitting to their task. Yet the game is at an impasse until the players decide which set of rules to receive as authoritative. Legitimate power as we have defined it, therefore, is necessary but not sufficient to establish genuine authority. Reception is also necessary. Each of these conditions is significant, moreover, in the question of what we mean when we affirm the authority of Scripture. To that question we now turn.

The Nature of Scripture's Authority

Affirming Scripture's authority is best understood as a means of expressing our relationship to the Bible in light of God's salvific purposes. We stand under the Bible as a bearer of both God's self-disclosure and God's transformative power—that is, as a means of grace. In light of the preceding discussion, we can locate Scripture as an auxiliary authority with all three of the requisite elements we have recognized. The power of Scripture is none other than the power of God, and particularly the person of the Holy Spirit, at work. The legitimacy of Scripture's power is grounded in its place in God's economy of salvation and recognized by the ecclesial act of canonization. The reception of Scripture's authority is marked by the engagement of the Bible by God's people, collectively and individually, with a posture of humility and a hunger to be immersed more deeply in the life of God. As we proceed to develop each of these dimensions more fully, let us aim to root them firmly in theological soil.

One might ask, first of all, why I have designated Scripture an "auxiliary" authority. My reason for doing so is simply to recognize that its authority falls in the category of a document or object rather than that of an agent or institution, as described above. A collection of sacred texts is not capable of action. To be sure, we are not wrong to use a phrase such as "Scripture judges our actions." But when we do so, we are recognizing the Bible's particular role in God's self-revelation and God's judgment—we are not actually suggesting that the Bible exercises volition. John Webster's concise statement is apt: "the authority of Scripture is the authority of the church's Lord and his gospel."[13] It is important to add that this recognition need not commit us to a purely extrinsic notion of Scripture's authority.[14] While we rightly could say that biblical authority is *grounded* extrinsically—in God's authority—we also should recognize that God's use of Scripture in drawing people to Godself endows it with intrinsic (if still auxiliary) authority. God's sanctification of *these* texts rather than some other texts, along with the Spirit's engagement of these particular texts in the life of faith, is confirmed not only by the church's canonization of them but also by our actual experience of Scripture. Moreover, such experience of the Bible's intrinsic authority (which should be understood in relation to the classical doctrine of illumination) is essential to the *reception* of Scripture's authority by the people of God. As Joel B. Green observes, "most Christians relate to the Bible by granting it some combination of intrinsic and extrinsic authority."[15] This combination fits naturally into the conception of Scripture's authority that we have been developing.

We are now in a position to see precisely how the authority of the Bible reflects the first essential component of authority, namely, power to effect change. Let us recall that for an auxiliary authority, power implies both the power of the agent or institution that has vested the object with authority and fittingness to its task. In this case, we speak of the transformative power of Scripture in reference to God's power active through our engagement of the biblical texts. N. T. Wright suggests that "the phrase 'authority of Scripture' can make Christian sense only if it is a shorthand for 'the authority of the triune God, exercised somehow *through* Scripture.'"[16] It is appropriate to emphasize in particular the third person of the Trinity in this regard. In the economy of salvation, the Holy Spirit is particularly associated with the transformative work of shaping us in the likeness of Christ.[17] Indeed, the Spirit's power to heal and transform creation was a crucial aspect of John Wesley's pneumatology.[18] His brother Charles echoed this dimension of the Holy Spirit's work in one of the stanzas of his hymn "Come, Thou Everlasting Spirit":

> Come, Thou Witness of his Dying;
> Come, Remembrancer Divine!
> Let us feel thy Power, applying
> CHRIST to every Soul, and mine![19]

To speak of the power of Scripture, then, is to speak of this sort of power effected by the triune God (and esp. the Holy Spirit) as we immerse ourselves in Scripture. Later in his discussion, Wright continues, "'The authority of Scripture' refers not least to God's work *through* Scripture to reveal Jesus, to speak in life-changing power to the hearts and minds of individuals, and to transform them by the Spirit's healing love."[20] As with any auxiliary authority, then, the power at work in and through Scripture is that of the one who vested it with authority.

The other requisite aspect of power in an auxiliary authority is fittingness to its task. Again, if an object or document is ineffective in fulfilling its purpose, it cannot be said to be authoritative. The crucial question with regard to the authority of Scripture is not *whether* it is fitting to its task, for any Christian community that affirms biblical authority will doubtless affirm that the Bible functions as it ought. The crucial question, rather, is what the Bible's task actually is. And it is here that the controversy over the authority of Scripture usually centers. For if the function of the Bible is conceived in primarily epistemological terms—say, of providing perfectly accurate information—then its authority is left on very precarious ground. For example, if one commits to the position that all historical and scientific claims found in the Bible are true,[21] then Scripture's fittingness to its task (and thus its authority) will depend on its correspondence with the results of critical historical inquiry and scientific investigation.[22] Or, if one argues that the task of Scripture is to provide a univocal set of doctrinal propositions that represent the cognitive content of the Christian faith,[23] then Scripture's fittingness to its task (and thus its authority) will be undermined if the multivalent theological witness across the canon of Scripture is acknowledged.

If, however, one articulates the Bible's function in soteriological terms, then we find ourselves in very different territory. Scripture's fittingness to its task will be confirmed by the actual experience of the community of faith as it draws closer to God through immersion in the biblical texts. Webster clearly takes his stand here: "The authority of Scripture is its Spirit-bestowed capacity to quicken the church to truthful speech and righteous action. Confession of Scripture's authority is avowal by the hearing church of that which the Spirit undertakes through Scripture's service of the Word, and its proper context is therefore soteriological."[24] In his remarkable theology of Scripture, *Living and Active*, Telford Work develops a vision of Scripture's purpose along similar lines: "Because the Bible acts in ways consistent with God's overall plan of salvation—mediating, demonstrating, and accomplishing it—the Bible's work can be understood according to soteriological categories. . . . The Bible operates both macrocosmically, altering the trajectory of human history, and microcosmically, altering the person who receives its message."[25] Such an understanding of the task of Scripture, I would suggest, better comports with the church's actual experience and engagement of the Bible than does a primarily epistemic framing of the Bible's task. This is not to imply that truth and knowledge are unimportant to God's saving purposes or to the place of Scripture within those purposes. The point is that the relationship between the Bible and knowledge is framed in terms of Scripture's role within the economy of salvation. Scripture's authority does not depend on its ability to yield accurate historical or scientific data. Scripture is authoritative because through it God speaks, heals, gives us hope, convicts us of sin, shapes our understanding of the world, and reminds us of God's saving actions.[26] In other words, it is fitting to its soteriological and formative task.

At this point an analogy is in order to help convey why purely epistemic accounts of Scripture's authority are inadequate. Consider the authority of a prescription. (For the purposes of this analogy, we will keep in mind the written prescription from the physician, the instructions from the pharmacist, and the medicine itself when referring to a prescription.) The power of the prescription lies in the combination of the physical properties of the medicine and the expert knowledge of the physician and the pharmacist. The legitimacy of that power is recognized by means of the social arrangement that has determined the appropriate protocols between the medical practitioner and the pharmacy (though, as always, these protocols are subject to a deeper ethical standard). The reception of the prescription involves the proper use of the medicine according to the instructions from the pharmacist. While knowledge is clearly important throughout the process—with the power to heal or harm the patient significantly—it would be quite odd to suggest that the *purpose* of prescribing medicine is to convey information to the pharmacist.[27] The purpose of the prescription is to help in the healing of the patient, and the knowledge involved is oriented toward that end. Moreover, the authority of a prescription would not be undermined if the zip code were incorrect on the written prescription or on the pharmacist's instructions. While it is certainly true that specifying the wrong medicine or an incorrect dosage could have devastating effects, the reason is that doing so would undermine the very purpose for the prescription in the first place. I would suggest that the authority of Scripture is similar in that the crucial dimension of knowledge involved is that which is directly connected to its healing function.[28]

We now turn to the second essential component of Scripture's authority: the legitimacy of the transformative power we have been exploring. The obvious point should be made up front that the recognition of legitimacy is distinct from the ground of legitimacy. As we have seen in a number of examples, the social conventions by which the legitimacy of any authority's power is recognized are held to a deeper standard of morality, justice, and/or truth. In the case of Scripture, the church catholic's reception of the Bible as canonical is the fundamental action by which legitimacy is recognized. The fact that the Epistle of James is part of the canonical New Testament while, say, *The Shepherd of Hermas* is not is a result of the church's careful discernment of the particular role the former plays in God's salvific purposes.[29] The actual *ground* of the legitimacy of Scripture's transformative power, then, is the triune God's use of the Bible in drawing people to Godself. In the richness of the Christian theological tradition, the ontology of Scripture has been framed in multiple ways within the economy of salvation.[30] I would suggest that this task is best served by employing the categories of both the word of God and the breath of God.[31] Using the former category, we can say that the Father speaks his word in various manifestations, most clearly in the incarnation of the Son in Jesus. The written word of God in Scripture is one such manifestation.[32] The Spirit connects God's people to this word by means of both inspiration of the biblical texts and the illumination of Scripture's readers. Utilizing the latter category, the Father breathes life into creation in various ways through the person of the Spirit. In light of the incarnation of Jesus, a fresh assortment of materials and practices is both given to the church and animated in the lives of its members by the Holy Spirit: Scripture, sacraments, liturgies, creeds, and icons would all be included in this category.[33] Locating Scripture within this dual theological landscape enables us to perceive the legitimating action of God that grounds the Bible's authority.

If the Bible is to fulfill its purpose in drawing people into the life of God, then it must be received by the community of faith as Scripture. It is here that we see the third requisite component of authority: reception. I suggest that reception is located in the church's actual engagement, in the Holy Spirit, of the biblical text and *not* in the act of canonization (which I connected to legitimation above). The recognition by the church of a particular set of texts as legitimately part of God's salvific work does not in itself bring about that salvific work;

those texts must be humbly and prayerfully engaged by God's people in each generation for them to fulfill their task.[34] Along with other means of grace, our immersion in Scripture is a way of welcoming the saving work of God into our lives. This is why Webster insists that the authority of Scripture cannot be disconnected from the life and activity of the church: "To lift the authority of Scripture out of the context of the church would be to formalise that authority by abstracting Scripture from its revelatory and therefore ecclesial setting."[35] Moreover, given the church's deep tradition of using biblical material in worship, the reception of Scripture is not merely a passive exercise. We receive this means of grace and then we respond doxologically, as Work observes: "our ecclesiology of Scripture focuses on the Bible as a means of God's presence to his earthly, eschatological community, and as an instrument of the worshiping community when it is present before God."[36] Of course, as ecclesial heirs of John and Charles Wesley, those in the Wesleyan tradition regard the engagement of Scripture in worship as particularly important. In this light, it is appropriate to turn now to the distinctively Wesleyan character of the vision of Scripture's authority we have been exploring.

The Authority of Scripture and the Wesleyan Ethos

While the foregoing reflections have drawn on the broader theological traditions of the church catholic, they have been articulated in a Wesleyan dialect. This is not to suggest that the account of biblical authority I have developed is identical to John Wesley's; it quite clearly is not. Wesley employed both epistemological and soteriological categories in giving an account of Scripture's authority. The ways in which he developed some of his epistemic categories, such as infallibility and clarity, were typical in eighteenth-century Protestantism.[37] While he seemed to be aware of some of the tensions that the text of Scripture itself raised for his views, he generally dealt with them by means of carefully developed hermeneutical strategies.[38] He could not, of course, have foreseen some of the ways in which later critical studies would raise further tensions for some of his affirmations about the Bible. It would be unfair and anachronistic to criticize Wesley for this, but it would also be unwise simply to transcribe his vision of Scripture into our (very different) context. Indeed, to be "Wesleyan" on any issue of doctrine or practice is less about simply repeating John Wesley's views than it is about engaging each context in light of Wesley's guiding commitments.[39] Given our earlier reasons for privileging Scripture's soteriological and formative purposes over epistemic purposes, it makes sense that a Wesleyan account of biblical authority at the present moment would privilege those streams of Wesley's thought. Among the best representative examples is his sermon, "The Means of Grace." In that sermon, he identified "searching the Scriptures (which implies reading, hearing, and meditating thereon)" as one of the three chief means of grace (along with prayer and receiving the Lord's Supper). He described these means of grace as "ordained of God, and appointed for this end—to be the *ordinary* channels whereby he might convey to men preventing, justifying, or sanctifying grace."[40] This description of the purpose of the means of grace correlates nicely with the vision of Scripture's authority that I have been articulating.

Along with emphasizing Wesley's understanding of "searching the Scriptures" as a means of grace, let me suggest two other ways in which our account of biblical authority reflects a Wesleyan DNA. First, the logic of "reception" in our reflection on authority corresponds directly to a Wesleyan framing of the divine-human relationship. As I have insisted, authority proper requires some degree of reception on the part of those under authority. When this element is missing, authority has given way to bare power. If this is granted, the implications for biblical authority are significant. If one has conceived Scripture's authority in terms of its ability to convey historically reliable information, then the human engagement of Scripture plays no role whatsoever in its authority. We might call this a monergistic understanding of Scripture's authority. But if one locates Scripture's authority in relation to its role in the economy of salvation, as we have done, then a Wesleyan soteriology becomes highly instructive. The gracious priority of the saving work of the triune God invites a grace-enabled response, which draws the believer ever deeper into God's transforming grace.[41] This dynamic interaction between God and humanity is echoed in our discussion of the power, legitimacy, and reception that make sense of the Bible's authority.

A second Wesleyan fingerprint in the vision of scriptural authority outlined here is its missional focus. The Bible is authoritative, we have argued, because of its place in God's salvific activity toward the world. Scripture is breathed and animated by the Holy Spirit for the purpose of enabling movement through the *via salutis*, toward the perfect love of God and neighbor; in other words, Scripture's role is dynamic. By contrast, a conception of Scripture's authority that emphasizes the Bible's propositional content is patently static. From its beginnings as a Methodist movement and into its various ecclesial iterations, the Wesleyan tradition has aimed to shape a people on the move toward the God who graciously moved toward us. In the "Large *Minutes*" of the 1763 Methodist conference, the following well-known exchange is illuminating: "*Q.* What may we reasonably believe to be God's design in raising up the preachers called 'Methodists'? *A.* To reform the nation, particularly the church, and to spread scriptural holiness over the land."[42] Later in those same *Minutes*, we find a section describing how the preachers' "helpers" were to be examined on their use of the means of grace. The section on "searching the Scriptures" outlines the questions to be asked regarding the helpers' reading, meditating on, and hearing the Scriptures. The last of those sets of questions makes it quite clear what sort of engagement of Scripture was needed to sustain such a holy and ambitious mission: "Hearing [the Scriptures]. Constantly? Every morning? Humbly? Uncritically, devoutly? Carefully? With prayer before, at, after? Fruitfully? Immediately putting into practice?"[43] A dynamic movement called for dynamic and consistent encounters with Scripture. One can hope that the vision of and immersion in Scripture embodied by the present-day heirs of the Methodist movement is sufficient to our calling as well.

10

THE HOLINESS OF SCRIPTURE

Jason E. Vickers

Wesleyans, like other Protestants, spend a great deal of time talking about the significance of Scripture. We talk about the authority of Scripture, the inspiration of Scripture, the infallibility or inerrancy of Scripture, and the sufficiency of Scripture.[1] From time to time, we even discuss the concept of Scripture as canon.[2] Most of all, Wesleyans like to discuss the place and function of Scripture in the Wesleyan quadrilateral.[3]

Curiously, for all the time that Wesleyans spend discussing the doctrine of Scripture, we have had relatively little to say about what it means for Scripture to be holy. To be sure, we pay significant attention to holiness *in* Scripture, but we say next to nothing about the holiness *of* Scripture.[4] This omission is surprising because, like most Christians, Wesleyans routinely refer to Scripture as Holy Scripture, the Holy Bible, Sacred Writ, and the like. Moreover, the "Holy Bible" is printed on the spine and covers of the vast majority of Bibles in Wesleyan church pews and in Wesleyan homes. So it is rather odd that, when we talk about Scripture, we do not begin by clarifying what we mean when we refer to the Bible as the Holy Bible or to Scripture as Holy Scripture.

What makes this omission really surprising, however, is that, while some Protestant traditions are purportedly tone deaf to holiness, Wesleyan ears are supposed to be especially attuned to holiness.

After all, Wesleyans are given to ritual recitation of John Wesley's declaration that it was for the propagation of the doctrine of holiness that God raised up the people called Methodists in the first place, and we regularly remind ourselves of the importance of both personal and social holiness. Yet, for all of our emphasis on holiness as the hallmark of the Wesleyan theological tradition, the best treatment of the holiness of Scripture currently available is the work of a Reformed theologian, namely, John Webster.[5]

In an effort to begin a conversation about the holiness of Scripture among Wesleyans, I will do two things in this essay. First, I will offer an explanation for the relative lack of theological reflection among Wesleyans on the holiness of Scripture. On this front, I will suggest that Wesleyans rarely think about or discuss the holiness of Scripture because, for the better part of our history, we have been held captive by an *epistemological* conception of Scripture and an *ethical* vision of holiness. Second, I will offer an alternative way of thinking about both holiness and Scripture, namely, from the standpoint of Methodist dogmatics. On this front, I will maintain that Wesleyans ought to conceive of holiness first and foremost in connection to theology proper, which is to say, to the doctrine of the Trinity. I will then suggest that, when we conceive of holiness as having fundamentally to do with the Trinitarian life of God, the stage is set for attributing holiness to creaturely realities, including the church, sacraments, Scripture, marriage, ordination, and human beings. Finally, I will conclude by suggesting that, in practice, Wesleyans routinely apprehend and approach Scripture (and other creaturely realities) as holy, which is to say, as a site in and through which the Holy Spirit enables us to encounter the real presence of our resurrected Lord and thereby to participate in the Trinitarian life of God.[6]

WESLEYAN CAPTIVITY TO EPISTEMOLOGY AND ETHICS

In its earliest form, Methodism was a renewal movement within the Church of England in the long eighteenth century.[7] This means that Methodism emerged during a period in English church history characterized by a political theology that revolved around subscription to the doctrine of the Trinity and participation in the sacraments.[8] It also means that Methodism came on the scene at roughly the same time as deism and Unitarianism, the two quintessential English manifestations of rational and ethical religion.⁹

Throughout the long eighteenth century, deists, Unitarians, and Protestant Trinitarians shared the same basic outlook with regard to Scripture. Theologians belonging to each of these groups insisted that Scripture, and not the doctrine of the Trinity, was the rule of faith. As a result of this move, Scripture was dislocated from its ancient home, namely, a Trinitarian vision of divine presence and action in human history and in the sacramental life of the church. Deists, Unitarians, and Protestant Trinitarians all viewed Scripture primarily, if not exclusively, as a repository of *rational* propositions necessary to be believed for salvation.

On this view of Scripture, the doctrine of the Trinity, like every other doctrine, was up for grabs. People had to embrace the Trinity only if it could be shown to be contained in or derived from "clear and intelligible" propositions in Scripture. In other words, the doctrine of the Trinity had to be proven rational. Discerning whether a given proposition or network of propositions was in fact rational was a complex and often subtle affair, having to do with these groups' relationships to the fast-emerging natural sciences and to historical criticism.¹⁰ In the end, theologians in all three groups consigned the doctrine of the Trinity (and the incarnation and resurrection) to one of two categories: they were either "contrary to" or "above" reason. Generally speaking, deists and Unitarians assigned the doctrine of the Trinity to the former category, while Protestant Trinitarians routinely assigned it to the latter.¹¹

The prevailing sense that Scripture was above all a repository of rational propositions was buffeted by a decline in sacramental vitality. This was due in part to widespread anti-Catholic sentiment, as evidenced by repeated attacks on the doctrine of transubstantiation, ad hominem labeling of appeals to early creeds and councils in the Socinian and Unitarian debates as "popery," and the rejection of the saints. Behind all of this was the Francophobia that haunted English society during much of the long eighteenth century.

When taken together, the commitment to an epistemic conception of Scripture and the decline in sacramental vitality led to a very different way of thinking about religion. What ultimately came out in the wash was an ethical vision of Christianity completely shorn of theology proper.[12] Indeed, rational religion in England was not unlike its Kantian counterpart in Germany: both reduced theology to ethics.

Like many other Anglicans, early Methodists were deeply concerned about the foregoing developments. Indeed, John Wesley was so concerned about deism and Unitarianism that he went out of his way to name deists and Unitarians as persons to whom he would not extend his hand of fellowship.[13] Moreover, Wesley commissioned John Fletcher and, following Fletcher's untimely death, Joseph Benson to write against the lunatic ravings of Joseph Priestley.[14] Wesley also repeatedly turned to the doctrine of the Trinity when he wanted to indicate what Methodists regarded as essential Christian doctrine.[15] Charles Wesley was no less concerned about deism and Unitarianism, frequently critiquing these movements in hymns and verse and taking the time to compose an entire collection of *Hymns on the Trinity*.[16] Even Thomas Coke, in his sermon at the Christmas Conference in 1784, warned the members of the new Methodist Episcopal Church in America against the dangers of Arianism, deism, and Unitarianism.[17]

In addition to their concerns about deism and Unitarianism, early Methodist leaders were also very worried about the loss of sacramental vitality. It is well known, for example, that John Wesley left the Fetter Lane Society in large part because they had abandoned the sacraments. Moreover, Wesley insisted that Methodists be most faithful to receive the sacraments as frequently as possible in their respective Anglican parishes. For his part, Charles Wesley wrote numerous sacramental hymns, most notably *Hymns on the Lord's Supper*.

Beyond all of this, the Wesleys and other early Methodists were especially sharp in their attacks on rational and ethical religion. For instance, John Wesley frequently rejected the notion that faith had primarily to do with intellectual assent.[18] He also insisted that religion did not have primarily to do with "a round of duties," or even with "honesty, justice, and whatever is called morality," but with the disposition of the heart toward God and one's fellow human beings.[19]

Despite their efforts to combat deism and Unitarianism, to defend and promote the doctrine of the Trinity, to foster sacramental vitality among Methodists *and* Anglicans, and to reject rational and ethical religion in favor of heart religion, the Wesleys and other early Methodist leaders could not avoid being caught up in the prevailing thought currents of the long eighteenth century, especially as these had to do with the conception of Scripture. Wesley himself articulated and defended a view of Scripture that placed an emphasis on the utter reliability of Scripture as a repository of truths. For example, in an infamous letter to William Law, Wesley says, "If there be one falsehood in the Bible, there may be a thousand; neither can it proceed from the God of truth."[20] Similarly, in response to William Warburton's assertion that there is "no considerable error" in the Bible, Wesley asks, "Will not the allowing there is *any error* in Scripture shake the authority of the whole?"[21] And while Wesley adhered to and defended the doctrine of the Trinity as contained in the Nicene Creed, he was also clear that Scripture, and not the creed, was the only true rule of faith. For instance, in setting out the fundamentals of Methodism, he declared that "the Bible is the whole and sole rule both of Christian faith and practice."[22]

When we shift our focus from the Methodist revival in England to early American Methodism, the basic conception of Scripture is the same. For example, in one of the first Methodist theological treatises written in North America, Asa Shinn could say, "Each one is bound under a sacred obligation, to go to the Bible for [one's] system of divinity, and so far as any is governed by a regard to any human creed, in the formation of [one's] religious opinions, so far [one] is deficient in the very principle of Christian faith; and pays that homage to human authority that is due only to the Divine."[23]

It would be easy to give additional examples of how Wesleyans continued to conceive of Scripture primarily in epistemological terms in the nineteenth and twentieth centuries. Over against this, some will insist that the emergence of the quadrilateral in the 1960s rescued Wesleyans from an epistemological conception of Scripture. My own judgment is that this has not in fact occurred. At its best, the quadrilateral has helped Wesleyans to acquire a bit of methodological sophistication in the area of hermeneutics. It has not altered the basic conviction that Scripture is above all a repository of rational propositions to which, following proper interpretation (i.e., following the consultation of reason, tradition, and experience), Christians ought to give their assent. Nor has it enabled Wesleyans to think carefully about the holiness of Scripture.

When Wesleyans conceive of and approach Scripture *primarily* as the rule of faith from which to derive true beliefs, Scripture's relationship to holiness is by definition one of a criterion or, more generally, a source for true beliefs *about* holiness. Consequently, Wesleyans have for centuries combed the pages of Scripture in order to ferret out what Scripture says *about* holiness. On this way of thinking about Scripture, one would think to inquire about the holiness *of* Scripture (i.e., how Scripture itself might be holy) only if Scripture plainly addressed the matter of its own holiness. It does not appear to do so. Indeed, holiness seems to be something that, together with other Christians, Wesleyans have attributed to Scripture without clear scriptural warrant.

Even if someone were to think of a proposition in Scripture that attributes holiness to Scripture itself, I am not convinced that this would lead to a profound vision of the holiness of Scripture among Wesleyans. On the contrary, I am convinced that there is a much deeper problem here than Scripture's failure to attribute holiness to itself. The deeper problem, as I see it, has to do with a subtle connection between epistemic conceptions of Scripture and what can only be described as functional deism among Wesleyans. To be sure, Wesleyans often insist on the *divine* origins of Scripture. Indeed, Wesleyans have developed doctrines of divine inspiration and revelation, and we have a long history of debate regarding the doctrine of inerrancy, theories of dictation, and the like. Yet, in a way that resembles the classical deist vision of the God-world relationship, Wesleyans, having insisted that God created the Scriptures, have little to say about God's ongoing relationship to Scripture. We insist that Scripture *contains* propositions given by God, but we are less certain that God dwells freely and faithfully among human beings today in and through Scripture.[24] Insofar as this is true, Wesleyans come dangerously close to embracing a view of Scripture that is fundamentally more deistic than Trinitarian in its logic.

The functional deism that so often accompanies epistemic conceptions of Scripture is further exacerbated by Wesleyan thinking about holiness. Generally speaking, Wesleyans conceive of holiness primarily in terms of separation. To be holy, we are prone to say, is to be set apart or to be consecrated. This way of thinking about holiness may be appropriate when we are attributing holiness to the church, the sacraments, marriage, Scripture, ordination, or Christians, but it can quickly become problematic when we extend this conception of holiness to God. To be sure, Wesleyans acknowledge that God is, *pace* the doctrine of creation ex nihilo, absolutely other than creation. Moreover, Wesleyans readily confess that God is entirely independent of creation. Similarly, Wesleyans believe that God is the transcendent and sovereign Lord over creation. As a result, most Wesleyans have deep problems with process theology or panentheism.[25] Yet, if we are not careful, our talk of God's holiness will register God's distance or separation from creation *and nothing more*. Having rejected one extreme in the form of process theology, we will quietly and unwittingly embrace another, namely, functional deism.[26]

I could say more about the causes of Wesleyan inattentiveness to the holiness of Scripture. However, I have said enough at this stage to indicate what I take to be the major sources of the problem. With this in place, the time has come to propose a solution. Like my analysis of the problem, the following proposal will be an outline for a solution. Nevertheless, the direction that I want to go on this front will be clear.

Methodist Dogmatics
The Holy Trinity and Holy Scripture

My own proposal for correcting the problem of functional deism and for fostering among Wesleyans a lively notion of both the holiness of God and the holiness of Scripture (and, by extension, of the sacraments, marriage, ordination, and believers) is at once simple and radical. I propose that Wesleyans undertake a new approach to theology, an approach that I like to call Methodist dogmatics. Initially, this undertaking will involve one thing, namely, the restoration of the doctrine of the Trinity to its rightful place as the rule of faith for theology proper.

At one level, this really is a relatively simple move. I am proposing that the Christian doctrine of God be the first word in theology *proper*. At another level, of course, this is a radical move, insofar as it appears to entail a significant demotion of Scripture. Surely this approach will lead not to a lively notion of the holiness of Scripture but to the evisceration of the authority of Scripture. For those who might have such worries, I can only ask for patience, though I would hasten to add that holiness, especially for Wesleyans, ought finally to be of even greater concern than authority per se.

Before I attempt to spell out in outline form what the restoration of the doctrine of the Trinity to its rightful place as the rule of faith entails for our understanding of both the holiness of God and the holiness of Scripture, it bears mentioning that such a move does not so much entail the demotion of Scripture as it does its relocation within theology proper. For that matter, the recovery of the doctrine of the

Trinity as the rule of faith does not even rule out appeals to Scripture in the epistemology of theology. If anything, such a move may open up new insights in this arena. To see this clearly, we need simply to get clear on what is meant by theology *proper*.

In the modern period, Wesleyan theologians, like most other Christian theologians, expended enormous amounts of time and energy on matters like prolegomena and theological method. The greatest evidence for this is the aforementioned Wesleyan quadrilateral. Whatever its merits or demerits, the quadrilateral does not belong to theology proper. Its proper home is in prolegomena, theological method, or perhaps in theological hermeneutics.

What, then, is theology *proper*? As I am using the term, theology proper has a basic shape or outline, as well as a basic content, namely, the doctrine of the Trinity. At first glance, this way of defining theology proper will no doubt strike some people as entirely too restrictive, insofar as it would seem to entail that doctrines like creation, human nature and sin, and salvation, not to mention Scripture, are not a part of theology proper. Are these doctrines not also a part of theology?

If the suggestion that theology proper just *is* the doctrine of the Trinity seems too restrictive, then it is no doubt because there is much misunderstanding about what the doctrine of the Trinity encompasses. And this misunderstanding is due in no small way to the identification of Scripture as the rule of faith, which is to say, as containing rational propositions ready made for intellectual assent. In the late seventeenth and eighteenth centuries, this way of thinking about Scripture led deists, Unitarians, and Trinitarian Protestants to conceive of the doctrine of the Trinity as having to do exclusively with the so-called immanent Trinity. In other words, they conceived of the doctrine of the Trinity as having to do with God *ad intra* (without reference to creation).

Sadly, this way of thinking about the doctrine of the Trinity lumbers on in many quarters within Wesleyanism today. One can easily observe this every time a well-meaning Methodist or Wesleyan attempts to "explain" the Trinity by way of an analogy to ice, water, and steam (or some other favored analogy). The point of these analogies is to account for how three things can be one and yet remain three. Invariably, however, the analogies fail to depict in any way the so-called economic Trinity. They say nothing of God's outgoing movement of reconciliation and redemption to creation and to human beings.

Rightly understood, the doctrine of the Trinity includes the doctrines of creation and salvation. Indeed, to speak of the Trinity is to speak of the God who, in Jesus Christ and in the Holy Spirit, creates, redeems, and sanctifies. In other words, it is impossible to conceive of the doctrine of the Trinity apart from God's coming to dwell among us in the incarnation and at Pentecost, which is to say, apart from the doctrines of creation, human nature, and sin, or apart from Christology, pneumatology, and eschatology. The immanent Trinity is the economic Trinity.[27]

If the best place to see the isolation of the immanent from the economic Trinity is in popular analogies, then the best place to see that the doctrine of the Trinity does have everything to do with creation and redemption, which is to say, with God *ad extra*, is the classical creeds, most notably, the Nicene-Constantinopolitan Creed. The classical creeds are clearly Trinitarian in structure, containing as they do three articles corresponding to Father, Son, and Holy Spirit. But the content of those articles and therefore of the doctrine of the Trinity as the rule of faith for Christian theology is none other than God's outgoing in and to creation—an outgoing that is "for us and for our salvation." This is what early Christian theologians called the rule of faith. And this is what I have in mind when I speak of theology *proper*.

What difference, if any, would the recovery of the doctrine of the Trinity as the rule of faith make for how Wesleyans understand the holiness of God? In raising this question, we are shifting our focus slightly from the doctrine of the Trinity to the doctrine of divine attributes. In doing so, we are entering tricky theological territory.[28] If we are not careful, as we have already noted, then our talk of God's holiness will leave us with a vision of God that has little to do with the God we have come to know, to love, and to worship in the coming of Jesus Christ and of the Holy Spirit at Pentecost. In other words, when the holiness of God is purely a function of God's otherness or difference, then we ultimately will have to do with any number of gods besides the Holy Trinity, or we will have to do with a doctrine of the Trinity that "makes no real difference."[29]

When it is the triune God of Christianity to whom we attribute holiness, then otherness or transcendence is always only part of the story. The doctrine of the Trinity, rightly understood, makes all the difference in the world for how we think about God's holiness precisely because it reminds us that the God who transcends the world and who is altogether different from creation is precisely the God who, in Jesus Christ, has taken on flesh and dwelt among us in order to reconcile us to God's self, to heal and to sanctify us, and the like. Indeed, it is precisely at this point that Wesleyans can learn from John Webster. He writes,

> Holiness, because it is the holiness of the God and Father of our Lord Jesus Christ now present in the Spirit's power, is pure majesty in relation. God's holy majesty, even in its unapproachableness, is not characterized by a sanctity which is abstract difference or otherness, a counter-reality to the profane; it is majesty known in turning, enacted and manifest in the works of God. Majesty and relation are not opposed moments in God's holiness; they are simply different articulations of the selfsame reality. For if God's relation to us were merely subordinate to his primary majesty, then God's essence would remain utterly beyond us, forever hidden; and if God's relation to us were not majestic, then that relation would no longer be one in which we encountered God. An essential condition, therefore, for making dogmatic sense of God's holiness is to avoid the polarizing of majesty and relation; the divine distance and the divine approach are one movement in God's being and act.[30]

A little later, Webster offers this helpful summary of what it means to speak of the holiness of God when God is taken to be Father, Son, and Holy Spirit: "God the Holy Trinity is known in his turning to us, and so to speak of God's holiness is to speak on the basis of his majestic self-communication and saving presence. God the Holy One is the Holy One *in our midst*."[31]

I can see little reason why Wesleyans would quibble with or reject this aspect of Webster's account of holiness. Here we have to do with the very heart of Trinitarian theology. The doctrine of the Trinity is not a puzzle in search of an explanation or a statement about the absolute otherness or incomprehensibility of God so much as it is a confession that in Jesus Christ and in the Holy Spirit we have come to know God's true nature and therefore the true nature of holiness. As things turn out, God's nature and holiness are never more manifest than in the economy of salvation, which is to say, in God's ongoing work of reconciling and sanctifying God's creation.

What does all of this entail for our understanding of Scripture? More directly, in what sense might we now speak of the holiness of Scripture? One of the interesting things about the classical creeds or early rules of faith is that they do *not* mention Scripture. At no point do we confess, "And we believe in Holy Scripture." But this should not be cause for alarm. Early Trinitarian rules of faith do not mention all sorts of things. For example, they do not mention the doctrine of original sin, and they do not contain any doctrine of the atonement. As the rule of faith, the doctrine of the Trinity does not address everything directly or explicitly. Rather, it provides the structure and fundamental content to which everything else must be annexed in due course.

How, then, might we develop an account of the holiness of Scripture by annexing it to the doctrine of the Trinity as expressed in, say, the Nicene-Constantinopolitan Creed? My own inclination here is to locate Scripture underneath pneumatology, as one of the Holy Spirit's gifts to the church. In making this move, however, we must be careful that we do not wind up with a conception of the holiness of Scripture that has to do with Scripture's epistemic role or with something like scriptural authority. After all, the link between the work of the Holy Spirit and Scripture is one that Protestant theologians normally make precisely with a view towards shoring up Scripture's reliability as an epistemic criterion. Let us be clear. That is not our concern in this case. Our concern is with Scripture's holiness and not with its ability to function as an epistemic criterion.[32]

At this stage, we must recall what we have said above concerning the holiness of God when God is understood to be Father, Son, and Holy Spirit. In sum, to speak of the holiness of God is to speak of God's turning to creation and of God's reconciling and transforming presence in our midst. On this view, creaturely realities, including Scripture, are not holy by nature. Rather, they are holy precisely insofar as God freely and faithfully chooses to dwell therein, which is to say, insofar as they mediate ongoing divine presence and action. On this view, Scripture is far more than a mere repository of true propositions. Rather, Scripture, together with the sacraments and other creaturely realities, is a site within the sacramental life of the church where the Holy Spirit condescends to dwell, enabling us to apprehend the real presence of our risen Lord, joining us to his broken body, and bringing about our reconciliation with God the Father. Accordingly, it may be that, when it comes to Scripture's holiness, the best analogy is neither the incarnation nor the church per se, but Holy Eucharist or iconography.[33] Indeed, I think Wesleyans could do worse than to conceive of Scripture as a sacrament or icon in and through which the Holy Trinity is present and at work in our midst.[34]

But what makes this a *Methodist* dogmatic account of the holiness of Scripture? For Wesleyans, God's free and faithful dwelling in the sacramental life of the church brings about our sanctification and perfection. This emphasis on sanctification and perfection as the purpose for which God dwells in our midst yields a more lively account of the holiness of God and the holiness of Scripture than would otherwise be possible. In other words, God's turning to creation and dwelling in our midst is not an inert kind of dwelling, as though God needed a place to lay God's head. Rather, Wesleyans believe and teach that God dwells among us *in order to* bring about our reconciliation, our sanctification, even our transfiguration.

If God is present in our midst in and through Holy Scripture, then Scripture is far more than a repository of propositional truths or a record of the religious experiences of ancient peoples.[35] It is a means through which the Holy Spirit speaks, comforts, convicts, sustains, calls, chastens, empowers, and sanctifies. In and through Scripture, the Holy Spirit enables us to discern the real presence of the risen Christ among us and unites us with Christ in such a way that we are knit together into Christ's body, the church. In and through Scripture, the Holy Spirit forms in believers the theological virtues, the mind of the Christ, and the fruits of the Spirit. In other words, what makes this a *Methodist* account of the holiness of Scripture is the conviction that in and through Scripture, God is present in our midst, making us perfect by making us one with each other and with God in Christ, so that the Holy Spirit might work through us to effect the healing of the whole world.[36]

Finally, we may anticipate one objection to what we have said here, namely, that we are blurring the lines between the proper function or role of Holy Scripture on the one hand, and the other means of grace in the life of the church on the other. It is precisely in response to this issue that I think more work needs to be done. My own inclination here is that, insofar as Scripture, baptism, Eucharist, and other means of grace can all be said to be sites in and through which God dwells in the sacramental life of the church for our sanctification and perfection and for the healing of the world, we ought to be cautious about drawing lines of demarcation with respect to what God does and does not do through this or that means. In other words, I think there is deep wisdom in John Wesley's observation that the Eucharist might be the means by which some people are converted. At this stage, I want simply to suggest that it would be in keeping with the spirit of generosity and humility that pervades all good Wesleyan theology to extend this notion across the board.

Conclusion

In conclusion, I want to note that there may be a large gulf between the way in which Wesleyan theologians conceive of and talk about Scripture on the one hand, and the way in which Wesleyans down through the centuries have actually apprehended and approached Scripture in the sacramental life of the church, as well as in their everyday lives, on the other. In actual practice, my own sense is that Wesley himself and many subsequent generations of Wesleyans routinely have apprehended and approached Scripture in ways that are strikingly similar to the brief account of the holiness of Scripture above. Indeed, I suspect that most Wesleyans across space and time have approached Scripture with a mixture of terror and excitement, fear and trembling, and with a spirit of humility and deep repentance before God.

At our best, we Wesleyans have approached and read Scripture sacramentally, which is to say, with attentiveness to the voice of the Holy Spirit, the sanctifying presence of our risen Lord, and the abiding love of God the Father. We have even understood that the purpose of Scripture entails being grafted into the communion of saints. Thus, from the beginning, Wesley and Wesleyans insisted on the importance of reading Scripture within bands and cell groups, and we maintained this practice well into the early twentieth century. Within these groups, we read Scripture in the context of prayer, mutual confession of sin, and fasting, and in the presence of a leader who underwent routine examinations for holiness of heart and life. In short, we understood that Holy Scripture was a part of a wider class of materials, persons, places, and practices in and through which the presence and power of the Holy Trinity was accessible within the order of creation in a special way.

As I say, this was Wesleyanism at its best. My deepest fear is that this way of thinking about and approaching Scripture has been gone from among us for so long now that it is virtually irrecoverable. Then again, from the standpoint of theology proper, it is a matter of sheer gratuity that it was ever there in the first place. And therein is my hope for the future of Wesleyanism.

11

SCRIPTURE AS CANON

David F. Watson

John Wesley was a man immersed in the Bible. It is hard to overstate the importance that he placed on Scripture, since he believed that Scripture showed the way to salvation, which meant a renewed life in the present and eternal life with God. He was committed to an understanding of scriptural holiness—a life guided by the statutes of Scripture and empowered and shaped by the work of the Holy Spirit. This vision of scriptural holiness would define the early Methodist movement. In fact, in his *Complete English Dictionary*, Wesley defines a "Methodist" as "one that lives according to the method laid down in the Bible."[1] Though he certainly saw some parts of the Bible as identifying most clearly the crucial components of the life of faith, Wesley nevertheless believed in the significance of the *whole* Bible. In his preface to *Explanatory Notes upon the New Testament*, he states, "The Scripture, therefore, of the Old and New Testament is a most solid and precious system of divine truth. Every part thereof is worthy of God; and all together are one entire body, wherein is no defect, no excess. It is the fountain of heavenly wisdom which they who are able to taste prefer to all writings of men, however wise or learned or holy."[2] Wesley emphasized the significance of the whole Bible for the life of faith while privileging some parts of Scripture as a hermeneutical lens. He did not discuss at length the canonicity of the Bible, but certain concepts that would come to the forefront of discussions of canon since the emergence of canonical criticism in the second half of the twentieth century were implicitly at work in his understanding of Scripture and the ways in which he used it.

In this essay, I will address the question: Given the ways in which John Wesley used and understood Scripture, what will it mean for us who are Wesleyans to engage the Bible as canon? In answering this question I will discuss three topics that I think were especially important for Wesley and remain important for Wesleyans today: reading in community, reading that shapes the community, and the relationship between the community of faith and the wholeness of Scripture. Before engaging these three topics, however, I will discuss the various ways in which "canon" functions in theological discourse and formation.

The Contours of "Canon"

When Wesleyans talk about "canon," we are most often talking about the canon of Scripture, the sixty-six books of the Bible. As Randy Maddox has pointed out, Wesley himself confined the canon of Scripture to the sixty-six-book Protestant canon. The KJV, which Wesley read (along with other versions of the Bible), did contain the Apocrypha in a separate section, but Wesley never preached a sermon on any of the apocryphal works, and in fact he explicitly rejected them as Scripture. While one may find references to apocryphal works scattered throughout his writings, they functioned in an essentially supplemental capacity and never for doctrinal instruction or argumentation.[3] The Wesleyan canon of Scripture, then, is the Protestant canon, which excludes the Apocrypha for purposes of teaching or establishing doctrine.

While Wesley did believe and engage in the practice of reading the whole Bible, he clearly assigned more importance to some parts of the canon than others. Put differently, Wesley had a "canon within the canon." Robert Wall holds that 1 John held special significance for Wesley and functioned as his canon within the canon. In other words, 1 John served as an interpretive lens through which Wesley read the rest of Scripture.[4] Steven J. Koskie has argued that, while it may be true that 1 John was of special significance for Wesley, he nonetheless read 1 John in light of a Pauline understanding of salvation, and Pauline themes do a considerable amount of heavy lifting elsewhere in Wesley's interpretation of Scripture.[5] Either way, what is clear is that

Wesley's reading of the Bible was deeply theological, and it was not constrained by the desire for "objectivity" that would come to characterize later historical-critical exegesis.

Wesley interpreted Scripture according to Scripture but also according to particular traditions of the church. This suggests a more complex notion of what it means to speak of "canon" and points us to what it means to "read Scripture canonically." It is common especially among Protestants to restrict the use of the term "canon" to Scripture. Historically, however, the term has been used much more broadly than this. One only needs to spend a bit of time with the *Oxford Dictionary of the Christian Church*, browsing various entries related to "canon," to get a sense of the complexity of this term. In addition to the basic entry for "canon," we find separate entries for "canon" as an ecclesiastical title and as a hymnological designation. There are also entries for "Canon Episcopalis," "canon law," "Canon of the Mass," and "Canon of Scripture."[6] In fact, the use of the term "canon" for Scripture is derivative of the use of this term for other aspects of the life of the church. As Bruce Metzger writes, "ecclesiastical writers during the first three centuries used the word κανών to refer to what was for Christianity an inner law and binding norm of belief ('rule of faith' and/or 'rule of truth'). From the middle of the fourth century onward the word also came to be used in connection with the sacred writings of the Old and New Testaments."[7] The term "canon" properly applies to Scripture, therefore, but it is also about more than Scripture. As Wall puts it, "The word 'canon' is a theological metaphor for a religious norm,"[8] and Scripture is not the only religious norm for the Christian church.

William J. Abraham has written extensively on the church's "canonical heritage," which consists of materials, persons, and practices that are binding on communities of faith.[9] Historically the church has incorporated these materials, persons, and practices into its life because they function as means of grace. A canon, then, is not just a norm, but a norm that does something, namely, leads people of faith more fully into the life of God. It is helpful for us who are Wesleyans to take seriously this notion of a canonical heritage, which we often identify with "tradition." Indeed, Wesley's own understanding of the Christian faith and life was deeply informed by various aspects of this canonical heritage, and we have noted that, although he did interpret Scripture in light of Scripture, he also interpreted Scripture in light of the church's broader doctrinal heritage.[10] In particular, Wesley was reliant on the orthodox tradition of the first five centuries and the traditions of the Anglican Church, especially as expressed in the *Book of Common Prayer*.[11]

Wesley himself would likely have said that the church of the first five centuries and the Anglican Church were simply accurate interpreters of Scripture, and that explains his reliance on them.[12] This explanation is historically implausible, however. The theologians of the early church were not simply reflecting on Scripture but reflecting on the apostolic witness embodied in the Rule of Faith and on writings that they understood to testify to that faith. Historically, they were determining the canon of Scripture as they were reflecting on the works that it would contain. Robert Jenson describes this process thusly: "the church recognizes authentic Gospels by coherence with its living grasp of the apostolic faith; and against deviation from that faith, it summons those Gospels as apostolic witness."[13] The Anglican Church was the recipient of important theological insights of the early church via its parent tradition, the Roman Catholic Church. Wesley, then, internalized the historic faith that he was taught in the home and the church, and this faith deeply affected his reading of Scripture.

To speak of a "canonical reading of Scripture," then, is to speak of Scripture as a means of grace that norms and shapes our lives together and that functions best when it is appropriated alongside other elements of our canonical heritage, such as creed, liturgy, sacrament, practices of prayer, and the writings of important teachers. For Scripture to function properly in this way, however, it should be read in community, it should shape the community within which it is read, and it should be taken seriously as a whole, even if some parts of Scripture occupy greater significance within the community of faith than others.

READING IN COMMUNITY

Private and Communal Readings

Wesley clearly ascribed importance to both private and communal uses of Scripture. On the one hand, he drank deeply from the cup of Reformation individualism.[14] His brand of evangelical Anglicanism was deeply individualistic and heavily dependent on the inner witness of the Holy Spirit. As he writes in his sermon "The Witness of the

Spirit," "the testimony of the Spirit is an inward impression on the soul, whereby the Spirit of God directly witnesses to my spirit, that I am a child of God; that Jesus Christ hath loved me, and given Himself for me; and that all my sins are blotted out, and I, even I, am reconciled to God."[15] He seems to have written his notes on the Old and New Testaments with the individual reader in mind, studying and meditating on Scripture, examining him- or herself, and seeking prayerfully the guidance of the Spirit. Yet Wesley also believed strongly that one should read the Bible in conversation with other Christian readers. As Maddox suggests, this is in part because Wesley recognized the limitations of human understanding and believed that we could arrive at fuller and more adequate interpretations of Scripture in consultation with other believers.[16] Wesley is clear that to be a Christian is to be a part of a community of faith. In his sermon "The Catholic Spirit," he writes that "every follower of Christ is obliged, by the very nature of the Christian institution, to be a member of some particular congregation or other, some church, as it is usually termed."[17] We should bear in mind, moreover, that Wesley was a far more prolific writer of sermons than he was a writer of notes on the Bible. One who reads through Wesley's sermons will find quotations of and allusions to Scripture as ever-present features. In other words, Wesley worked far harder at the task of using Scripture in public proclamation than he did at creating notes for private devotion and study. Likewise, one finds the hymns of John and Charles shot through with scriptural references. The communal use of Scripture included reading Scripture in dialogue with the historic Christian faith, the reading of Scripture within gatherings such as class meetings, the liturgical practices of the church, hymnody, and the use of Scripture in sermons.

Today, as in Wesley's day, the reading of Scripture takes place privately and communally. For purposes of reading the Bible canonically, there must be strong and wide representation of Scripture within the community of faith. This is not to diminish the significance of private, devotional reading, but rather to note that it must be complemented by participation in a community of faith that is also engaging the Bible on a variety of levels. The Reformation emphasis on *sola Scriptura* and Enlightenment individualism have come to bear in significant ways on the prominence of private devotional reading of Scripture. Private reading was not, however, the primary intention of collecting sacred writings into a canon. During the years when the writings of the Christian biblical canon were collected and agreed upon (the first five centuries), the use of Scripture was primarily corporate. Most people during this period were illiterate, the production of books was far more limited and difficult, and the ethos of the Mediterranean world in which the canonization process took place was primarily collectivistic rather than individualistic. Scripture was made for community, and while there is nothing wrong with private reading, the less we read Scripture in community, the more we remove it from its intended location—the gathered body of Christ.

Biblical scholars engaged in the work of canonical criticism have often pointed out the essential connection between canon and community. We read Scripture within our liturgical and collective devotional practices. We attempt to discern the truths of Scripture within our communities of faith. The Bible is not just a book that one uses in one's personal journey of faith, nor is it simply a repository of more or less historical information and theological perspectives from Israel and the early church. For Christians, it is not a disparate collection of *works*, but a single *work*, because the historic church of which we are a part has authorized it as such.[18] The Bible is the primary text of the church's life together. The reading of the Bible in corporate worship, preaching that is rooted in Scripture, music that draws on biblical words and themes, the biblical references and recitation in the Great Thanksgiving, responsive readings from the Psalter, communal Bible study, and other corporate practices—these are all ways in which we collectively engage the Scripture for the formation of our beliefs, practices, and character. To read Scripture as canon means that we read in community. As Wall has put it, "The Bible is not for lone rangers; it belongs to the Church and so its interpretive practices are communal, conversational, and participatory. We learn Scripture in the company of saints. Although somewhat autocratic as a leader of the Methodist movement, Wesley received and studied Scripture with other interpreters on whom he depended and from whom most of his explanatory notes derive."[19]

The Communion of Saints as Present Community

In keeping with the Wesleyan tradition, the faith learned within our communal practices should shape our private devotional readings of Scripture. In that sense, the individual's reading of Scripture is tied closely to the faith of his or her community. To be a part of a church means in part to assent to various historic tenets of the faith. The "catholic spirit" is not "speculative latitudinarianism" or "an indifference to all opinions." "This," said Wesley, "is the spawn of hell, not the offspring of heaven."[20] Rather, one who is truly of the catholic spirit "has not now his religion to seek. He is fixed as the sun in his judgment concerning the main branches of Christian doctrine."[21] For Wesley the individual application of Scripture was shaped by the beliefs of the historic faith of the church. God works through the Bible within the life of the believer, shaping him or her in Christian character and testifying within him or her to a faith that has been expressed through the major doctrines of catholic Christianity. Put differently, our reading of Scripture as canon is not simply within our present-day and local communities of faith, but with the communion of saints. The very list of works that make up the canon comes from the corporate discernment of Jews and Christians over a number of centuries. Within the early church, coherence with a community's rule of faith would help to determine the usefulness of a writing for that community's liturgical life. Works that found widespread use in the liturgical life of Christian communities tended over time to become canonical.[22] The canon is the product of a historic community, and the canon properly functions when we read it in dialogue with that historic community.

Scripture, therefore, should not be severed from the interpretations of worshipping communities, past and present. Scripture stands within the canonical heritage of the church and cannot be properly understood for the life of faith apart from it. The church has, after all, handed on to us a vast canonical heritage to lead us ever more fully into salvation. This issue has been brought forward forcefully in the book *Canonical Theism: A Proposal for Theology and the Church*. At the outset of this volume are thirty theses, the ninth of which states, "The church possesses not just a canon of books in its Bible but also a canon of doctrine, a canon of saints, a canon of church fathers, a canon of theologians, a canon of liturgy, a canon of bishops, a canon of councils, a canon of ecclesial regulations, a canon of icons, and the like. In short, the church possesses a canonical heritage of persons, practices, and materials."[23] What do these various canons have to do with Scripture? They testify to and can lead us more fully into the life of the same God testified to and made available to us in Scripture. To be clear, none of these resources may supplant Scripture, but Scripture works most perfectly in cooperation with these other elements of the canonical heritage, just as a body cannot function without the heart, but the heart functions best when the rest of the body is in good shape.

To read in community, then, is to read not just with the living members of our communities of faith but in dialogue with those who have gone before us in the faith, on whose insights into the life of God we can draw. To read the Scripture in dialogue with the ways, say, Augustine or Julian of Norwich or John Wesley read and appropriated Scripture can build us up in the faith. To read the Bible in the knowledge that the God attested to in these writings would, over time, come to be properly understood as the Holy Trinity is a way of acknowledging both the historical situatedness of the biblical texts and the development of our corporate understanding of God over time. To sing passages of Scripture helps us to learn and internalize them. To see stories of Scripture portrayed in pictorial representations, whether ancient icons or modern works of art, helps us to meditate on and be formed by the Scriptures portrayed. As we prepare to partake of the Eucharist, we remember the words preserved in Scripture whereby Jesus instituted this blessed practice. To read Scripture as canon is to read it within the larger canonical heritage, not simply as a resource that I encounter on my own for my individual growth as a believer but as a powerful means of grace situated within a historic communion of saints, saints whose insights we may utilize for our growth in the faith.

READING THAT SHAPES THE COMMUNITY

Hearing the Good News for Salvation

Wesley wrote his *Explanatory Notes* precisely because of his belief in the centrality of Scripture in shaping the faith and character of a Methodist. As his prefaces to these works indicate, he felt that he lacked both the time and the skill necessary to complete this task in the way he thought it deserved. Nevertheless he did write out of a pastoral concern for the salvation of all who would earnestly seek God. He was especially concerned about people who were not well educated or wealthy and who would not have the training and abundant time necessary to work through technical and meticulous commentaries. It was crucial for him that all people, regardless of education or class, encounter the message of salvation conveyed by the Bible. Scripture shows "the way to heaven," though we should not understand this as simply glorification. Rather, as we read in Wesley's sermon "The Scripture Way of Salvation":

> The salvation which is here spoken of is not what is frequently understood by that word, the going to heaven, eternal happiness. It is not the soul's going to paradise, termed by our Lord, "Abraham's bosom." It is not a blessing which lies on the other side of death; or, as we usually speak, in the other world. The very words of the text itself put this beyond all question: "Ye *are saved*." It is not something at a distance: it is a present thing; a blessing which, through the free mercy of God, ye are now in possession of. Nay, the words may be rendered, and that with equal propriety, "Ye *have been* saved"; so that the salvation which is here spoken of might be extended to the entire work of God, from the first dawning of grace in the soul, till it is consummated in glory.[24]

From a Wesleyan perspective, Scripture teaches us the way of salvation, which includes all of God's work in the life of a Christian. Faith and salvation were for Wesley "the substance of all the Bible, the marrow, as it were, of the whole Scripture."[25] He believed that Scripture, properly interpreted, gives us all we need to know in order to receive God's saving grace in our lives. To be the community that hears the gospel is to be a community that is saved, that is, experiencing the justifying and sanctifying work of God. Our lives as individuals and our life together should look different because of our engagement with the Bible.

Scripture, for Wesleyans, should find its primary use and interpretation within the life of the church, and the church, in turn, should be shaped by the witness of the canon. As the Anglican theologian John Webster put it, "The definitive act of the church is faithful hearing of the gospel of salvation announced by the risen Christ in the Spirit's power through the service of Holy Scripture. As the *creatura verbi divini*, the creature of the divine Word, the church is the hearing church."[26] The church must be a *hearing* church because, through our hearing of the good news of God announced in Scripture, we are formed more perfectly in God's ways of truth and righteousness. The canon shapes the community. Communally, Wesleyans should be formed by Scripture and particularly by Scripture as interpreted through the lens of God's saving work. It is both necessary and acceptable to identify certain core Scriptures and beliefs that form our interpretive framework as we engage the Bible. Wesley certainly did this. It is primarily through this interpretive process, which we pray is guided by the Holy Spirit, that we are formed as a gospel people. Originally, "canon" meant "measuring rod," and indeed we should measure our lives personally and corporately according to the teachings of the Bible. And yet without a proper interpretive framework, this task is impossible.

Prima Scriptura

Strictly speaking, this is not *sola Scriptura* but rather *prima Scriptura*.[27] A Wesleyan community should be one that is formed by the words of Scripture for teaching and reproof so that we might know "the way to heaven" and as a means of grace. Nevertheless, judicious application of the traditions of the church, some of which in fact helped to determine the canon of Scripture, aid us as we interpret the Scripture for Christian faith and life. Scripture is therefore the final norm for our theological and ethical judgment, but it cannot function properly apart from the collective wisdom of the Christian tradition. When separated from the tradition, the interpretation of Scripture for the life of faith can easily become arbitrary and idiosyncratic. To be the church is to be the hearing church, but to be a Wesleyan is to hear in a particular way. In other words, we read the Scriptures in dialogue with the tradition, and through these voices we are shaped by the gospel as people of faith.

Among Wesleyans, Scripture has not always performed this soteriological function. Especially among academics, we have, at times, emphasized historical-critical issues to such an extent that we have neglected to attend to Scripture's soteriological function. In the interest of historical concerns and ostensibly intellectually responsible readings, we have at times assumed an epistemological skepticism that has eliminated from consideration some of the very issues that Wesley thought most important. To disallow claims of God's intervention into the cause and effect of history is to disallow the classical Christian economy of salvation. To the extent that we have adopted this perspective, Wesleyans have read the Bible in ways that *could not* speak meaningfully to the life of faith as Wesley understood it. It is little wonder, then, that among many Wesleyans a crisis of biblical literacy has emerged. Why read the Bible when its relevance to the faith that Wesley proclaimed, a particular brand of the classical faith of the church, is so unclear? When the Bible no longer shapes our communities, when it no longer functions as canon for us, we can easily lose our focus on and awareness of the salvation that is ours in Jesus Christ. Indeed, we put our very salvation at risk.

To be clear, the problem to which I am pointing here is not with readings of Scripture that incorporate tools from history, literature, the social sciences, or other helpful disciplines. Rather, the problem has to do with readings that are removed from the life of faith and the historic witness of the church. Nor does this preclude our engaging the text at times with a healthy hermeneutics of suspicion. Indeed, sometimes our commitments as Christians, commitments that are shaped by portions of the Bible, compel us to read Scripture critically. A hermeneutics of suspicion may be a natural response to passages of the Bible that seem to be in conflict with our Christian values. To be able to confront these passages, wrestle with them honestly, refuse to ignore them, and consider them in light of our core faith commitments is to deal with them canonically. Our relationship to Scripture is therefore dialectical: we read Scripture in light of our faith commitments, while Scripture consistently shapes, reshapes, and challenges those commitments. For example, it is interesting that in his *Explanatory Notes* Wesley scarcely touches on slavery as a moral issue (see the discussion of Wesley's treatment of slavery in ch. 5).[28] Nevertheless in his "Thoughts upon Slavery," he uses Scripture to condemn a practice that Scripture itself allows. Wesley quotes, for example, from Jas 2:13, "He shall have judgment without mercy that showed no mercy," to condemn the practices of slavers.[29] Likewise he quotes from Gen 4:10, "The blood of thy brother crieth against thee from the earth."[30] Here Wesley is engaging in an act of biblical interpretation whereby he reads Scripture through a particular moral lens, a lens that is in large part formed by Scripture. It is out of his Christian commitments that Wesley speaks against slavery. "May I speak plainly to you?" he asks the slavers. "I must. Love constrains me; love to you, as well as to those you are concerned with."[31] We are back, then, to a canon within the canon, the use of particular Scriptures that function as an interpretive lens by which one interprets the whole.

Scripture and the Life of God

Holy Scripture, shaping our communities of faith, leads us corporately and individually into the life of the Trinity. This is another way of understanding Wesley's belief that Scripture shows "the way to heaven." Scripture is a means by which we participate in the Trinitarian life of God. One way in which this takes place is by Scripture's mediation to us of the reconciling presence of Christ. Scripture is the primary resource by which we learn the story of God's saving work in history. It is the primary resource by which we learn the significance of Christ's ministry, death, resurrection, and eschatological promise. In other words, by reading the Bible, and in particular by reading in dialogue with the communion of past and present saints, we gain knowledge that leads us to salvation. Yet knowledge of salvation is not enough for salvation to take place. For Scripture to mediate Christ to us and to be a mechanism through which Christ reconciles us to God the Father, the Spirit must draw us into that reconciliation. The Spirit may work through Scripture in a variety of ways: through the word spoken aloud in worship, through the preached word, through practices of meditation on Scripture, through Scripture as expressed and learned through hymnody, through private reading, through practices of prayer over Scripture, and in other ways as well.

If the Spirit does not work through the Bible to lead us into the life of God, then the Bible is of little use. Human beings are finite and sinful, and to do God's will we need God's help. We need help, first, in discernment. To discern God's will as spoken through the Scriptures, even in cooperation with the communion of saints, we need the Spirit's guidance. Yet even if we could read Scripture perfectly in keeping with God's will in ways that built up the life of the church, we as Wesleyans believe that we could not live as Scripture so instructed. Rather, we need, second, the sanctifying work of the Spirit to create in us a character that is willing and able to live faithfully and overcome our propensity to sin. To read Scripture as canon means that we are a community formed by the Scripture, and yet Scripture can do nothing on its own but only by way of the Holy Spirit working through it, mediating to us Christ's work of reconciliation with the Father.

The Community of Faith and the Wholeness of Scripture

Our Hermeneutical Lenses

John Wesley was very much a believer in reading the whole Bible.[32] In keeping with this practice, we who are Wesleyans would do well to engage the whole of the canon, even those parts that we do not like or in which we may find little potential for spiritual edification.

Wesley could affirm this type of position, not because he believed that every passage of the Bible, taken on its own, clearly testified to the salvation available to us in Jesus Christ, but because he had an interpretive lens, determined in large part by 1 John and Pauline soteriology, that came to bear on his reading of the whole work. Wesley at times spoke of the "whole tenor of Scripture" (or the "general tenor of Scripture"). The "whole tenor of Scripture" was a name for its overarching message, which Wesley believed was a message about salvation. Individuals are born into sin, need God's justifying grace, and receive new birth and enter a life of holiness by their faith in Christ. As Scott J. Jones puts it, "For Wesley, the general tenor of Scripture teaches the analogy of faith: the system of doctrine whose content is the order of salvation and whose function is to serve as a normative guide and limit for theology and as a rule for interpretation."[33] Wesley therefore engaged in the Reformation practice of interpreting Scripture according to Scripture. One interpreted the whole of Scripture according to those parts that clearly pointed to the way of salvation, most clearly articulated the analogy of faith, and therefore served as a hermeneutical lens.

A consequence of this way of interpreting Scripture was that Wesley did not acknowledge the plurality of voices within the Bible. I intend no criticism of Wesley here; to a considerable extent this was simply a function of his historical and social location. Wesley lived just as historical-critical scholarship was in its infancy. Scholars such as J. S. Semler and J. D. Michaelis worked during Wesley's lifetime, and their work would give rise to more developed historical scholarship, such as that of J. J. Griesbach and J. G. Eichhorn.[34] William Baird describes this era as confirming a "shift in biblical studies undertaken by the earlier Enlightenment scholars: the shift from doctrinal to historical exegesis."[35] The historical-critical method that would emerge was resistant in principle to the imposition of theological schemata on the biblical texts, and therefore contributed in significant ways to an awareness of the plurality of voices within the canon. By contrast, while Wesley did make use of historical information that was available to him, he did so within a confessional theological framework.[36]

The Plurality and Unity of the Canon

To be sure, a canonical reading of Scripture will depart in particular ways from the historical-critical method. A canonical reading is incompatible with an exegetical method that precludes confessional, theological readings of the Bible. Any normative claim about canonicity is in fact a theological claim. This does not mean, however, that we must neglect the variety of voices that we find in the biblical canon. If we are to read the Bible as canon then we must take seriously the entirety of the canon. We must attend to those passages of Scripture that challenge our core values and beliefs, which puzzle us, even anger us. We must wrestle with these texts, embrace their ideas, reject their ideas, assess them and reassess them, and, most importantly, pray over them. We must recognize what James Sanders has called the "pluralism" of the Bible in all its sacred tension. He writes, "There is no program that can be constructed on the basis of the Bible which can escape the challenge of other portions of it: this is an essential part of its pluralism. No one person, no denomination, no theology, and certainly no ideology can exhaust the Bible or claim its *unity*. It bears with it its own redeeming contradictions, and this is a major reason it has lasted so long and has spoken effectively to so many different historical contexts and communities."[37] Sanders elsewhere refers to Scripture's "self-correcting" function.[38] We must attend to the entire Bible, but this does not mean that we consider the entire Bible normative. In fact, such a position would be utterly incoherent.

Are we at a loss, then, with regard to the unity of Scripture? One way to address the tension between unity and plurality in Scripture shows up in the field of "biblical theology." Often works in this field attempt to identify a thematic theological unity that one may trace through the various parts of the canon. A number of biblical theologies have been written since Wesley, including many within the twentieth century, that would identify a thematic unity inherent to the writings of the Bible themselves. Yet there is no consensus regarding the essential unity of the Bible's message, the content of which that unity might consist, or under what circumstances such unity might obtain. As James Barr writes, "It is, I think, now agreed among most biblical theologians that there is a plurality of theologies within the Bible; at least, this is not the dominant use of the term 'theology' with reference to biblical texts."[39]

Barr does not consider the matter closed with regard to the unity of Scripture, however. He writes, "I want to argue that the locus of the 'unity' we seek lies, not in the collection of books, even if we view their contents 'holistically,' but in the relation of the biblical collection to the formation of doctrine, of theology, of law, or of whatever it may be. Specifically, the locus of 'unity' lies in the regulative decisions that, though arising in part of the Bible, become the interpretive guide for the religion afterward."[40] In other words, the unity of the canon is something that happens in dialogue with the later reflection of the church on God's saving work in history. It involves reading the Bible with an eye toward the ways in which the tradition has discerned its meaning. This, in my opinion, is what Wesley did, though he did not normally do so explicitly.

Wesleyan readers of the Bible may do so fully cognizant of their particularly Wesleyan faith commitments while remaining simultaneously cognizant of the fact that Scripture speaks in many voices, some of which challenge our faith commitments and force us to come to terms with the fact that God is not confined to our theological schema. While we take our Wesleyan faith commitments seriously, the plurality of Scripture helps us to remain humble and self-critical, aware of the mystery of God's work in the world and plan of salvation for all of creation. We therefore read the canon—the whole of the canon—aware that our own faith commitments reflect certain theological constructs of the early church, the Anglican Church, the Reformers, Wesley himself, and our contemporary believing communities. These theological constructs are related in various ways to Scripture but are not exhaustive of Scripture. They are not the product of a perspicuous and autopistic canon but the product of theological decisions made in dialogue with the canon, and they stand in tension with some parts of the canon. We can therefore claim that our theological positions are biblical and lead us more fully into God's saving work, while simultaneously acknowledging the work of God attested to in Scripture that transcends any and all theological constructs.

Conclusion

The issue of Scripture as canon is a complex one, made even more so by asking the question of what it means to read Scripture as canon *as Wesleyans*. In this essay I have identified three main issues that I believe are crucial for reading Scripture canonically in the Wesleyan tradition. First, to engage Scripture as canon means that we read in community. The writings that today make up our canon were not written or adopted primarily for private reading. Rather, they were used within the corporate life of Jews and Christians. The very process of canonization took place primarily within the liturgical life of early Christian communities. Yes, private reading of the Bible can be an enriching, edifying practice, but it is no substitute for the use of the Bible in worship, preaching, teaching, music, and other aspects of our life together as Christians. The church was the original setting of the use of Christian Scripture, and it continues to be the most essential setting today.

Reading Scripture as canon also means that we are shaped by Scripture within our communities of faith. The purpose of the Bible is to lead us into salvation, but salvation here entails much more than "going to heaven." It involves the whole process from God's call through repentance, justification, new life and sanctification, growth in grace, and finally glorification. Salvation affects the way we live in the here and now, and Scripture is a key resource in determining what that life looks like. Another way of putting this is to say that the Bible leads us into the life of God. Through Scripture we learn about the salvation that we have in Jesus Christ. We learn that we are reconciled to God through Christ, who has called us out of sin and offers us new life. The Holy Spirit mediates Christ to us and allows us to respond to God's calling of us into salvation.

Finally, reading Scripture as canon means that we take seriously the whole of Scripture. The witness of Scripture is wide and varied. Parts of the canon stand in tension with one another. Scripture speaks with many voices. The unity of Scripture is not clear within Scripture itself but involves reading Scripture in dialogue with the historic faith of the church. As post-Enlightenment readers, we can recognize the writings of Scripture as having their own concerns, contexts, and agendas that are at times very different from one another, and yet we realize that the God attested to in Scripture is clarified for us in the traditions of the church. These traditions are rooted in Scripture but are not themselves Scripture. Rather, they emerged precisely because of Scripture's variegated witness.

PART III

Wesleyans Working with Scripture

12

SCRIPTURE AND SOCIAL ETHICS

D. Brent Laytham

Like Lotto balls fluttering in their hopper, this essay begins with the question of the ordered relationship of several intellectual arenas. Are we playing "Pick 3"—investigating the proper interaction of Scripture, "social ethics," and the Wesleyan tradition? Or are we hazarding the longer odds of "Pick 4"—seeking the winning combination of Scripture, "social ethics," and Wesleyanism with a pressing "moral issue"? Either way, do we bet on the balls aligning according to our lucky number four (a "quadrilateral"[1]), do we "stand pat" with our "Old Daddy's" convictions and principles,[2] or do we need a new horse for the race, a more modern method that avoids anachronistic embarrassment?

I am convinced that starting with such metaethical questions about how to relate Scripture, Wesley, church, and social ethics already cedes territory that is and should be contested. For example, "social ethics" is often defined as an ethical subdomain differentiated from "personal ethics" and distanced (or even divorced) from communally particular convictions. So its subject becomes matters social, economic, and political in isolation from the formation of moral character (or sanctification). Its discourse becomes generic and procedural in refusal of a shared account of the good (or theology). Its "community" of reference becomes nations, markets, media, or globe, rather than the church. Positioning social ethics that way shatters the singularity of Wesley's affirmation, "the Gospel of Christ knows of no religion, but social; no holiness, but social holiness."[3] If "social ethics" defines Christian conviction and community as preemptively exterior to its work, then conjunctive titles like "Scripture and Social Ethics" or "Wesley and Social Ethics" are unavoidable, and, before we get to work on questions of how to live and love, we are required to first figure out how to reconnect what should never have been disjoined![4]

We must not acquiesce to a reframing of the task so substantive that it tears asunder what is rightly whole cloth not only for Christians in the Wesleyan tradition but for the entire church catholic. So this essay will place a different bet, namely, that consulting Wesley on one of our moral challenges will draw us deeper into God, deeper into Scripture, and deeper into church.

Gambling on Gambling

Specifically, I want to play with the conundrum of a gracious understanding of gambling. The vocabulary of this sentence is carefully chosen. I want to "play" because traditional arguments against gambling were often rooted in an unreflective embrace of a Protestant work ethic along with a deep suspicion of populist forms of recreation and because current acceptance of gambling has roots in its public image as a form of recreation or entertainment—of play for grownups. I call gambling a conundrum because so often rubbing together its partial truths generates heat rather than light. Lotteries provide money for education but also mislead the uneducated. Casinos stimulate the economy yet drain public and private social aid funds. Native American gambling offers redress for centuries of economic disappropriation by disappropriating other economically vulnerable groups. I seek a "gracious" understanding of gambling that repents of Protestant diatribes against Catholic bingo, of petty moralisms masquerading as sanctification, and of a position on gambling that stops short of the gracious news of the death and resurrection of Jesus Christ.

I am wagering that gambling provides an excellent test case for a "practical divinity" that engages Scripture seeking a Word written on our hearts, "a letter of Christ, . . . written . . . with the Spirit of the living God," an epistolary ecclesial performance (2 Cor 3:3). Here is why. First, Scripture has no direct and obvious word on gambling.[5] But Scripture does have a pointed and pervasive concern for righteous economics. Second, Christian traditions have disagreed, at times vociferously, about the morality of gambling. But these disagreements have seldom elicited high-quality engagements with Scripture. Third, recent changes in the legality, modes, and accessibility of gambling have exponentially increased its social, economic, and political status, impacting not only how but whether many Christians consider it a moral matter in need of Scriptural guidance.[6] Finally, gambling is a diversified reality that resists efforts to classify it as mainly personal ethics or primarily social ethics; it is nearly always both at the same time.

Where are we Wesleyans on gambling? We are heirs of a tradition whose founder called gamblers "*sharpers* and *gamesters*—those public nuisances, those scandals to the English nation."[7] In celebrating the reconstitution of the Society for the Reformation of Manners, Wesley commends them for taking on "another sort of offenders as mischievous to society as any, namely, *gamesters* of various kinds. Some of these were of the lowest and vilest class, commonly called 'gamblers,' who make a trade of seizing on young and inexperienced men and tricking them out of all their money. And after they have beggared them, they frequently teach them the same mystery of iniquity."[8] Although Wesley did not explicitly mention gambling in the General Rules, this simply indicates that he took it for granted that gambling counted among "such diversions as cannot be taken in the name of the Lord Jesus."[9]

In the century following Wesley, disapproval of gambling continued, but modified by a tendency toward moralism. Whereas Wesley's prohibitions in the General Rules were staking out space to *pursue* holiness (and happiness), his heirs sometimes used specific prohibitions as a template to *define* holiness. So the "Special Advices" section of early twentieth-century Methodist *Doctrines and Disciplines* condemned the "unholy three": dancing, theater-going, and games of chance.[10] Gambling was especially easy to refuse, however, since it was almost universally illegal and unsavory.

A century later, circumstances have changed dramatically. Today most American and British churches that are heir to Wesley no longer prohibit or oppose "diversions" like dancing, drama, cinema, radio, and television, although they may still warn against specific trends, particular artists, or salacious content. Most Wesleyans "are a bit embarrassed" by that earlier history, which suggested that "how we are to entertain ourselves" has something to do with perfect love.[11] The one "diversion" that remains on the "unholy" list in American strands of Wesleyanism, however, is gambling.[12] Yet because wider culture classifies gambling as "just entertainment" and because our churches have mostly abandoned a stance of moral suasion regarding entertainments, the churches' capacity to foster significant moral reflection and formation in regard to gambling has experienced a real loss of traction. British Methodists have argued that this is exacerbated only when churches fail to distinguish between serious and trivial forms of gambling, which further weakens the church's moral authority.[13]

Before my own effort to reflect on gambling scripturally, it will be helpful to notice the variety in some existing approaches that position gambling in the Decalogue. Catholicism thinks about gambling as a matter of economic justice in light of the commandment "You shall not steal."[14] From this perspective, gambling becomes morally unacceptable only when someone is deprived of life's necessities, when there is cheating, or in addiction. Conservative Protestants usually press on toward the tenth commandment "Do not covet" as basis for a wholesale refusal of gambling.[15] From this perspective, gambling is both inducement to and expression of greed, and its corollary, the fantasy of "something for nothing."[16] United Methodists also reject gambling completely but do so not only in relation to the second table of the law summarized as loving neighbor but also to the first table. Its 2004 Resolution on Gambling says gambling "invites persons to place their trust in possessions rather than in God. It represents a form of idolatry that contradicts the first commandment."[17]

What each of these positions has in common is distance and abstraction from Scripture. The biblical Word has been abstracted into moral vocabulary (idolatry, covetousness, greed, economic injustice) and ethical principles (loving neighbor, the work ethic) at considerable remove from the actual text, especially its narratives. Even where such abstractions are faithful to a plain sense reading of Scripture, they work against scriptural engagement in multiple ways. As summaries abstracted from the text, they substitute for real readings and preempt rereadings of the text. As moral vocabulary that funds moral perception and description, they bypass canonical investigations of that vocabulary's full scope and nuance, driving us too quickly toward empirical adjudications about the attitudes of gamblers and the effects of gambling. As ethical principles guiding reflection and action, they float above the biblical story, entirely detached from canonical orientation in the Triune economy and from christological specification in Jesus, and largely impotent in the task of forming moral agents. As statements of ecclesial position, they offer ethical conclusions and applications without displaying the process of moral reasoning, a process that is centrally a way of reading Scripture together. What is not displayed to the church is not inculcated in the church, meaning we continue to reason poorly and ascripturally, or, more often than not, we do not reason at all about matters like gambling.

I want to attempt a reflection on gambling grounded in a close reading of Scripture and guided by our Wesleyan tradition. Such a reading will focus on a limited portion of Scripture, eschewing comprehensiveness for the sake of depth. Because gambling as an activity is not the focus of a single biblical passage, there is no key text for focus. As mentioned above, the Decalogue has been an important passage for many traditions. Given Wesley's sermonic series of "discourses on the Sermon on the Mount," Matthew 5–7 would be a more ideal passage for Wesleyan focus. Nonetheless, I have chosen a different tack, prompted by the way our culture presently understands gambling as a leisure activity.

Trusting Time

The growth of gambling in the U.S. over the past half century has been accompanied by a correlative change in status, becoming not only legalized, but legitimated, normalized, at times routinized.[18] That is, in fewer than fifty years, public opinion about gambling has gone from a majority considering it to be a sinful activity to a majority seeing it as a valid form of entertainment, a fun way to spend leisure time and expendable income.[19] The congeries of dimensions in this perception immediately catches a Wesleyan's attention. It invites us to reflect on the pursuit of happiness, the rhythms of holiness, and the character of money.

Our way in is Wesley's "Appeal to Men of Reason," where he asks the virtuous person who does no harm (§41) but lacks faith, "Are you *now* happy?" (§42).[20] Wesley argues that the answer is "no," because neither work nor leisure brings satisfaction. Working is a means to an end, "the enjoying yourself, . . . the taking your pleasure" (§44). But supposedly enjoyable leisure activities are actually an endless round of pleasures that cannot satisfy (§§43, 45). For Wesley, this restless quest for happiness is a problem of time—its present use (§§42–45) and future goal (§46) in their divinely ordained interrelation. For our purposes, Wesley's socio-economic comment is telling: "the earth as it is now constituted, even with the help of all European arts, does not afford sufficient employment to take up half the waking hours of half its inhabitants" (§45). Here Wesley identifies the advent of leisure culture as compounding the problem of "time that lies so heavy upon your hands" (§45). In the ensuing 268 years, this dilemma of too much time to achieve happiness has grown exponentially, as the industrial economy whose excess production created more time for leisure has given way to an information economy whose primary product is entertainment.

Wesley's solution to the unhappy dilemma of leisure time is "the religion we preach. That leaves no time upon our hands. It fills up all the blank spaces of life. It exactly takes up all the time we have to spare, be it more or less, so that 'he who hath much hath nothing over, and he that has little has no lack'" (§45; quoting Exod 16:18). As a Wesleyan proof text, this might suggest that a Wesleyan response to gambling is "we don't have time for that" or for any other diversions from our true happiness. But in fact, Wesley does recognize the need for "intervals of diversions from business" that relax body and mind.[21]

The more interesting question is whether Wesley's paraphrase of Exod 16:18b is irresponsible proof texting or something more significant and suggestive.[22] Like Paul's metaleptic use of this same verse in 2 Cor 8:15, I believe Wesley's use has "resonant significations" for the question of leisure time.[23] As it stands, the verse points to one of manna's intrinsic oddities: no matter how much or little of it one tried to grab, by God's beneficence everyone had an equal portion in the end. This alone makes manna a fitting *metaphor* for time, because no matter how much time we waste or save, everybody has just twenty-four hours a day. Apparently "time is manna,"[24] rather than money.

Attention to the larger narrative of Exod 16, however, shows that manna has everything to do with time and trust or, more accurately, with the timely enactment of trusting obedience. Manna is intrinsically temporal. Manna observes God's daily and weekly schedule over a forty-year term. Manna faithfully appears "morning by morning" (16:21), it obediently rots if stored overnight (16:20), it punctiliously keeps (16:24) and rests (16:27) on the Sabbath. It manifests God's faithfulness in a temporal modality that tests (16:4) Israel in the best possible way, by inculcating in Israel what it asks from Israel,[25] a generationally extended following and trusting of the Lord through this obedient rhythm of daily bread and weekly Sabbath.[26] Reading the verse in its cotext, Wesley's metalepsis brings us to a proper narrative moment for considering the problem of timeful trust in the pursuit of holiness.

Yet there is a problem with Wesley's approach that sorely needs correction. One hears in his claim that pursuing the conjoining of holiness and happiness "leaves no time" and "takes up all the time we have to spare." Wesley's tone implies that time is demanded from us, rather than given to us.[27] He says that all our temporal activities, including "our diversions as well as refreshments," are to be done "with a single view to the will of God . . . [who wills that] you should use them in such a manner and measure as they prepare you for business or devotion. So far therefore as your present weakness makes them necessary to this end you are to use them, but no farther."[28] Notice two important implications. First, all recreational activity is given as a concession to our weakness. Recreation compensates for creaturely inadequacy rather than celebrates creation's goodness. Second, all recreational activity is preparatory. It is a means to the extrinsic goals of business and devotion rather than an end valued for intrinsic goods or pleasures.[29] To put the two points together as starkly as possible, we do not play for the fun of it, but (1) to repair our inadequacies and (2) to prepare for more "heavenly" pursuits. Holiness would seem to lie outside whatever intrinsic pleasures our recreations afford.

Here Wesley's metalepsis is serendipitous, for it invites us to notice the difference between his emphasis that pursuing holiness *claims all our time*, and the manna story's narration of a holy God who *gives Israel time—sanctified and sanctifying time*. The manna story certainly knows that time is God's, claimed entirely for our transformation. It presents this claim as the question of whether Israel will listen to God (16:4) day by day, in its weekly rhythm, and over the duration of the wilderness generation. Nonetheless, the heart of this story is not claim but gift: God gives Israel not only bread (16:15) but *time*. "See! The Lord has given you the Sabbath" (16:29).[30] Its proper form is shared rest (16:23, 30) from striving, and its tone is joyful celebration of the Giver in the gift. Brevard Childs describes this as God's giving Israel a "surprise party" with a "festive ring."[31] As such, the goodness of keeping the Sabbath was not extrinsic (resting today so that tomorrow we can work harder) but intrinsic (resting today participates in God's holy joy). Keeping Sabbath teaches Israel that all time is God's good gift *to and for us*, a gift reclaimed *from us* in the dialectic of working and resting, striving and ceasing, pursuing the holiness that makes us happy and enjoying the happiness that makes us holy.

In other words, Exod 16 forces us to notice how Wesley underestimates the gift of time as a sanctified and sanctifying dialectic of doing and ceasing.[32] Admittedly, Israel's Sabbath is a far cry from the leisure pursuits of Wesley's day or ours.[33] Nonetheless, Sabbath forces open the question of what other pleasurable ceasings from "gathering" bring happiness that makes us holy. Such activities would not be "diversions" from more important matters nor false turns on "the way to heaven." They would be "enjoyments" and "recreations," for in them we enter into God's re-creating joy. More fully than Wesley, we must explore which pleasures and what kinds of play can function as means of grace. We must proceed carefully, recognizing that some entertainments are ennobling, some debasing.[34] Entertainments that gratefully receive time as a gift, that trustfully rest from labor, that enjoy the Giver present in the giving, will be sanctifying. They will be a foretaste of "continual enjoyment of the Three-One God, and of all the creatures in him."[35] So perhaps now we can play hearts with a clear conscience, but that does not decide the matter of blackjack.

Nor will it, because Exod 16 has far less to say about casino gambling than it does the lottery. It is a matter of great significance that God has woven together time, trust, and enjoyment. Sabbath is a rhythmic celebration of God's providence (as well as of creation and redemption, cf. Exod 20:11; Deut 5:15), a rhythm of enjoyable trust. Manna is a daily cycle of provision, labor, and enjoyment; it is a weekly cycle of profitable work followed by pleasurable ceasing. On the Sabbath the absence of manna and the ceasing from work signify trust that the daily divine provisioning will continue tomorrow; the Lord will provide. The proximate eschatological horizon of this manna-Sabbath cycle is a land flowing with milk and honey; its ultimate horizon is that city not built with human hands.

Lotteries parody manna and Sabbath. Nearly all U.S. lotteries run on a weekly cycle, and the majority of lottery revenue comes from people who play weekly (often ritually). Lotteries lure play with the promise of extravagant jackpots, often advertised as the pleasures of permanent *freedom from* employment and *for* extravagant consumption. It is these grand prizes that motivate play (although small prizes are the "tease" that keeps players in the game). The permeation of society by lotteries then begins to shape a societal eschatological imagination in which hope for a better future centers on "winning the lottery," not on the better education (and subsequent employment) that lotteries ostensibly are meant to fund. That is, lotteries direct hope toward money as purveyor of happiness, and lotteries individualize rather than socialize hope. Thus, although spending $10 a week on lottery tickets looks economically insignificant for middle-class persons, in fact it is a ritual of complaint and a rhythm of distrust. Just as Israel complained about its present circumstance (Exod 16:2-3; cf. Num 21:5), longing to taste again the fleshpots of Egypt, so a weekly lottery ticket is a ritual complaint about our present circumstance, a ritual longing to taste the jackpots of wealth and ease. Whereas Israel's Sabbath was a trustful, rhythmic celebration of provision past, present, and future—a weekly celebration of "daily bread," weekly lottery play is a rhythmic denigration of past provision and its Provider. Unlike Sabbath, where weekly rest from labor also celebrates liberation from slavery (Deut 5:15), lottery play is a weekly ritual searching for liberation from all work. Sabbath rest says to Yahweh, "Because you provide, we can rest." Lottery play says to Luck, "If you provide, I will rest." Playing the lottery is one place we had best not "plunder the Egyptians."

To this point, we have followed Wesley into the wilderness of Sin, where Israel's unhappy complaint against Yahweh elicited not a return to the putatively satisfying fleshpots of Egypt but a rhythmic discipleship of divine provision and trusting celebration, a temporally structured and extended journey into the conjoining of holiness and happiness. We have suggested that this positions us to resist Wesley's prejudice against "diversions" without thereby sanctifying everything people do to have fun. Some parties will always be wrong (Exod 32:6), and probably the weekly lottery ticket is too.

Wagering Grace

Are other forms of gambling, properly tempered, as appropriate for Christians as listening to the radio? Answering turns us to Paul's metaleptic use of Exod 16:18 in his most extensive discussion of the Jerusalem collection, 2 Corinthians 8–9. This collection was Paul's commitment that he and his Gentile churches "remember the poor" (Gal 2:10). A wooden Wesleyanism might read no further, deducing from the prevalence of poverty in our world a claim that Christians with "entertainment budgets" are failing to "save all they can" in order to "give all they can" to the poor.[36] Paul's argument in these chapters is far more supple and subtle, inviting Wesleyans to read their way into the text before they read out of it obligations or refusals.

Indeed, one of the striking things about this passage is that Paul appeals but does not command (2 Cor 8:8a; cf. 9:7). He calls it a *test* of their love (8:8b; cf. 8:24; 9:13). A hermeneutics of suspicion hears in that move crass manipulation. A canonical hermeneutics can ask whether Paul's metalepsis echoes Yahweh's testing Israel (Exod 16:4), remembering that testing intends transformation. Like manna in the wilderness, the collection is a weekly cycle (1 Cor 16:2) with sufficient duration for the Corinthians to learn generous love by participation.[37] Notice the emphasis on the affective dimension; Paul's exhortation is for a performance sourced in and surrounded by generosity, joy, eagerness, earnestness, cheerfulness, and thanksgiving.[38]

In a historical sense, their test has now ended. Paul envisioned that reality with his advice that they "now finish" what they started (8:11); he enacted it when he carried the collection to Jerusalem (Acts 24:17) at great personal cost. Theologically, however, their test is our test, and it is ongoing. We belong to the same church addressed and invited by God in 2 Corinthians to participate in "this generous undertaking."[39] Now as then, impoverished churches bring into question the gospel's truth (9:13), God's glory (8:19; 9:13), and the church's apostolicity.[40] Now as then, collections to "remember the poor" contribute to the free circulation of economies of blessing (8:14; 9:8), to an abundant harvest of Christ's righteousness and God's glory (9:8-13). So for us, as for Corinth, the extra that we earn (1 Cor 16:2) in a world of impoverished churches constitutes a test of the genuineness of our love (8:8). We, too, must "remember the poor."

Of course, that is precisely what politicians and promoters tell us we are doing when we institute or support an education lottery or legalize casino gambling as an economic stimulus. And that is sometimes the stated motive behind mission raffles or congregational bingo. Do such contemporary arrangements constitute a "prudential means of grace" not unlike Paul's advice on how best to prepare for his collection (1 Cor 16:1-4)? No! They do not precisely because of the disconnect between policy ends (addressing poverty) and player motivations (the thrill of risk, the hope of fortune). Means of grace have no such disconnect between means and end, impact and affect, motivation and formation. Rather, the means of grace perfect love through loving action. Gambling as a means of remembering the poor fails Paul's test of "the genuineness of our love" (8:8), since it is public policy rooted in voters' unwillingness to be taxed to relieve poverty, and it is church practice rooted in disciples' unwillingness to give freely and generously to the poor.[41] As such, the only loves gambling is likely to increase are the loves of pleasure and money.

To think our way deeper into the passage requires that we notice the "density of grace language in these chapters."[42] We will consider this first as a matter of vocabulary and then of the logic of grace. First, consider that grace (*charis*) is one term Paul uses in these chapters to speak about money. He also calls money everything from gift (2 Cor 8:12, 20; 9:5), abundance (8:14), proof of your love (8:24), and ministry (9:1, 12), to seed for sowing (9:10). In short, Paul calls money everything but "money." This is not a rhetorical trick but a theological revelation: the true identity and real meaning of money is intrinsic to its use within a structured exchange or relationship. Notice how that same dynamic plays out in the gambling industry, where money is a "stake," "bet," "wager," "jackpot," "prize," "winnings." The key question is whether money that is rightly recognized as *grace* ought to be shifted into an exchange where its identity becomes *wager*. Does that not risk (or destroy) its character as grace? Adjudicating this question is more a matter of nurturing scriptural imagination and Christlike character than a matter of logical conclusion or empirical assessment, but I strongly suspect that moving from "it's only money" to "it's actually grace (and gift and ministry and love)" will considerably up the ante of responsibility to live as those who have not received grace in vain.

Now let us follow the "density of grace" through to its theological structure. Paul uses the word *charis* ten times in two chapters, with a semantic subtlety that leads to variability in translations; for example, the NRSV renders *charis* "grace" (2 Cor 8:1; 9:14), "privilege" (8:4), "generous undertaking" (8:6, 7, 19), "generous act" (8:9), "thanks" (8:16; 9:15), and "blessing" (9:8). The overall claim Paul makes is that participation in the collection is participation in the divine economy of grace. Indeed, it *is* grace and is *graced*. It *is* grace, not merely *like* grace (a material analog to a spiritual benefit) or *because of* grace. Rather, Paul is expressing the tangible truth that grace has material, even monetary dimensions. (Anything less becomes a Nestorian theology of grace.) But the Corinthians' gift *is* grace only because it is *graced*;

that is, it is a graciously enabled human response, it is a christologically positioned and pneumatologically perfected response.[43] Though the Spirit is not explicitly named, the Spirit's gifts are named as that in which the Corinthians excel as part of the logical implication that excelling in "this grace" will also be the Spirit's gift (8:7).[44]

Christ is named explicitly in the pithy plot summary of 2 Cor 8:9, which many commentators wrongly take as a mere exemplification of and motivation for generosity. It is certainly both example and motive, but it is also something far more basic. This "interchange"[45] Paul describes is not a simplistic trading of places nor a forensic trading of statuses. It is a real (as well as relative) change that takes place "in [Christ so that] we might become the righteousness of God" (5:21). *In* Christ, the interchange includes both our participation in the grace/generosity of his impoverishment (as Paul did, 6:10), as well as our participation in his enrichment ("you will be enriched in every way," 9:11).[46] Thus, if the word of God—"he scatters abroad, he gives to the poor, his righteousness endures forever" (Ps 112:9)—is written on our hearts (2 Cor 3:3), as it was on Jesus' heart,[47] it is because we are "in Christ" (5:17 NRSV).

Finally, let us recognize the death at the heart of Paul's claim that Christ "became poor." Whether one reads as commentary Phil 2:5-8 or the second article of the Apostles' Creed, "the grace of our Lord Jesus Christ" leads to and through a tomb. Christ's death "for all" (2 Cor 5:14) brings to us a life lived no longer for ourselves but for him (5:15) and thus for others. Facing the shape of his death positions us to consider gambling again in terms of loss and gain.

Nigel Turner sees gambling as a legitimate form of play belonging to the larger category of things "we do to momentarily forget our mortality." Paradoxically, he suggests that "part of the thrill of gambling is the potential for loss" and harm.[48] Gambling is similar to "extreme sports"—e.g., mountain climbing or grizzly tipping, in which an important part of the excitement correlates with the risk of harm. Christian moral analysis must not underestimate the positive significance of a strong human attraction to risk. If Paul's account of his own ministry is any indication, "missionary to the Gentiles" counts as an extreme sport (2 Cor 4:8-12; 6:3-10; 11:23-33). Our calling is not to avoid risk but to carry crosses toward Christ's kingdom.[49]

It is not the threat of loss that keeps people coming back to the tables, Turner says, but "the dream of the big win"—the desire to become rich.[50] So gambling engages the same dynamics of becoming poor and getting rich as Christ's interchange but with key differences. In Christ, he becomes poor so that you (plural), many, all can become rich. In gambling, many become poor so that a few can become rich. There is a different logic at the heart of gambling than the logic of the cross. That becomes most obvious in two particular forms of gambling: "true poker" and slot machines. "True poker is played between players"[51] rather than against the house, which means that the winner is enriched at the direct cost of the losers' impoverishment. It enacts a parody of the cross:

> Winner: . . . yet for his own sake he became rich, so that by his winnings you might become impoverished.

> Messiah: . . . yet for your sake he became poor, so that by his poverty you might become rich.

Is this categorically different from playing any game in which only one can win? Perhaps not if there are truly low stakes and unbreakable limits; this may be the wisdom of the Catholic position, that Thursday night poker with a $20 limit is just a few people having a good time. But even here, there is a difference. Whereas in most games the benefits of winning are intrinsic to the game itself and endure after the game only as status (bragging rights) or record (undefeated), with poker and other gambling games the fun of winning is *the winnings*, which become an extrinsic, enduring benefit. However one thinks about small stakes games, it is crucial to realize that "poker can be very predatory."[52] The skills involved in playing well are not simply mathematical understanding of probable outcomes but the psychological skill of misleading (bluffing) or even intimidating other players. In a society where poker is the most common gateway for underage gamblers, where high-stakes poker is romanticized and fetishized in movies and through televised poker tournaments, and where online poker allows anonymous play apart from socially stabilizing and restraining factors, Paul wants us to recognize the dis-grace of poker, that ungenerous act of seeking to become rich by the neighbor's impoverishment. That recognition will entail a "lifestyle" of *restraint from* rapacious entertainments but, more importantly, one of *risk for* the poor and the vulnerable.

Slot machines are the antithesis of poker in two ways. First, they are entirely random games that require no skill, which means that the "fun" has to be part of the device design or the mode of play, or rests entirely on the thrill of chasing a jackpot or "the fleeting sense of immersion in pure possibility"[53] that accompanies each spin. Second, one plays the "house" rather than other people, which means that slots are solitary endeavors against an opponent without the moral restraint of a face-to-face encounter. Put these two facts together in the era of modern gambling, and we get predatory slot machines that are intentionally designed to induce players to "play to extinction." That euphemism means to entice the slot machine player to spend "everything she had, all she had to live on" (Mark 12:44 NRSV). Though the widow that Jesus observed giving her two coins in the temple can be read as a type of his cruciform self-giving, she can also be seen as a victim of economic exploitation by religious leaders.[54] In modern casinos she becomes a representative victim devoured by corporate greed and social indifference. In a society where most of the population is an easy drive from a casino, where slot machines now cover most of casinos' floor space, where slots take debit and credit cards instead of quarters, Paul wants us to recognize the dis-grace of slots, that ungenerous mechanism for disgracing and devouring the poor.

Jackson Lears, a penetrating social observer, suggests, "There are powerful links . . . between the gambler's longing for luck and the believer's longing for grace—which, as a free gift of God, has always been a kind of spiritual luck."[55] We Wesleyans should see in the proliferation of gambling a quest for happiness led astray by parodies of grace. The true logic of grace conjoins happiness and holiness, poverty and riches, Christ and the church, even Scripture and social ethics.

Betting on the Bible

I conclude with theses and dicta extracted from the work above.

1. Holy Scripture is God's gift, a means of grace given by God for our transformation. Therefore, *read trustfully and repentantly! And reread, humbly and joyfully expecting to encounter God.*[56]
2. Holy Scripture is God's sanctified and sanctifying gift in its entire two-Testament unity.[57] Therefore, *read "the whole scope of Scripture" and attend to intertestamental conversations.*
3. Scripture plots the triune God's story of creating, redeeming, and perfecting our world.[58] Therefore, *we read to figure ourselves* into *Scripture's story, not to figure* out *principles that replace reading Scripture.*

4. The "grace of our Lord Jesus Christ" is the hermeneutical key to Scripture (and the cosmos). Therefore, *read Scripture as ordered to as well as through Christ.*
5. Scripture already is theology and ethics (not raw material for them).[59] Therefore, *read for Scripture's theological interests and moral intent in their interrelation, noticing that God is Scripture's primary moral agent.*
6. Scripture is written to and for the church. Through it Christ's rule is manifested in the church. Therefore, *search the Scriptures in and with the church seeking his wisdom and way, a practical divinity uniting truth and goodness in the beauty of a holy people.*
7. Scripture's theological vocabulary and grammar shape moral perception, feeling, and action. Therefore, *read praying "that what we read may be written on our hearts."*[60]
8. Scripture itself refuses "to divorce holiness and happiness."[61] Therefore, *read with soteriological aims attentive to the uniting of divine perfections and human passions.*

Wesley's well-known expostulation, "At any price give me the Book of God!"[62] suggests the intensity of his wager that Scripture is sufficient to its task of drawing us into God's abundant life of holiness and happiness. That remains a safe bet for Wesleyans today. Indeed, considering the grace of our Lord Jesus Christ, it is no gamble at all.

13

CAN WE SPEAK OF A WESLEYAN THEOLOGICAL HERMENEUTIC OF SCRIPTURE TODAY?

Steven J. Koskie

Are Wesleyans still a people of one book? If so, do they know how to read that one book? This seems to be part of the issue surrounding the recent interest in developing a Wesleyan theological hermeneutic of Scripture. How we read, to what end we read, and whether all of this reading can be labeled "Wesleyan"—such questions have only grown in fervor of late.[1] Here I will try to clarify some of the issues involved if we are to speak of a Wesleyan theological hermeneutic of Scripture today.

As a preliminary, let me clarify the term "theological hermeneutics." What I do not mean by theological hermeneutics is an intermediate, descriptive step between biblical studies and systematic or dogmatic theology. Theological interpretation of Scripture is not a series of steps from, say, grammatico-historical exegesis to theological description to constructive theology. Instead, the term refers to theological reflection as biblical exegesis (or vice versa). Reflective of so much premodern theology, this biblical-exegetical mode of theology reads the Bible as the church's Scripture, bringing all manner of commitments—credal, ethical, sacramental—to reading the Bible. Historical, literary, and other types of "critical" approaches to the Bible are not disqualified, but they are subsumed to the goals of theological interpretation. Modernist academic divisions between theology and biblical studies are left behind in theological hermeneutics, and the chasm between academy and church is bridged.

Can we speak of a *Wesleyan* theological hermeneutic today? We can, if as Wesleyans we are willing to confront certain issues, as I will do here. First, there is the problem of Wesley's own texts. Since Albert Outler, Wesleyans have struggled with how to read Wesley in the service of constructive theology, either trying to systematize doctrines from his occasional writings or reading "through" his texts to uncover his socio-historical and literary influences. Looking to Alasdair MacIntyre, I will offer a third way that is better suited to developing a Wesleyan theological hermeneutic. Second is how contemporary accounts of meaning as produced rather than discovered require Wesleyans to retool certain hermeneutical commitments of Wesley's, especially to the literal sense and the unity of Scripture and perhaps to certain readings that have been basic to the Wesleyan tradition. Finally, there is the role of the reader. How does the Wesleyan identity shape a soteriological reading of Scripture's literal sense, and how does that same reading in turn shape the Wesleyan identity? Here I will examine the soteriological commitments of Wesleyan theological hermeneutics. Although neither exhaustive nor definitive, I hope my treatment of these issues will add to and move forward the conversation around a contemporary Wesleyan theological hermeneutics of Scripture.

Reading Wesley to Read Scripture

In one exploration of Wesleyan hermeneutics, Robert W. Wall argues that because any biblical interpreter also belongs to a particular tradition, a Wesleyan interpretation is one interested in "rendering the (esp. soteriological) accents of the Wesleyan theological tradition."[2] But although Wesleyans stand in a history of interpretation whose font is John Wesley, they cannot "simply adopt as normative Wesley's particular reading of Scripture."[3] Modern-day Wesleyans live in a different context from Wesley, so even if some of Wesley's methodological and theological interests can be retained, other interests must be modified or abandoned. In part, it is the question of how to navigate this issue that leaves Wall at a loss about how to move forward with a Wesleyan hermeneutic, despite his enthusiasm for the subject.[4]

Questions about how Wesleyans relate to Wesley have been long-standing in the tradition, and modern Wesleyan studies has been unable to answer, despite making John Wesley *the* object of investigation. It has long been observed that contemporary Wesleyan theology owes its defining marks to Albert Outler.⁵ Recently, both William J. Abraham and Jason E. Vickers have taken up this observation, if only to note Outler's agenda is exhausted.⁶

Whether this is true, Abraham helpfully discerns that the driving motivation of contemporary Wesleyan theology since Outler has been to present John Wesley (and by extension the tradition that springs from him) as a theological voice with which it is worth reckoning.⁷ From this motivation sprang a program to recover Wesley the theologian by first establishing his theological prowess in fusing multifarious strands of the Christian tradition, East and West, then adapting his ideas from the occasional genres in which he wrote as a "folk theologian" to those more amenable to the modern academy and ecumenically minded church.⁸ The outworking of this program has been twofold: one a form of scholasticism, the other a form of historical criticism.

As scholasticism, Wesleyan theology has distilled and systematized Wesley's doctrine, commending it as the baseline for Wesleyan belief, and it has devised a supposedly distinctive Wesleyan theological method, the quadrilateral, to go with it.⁹ The quadrilateral, a matrix of Scripture, tradition, reason, and experience, has been embraced,¹⁰ criticized,¹¹ and defended¹² since its introduction by Outler. Instead of entering directly into that debate, my primary reservation is not with the quadrilateral per se but with the larger venture of systematization. By separating out Wesley's doctrines from the exegesis that he both assumed in reading Scripture and believed resulted from that same reading, Wesleyan theologians have adapted Wesley's thought to the modern academic arena in a way that yields a theological practice quite different from Wesley's, a theological practice more at home among the divisions of the academy—divisions, for example, between biblical exegesis and systematic theology—than what Wesley, writing in the eighteenth century, would have understood. More to the point, the scholastic method has perhaps limited Wesleyan theologians' ability to query whether Wesley's own mode of theological reflection, as exegetical theology, has anything to offer.

Also stemming from Outler is what we might call the historical-critical approach to Wesley. Here Wesley's writings are seen as doorways through which their socio-historical background can be reconstructed and their various sources catalogued. Nothing exemplifies this approach better than the Bicentennial Edition of Wesley's

Works. Outler gives the motivation for the Bicentennial Edition's methodology in his introduction to the first volume: "The credibility of any such perspective [of Wesley as a theologian worthy of serious scholarly attention] . . . depends upon an adequate display of Wesley's sources, and a demonstration of his way with the diverse traditions that converged in him."[13] Again, if Wesley can be shown to be a significant theological voice in the tradition through his encyclopedic and skillful use of diverse sources, credibility is transferred to the tradition he founded.

The Bicentennial Edition is a magisterial accomplishment, but there is a difference between reading a text as an entryway to the past and reading it formatively for the present.[14] If distilling doctrines from Wesley's writings and systematizing them short-circuits how we might learn Wesley's theological interpretation from Wesley, the archeological approach exemplified in the Bicentennial Edition bypasses the same opportunity by reading "through" Wesley's texts into their past. These critical remarks are not made to claim the Bicentennial Edition is somehow *wrong* (it is uncertain what such a judgment would mean) but only to demonstrate that the kind of reading found in the Bicentennial Edition has limits; it is not omnicompetent for every way of reading Wesley.[15]

Both the scholastic and the historical-critical approaches have their place in Wesleyan studies, but at issue here is whether either procedure helps us wrestle with how to learn theological interpretation from Wesley. The scholasticism that elaborates on Wesley's doctrines apart from his interpretive practices can be helpful, perhaps especially for catechetical purposes, but how does this help us read Scripture as Wesley does? Showing that Wesley takes some of his exegetical moves from Bengel can be insightful but may not help us deal with whether we can follow in Wesley's stead and pattern our interpretation similarly. The limitation of these approaches is that neither of them helps us make judgments about how to appropriate Wesley's practices in light of changes that have occurred in hermeneutics in the more than two hundred years since Wesley's death. It may be helpful, therefore, to recontextualize Wesley's writings away from the questions and concerns that have animated Outler-inspired scholarship and toward the questions and concerns of this essay, for they are different.

Let us return to Wall's comment about how Wesleyan interpreters stand within a certain tradition. Alasdair MacIntyre argues that a tradition exists within a community and extends through time; said differently, tradition-constituted knowledge is historical knowledge. Every tradition changes over time, and these changes are the result of needed adaptations to novel situations that often are beyond what could have been envisioned by a tradition's founders. New situations create problems for the interpretation of authoritative texts, beliefs, and practices. For a tradition to survive a "rupture," it needs skilled adherents who can address past inadequacies and keep intact the tradition's core beliefs.[16] A resourceful enough tradition can treat problems as an opportunity to develop, but a crisis for a tradition lacking resources could be fatal.[17]

If MacIntyre is correct, reports of Wesleyan theology's demise may be premature. Whereas Abraham especially judges the failure of Outler's agenda to be the end of Wesleyan theology, a MacIntyrean analysis might say that Abraham's critique merely signals the death throes of one stage of the Wesleyan tradition, but that another is ready to break forth.[18] In fact, Abraham's argument that Wesley should be venerated as a church father who offers a nourishing spirituality, rather than as a source for theology (a distinction Wesley might have found foreign), may in fact open an opportunity to learn theological interpretation from Wesley.[19]

Consider MacIntyre's idea of learning a craft. In order to become a skilled practitioner, a person must submit to an authority, as this authority is someone who knows how to initiate a student into the craft to be learned. As MacIntyre frames it:

> The authority of a master within a craft is both more and other than a matter of exemplifying the best standards so far. It is also and most importantly a matter of knowing how to go further and especially how to direct others towards going further, using what can be learned from the tradition afforded by the past to move towards the *telos* of fully perfected work. It is thus knowing how to link past and future that those with authority are able to draw upon tradition, to interpret and reinterpret it, so that its directedness towards the *telos* of that particular craft becomes apparent in new and characteristically unexpected ways.[20]

Moreover, "we shall have to learn from that teacher and initially accept on the basis of his or her authority within the community of a craft precisely what intellectual and moral habits it is which we must cultivate and acquire if we are to become effective self-moved participants in such enquiry."[21]

MacIntyre provides a reorientation away from modes of reading Wesley derived from Outler but also a different solution—even a different way of understanding the problem—than some criticisms of Outler's agenda. First, MacIntyre helps us see that the frustrations of both Wall and Abraham are a natural part of the lifespan of a tradition. The question is whether the Wesleyan tradition has the resources to survive. Second, MacIntyre gives more substance to Wall's point that a Wesleyan theological hermeneutic of Scripture is rooted by definition in the Wesleyan tradition, which is embodied in Wesleyan communities. On this account, reading Wesley in light of contemporary issues is what transmits the craft of theological interpretation and the beliefs and practices that compose it from Wesley to Wesleyans. And since Wesley would have separated his exegesis from neither his theology nor his spirituality, we can follow Abraham's commendation to venerate Wesley while also reading him constructively for Wesleyan theology.

The critical differences Wall detects between past founder and present followers need not stymie a Wesleyan theological hermeneutic. Instead, for the skilled practitioner formed in the Wesleyan tradition, difference creates an opportunity to move things along. For our purposes, then, being conversant with both Wesley's hermeneutics and contemporary hermeneutics allows the Wesleyan interpreter to, as MacIntyre says, "link past and future" toward "the *telos* of fully perfected work"—Wesleyan language if ever there was any.

Reclaiming Wesley's Hermeneutics

As Hans W. Frei showed in *The Eclipse of Biblical Narrative*, for so much premodern exegesis meaning was found in the biblical text itself; it was with modernism that meaning was wrenched from the literal sense of Scripture and located in abstract concepts or in a reconstructed history of the text's composition, only to be moved in postmodernism to the subjectivity of the reader.[22] Modernist criticism keyed on the problem of unity and diversity and allowed its own type of historical consciousness to fragment the NT into a cacophony of different traditions or schools, whether Pauline, Johannine, or some other. The Bible was now a hodgepodge of competing "preorthodox" versions of the faith.

Contemporary theological hermeneutics has sought to reclaim both the literal sense and the unity of Scripture, but according to a view of meaning as something dynamic arising from the interaction of reader, text, and context and while finding strategies to reunite diverse voices in Scripture without conflating or silencing. Texts are not inert objects acted on methodologically by a reader who discovers the one correct meaning, nor are they occasions for simply displaying the reader's perspective. Rather, texts have numerous (though not infinite) meanings. A reader comes to the text from a particular point, with questions, and this stimulates the interpretive process that births meaning. The inexhaustible nature of a text, its polysemy, permits continued rereadings, the occasion for which is created by the context of the reader. Any Wesleyan theological hermeneutic that wishes to hold to Wesley's formal commitments to the literal sense and the unity of Scripture will need to appropriate his hermeneutics in light of these issues.

Wesley lived in the time when the cleaving Frei documents was under way, but he made a priority of adhering to the literal sense of Scripture, which for him was primarily the verbal sense of the text.[23] This is clearest when he runs into a problem with the literal sense and needs to depart from it. Wesley assumes that meaning is typically found in the words on the page, neither "behind" the text (as in so much modernist criticism) nor "in front of" the text (as in so much postmodernist criticism). The exception proves the rule. In situations where the literal sense resulted in contradiction or absurdity, Wesley resorted to a "spiritual sense" of the text. In his sermon "Of the Church," he says, "It is a stated rule in interpreting Scripture never to depart from the plain, literal sense, unless it implies absurdity."[24] Elsewhere he claims that tensions with the literal sense permit him to seek "a looser meaning," that is, a spiritual one—something figurative or allegorical.[25]

With the introduction of reader and context into hermeneutics, the literal sense today is understood as the community's conventional reading of Scripture. The literal sense is not a property of the Bible but rather a certain type of interaction between the community and text. The life of the community, those beliefs and practices that comprise its identity, is thus interwoven with what it is that the community understands the literal sense to be. Charles M. Wood makes this point when he asserts that, although the literal sense is the second-nature, obvious reading of Scripture, "what is obvious to a reader depends a great deal on how the reader has been schooled to approach the text." The literal sense is therefore "intimately bound up with the conventions of reading, with the capacities and dispositions, linguistic and personal, which the reader brings to the text, by virtue of having been formed in a community with a fairly secure style of interaction with this material."[26] Biblical interpretation cannot be abstracted from the aims, interests, and practices of the community. Bible and church are therefore "dialectically related," as David H. Kelsey says, and ordered to particular ends.[27]

The community's grammar of faith, the internal logic that norms its self-understanding, enjoins and regulates this dialectical relation. According to Paul L. Holmer, "The grammar of a language is that set of rules that describes how people speak who are doing it well and with efficacy. A logical schematism is also that set of criteria and law-like remarks that describe how people think when they make sense." Theology uses a grammar to give believers "the order and priorities, the structure and morphology, of the Christian faith. It does this by placing the big words, like *man, God, Jesus, world*, in such a sequence and context that their use becomes ruled for us."[28]

Hermeneutically, the grammar functions as a rule or canon that regulates interpretation, activating a normative, literal sense. As Frei argues, traditionally "the creed, or 'rule of faith' or 'rule of truth' which governed the Gospels' use in the church asserted the primacy of the literal sense."[29] According to its typical use in premodern interpretation, the rule of faith was considered a hypothesis about the substance of the biblical narrative, functioning as the first principle that made knowledge of God through Scripture possible.[30]

For Wesley, the analogy of faith is the grammar that rules his reading of the literal sense. In his comments on Rom 12:6, Wesley describes the analogy of faith as follows:

> St. Peter expresses [the analogy of faith], as the oracles of God: according to the general tenor of them; according to that grand scheme of doctrine which is delivered therein, touching original sin, justification by faith, and present, inward salvation. There is a wonderful analogy between all these; and a close and intimate connection between the chief heads of that faith "which was once delivered to the saints." Every article, therefore, concerning which there is any question, should be determined by this rule: every

doubtful scripture interpreted, according to the grand truths which run through the whole.[31]

Although there are variations on the analogy in Wesley's writing, none of them are theologically contradictory.[32] Most obvious is the clear soteriological content of the analogy of faith. Perhaps less obvious is that the analogy of faith is neither a systematic theology nor a doctrinal scheme laid over Scripture—a point that might be obscured by Wesley's calling it "that grand scheme of doctrine." This should be balanced with a phrase at the quotation's end, that unclear Scripture should be interpreted "according to the grand truths which run through the whole." These are not doctrines arranged systematically like beads on a string. Instead, they are a précis of the whole of Scripture, which is sometimes referred to as the "whole" or "general tenor" of the Bible. The concept of the general tenor combines naturally with the analogy of faith for Wesley. In the quotation above, from Romans 12:6, the general tenor and the analogy of faith are mentioned in parallel ways to elaborate a point about Scripture's message.

The dynamic at play here is a circular one. On the one hand, the analogy of faith makes it possible to interpret Scripture as having one soteriological message. The analogy of faith is the "structure and morphology" Holmer describes. Instead of the big words "man, God, Jesus, world" of Holmer's example, Wesley's grammar arranges words like "original sin, justification, new birth, and sanctification." The analogy of faith is a pattern for seeing how all of Scripture fits together as a whole in the economy of salvation, and its sense of moving from a beginning through to an end gives the analogy its grammatical force. Exegetically, the analogy of faith allows Wesley to extend the literal sense figurally or typologically, so that he can interpret OT texts christologically, as he does in Genesis 3:15 or Isaiah 7:14, or claim that both Testaments of Scripture together are "the history of God."[33] On the other hand, reading Scripture is a way of elaborating on, or even exegeting, the analogy of faith, which is a summation of the gospel message everywhere attested to in Scripture.

But, as with the literal sense, the analogy of faith for Wesley simply is the message of the text, a difference from today when ruled readings are seen as just that: readings. Other readings of the Bible are possible, but a Christian ruled reading is the most appropriate one within the context of the church, and the church can claim a privileged seat at the table of biblical interpretation because the Bible is the church's book, its Scripture. As Richard Hays argues, the narrative shape of the Bible, which results from the church's work of collection, preservation, and handing down, indicates how the church wants the Bible read as a unified text.[34]

To this point I have tried to exhibit Wesley's reading of the literal sense according to the analogy of faith. If we follow Charles Wood in calling the literal sense a "style" of reading, what can we say about the style of Wesley's reading Scripture, especially as a practice Wesleyans will want to appropriate? Based on my admittedly cursory overview, a few observations can be made.

First, for Wesley the literal sense of Scripture is its soteriological sense. When Wesley reads Scripture, he does so assuming that all of it contributes to the economy of salvation, as is evident in the way he brings various texts throughout Scripture to bear on a particular theme in his sermons. Wesley assumes the unity of the divine purpose to bring salvation to fallen humanity, so that the unity of the Trinitarian missions is reflected in the unity of the entire Bible. Scripture is open to all persons seeking salvation through it because God addresses them through Scripture. The literal sense is the instrument by which God reveals both who he is and who humanity is as well. The analogy of faith is obviously at work here, patterning Wesley's perception of the divine intent throughout the Bible.

Second, we can note that Pauline themes dominate Wesley's hermeneutics by virtue of his Augustinian-Protestant heritage. They shape his analogy of faith, determining his style of interpretation. Even when Wesley uses other passages in key places, such as when he invokes John 3:7 to head his sermon "The New Birth," the content of new birth comes from Paul. And when Wesley arrives at the end of Ps 22, his remarks are basically a summary of Rom 9. Wesley's understanding of original sin and justification both come from the Augustinian-Protestant tradition that privileged Pauline writings, and the two doctrines are at least conceptually prior to entire sanctification in Wesley's soteriology. At the very least, it seems correct to claim that this reading of Paul set a trajectory for how Wesley reads the rest of Scripture.[35]

The first characteristic of Wesley's style may be more easily adapted than the second. Although modernist criticism tried at times to read the Bible without subjective faith commitments and postmodernist criticism has at times reveled in subjectivity, within the life of the church a soteriological reading is more than appropriate; it is assumed in the very composition of the biblical canon itself. If Christian hermeneutics since Christ has had any continuity with him, then beginning with the New Testament authors' reading of the Law, Psalms, and Prophets, Christians have always read the Bible soteriologically. From within the church catholic, it is only natural for Wesleyans to follow suit.

The Augustinian-Protestant predominance of Pauline theology is more difficult. To focus the problem, consider how our understanding of justification by faith has changed since Wesley. Following Protestant precedent, Wesley considered justification by faith the central doctrine of Scripture. The presence of original sin made all guilty before God and in need of salvation. The grace that came with justification was what Wesley called a "relative" change, giving believers a new standing before God. It is a gift that cannot be earned by works. Justification removes the guilt of sin, and regeneration removes the power of sin in one's life. This is the soteriology reflected in the analogy of faith, which of course rules Wesley's reading of Scripture. Despite the biblical and doctrinal centrality (which for Wesley would be an artificial distinction) of justification, two points suggest that Wesleyans can no longer assume Wesley's view.

The first point regards the unity and diversity of Scripture. I have already mentioned how the modernist version of this problem fractured the Bible into different sources, sacrificing the theological unity Wesley assumed. As late modern or postmodern biblical scholarship has changed its ideas about history and applied more recent literary studies to Scripture, the particularity of the final form of the text has made gains on (though by no means supplanted) "behind the text" studies. Consequently, the distinctiveness of different biblical writers has become better appreciated, including how each depicts salvation. This does nothing to how the concept of justification itself is understood, but it does relegate it to the Pauline texts in which it is prominent (viz., Romans and Galatians). Whatever the meaning of justification in Paul, one should not presume Romans speaks for other NT books about salvation.

Moreover, if modern and postmodern ways of handling canonical diversity have challenged the hermeneutical priority of justification by faith, what justification means within Paul's writings has also come under reexamination. Thus the second factor that indicates a change in hermeneutical context from Wesley's is the "new perspective," as it is known.[36] Adherents to this position have variously asserted that justification by faith is not based on a dichotomous paradigm of faith versus works. Rather, Jews observed the law in response to God's gracious initiative, and Christ's mission was the covenantal restoration of God's people. Far from being the private gospel of Protestantism, the gospel is a social reality ultimately cosmic in scope.

In general, new perspective scholarship, thanks to socio-historical insights not available to Wesley, has redefined justification by faith significantly enough to create a real difference between it and Wesley's doctrine. The faith versus works polemic has been disarmed, and the communal dimension of justification has emerged. Any theological hermeneutic that wishes to stand in the Wesleyan tradition will therefore have to account for this difference.[37]

Whenever a decision is made to interpret a text a certain way, the decision acts as closure on that text. A tradition that makes a certain closure definitive identifies itself from that point on with that interpretive decision, which may create a tension with the text, especially if that text's interpretation is also fundamental to the tradition's identity. In the Wesleyan tradition, a certain reading of justification by faith is a closure on the text, and it remains closed when this reading becomes assumed and is developed systematically apart from Scripture. But as times have changed, so have some of the assumptions and questions, and new factors have reopened how justification is read. If this reopening presents a potential threat to the Wesleyan tradition, it also creates an opportunity (to recall Alasdair MacIntyre) to creatively extend itself through a context different from Wesley's.

Identifying the Wesleyan Interpreter

Joel B. Green wants Wesleyan hermeneutics to move away from techniques and toward recognizing the priority of identity formation: "much of what characterizes a Wesleyan hermeneutic must be that Wesleyans do it."[38] He emphasizes how the presence of reader and context in contemporary hermeneutics moves away from meaning as something discovered in the text toward something that is produced. Instead, priority should be given to a literal sense that both addresses readers and allows for multiple interpretations. I have dealt with this latter point above, but, combined with the preceding section, we must realize that to recover a ruled reading of the literal sense in conversation with Wesley is also to recover the ruled way of life in which he interpreted Scripture. This being the case, what are the aims, dispositions, and practices that make a Wesleyan interpreter of Scripture Wesleyan?

Essentially it is the identity of Christ as revealed in Scripture that defines the identity of the Wesleyan interpreter. Through the Spirit the Father invites us to meet Christ again and again through Scripture, continuing to take on his attributes. This is especially evident in Wesley's thirteen discourses, *Upon Our Lord's Sermon on the Mount*, where he examines Christ's teachings on "true religion."[39] To be changed into the image of God means we are to live like him, to imitate him; we are to be what we were created to be originally;[40] we are to love and enjoy God forever.[41] To imitate God is to be holy and perfect as God is holy and perfect,[42] and, since God is revealed in Christ so that through him we see "the fountain of beauty and love, the original source of all excellency and perfection,"[43] then the imitation of Christ is the appropriate response to Scripture.

The nature of this imitation can be found in Wesley's *The Character of a Methodist*, where he sets out "the *principles* and *practice* whereby those who are called 'Methodists' are distinguished by other men."[44] After setting aside misconceptions of Methodism as being defined by "opinions of any sort," "*words* or *phrases* of any sort," "*actions, customs*, or *usages* of an *indifferent* nature," or "by laying the *whole* stress of religion on any *single part* of it,"[45] Wesley argues that "a Methodist is one who has 'the love of God shed abroad in his heart by the Holy Ghost given unto him'; one who 'loves the Lord his God with all his heart, and with all his soul, and with all his mind, and with all his strength.'"[46] What follows is an elaboration on the love of God that reads like a scriptural collage of nearly forty biblical quotes and allusions, encompassing rejoicing, thanksgiving, hope, praise, and ceaseless prayer.[47] Wesley spells out love of neighbor similarly. At the core of love for others is purity of heart, achieved because God's love has purged the Methodist of sinful behaviors and attitudes in exchange for "bowels of mercies, kindness, humbleness of mind, meekness, long-suffering," and the ability to forgive.[48] Wesley claims that a Methodist not only aims at, "but actually *attains*" living a life "all to the glory of God."[49] These are not merely ideas, in other words, but descriptions of actual beliefs and practices of Methodism, which in the end Wesley indicates is simply "real Christianity."[50]

The impressive collection of quotations and allusions here and in *The Character of a Methodist* is hardly haphazard but reflects the internal logic of the analogy of faith governing Wesley's language about God and Christian life. Considering that Wesley believed the Methodists actually attained what they set out for, it follows that the aim of a Wesleyan hermeneutic is no less than the attainment of the perfect love of God and neighbor in the heart and life—Wesley's doctrine of Christian perfection.

We can confidently say, therefore, that Wesley teaches Wesleyans to approach the Bible soteriologically. The ultimate goal or aim of theological interpretation is traversing "the way to heaven" to reach that "happy shore" Wesley writes about in the preface to his *Sermons*.[51] It is a journey that changes us. For Wesley, the act of interpreting Scripture is a means of grace, an ordinary channel through which the Holy Spirit effects salvation in the heart. Through the means of grace, a person is transformed from slave to sin to child of God as he or she is inducted into the communion of Father, Son, and Holy Spirit.[52] This ontological and filial identity is rooted in the person and work of Christ as he is found in Scripture, so that for Wesleyans the identities of Jesus and readers of Scripture are closely bound to the text. Wesleyans interpret Scripture in concert with the Spirit's work of sanctification, so that as Wesleyans interpret Scripture, the Holy Spirit reinterprets their identities as children of God.

Hermeneutically, the way by which the identity of the Wesleyan reader is transformed from slave to child—someone in whom the image of God is restored—is figural reading. Above I noted how figural reading extends the literal sense, allowing Wesley to read one soteriological message in the Bible. But figural reading goes beyond prophecies and their fulfillment, types and antitypes in the text. Frances Young, commenting on the traditional place of figural reading in Christian identity, writes, "The way that people understood their own lives was once shaped by patterns and models found in Scripture, and, conversely, people read their own lives into Scripture."[53] Along these lines John David Dawson gives a soteriological definition of figural reading that is useful for Wesleyan theological hermeneutics:

> Figural reading in the Christian tradition seeks to express the dynamic process of spiritual transformation in ways that respect the practitioners' commitment to both past and future, both old

identity and newly refashioned identity. Imbedded in figural practice is all the drama of discerning the point of existence and identifying one's place in it, figured as a journey from a former mode of existence through various states of transformation toward some ultimate end.[54]

For Wesley, this ultimate end is happiness ("the end of religion"), that is, the knowledge and love of God, for which we are created.[55] This experience of happiness occurs when the Holy Spirit sheds God's love in our hearts and adopts us as children of God, renewing the image of God, Christ, within us. Figural reading for Wesleyans is about their location within the whole of Scripture, and it is able to truthfully describe the soteriological state of persons before God regardless of historical location, for God is author not only of Scripture, but also of life, faith, and salvation.[56]

To put it concisely, the aims, dispositions, and practices of the Wesleyan interpreter are otherwise known as holiness. Because God is the author of both Scripture and life, Wesleyans are to read Scripture as offering an accurate understanding of who they are before God, as God is identified in that same Scripture. And because it is in the act of reading that meaning is produced and because the reading of the Bible as a means of grace opens the Wesleyan interpreter to the work of the Holy Spirit, we cannot talk about meaning in a Wesleyan theological hermeneutic apart from a changed life. Holiness, in other words, is to a large extent the meaning produced in a Wesleyan interpretation.

Conclusion

Yes, we can speak of a Wesleyan theological hermeneutic of Scripture today, at least as long as we can speak of Wesleyan communities of faith that continue to read the Bible as the text that shapes their lives. Theological interpretation cannot be boiled down to techniques, but as a means of grace it is part of a larger, textured life lived together in a trajectory set by John Wesley in the eighteenth century. Over the course of that trajectory, changing times and ongoing biblical interpretation create both continuity and discontinuity with Wesley himself. To the extent that these hermeneutical judgments are part of a larger life that is pressing on to attain the knowledge and love of God, though they might depart from Wesley, they are nevertheless Wesleyan.

14

READING SCRIPTURE FOR CHRISTIAN FORMATION

Elaine A. Heath

What does it mean to read the Bible for Christian formation as Wesleyans? How did John Wesley engage formationally with Scripture, and what did he teach others to do? How have Wesley's theological descendents—teachers and practitioners of Wesleyan Christian formation—carried Wesley's "scriptural DNA" forward into contemporary methods for reading and praying with the Bible? In this essay we will consider these questions, beginning with John Wesley's principles and practices. Our goal is to identify and critically consider distinctly Wesleyan practices of reading, praying with, and being shaped by the Bible.

While it is true that John Wesley never produced a treatise on his doctrine of Scripture, nor did he preach a sermon focusing exclusively on this topic, the primacy of Scripture in his theology is clear. For Wesley the Bible is the ultimate guide to Christian faith and practice. Since other essays in this volume explore in detail what Wesley understood to be appropriate tools for exegesis and hermeneutics, I will not repeat that information in detail here. It is wise to remember for our focus on Christian formation, however, that the Articles of Faith and the Confession that guided Wesley's doctrine of Scripture never refer to the text of Scripture as "inspired," nor do they call the Bible "the Word of God."[1] The Confession states that the Bible "reveals the word of God."[2]

Though Wesley was certain that the Bible is inspired, Randy Maddox comments that "it is doubtful that he should be characterized as an inerrantist in the contemporary sense of the term."[3] Wesley read the Bible in its original languages, appreciated the biblical scholarship available to him, and drew heavily from others' exegetical work in drafting his *Explanatory Notes*. As Robert Wall notes, "Wesley was shaped by the Enlightenment projects and embraced the critical methods of his day, including a lifelong interest in textual criticism and the importance of reading sacred texts in their linguistic and historical contexts."[4] Thus, when Wesley describes himself as "a man of one book," he means a book interpreted in community with many other scholars and practitioners of the Christian faith. He also means a book that is different from the many other books in his impressive library, for Wesley understood the Bible to be uniquely sacred writ. We would be in error however, to think that Wesley's approach to Scripture for Christian formation was naïve, fundamentalist, or uninformed by the emerging critical scholarship of his day.

Robert Wall identifies ten interpretive principles Wesley uses in his reading of the Bible for Christian formation.[5] To summarize:

1. The Holy Spirit illumines the reader to discern the spiritual truth in Scripture. While the Holy Spirit also inspired the authors of Scripture, the emphasis is on the illumination of readers' hearts and minds to receive the spiritual meaning of the text.
2. Wesley refers to reading the "naked Bible," meaning the plain sense of the text has primacy over "abstract reasoning" substituted for reading what is actually there.
3. Wesley's understanding of the formation of the canon of Scripture is nuanced, demonstrating that he knows that the various "collections were arranged to perform together as an integral whole."
4. The Bible is a communal text; "its interpretive practices are communal, conversational, and participatory."
5. The reading and interpretation of the Bible are for purposes of salvation, for the spiritual formation and maturation of disciples.[6]
6. Preaching, even in academic settings like the university classroom, is the best way to share with others inspired interpretations of the Bible. The bifurcation of academic biblical studies from spiritual formation-oriented readings common today would have been unthinkable to Wesley.

7. Wesley expects the biblical text to challenge and change the reader. Critical, suspicious, or detached readings of the Bible are unacceptable.
8. The biblical text causes a change in the life of the Spirit-illumined reader, including attitudes, affections, thoughts, speech, and behaviors.
9. The Spirit-illumined reader is also missionally aware of her or his own cultural environment and thus reads the Bible with neighbor in mind, as to how to live the text faithfully among neighbors so that neighbors come to experience the saving love of God and find answers for their theological questions. This means that preparation for evangelism is inherent to a Wesleyan reading of the Bible.
10. Wesley's own speech was profoundly shaped by the rhythms and language of the Bible. "Wesley's prolific use of Scripture turned his sermons into sacraments, means for the body of Christ to ingest the sacred words and to experience in them afresh the Holy Spirit's active presence in our hearts."

In addition to these principles, which can be discerned by reading Wesley's *Sermons*, the Preface to *The Explanatory Notes upon the Old Testament*, and the Preface to *The Explanatory Notes upon the New Testament*, Wesley includes two forms of Scripture reading in his list of the six ordinances of God within his General Rules. The General Rules were Wesley's "rule of life" for the people called Methodists.[7] The first of the two ordinances having to do with Scripture is "the ministry of the Word, either read or expounded." Thus for Wesley the reading and exposition of the Bible are primary means through which God's grace is given to human beings, leading them to salvation and holiness of heart and life. The second method of Scripture reading as an ordinance or means of grace is "Searching the Scriptures," a way of reading that is similar to *lectio divina*, as we shall see. This ordinance, too, is designated as a primary means by which God's saving and sanctifying grace is distributed to willing hearts. Because reading the Bible for Christian formation was so important to Wesley, his catechism for children *Instructions for Children* lists "Searching the Scriptures" as one of five "chief means of grace."[8]

A significant motivator for Wesley in writing his sermon "The Means of Grace" (1746) was that some Methodists under the influence of quietism had abandoned "outward observances" of religious practice, especially reading the Bible and the sacraments of baptism and the Eucharist. In response to what Wesley felt was a dangerous form of enthusiasm, he wrote "The Means of Grace" to insist that the three "chief ordinances"—prayer, searching the Scriptures, and the Eucharist—were necessary for Christian formation.[9] While acknowledging that God is able to mediate grace directly to humans without these ordinary means, for example, in times of imprisonment or other circumstances preventing access to the Bible or Holy Communion, Wesley stresses that it is folly to abandon the chief ordinances when they are available. Even so, in this sermon Wesley also asserts that all the means of grace ordained by God are "dung and dross" unless they are undertaken intentionally in submission to the Holy Spirit for the purpose of holy transformation.[10] With regard to reading the Bible, Wesley is clear. To read the Bible without the goal of holy transformation is to abuse the means of grace.[11]

Wesley's Instructions for Reading the Bible

In his Preface to the *Explanatory Notes upon the Old Testament*, Wesley advises the following method to ensure that the reader experiences the text for transformation and not just information. First, the reader should set aside time morning and evening, habitually, to read a full chapter each from both the Old and New Testaments. If there is not time for two chapters, the reader should select one chapter or a portion of one chapter. The goal in this reading is for one purpose: *to know and do the will of God*. Because of this goal of Christian formation, Wesley urges readers to keep in mind at all times the overarching themes and doctrines of the Christian faith, including original sin, justification by faith, the new birth, and inward and outward holiness. The reader must pray for the Holy Spirit to illumine his or her mind to receive the spiritual understanding of the text, something that does not happen automatically and without which the reading will be useless. While reading, one should move slowly through the passage, pausing to reflect often so that the text can aid the reader in self-examination, with the Scripture sometimes comforting, sometimes challenging, and sometimes convicting the reader of the need for change. Finally, one should immediately put into practice any guidance or instructions that come through this twice daily practice of searching the Scriptures.[12]

In Wesley's Preface to *The Explanatory Notes upon the New Testament*, he describes both his purpose for writing the notes as well as the array of sources he has consulted from other Bible commentators. The notes, he says, are not written for the learned, but for "plain unlettered men, who understand only their mother tongue, and yet reverence and love the word of God, and have a desire to save their souls."[13] The only reason to read the Bible, in other words, is for Christian formation.

These instructions, emerging from Wesley's own discipline of reading the Bible daily for Christian formation, have much in common with the ancient contemplative method of praying with Scripture called *lectio divina*, or sacred reading.[14] The tradition of *lectio* goes back to before the sixth century, originating in the Benedictine-Cistercian traditions. It is a practice of contemplative prayer based on Scripture that is accessible to almost anyone, and it seems that this method may have influenced Wesley's structure for searching the Scriptures, though he does not use the term *lectio divina*.

Lectio divina has four movements, which do not always follow in the sequence I am going to enumerate. After all, the Holy Spirit is in charge of what happens in prayer. The reading is done with an orientation toward listening to the Holy Spirit who may speak through the text. This principle is in keeping with the Confession that guided Wesley, that the Bible reveals the word of God. To prepare for reading, one should quiet oneself and open one's heart to the Holy Spirit in readiness for whatever may be given. The intention is to hear whatever the Holy Spirit may say through the text, and to pray with it and then live it. As in the case with Wesley's instructions, the practice of *lectio* should be habitual, at least once a day, preferably twice.

Lectio is the first movement. A short passage of Scripture, no longer than one chapter and preferably just one pericope, is read through slowly at least twice. As Thelma Hall notes, "When in 'hearing' scripture we are receptive to the One who speaks in us, what we hear may be more than the words in themselves convey. The Spirit who vivifies them is himself the meaning, expressed *through* the words even more than by them, just as a lover may convey volumes in a phrase that would be mere convention when spoken by another."[15] As the reader moves slowly, in a listening manner through the text, he or she may sense a phrase, word, sentence, or concept emerging from the text, drawing the reader's attention. At that point the reader should pause. As Wesley instructs in his Preface to the *Explanatory Notes upon the Old Testament*, the pause allows the text to examine the reader.

This pause is the second movement of *lectio*: *meditatio* or meditation. In this part the reader reflects on the word, image, or phrase that has surfaced from the reading. It is time for a deeper listening to what God wants to share from that word. What and how a reader experiences *meditatio* is unique to each person and to each text. For some persons the experience will be more rational and reflective, pondering, for example, what it means to worship in Spirit and in truth (if the reading is John 4). For others the experience will engage the imagination more vividly, so that the reader especially notices the heat of the day and Jesus' thirst as he sits down at Jacob's well and sees the woman coming to draw water (also from John 4). Once the reader has experienced the emergence of the Word from the text and has paused to allow the Word to speak in some way, he or she is ready for the third movement of *lectio*, which is *oratio*, or prayer.

Oratio is similar to Wesley's instructions for allowing the biblical text to search one's heart and to comfort, convict, challenge, or instruct the reader in the way of holiness. With *oratio* the reader begins to pray with whatever has been revealed from the text during *meditatio*. Thelma Hall writes eloquently of the transformation and holy disillusionment (the removal of illusions that we have about God, ourselves, and the world) that take place as we pray during *oratio*:

> In this prayer, our hearts are opened to him and by him, so that his light may enter. Because he loves us too much to leave us in our illusions, which are obstacles to his grace, sooner or later they will begin to be revealed to us for what they are: the conscious and unconscious claims of the false self to autonomy, self-sufficiency, control, pride, role playing, or limits to our generosity. The list is unique to each, but its effect is the same, to impede the life of grace and the gifts of the Holy Spirit within us. . . . If we fail to act upon whatever he is revealing or asking of us, our prayer will be to that extent untruthful.[16]

The commitment to live what has been revealed, as a response to God's love and grace, undergirds the fourth movement of *lectio*, which is *contemplatio* or contemplation. It is also consistent with Wesley's instructions to immediately put into practice whatever has been given to us as we read the Bible. Yet there is a difference in *lectio divina*, as it goes beyond obedience to instructions that might surface in the first three parts of *lectio*. In *contemplatio* the reader has moved deeper than words, ideas, reflections, discursive prayer, and actions and is simply resting in God's love, attentive to God's presence. *Contemplatio* is a fundamental orientation of surrender to and adoration of God. While at times one may have emotional experiences related to *contemplatio*, this element of *lectio divina* is not really about emotions. It is about orientation toward God. Thus, whether the one praying has affective experiences (kataphatic prayer) or has no affective experience (apophatic prayer) the commitment is the same, to love, honor, serve, and rest in God, to find one's home in God. Whether one experiences a Word of God when reading the text or nothing happens during a particular reading, one remains grounded in true worship of God. Union with God, not experiences from God, is the purpose of *lectio divina*.

This final movement of *contemplatio* brings us to a disjunction with Wesley's early teaching on searching the Scriptures, because Wesley was not able to come to terms with Christian apophatic spirituality until very late in life. Though early in his ministry Wesley was drawn to the contemplative spirituality of William Law and other Christian mystics, he became frustrated with the apophatic element of their practice and ultimately denounced them. For many years Wesley wrote and spoke harshly against Christian mysticism because he did not understand apophatic spirituality. As noted earlier, because of his resistance to certain groups of Methodists under the influence of Moravian "enthusiasts," Wesley rejected all apophatic contemplative spirituality. Partially in reaction to them, he emphasized the necessity of "assurance," or kataphatic spiritual experience, in response to prayer and Bible reading. Yet, by the end of his life, Wesley underwent a transformation in his understanding of apophatic spirituality. As Jean Orcibal comments, by 1783 Wesley "retracted the [anti-mystical] expressions which had come from his own pen on the subject of the mystics."[17] Even Madame Guyon, whose apophatic mysticism caused her imprisonment as an alleged quietist in the seventeenth century, had become an exemplar of holiness for Wesley by the end of his life.[18] Guyon's best known work, *A Short and Very Easy Method of Prayer*, is entirely consistent with the tradition of *lectio divina*.[19]

HYMNODY, SCRIPTURE, AND CHRISTIAN FORMATION

One of the stellar features of Methodism from its inception has been the role of music in celebrating and teaching the Bible through psalms, hymns, and spiritual songs. Charles Wesley wrote as many as 9,000 poems during his lifetime, most of them expressing Methodist theology based on Scripture texts. Of these thousands of poems, several hundred became hymns widely sung in the church, with many of them still regularly used in worship. Though Charles was not a musician, with most of his songs being set to music others had composed, the legacy of his musical work in hymnody cannot be overstated.[20] Some of the best known include "Christ the Lord Is Risen Today," "O for a Thousand Tongues," and "Hark, the Herald Angels Sing."

Not only are Charles Wesley's hymns based on Scripture—often drawing words directly from the text—a number of them focus on the Bible. "Whether the Word Be Preached or Read" captures John Wesley's instructions for reading the Bible, and the powerful role of illumination in the reader's ability to receive divine revelation through the text:

[1.] Whether the Word be preach'd or read,
   No saving benefit I gain
From empty sounds or letters dead;
   Unprofitable all and vain,
Unless by faith *thy* word I hear
And see its heavenly character.

2. Unmixt with faith, the scripture gives
   No comfort, life, or light to me,
But darker still the dark it leaves,
   Implung'd in deeper misery,
Or'whelm'd with nature's sorest ills.
The Spirit saves, the letter kills.

3. Most wretched comforters are they
   Who bid "On the bare word rely!"
Physicians of no price, they say
   I must the promises apply,
And, destitute of inward sense,
Draw all my consolations thence.

4. Their counsels aggravate my grief,
   (But never move the heart of stone)
Insult my helpless unbelief,
   Who cannot find a God unknown,
While without eyes they bid me look
And read the seal'd, unfolded book.

5. If God inlighten thro' his word,
   I shall my kind Inlightener bless:
   But void, and naked of my Lord
   What are all verbal promises?
   Nothing to me, till faith divine
   Inspire, inspeak, and make them mine.

6. Jesus, th' appropriating grace
   Tis thine on sinners to bestow.
   Open mine eyes to see thy face,
   Open my heart to thyself to know.
   And then I thro' thy word obtain
   Sure present, and eternal gain.[21]

Charles Wesley's hymn "Come Divine Interpreter" explicitly describes the Bible as a mystical text that is only understood by illumination. Moreover, the reception of divinely interpreted Scripture has eschatological import—the one who searches the Scriptures, prays, and is obedient to what is revealed will reign with Christ in glory:

> Come, divine Interpreter,
> Bring me eyes thy book to read,
> Ears the mystic words to hear,
> Words which did from thee proceed,
> Words that endless bliss impart,
> Kept in an obedient heart.
>
> All who read, or hear, are blessed,
> If Thy plain commands we do;
> Of Thy kingdom here possessed,
> Thee we shall in glory view
> When thou comest on earth to abide,
> Reign triumphant at thy side.[22]

The vast majority of hymns that Wesleyans sing are based either loosely or explicitly on biblical texts, making hymnody one of the primary ways that Wesleyans engage Scripture for Christian formation. In addition to traditional hymns such as "Holy, Holy, Holy" (written by Reginald Heber), Wesleyans within and beyond The United Methodist Church use many other contemporary worship songs that are based on Scripture or that teach a biblical text. While some liturgically oriented Wesleyans criticize all contemporary worship (anything written after 1965 and meant for accompaniment with a guitar or band) as being theologically vacuous, a large number of newly composed worship songs are Scripture set to music.

Today, as in the beginnings of the Methodist movement, the use of music to embed theological beliefs in the community of faith cannot be overestimated. We should not be surprised at the "worship wars" experienced in Wesleyan churches over the past two decades, as new songs and styles of music have made their way into staid, traditional churches. Charles and John Wesley experienced the same kind of resistance upon introducing "Christ the Lord Is Risen Today" to a skeptical and entrenched church.

Phoebe Palmer and Naked Faith in the Naked Word

As we move forward in the unfolding Methodist story, we come to the rise of the American Methodist Holiness Movement, whose mother is Phoebe Palmer. With Palmer (1807–1874), whose greatest stated goal in the Christian life was to be a "Bible Christian," we once again encounter the tension between kataphatic and apophatic spiritualities with regard to reading, praying with, and living God's Word revealed in the Bible.[23] Like Wesley before her, Palmer publicly eschewed what she thought of as mysticism and would never have called herself a mystic. In her quest to be a Bible Christian, however, she became a Christian mystic on par with St. Catherine of Genoa, St. Thérése of Lisieux, and many other spiritual giants over the ages. What is pertinent to our discussion is that Palmer's Wesleyan spirituality is focused on reading, believing, praying with, and living into what is revealed in the Bible. Being a "Bible Christian" is all about sanctification—holiness of heart and life.

Palmer, along with her sister, Sarah Lankford, led the Tuesday Meetings for the Promotion of Holiness and was the first woman to lead a mixed-gender class meeting in New York (beginning in 1839). Eventually Palmer became a highly sought-after speaker at holiness camp meetings, the author of eighteen books and numerous articles on holiness, the editor for *Guide to Holiness*, the cofounder of Five Points Mission, which was the first Protestant inner-city ministry in the United States, and many other justice ministries. By the time of her death, Palmer is credited with having led more than 25,000 people to faith in Christ.[24] All of these accomplishments were outgrowths of her determination to be a "Bible Christian."

Palmer's move into the public arena took place after a crisis of faith during a time of deep grief in 1837. Out of a series of personal tragedies involving the deaths of three of her children, combined with her inability to make sense of her inherently apophatic spirituality in a kataphatic Methodist revival context, Palmer developed a method of prayer and sanctification called "the shorter way." The shorter way and its corollary "altar theology" became the foundation for her extraordinary influence over the development of the Holiness Movement. Both of these were built on what Palmer called "naked faith in the naked word of God."[25] By "naked faith" Palmer meant faith in God's word apart from one's affective state, apart from whether one felt "assurance" or not. (Here she differed from Wesley, who through most of his years of ministry focused on the need for assurance because of his distaste for apophatic spirituality.) By "naked word" she meant the Bible functioning as the voice of the Holy Spirit, speaking clearly and nakedly to the open-hearted reader. Palmer's exegetical method was patterned after Wesley's in that the plain sense of the text (the naked word) was to be preferred over abstract reasoning that obscured the meaning of the text. In a way, "naked word" was a hermeneutical version of Ockham's razor, where the simplest and most obvious meaning that makes the least amount of new assumptions is usually the right one. "Naked word" did not refer to a fundamentalist reading of the text.

Sadly, the profound insight Palmer discovered about trusting in God's word revealed in the Bible, regardless of the presence or absence of affective phenomenon, caused subsequent interpreters of Palmer to distort her theology. Many of them were holiness camp meeting preachers and teachers who advanced a naïve, literalist reading of the text so that "naked faith in the naked word" came to be seen as a rejection of anything except a simplistic, fundamentalist reading of the Bible. Palmer's apophasia, born in the depths of her own dark night of the soul, became in many of her theological descendants a clichéd resistance to all critical thought or nuanced readings of Scripture. It became a quick-and-easy formula for claiming that one had received "entire sanctification."

One of Palmer's greatest achievements was in writing *Promise of the Father,* an unprecedented, protofeminist apologetic for women's right to engage in public ministry. Based on careful and critical biblical exegesis and a strong pneumatology, Palmer argues that because the Holy Spirit gifts and calls women as well as men to prophetic and evangelistic work, the church has no right to suppress the public ministry gifts of women, including speaking ministries.

Promise of the Father is important to our understanding of Wesleyan approaches to reading the Bible for Christian formation on several levels. First, it demonstrates that she was not promoting fundamentalist, naïve methods of biblical interpretation. She was following Wesley in her method of searching the Scripture and in her use of many of the critical tools of her day for Bible study.

Second, Palmer's reading of the Bible led her to advance gender equality in the church and in society at large. Among her disciples were women's suffrage leader Francis Willard (1839–1898), who was influenced by Palmer's Christian formation with regard to justice for women. Other faithful followers of Palmer were William and Catherine Booth, founders of the Salvation Army. It is clear that for Palmer, as for Wesley, the Bible was not just a means for private spiritual growth and comfort. It was the voice of God calling people to prophetic words and actions even in the face of harsh opposition.

Third, Palmer's apophatic spirituality was based on her deep conviction that God can and will speak a living word through the Bible to the reader whose heart is open and listening. Palmer teaches that the Christian's responsibility is to exercise naked faith in that naked word, because God, not our shifting experiences of God, is the one we worship. These three principles remain at the core of Wesleyan approaches to reading the Bible for Christian formation.

Contemporary Trends

During the final decades of the twentieth century, a number of renewal movements and efforts sprang up in Methodism, all of them in one way or another harkening to Wesley's principles and practices for reading the Bible for Christian formation. Some of these renewal efforts included Good News and the Confessing Movement, and the charismatic Aldersgate Renewal Movement. These groups express an evangelical form of Methodism that is somewhat closer to Wesley's original understanding of the Bible as revealing the word of God, though there is still a strong element of biblical inerrancy to these movements. There is also among these groups a more concerted effort to reunite personal piety with social holiness in the manner of Wesley's original vision for scriptural holiness.

In the late 1980s, the first phase of the *Disciple Bible Study* curriculum was created to provide Methodists of diverse theological commitments a means to re-engage Scripture in depth for the purpose of growth in Christian formation.[26] The resource swept the nation, bringing many Methodists back to a rigorous practice of daily Bible reading and reflection in order to prepare for each week's class. *Disciple Bible Study* resources include video recordings of professional theologians as well as other Bible study tools to provide congregations with up-to-date scholarly information about each text. Persons leading the Bible studies are required to go through training in order to maximize the effectiveness of the materials in congregants' lives. By 2001 the final installment of *Disciple Bible Study* curriculum was published. At the time of this writing, more than 1.5 million people have participated in *Disciple Bible Studies*, the series has been translated into Spanish, and additional curricula have been developed to further aid congregations in ministries of Christian formation.

Additional ways that many contemporary Methodists read the Bible for Christian formation include the use of a daily office such as the Orders of Daily Praise and Prayer found in *The United Methodist Hymnal*.[27] Other widely used Methodist daily devotional resources include *A Guide to Prayer for Ministers and Other Servants*, which has Scripture readings arranged according to weekly theological topics but includes Sunday readings based upon the New Common Lectionary.[28] A more recent prayer guide that uses daily Scripture readings is *This Day: A Wesleyan Way of Prayer*, organized according to days of the week, the liturgical calendar, and with special attention to occasions such as grief and prayers for those with mental illness.[29] There are, of course, a host of other devotional materials that are regularly used by Methodists that include Bible reading, most notably *The Upper Room*, which is a quarterly guide that provides a short reading, Scripture passage, and very brief prayer. Many of these short devotional tools can be used in just ten minutes per day, a practice that is better than nothing but a far cry from Wesley's process of "Searching the Scriptures."

One of the most widespread means of providing Christian formation through Scripture in Wesleyan congregations is through the use of the *Revised Common Lectionary* in preaching and teaching within the church. The *Lectionary* is organized into cycles of three years so that over the course of three years most (but not all) of the Bible is read and used in teaching and worship. While many in the Wesleyan traditions use the *Lectionary* faithfully, its use is not required in The United Methodist Church. A substantial number of clergy prefer to use systematic readings, preaching series, and teaching methods that engage congregants with the entire text of the Bible, teaching through whole books of the Bible for example. For these Wesleyans, the *Lectionary*'s omission of troublesome verses in the Psalms of lament, for example, is unacceptable because it prevents readers from grappling with the whole text of the Bible. It is hard to imagine John Wesley or Phoebe Palmer agreeing to these omissions.

Seven Practices for Wesleyans Today

This brief overview of ways in which the Bible has been used for Christian formation in Wesleyan contexts is not exhaustive. It should suffice, however, as an orientation toward Wesleyan methods for the formative reading of Scripture. Seven practices mark a truly Wesleyan approach to reading the Bible for Christian formation:

1. Approach the text *regularly* and *faithfully*. A practice requires just that—practice. There is no substitute for regular time apart for prayer and searching the Scriptures. As in Wesley's Preface to *The Explanatory Notes upon the Old Testament*, it is best to cultivate a daily habit, to find a quiet place with minimal distractions, and to be faithful to the practice over the long haul.
2. Approach the text *respectfully*, in order to grow in holiness of heart and life. Though it is certainly possible to study the Bible as literature or to approach it in any number of critical stances, the truly Wesleyan orientation is toward holy transformation for the salvation of the world. This means coming to the text with our hearts and lives as well as our minds.
3. Approach the text *prayerfully*, asking the Holy Spirit to illumine our reading. There is an inherent mysticism to the Wesleyan way of searching the Scriptures because the prayer, hope, and expectation is that a faithful practice will result in transformative encounters with God. Simply put, praying with Scripture will change our lives and help us to become more like Christ.
4. Approach the text *responsibly*, using sound exegetical and hermeneutical practices and all the tools of research that are at our disposal.

Wesleyans do not fear academic rigor when applied to the biblical text. But the tools of scholarship are used to further open the meaning of the text so that readers can deepen in holiness of heart and life.

5. Approach the text *hospitably*, listening to and learning from the voices of others in communities of interpretation, so that we may gain wisdom from one another. In Wesley's day this meant consulting Bible commentaries from antiquity up to his own time and learning from their insights. In our day this means learning from other scholars and official commentators as Wesley did but also learning from communities of interpretation that have been historically overlooked or silenced, including women, racially, ethnically, and culturally marginalized people, incarcerated persons, survivors of violence, and others.[30]

6. Approach the text *humbly*, willing to be challenged, comforted, convicted, and given guidance for our lives individually and for us as communities of faith. Wesleyans today are ready to be "shaped by the word," to borrow from the title of Robert Mulholland's book about reading the Bible for Christian formation.[31]

7. Approach the text *incarnationally*, ready to live into whatever the Holy Spirit reveals through the Bible. Here the Wesleyan approach is very much the same as *lectio divina*. It is a contemplative life that is grounded in the love of God, anchored in a posture of worship; a life oriented toward God in all things, ready to live the healing, liberating, renewing, and forgiving gospel of God revealed in Jesus Christ. The Wesleyan approach is one of radical commitment to participate in the life of Christ in the world.

In the end, the test of a particular method of reading the Bible for Christian formation is whether readers are actually being formed into faithful Christians by their practice. Is *Disciple Bible Study*, *The Upper Room*, *This Day*, *lectio divina*, or simply reading the Bible day in and day out changing Christians' lives? Are they becoming more loving, more compassionate, more truthful, more prophetic as a result of their engagement with Scripture? A truly Wesleyan practice of reading the Bible for Christian formation is one in which the reader prays and takes action as a result of what is read. Increasing holiness of heart and life—a holiness that is deeply personal and inward and is profoundly social and outward—is the test of whether one's approach to Scripture is in keeping with a Wesleyan vision.

15

THE PLACE OF SCRIPTURE IN WORSHIP

Karen B. Westerfield Tucker

Scripture and Worship
Warrant, Example, Substance

"It is written, 'Worship the Lord your God, and serve only him'" (Matt 4:10; Luke 4:8, NRSV; cf. Deut 6:13-14). With these words, spoken in the context of his dispute with the Adversary, Jesus summarized the principle repeated throughout the OT: that the people of God—along with the rest of the inhabitants of earth and heaven—are meant to ascribe worth and adulation to the one true God. This precept was reiterated in the NT, though now that worship was redefined to include God revealed both as the one sought by magi (Matt 2:2) and enthroned as the Lamb (Rev 22:3), and as the one who by his Spirit teaches us from the very depths of the divine being (1 Cor 2:10-12; cf. Matt 28:19; 2 Cor 13:14). Scripture supplies the warrant for worship, which in the Christian dispensation is to be done "in spirit and truth" (John 4:23-24, NRSV).

Scripture identifies and describes practices related to worship. The OT furnishes detailed directions for occasions of worship (e.g., Exod 40:1-33; Lev 1-7, 16), but such instructions or models are absent relative to Christian worship. The NT does speak of worship on the Sabbath (and discloses the controversies Jesus provoked by performing certain actions on that day, e.g., Matt 12:1-14) and also on the first day of the week (cf. Acts 20:7; 1 Cor 16:2). Temple, synagogue, private homes (e.g., Acts 2:46-47), and even a jail (Acts 16:25) were among the venues for Christian gatherings characterized by thankfulness (Col 3:15-17; 1 Thess 5:16-18), spiritual sacrifices of praise (Rom 12:1; Heb 13:15), and encouragement of the ethical concern for neighbor (Luke 10:27; Acts 2:44-45; Heb 13:16). In his first letter to the church at Corinth, Paul comments on components of worship engaged in by that community: prophecy or revelation, speaking in tongues, and their interpretation; the exposition of Scripture; the singing of hymns; and a Lord's Supper with a meal (11:5, 17-34; 14:1-19, 26-33; cf. Acts 2:42, 46; Eph 5:19-20; Col 3:16). Other worship practices that can be ascertained include prayer (e.g., Matt 6:5-8; Acts 2:42), preaching (e.g., Acts 13:16-41), fasting (Acts 13:2-3; 14:23), and baptism (Rom 6:5; Eph 1:5-6; Col 2:14).

Scripture also provides the substance of worship—both in antiquity and over the course of Christian history. The NT itself appears to contain fragments of liturgical texts known to the communities of the authors and redactors: sermons (e.g., perhaps the four Gospels themselves), prayers (e.g., the initial and concluding greetings in the epistles), hymns (e.g., John 1:1-5; Phil 2:5-11; Col 1:15-20), and confessions of faith (e.g., Matt 16:16; Rom 10:9-10; 1 Cor 12:3). Paul's version of the Last Supper account likely has a liturgical origin (1 Cor 11:23-26) as do the "in the name" phrases stated in relation to baptism (e.g., Matt 28:19; Acts 2:38-39). Christians of later generations have quoted, paraphrased, or alluded to these and other scriptural texts in developing the contents of their own worship. Across the span of time and geography, there has been widespread (though not universal) use in Christian worship of the Psalms, scriptural canticles, the Lord's Prayer, and the NT "formulae" for baptism and Supper.

These three connecting points between Scripture and worship—with Scripture providing the warrant for worship, examples and descriptions of worship, and the substance and content of worship—shaped the worship praxis that emerged within the Methodist movement. John and Charles Wesley commented in prose and poetry on these multiple layers of connection between Scripture and worship, and they also took up practices developed from those connections, thereby laying what may be identified as a theological and liturgical foundation for worship in what would become the Methodist denominations. Following an examination of this foundation, these Wesleyan "principles" for Scripture and worship will be considered in relation to current worship practices within the Wesleyan/Methodist family in the U.S.

SCRIPTURE AND WORSHIP
The Wesleys

Scripture as Warrant for Worship

As children growing up in an Anglican rectory, the brothers Wesley learned that the family and public worship led by their father (and mother) was offered in response to the mandates of God recorded in Scripture.[1] In the 1662 *Book of Common Prayer*'s offices of Morning and Evening Prayer, they repeatedly heard about God's directives for confession ("the Scripture moveth us, in sundry places, to acknowledge and confess our manifold sins and wickedness") and for praise (Psalms 67, 95, 98, 100; and the canticles Benedicte, omnia opera,[2] Benedictus,[3] Magnificat[4]).[5] During the liturgy for Holy Communion, in which the Decalogue was recited in the form of a litany, they listened to the reading of the fourth commandment to "keep holy the Sabbath day" and replied, "Lord, have mercy upon us, and incline our hearts to keep this law."[6] While preparing for the rite of confirmation, they memorized the scripturally based answer to the Catechism's question, "What is thy duty towards God?": "My duty towards God, is to believe in him, to fear him, and to love him with all my heart, with all my mind, with all my soul, and with all my strength; to worship him, to give him thanks, to put my whole trust in him, to call upon him, to honour his holy Name and his Word, and to serve him truly all the days of my life."[7] Direct study and reflection on the Bible deepened for them what was briefly stated as scriptural warrant in the Church of England's liturgy and catechism. Thus, for the Wesley brothers as adult churchmen, the scriptural basis for Christian worship of the Three-One God was assumed and thus needed no elaboration, and could be firmly taught to the worshiping people.[8]

What did require amplification and comment was the exercise of worship by clergy and laity in their day. Uninspired and perfunctory worship—which was how the Wesleys and others assessed the situation, especially within the Church of England—was little better than no worship at all. The Methodist movement therefore arose in part with the intention of applying a scriptural corrective: to "stir up all parties, Christians or heathens, to worship God in spirit and in truth."[9] The necessity of worship offered "in spirit and in truth" (cf. John 4:23-24) permeated the writings of both brothers and thus formed a central theme in Methodist worship praxis and liturgical identity. Charles, referencing both John 4:24 and 2 Tim 3:4, defined this preferred approach to worship: "God is a Spirit, and they that worship him must worship him in spirit and in truth. He requires the heart; a spiritual not a mere literal obedience, the power of godliness and not the bare form."[10] John provided a fuller interpretation of the biblical directive by referencing additional scriptural sources:

> "What is it to worship God, a Spirit, in spirit and in truth?" Why, it is to worship him with our spirit; to worship him in that manner which none but spirits are capable of. It is to believe in him as a wise, just, holy being, of purer eyes than to behold iniquity; and yet merciful, gracious, and longsuffering; forgiving iniquity and transgression and sin; casting all our sins behind his back, and accepting us in the beloved. It is to love him, to delight in him, to desire him, with all our heart and mind and soul and strength; to imitate him we love by purifying ourselves, even as he is pure; and to obey him whom we love, and in whom we believe, both in thought and word and work. Consequently one branch of the worshipping God in spirit and in truth is the keeping his outward commandments. To glorify him therefore with our bodies as well as with our spirits, to go through outward work with hearts lifted up to him, to make our daily employment a sacrifice to God, to buy and sell, to eat and drink to his glory: this is worshipping God in spirit and in truth as much as the praying to him in a wilderness.[11]

Such a heartfelt and grateful approach to God "in spirit and in truth" was to characterize the Lord's Day and other occasions of corporate and private worship. This attitude, according to John, had already been appropriated by Methodist assemblies:

> The persons who assemble there are not a gay, giddy crowd, who come chiefly to see and be seen; nor a company of goodly, formal, outside Christians, whose religion lies in a dull round of duties; but a people most of whom do, and the rest earnestly seek to, worship God in spirit and in truth. Accordingly they do not spend their time there bowing and courtesying, or in staring about them, but in looking upward and looking inward, in hearkening to the voice of God, and pouring out their hearts before Him.[12]

However, personal and corporate practices of prayer were only one piece of worship "in spirit and in truth," for such a "godly" orientation was to be directed toward both God and neighbor in every aspect of life ("to buy and sell, to eat and drink to his glory"). The Wesleyan admonition that Methodists engage both in works of piety (e.g., prayer, attendance at public worship, and the sacrament) and in works of mercy (e.g., care for the poor, sick, and needy) was doubtlessly derived from this fuller understanding of engaging in worship "in spirit and in truth." Thus, for the Wesleys, the scriptural warrant was interpreted to mean a worship that took literally and expansively Jesus' word to the Adversary: "Worship the Lord your God, and serve only him."

Scripture as a Resource for Worship Practices

In summarizing his defense of Methodist practices to Scottish detractors, John recorded in his Journal for May 5, 1766:

> My ground is the Bible. Yea, I am a Bible-bigot. I follow it in all things, both great and small.
>
> Therefore, (1) I always use a *short, private prayer* when I attend the public service of God. Do not *you*? Why do you not? Is not this according to the Bible?
>
> (2) I *stand* whenever I sing the praise of God in public. Does not the Bible give you plain precedents for this?
>
> (3) I always *kneel* before the Lord my Maker when I pray in public.
>
> (4) I generally in public use *the Lord's Prayer*, because Christ has taught me when I pray to say . . .
>
> I advise every preacher connected with *me*, whether in England or Scotland, herein to tread in my steps.[13]

As a "Bible-bigot," John saw the Scriptures as a measure for the selection of worship practices, including the use of creeds.[14] Rules established for the Methodists from the 1740s prescribed worship and devotional practices justified according to "God's ordinances," which included attendance at public worship and the Lord's Supper; hearing, reading and meditating on Scripture; private and family prayer; and fasting.[15] The compatibility of worship practices with Scripture was critically important for the Wesleys as was the opposite—the avoidance of practices deemed contrary to Scripture. Charles' hymn based on Isa 8:20 in his *Short Hymns on Select Passages of the Holy Scriptures* (1762) signals the importance of the "sacred standard":

> Doctrines, experiences to try,
> We to the sacred standard fly,
> Assur'd the Spirit of our Lord
> Can never contradict his word:
> Whate'er his Spirit speaks in me,
> Must with the written word agree;
> If not: I cast it all aside,
> As Satan's voice, or nature's pride.[16]

It was on the basis of a perceived contradiction with Scripture that many Methodists took issue with some contents of the *Book of Common Prayer*—for example, the so-called damnatory clauses in the Athanasian Creed, certain prayers in the burial rite, and the absence of a rubric allowing prayer ex tempore—even though on the whole they regarded the Prayer Book as scripturally sound.[17] In 1784 John published an abridgement of the Prayer Book under the title *The Sunday Service of the Methodists* that addressed these and other textual and rubrical problems, yet he still identified the *Common Prayer* as possessing a more "solid, scriptural, rational piety" than any other liturgy he knew.[18]

Biblical evidence, however, did not necessitate employment of a practice. A particular case for John was prayer *to* the saints or the general dead, which was usually defended by reference to the parable of the rich man and Lazarus in which Abraham is invoked (Luke 16:24). In comments on Luke's verse in his *Explanatory Notes upon the New Testament*, John acknowledged the scriptural precedent but then dismissed it, noting, "but who is it that prays, and with what success? Will any, who considers this, be fond of copying after him?"[19] The motivation for rejecting prayer to the dead may in reality have had more to do with ecclesiastical concerns (i.e., identification with Roman Catholic practice) than with scriptural context. Yet John was willing to offer prayer *for* the faithful departed, citing the phrase "Thy Kingdom come" from the Lord's Prayer as proof, since it concerned the "saints in Paradise, as well as those upon earth." The validation of prayer for the departed was also substantiated by a source that, although less an authority than Scripture, carried significant weight: the theology and customs of Christians from the first three centuries.[20]

The Wesleys' desire to appropriate the practices of what they perceived to be true, uncorrupted, and "scriptural" Christianity meant that Christian worship could include services, ritual components, or actions for which there was no specific biblical warrant—as long as God's word was not contradicted. Methodists, drawing on hints in Scripture as well as early Christian praxis for their models, worshiped at love feasts (the ancient agape) and watch nights (vigils) that were judged to be both scriptural and apostolic.[21] With this approach to Scripture, the Wesleys stood apart from the Puritan wing within the Church of England (with which they were sometimes associated) and others that held the belief that God forbade anything that had not been explicitly commanded in Holy Writ (*Quod non jubet, vetat*). The Bible, insisted John, was the "supreme" rule of Christian worship but not the only rule; indeed "there may be a thousand rules subordinate to this, without any violation of it at all." Paul's assertion that "all things should be done decently and in order" (1 Cor 14:40) when speaking to the Corinthians meant that Christians of other places and of later generations could take up different practices while conforming to Paul's directive: thus, "not repugnant to, but plainly flowing from this, are the subordinate rules concerning the time and place of divine service."[22] Christian communities could engage in unique or shared practices of worship as long as they were judged to conform to and not violate scriptural intention; a shared scriptural methodology across communities—a "catholic spirit"—might have the added result, John posited, of a deepened Christian unity.[23]

Scripture as the Substance and Content of Worship

Words from Scripture permeated the Lord's Day liturgy of the Anglican cathedral and parish church, which typically was Morning Prayer followed by the Order for the Administration of the Lord's Supper up to the beginning of the communion liturgy proper (the "antecommunion"). At a minimum of three times each year, the Lord's Supper order was done in its entirety. Scripture was heard by direct quotation: in single verses (at the beginning and end of Morning Prayer and during the collection of alms and other monies in the antecommunion), in short passages (e.g., the Decalogue litany, the Lord's Prayer, and the eucharistic words of institution), and through large sections of the NT and chapters from the OT and Psalms as determined by the lectionary. Biblical phrases were scattered in collects and longer prayers, and interwoven to create a new composite text (e.g., the *Gloria in Excelsis Deo*, which borrows from Luke 2:14; John 1:29; Heb 10:12). Other liturgical components, such as the Apostles' and Nicene Creeds, were derived from scriptural texts and their exegesis. The priest's sermon referenced Scripture as might the anthem of a choir. In some parishes, tablets on the wall displayed the words of the Ten Commandments.

Methodist public worship was originally intended to supplement the Anglican liturgy; its simplicity presupposed attendance at the Church's public prayer, for if it had been "designed to be instead of Church Service, it would be essentially defective."[24] Even so, the leaders of the preaching services and the more access-restricted love feasts and watch nights still stressed the reading and hearing of God's word, although a fewer number of Scripture texts were offered when compared to the parish liturgy. A Psalm or a chapter from the Old or New Testament might be read and expounded, though the Methodist preachers often simply "took a text"—one or more verses on which they would sermonize or exhort. Methodist personal and family worship, and worship within the bands and societies, complemented the public gathering, for Bible reading and meditation on the Scriptures were expected as part of the twice daily engagement of worship "in spirit and in truth." John Wesley, by both personal example and practical advice, encouraged the reading of a chapter from each of the Testaments, a practice he had known since his childhood.[25] Serious and earnest prayer was to precede and follow the readings, since Scripture could "only be understood thro' the same Spirit whereby 'it was given.'"[26] Scrupulous Methodist individuals and families that coupled more informal worship with Morning and Evening Prayer would have read or heard several biblical chapters and selected verses each day.

Scripture was also heard at Methodist public worship by other means. If the worship leaders so desired, the Prayer Book's collects (with their scriptural snippets and allusions), and the Lord's Prayer might be used.[27] The extemporary or spontaneous prayer offered might employ the style preferred by many Methodists that interspersed biblical paraphrases and inferences and sometimes pseudo-direct quotation (on account of faulty memory).

No Methodist gathering for prayer and praise was without Scripture-rich hymns by Watts, the Wesleys, and other evangelical poets.[28] The hymns of Charles Wesley in particular were a catena—a chain—of Scripture phrases and paraphrases designed to speak to the human spirit and to a range of theological, spiritual, liturgical, and practical topics. Portions from Old and New Testaments were woven together to create a lyrical fabric of praise, confession or petition. Thus, for example, Deut 28:65; Ps 106:4; Isa 57:15; and Matt 9:36 are embedded in

> Love divine, all loves excelling,
> Joy of heaven, to earth come down,
> Fix in us thy humble dwelling,
> All thy faithful mercies crown;
> Jesu, thou art all compassion,
> Pure, unbounded love thou art,
> Visit us with thy salvation,
> Enter every trembling heart.[29]

Charles also engaged in intentional poetic exegesis by paraphrasing and amplifying scriptural passages in verse. For example, a hymn from the *Hymns on the Lord's Supper* (1745) interprets the Emmaus narrative (Luke 24:13-35, esp. vv. 30-32) as an encounter of present-day disciples with the risen Lord:

> O thou who this mysterious bread
> Didst in *Emmaus* break,
> Return herewith our souls to feed
> And to thy followers speak.
>
> Unseal the volume of thy grace,
> Apply the Gospel-word,
> Open our eyes to see thy face
> Our hearts to know the Lord.
>
> Of thee we commune still, and mourn
> Till thou the veil remove,
> Talk with us, and our hearts shall burn
> With flames of fervent love.
>
> Inkindle now the heavenly zeal,
> And make thy mercy known,
> And give our pardon'd souls to feel
> That God and love are one.[30]

Charles' two-volume exegetical *Short Hymns on Select Passages of the Holy Scriptures* (1762) was not intended only for reflection on the Scripture text and for song, but also, as he noted in the preface of the first volume, to prove and to guard the doctrine of Christian perfection through several of the hymn texts.[31] Yet, even in these hymns, as was true for the *Lord's Supper* hymn, Charles drew on a wealth of scriptural language and images. The so-called "covenant hymn," used at least from 1778 for the annual Methodist service of covenant renewal,[32] came from Charles' *Short Hymns* setting of Jeremiah 50:5 that focused on the second half of the verse: "they shall come and join themselves to the Lord by an everlasting covenant that will never be forgotten" (NRSV). The first stanza neatly places verse 5 in meter and concludes with an allusion to Rom 14:8:

> Come, let us use the grace divine,
> And all, with one accord,
> In a perpetual covenant join
> Ourselves to *Christ* our Lord,
> Give ourselves up thro' *Jesu's* power
> His name to glorify,
> And promise in this sacred hour
> For God to live, and die.

As the hymn develops in the second stanza, Scripture from other sources is drawn upon to support the supposition in the first stanza, such as Exod 25:22; Josh 24:16; 1 Chr 16:15; Job 15:4; and Pss 50:17; 61:5:

> The covenant we this moment make
> Be ever kept in mind!
> We will no more our God forsake,
> Or cast his words behind;
> We never will throw off his fear,
> Who hears our solemn vow:
> And if thou art well-pleas'd to hear,
> Come down, and meet us now![33]

Since in the eighteenth century hymn singing was not permitted during the Church of England's services (there was, however, an allowance for hymn singing before or afterwards), those who attended Methodist public worship and sang the hymns experienced and engaged with Scripture in a new way. Placed with a suitable and engaging tune, the metrical paraphrases of Scripture were believed to be capable of raising or quickening the spirit of devotion, confirming faith, enlivening hope, and kindling or increasing love to God and neighbor.[34]

Worship specifically designated as "Methodist" took on a new dimension with John Wesley's publication of *The Sunday Service of the Methodists* in 1784. Although at the beginning of the Methodist movement most participants in "Methodist" worship were familiar with the Anglican liturgy, by 1780 those numbers had decreased, and the simple Methodist components of prayer, Scripture reading, preaching, and hymn were the extent of their liturgical diet. Certainly many Methodists in the newly emancipated U.S. by choice or geography did not affiliate with the parish church. Nevertheless, John believed that worship according to the Prayer Book, even an abridged book, to be best suited for the Methodist people in America and in "His Majesty's Dominions."

Remarkably, among the alterations John made to the Prayer Book was a reduction in the number of Scripture readings—in Morning and Evening Prayer, in the alternative texts supplied in occasional services (e.g., the burial rite), and in the lectionary (for saints days and holy days).[35] There had been a long-standing concern about the "longsomeness" of the Prayer Book liturgies, and that may have been the rationale. Despite the deletions, Scripture readings still were plentiful with OT readings designated for Morning and Evening Prayer on Sundays, Sunday Epistles and Gospel lections as per the Prayer Book, and a thirty-day cycle of Psalm readings specified for morning or evening use.

Two other changes in the *Sunday Service* in regard to Scripture are particularly worthy of note. First, all readings from the Apocrypha were omitted, with one (inexplicable) exception: Tob 4:8-9 remained among the offertory sentences in the Order for the Lord's Supper. John had previously objected to classifying the Apocrypha as Holy Scripture,[36] and his revision of the Thirty-Nine Articles in Religion (located in the final pages of the *Book of Common Prayer*) deftly removed the listing of the Apocrypha from under the article "Of the Sufficiency of the Holy Scriptures for Salvation."[37] Second, Wesley deleted thirty-four Psalms from the Psalter and altered fifty-eight others because he found the material "highly improper for the mouths of a Christian Congregation."[38] Editing of the Psalter, and particularly the excision of the so-called "cursing" or "imprecatory" psalms, had been done prior to Wesley's time and concerns had again arisen about the matter in his day. A book Wesley read in 1750,[39] *Free and Candid Disquisitions* by John Jones, suggested that to avoid unsuitable material certain Psalms could be selected for the church's liturgical use in the same fashion that Epistle and Gospel lessons had been chosen,[40] and Wesley's inspiration may have come in part from that source. "Select Psalms" constituted the largest section in the *Sunday Service*, thereby indicating Wesley's desire to keep the long-standing Christian tradition of psalmody—even in an edited form—in Methodist devotional and liturgical practice.

SCRIPTURE AND WORSHIP
The Inheritance

The various contributions of the Wesleys that speak to a scriptural accounting of worship and the selection of Scripture-derived components of worship, when taken together, could be said to constitute a theological and liturgical foundation of worship for the people called Methodist. The Wesleys observed that Scripture identified worship as a gift—as well as an ordinance—from God: "to be admitted to worship his God is doubtless the highest honour wherewith a creature can be blest and to devote ourselves entirely to his service is only to be secured of our title to this dignity and prominence which the king of heaven and earth allows us."[41] The gift of worship was to be received and utilized by the entirety of creation, and especially the human creature, whose performance of this duty and delight was to permeate all of life and so shape interactions with both God and neighbor. Liturgical forms provided structure and substance for this worship, but such forms, though useful, could not substitute for the power of godliness found in a penitent, obedient, and generous heart. The Bible (without Apocrypha) set the standard for the forms to be used by providing specific models and conceptual ideals against which practices could be judged. Since Scripture had been provided by God to make known God's love, mercy, and justice, Scripture was accorded a central place in public and private worship through reading, exposition, and poetic paraphrase. In worship the faithful as well as inquirers could "hear, read, mark, learn, and inwardly digest" God's word in order to "embrace and ever hold fast the blessed hope of everlasting life" given in Christ,[42] and anticipate the coming day of "continual enjoyment of the Three-One God, and of all the creatures in him."[43]

By 1784 the Methodists in North America had received through several means this theological and liturgical foundation and inherited two quite different styles of worship for the Lord's Day: the informal preaching service and other services of similar construction and ethos, and the formal liturgies of Morning and Evening Prayer and the Order for the Administration of the Lord's Supper from the *Sunday Service*. Methodists in Britain, as "culturally" Anglican, were, for the most part, able to hold together the two different types of worship, and many preferred the Prayer Book to Wesley's version. Not so in the U.S., where although the *Sunday Service* had been officially adopted in 1784 at the founding of the Methodist Episcopal Church, the majority of Methodists keenly preferred "freedom" to "form." Thus in 1792, the year after John Wesley's death, the Sunday-related liturgies and liturgical aids in the *Sunday Service* were laid aside, and in their place extended rubrics were supplied in a section on "Public Worship" in the *Doctrines and Discipline of the Methodist Episcopal Church* that outlined the four components of Lord's Day worship specified for the sake of uniformity across the denomination: singing, prayer, Scripture reading, and preaching. Despite the loss of lectionary and Select Psalms,[44] John Wesley's ideal of two chapters daily persisted for the Sunday morning service (one from each Testament); the afternoon service was to include "one chapter out of the Bible," and no Scripture reading was recommended for the evening service. An additional instruction stating that "on the days of administering the Lord's Supper, the two chapters in the morning-service may be omitted" had the unfortunate result of separating word from sacrament.[45] In their interpretation of these directions, the bishops of the young denomination nevertheless stressed the importance of Scripture in corporate worship:

> Our church insists on the reading of the Scriptures in the congregation, and gives directions accordingly. This is of the utmost consequence, and we trust will be most sacredly observed by all our ministers and preachers. A peculiar blessing accompanies the public reading as well as preaching the word of God to attentive, believing souls. And in these days of infidelity, nothing should be omitted, which may lead the people to the love of the holy bible.[46]

With some adjustments (e.g., the expectation of a concluding "Apostolic Benediction" [2 Cor 13:14]), the rubrical guidelines persisted throughout the nineteenth century in the Methodist Episcopal *Discipline* and in the books of polity of other Wesleyan/Methodist denominations as they emerged, though in reality congregations likely heard far less than the prescribed norm, given the custom of reading only a sermon "text." By the end of the nineteenth century, the word "chapter" was replaced with "lesson," perhaps in acknowledgement of the common practice.[47] At the same time, the responsive reading of the Psalms started to figure in many congregations whose worship also added other scripturally related elements (e.g., Apostles' Creed and Gloria Patri) to expand beyond the simple four stipulated in 1792. Scripture and its interpretation remained arguably the single most important feature of worship throughout the twentieth century (with the sermon/meditation/homily typically given more weight than the scriptural text[s] by both preacher and congregation) even as the level of biblical literacy in the pew (and perhaps also in the pulpit) declined.[48]

Scripture and Worship
The Current Reality

In the second decade of the twenty-first century, worship in the broad Methodist family in the United States can best be described as diverse since, despite the presence of denominationally "authorized" orders of worship, no liturgical form is mandated. Worship styles range from the traditional (and simple) four-component Methodist preaching service amplified with an array of musical instruments and technological innovations to a (more complex) format of "word and sacrament" that, in reaping the harvest of the liturgical and ecumenical movements, recapitulates the experience of the disciples on the road to Emmaus who perceived Christ in the breaking open of the word and in the breaking of bread. Services may be intentionally designed to appeal to the spiritual, emotional, and musical preferences of worshippers (churched and seeker)—addressing in addition concerns related to evangelism and institutional survival. Scriptural precedent is sometimes argued by worship's planners to be the basis of or inspiration for a particular style, with, for example, selected Psalms cited to justify a "praise and worship" scheme. The reading of Scripture has a place in each arrangement: on a given Sunday, OT, Psalm (perhaps chanted by using a psalm tone), Epistle, and Gospel lections may be heard in one congregation (likely following the calendar and table of readings in the Revised Common Lectionary[49]); in another, a single verse is announced as the springboard for the sermon (which itself may contain a smattering of Scripture citations); in yet another, there may be one or more readings chosen from a lectionary or selected according to the inclinations of pastor and/or congregation. Reversing the nineteenth-century rubric on Scripture reading, the *Book of Worship* of the African Methodist Episcopal Zion Church advises: "This should not be a random passage, but should include the text of the sermon. A 'passage' is not an entire Chapter. Lengthy readings, 20 verses or more, destroy the congregation's ability to focus on the textual reference."[50] Scripture may be read from a Bible located on lectern, pulpit, ambo, or altar-table as an unspoken statement of the status of God's word, or the Bible may be read from the congregation, suggesting God's presence in the midst of the people. For the most part, the Wesleys' desire for worship that adheres to scriptural norms and includes the reading of God's word has been maintained. However, in general the quantity of Scripture read as part of worship in congregations, in families, and in private pales in comparison to what the Wesleys knew and advocated: the competing complexities of modern life have often reduced to a single hour what were once multiple occasions for the worship of God and hearing of God's word.

Remedies to the lean diet of Scripture and the biblical illiteracy that results are already available in the form of liturgical resources provided by many of the Methodist-Wesleyan denominations for their congregations. Lectionaries—the aforementioned Revised Common Lectionary,[51] its predecessor the Common Lectionary (1983),[52] and others[53]—facilitate the systematic hearing of texts from the biblical treasury, including the "hard" texts difficult for the ears of Christian congregations. With the lectionary's assignments, preachers are confronted by the Scripture text and made to consider it as opposed to selecting a passage based on a preconceived agenda. Employment of the lectionary, which is aligned with the ecumenical Christian calendar or liturgical year, allows the readings of the day to be situated within the broader narrative of salvation history, thus enabling a "double" encounter with God's word. Wesleyan/Methodist pastors and congregations from the 1980s have increasingly taken up the discipline of the lectionary but often only read in worship one or two of the provided texts. The notion of a sermon "text" has been slow to put to rest, and many congregations and pastors have yet to appreciate the hearing of Scripture on its own merits independent of development in a sermon. Given that Sunday morning for many in the congregation may be the only time when the Bible is heard, recovery of the Wesleys' practice of having multiple readings would be beneficial at multiple levels. Postmodern questions about authority—including the authority of the Christian Scriptures in relationship to the sacred writings of other traditions—may challenge the liturgical use of Scripture and thereby call for greater attention as to how Methodist-Wesleyan communities understand the Bible to be God's word.

It has already been observed that the embedding of Scripture quotations or allusions in prayers or other liturgical components permits a different manner of engaging the biblical text than does a verse-by-verse reading. The inclusion of texts that are Scripture-rich provides another remedy to minimal exposure, even though the allusions or references may not be immediately identified as scriptural. Since 1972, The United Methodist Church has made available eucharistic prayers (Great Thanksgivings) that knit the biblical narrative into the prayers' structure and content.[54] Truly following John Wesley's advice that worship should "follow the Scriptures and the Primitive Church,"[55] the Great Thanksgivings imitate the classic West Syrian/Antiochene pattern of eucharistic prayers that are Trinitarian in shape and rehearse the story of salvation, concluding with allusions to the messianic banquet yet to come. The United Methodist prayers intentionally incorporate material from the OT (e.g., creation, the prophets) prior to the Sanctus; after the Sanctus, the work of Christ is remembered, and Christ's continuing presence by the power of the Holy Spirit is affirmed. The Lord's Supper prayers are thus credal as well as doxological, and the "remembrance" they offer brings that which was and that which is to come into the sacramental present.

The Holy Spirit has continued to inspire "new songs" in each generation, and the current time is no exception. Scripture is present in various ways in these new hymns and songs; some poets, for example, take up the traditional method of retelling a single scriptural pericope but through the use of language and imagery accessible to the present generation. Because songs may be the principal means by which Scripture is accessed in certain styles of worship, serious attention needs to be given to the text, especially since modern technology has made instantly available songs that likely have not had the benefit of literary or theological review. Scripture may have been used as a proof text to express the particular theological perspective of the writer instead of the comprehensive "rule of faith" professed by the church. The talent of a Charles Wesley, who wove together of disparate strands of Scripture into a multihued tapestry which matched the diversity and unity of the biblical canon, is, unfortunately, rare.

The current reality is that Methodists/Wesleyans, to varying degrees, turn to Scripture for models of their worship and for the substance of their worship. But does Scripture serve as the "warrant" of their worship? Certainly for some. But it appears that such is not the case for others, for, similar to other Christians in the U.S., some are "consumerists" and "individualists" in their approach to worship, electing to attend services in those congregations where personal needs for spiritual direction, emotional affirmation, fellowship, religious education, and the like, can best be met. Worship is measured by what one "gets" out of it, rather than what one offers to almighty God and, subsequently, shares with the neighbor as a gesture of gratitude. Rather than a Godward orientation—"Worship the Lord your God, and serve only him"—worship is about how it makes one feel. Perhaps the time is ripe for a revitalization of Methodism's original intention, to "stir up all parties, Christians or heathens, to worship God in spirit and in truth."

16

THE PLACE OF SCRIPTURE IN PREACHING

Michael Pasquarello III

A recently published collection of essays on the pastoral use of Scripture describes the practice of John Wesley (and Charles) in the following manner:

> While preaching remained central to their project, Sacraments and a high view of the church office fell by the wayside; and for all of the education of the leadership, the incipient experiential pragmatism of the movement raised obvious questions about the need for education over against the ability to produce the desired effect. It was, one might say, at root an anti-intellectual and therefore anti-doctrinal movement. The exegetical and theological skills . . . crucial for any kind of pastoral ministry was ultimately to prove unnecessary within a Christianity conceived of in terms of revivalism.[1]

While I do not think this assessment does justice to Wesley's wisdom and practice, I would agree that it provides a valid description of how he has often been perceived within the tradition that bears his name. What has evolved into a kind of conventional wisdom presents a significant challenge to discerning the place of Scripture in preaching as Wesleyans. And it is true that one of the most challenging obstacles to appreciating Wesley's sermons as authentic theological and exegetical discourse may be the North American tradition of populism, which has its roots in nineteenth-century revivalism. Brooks Holifield writes of American Methodists who largely ignored Wesley's Anglican admiration for patristic sources, his sacramentalism, and his liturgical piety; they appropriated his anti-Calvinism, his revivalism, and his perfectionism, and they reshaped even that by filtering it through the lens of Scottish philosophy, mental science, and the free-wheeling denominational polemics of American popular Christianity.[2]

Wesley's wisdom and practice appear very different if we approach him as a member of the Anglican tradition, as an evangelical and catholic voice who preached during a time when more and more preachers were thinking out their theology—the knowledge of God and the ways of God—in sermons, that is, in "homiletic theology." Seen from this perspective, Wesley was neither a rationalist (reason without revelation) nor enthusiast (revelation above reason); rather, his preaching unites the intellect with will, knowledge with love, in responding to the truth and goodness of God revealed in the whole of Scripture. His was a form of theologically oriented popular preaching that reached thousands of people over the course of more than six decades.[3] This preaching was situated within a life of prayerful study and diligent interpretation of the truths of Scripture that he communicated in a plain style characterized by clarity of thought and simplicity of devotion. This elevation of the Word was accompanied by deep hunger for the church's sacramental life and desire for the rehabilitation of its doctrinal substance to bring about spiritual and moral renewal in the knowledge and love of God.[4]

As a priest of the Church of England and reluctant leader of a movement that sought its evangelical reform, Wesley was "traditioned" into the life of the church within a practical context constituted by Scripture, the confession of doctrine, the liturgy and sacraments, and works of piety and mercy—all means of grace through which the Spirit creates a holy people across time.[5] In many ways, Methodism was a consequence of a reform that began in England at the turn of the sixteenth century and served as a renewing force in parishes, working with common pastoral aims and participating in an educational and missional endeavor that underwrote the dissemination and transmission of evangelical faith and life.[6] Albert Outler writes,

> In the Methodist traditions after his death . . . the rationalists of the Enlightenment discounted tradition, experience and even Scripture, save where it squared with their reading of right reason. Romantics and pietists discounted tradition and reason, except for the purpose of polemics, and turned to experience as their

touchstone for Christian truth, including the truths of Scripture. They boldly appealed to Wesley himself for this privatizing move away for objective standards of doctrine and morality. They could do this, of course, only by ignoring the most distinctive elements in his theology (concealed from them by his chosen habits of simplifying issues.) And yet, one cannot point to another theologian in the eighteenth century with a stronger sense of tradition, in a very broad sense, or whose popular theology was more heavily influenced by what he had learned from his Christian ancestors, both immediate and remote.[7]

Remembering the Wesley in "Wesleyan"

John Wesley was not a good "modern" theologian, exegete, or preacher. Rather his life and ministry unites these modern disciplines in devotion to God and service to others. His work may yet challenge us to see that modernity's advances in empirical knowledge, its increasing dependence on efficient power, and its orientation to the logic of technological thinking, ingenuity, and skill have not nurtured the virtues of faith, hope, and love that engender the "mind of Christ"—that is, the pattern of knowing and loving that, as human creatures, we have been called and redeemed by God to share.[8]

This essay calls attention to the continuing significance of John Wesley as an exemplar of preaching through which the Spirit awakens us to hear with joy the Word God speaks in Scripture. Such enjoyment constitutes a useless, noninstrumental, participative activity with no purpose other than delighting in the extravagant outpouring of love through which the Father communicates his being and life to the Son, who through the work of the Holy Spirit restores human creatures to the divine image.

Because Wesley understood the end of human life as the restoration of the image of God through the gifts of justifying and sanctifying grace, human actions—including the activities of speaking and hearing Scripture—are true and good when directed to God who is known and loved for his own sake, rather than as a means to achieving something else. At the heart of Wesley's vision is a conviction that our truest end is to know, love, and enjoy God so that the witness of preaching springs from and leads back toward doxology, the praise of God's glory. In other words, the content and purpose of preaching are one: bearing faithful witness to the gospel of Jesus Christ through the grace of the Holy Spirit in the church's self-offering of thankful praise to God.[9]

Rather than attempting to repeat what Wesley did, said, and accomplished, our task is to learn from the character and wisdom of Wesley's practice so that we may discern more clearly how to speak in ways that are faithful to God and also fitting for the church's vocation within the particular conditions of our time. Addressing the church's "effectiveness" in terms of its faithfulness, Wesley raises questions worth our consideration in thinking about the place of Scripture in preaching.

> Why has Christianity done so little good in the world? Is it not the balm which the Great Physician has given to men, to restore their spiritual health? . . . I am bold to affirm, that they [who live within Christendom] are in general totally ignorant both as to the theory and practice of Christianity; so that they are "*perishing* by thousands 'for lack of knowledge,' . . . justification by faith, the new birth, inward and outward holiness."[10]

Wesley may yet guide us to see more clearly the practical wisdom of Christian doctrine—the truth confessed by the church according to the scriptural witness to God's gracious work in the narrative of creation, fall, incarnation, and new creation. Faith and practice are united in a way of being and living that is cultivated by coming to know and love the Father through the Spirit who illumines our minds to perceive the form of Christ in particular times, places, and situations. Wesley writes,

> We may learn, hence . . . that this happy knowledge of the true God is only another name for religion; I mean Christian religion, which indeed is the only one that deserves the name. Religion, as to the nature or essence of it, does not lie in this or that set of notions, vulgarly called "faith"; nor in a round of duties, however carefully "reformed" from error or superstition. It does not consist in any number of outward actions. No; it properly and directly consists in the knowledge and love of God, as manifested in the Son of his love, through the eternal Spirit. And this naturally leads to every heavenly temper, and to every good word and work.[11]

Learning to hear and speak God's Word is primarily a matter of having our judgment formed in congruence with the whole witness of Scripture according to the analogy of faith. Moreover, learning to read Scripture according to the analogy of faith engenders preaching that is shaped by the incarnate Wisdom who is the purpose of creation and redemption. The message of preaching—"Scriptural holiness"—is also the medium of preaching. For this reason, there will be congruence among Scripture, what is preached, and the life of those who preach and hear: the restoration of human creatures to the image of God who transforms us from original sin through repentance, justification, and the new birth to entire sanctification.[12] As Wesley happily describes the analogy of faith, which serves as a guide through the whole of Scripture,

> There is a wonderful analogy between all these; and a close and intimate connexion between the chief heads of that faith "which was once delivered to the saints." Every article, therefore, concerning which there is any question should be determined by this rule; every doubtful scripture interpreted according to the grand truths which run through the whole.[13]

Within the Wesleyan tradition, discerning the place of Scripture in preaching is primarily a matter of vocational holiness. By vocational holiness I mean the integrity of personal faith and pastoral vocation: proclaiming a holy gospel will nurture a holy life.[14] As an exemplar of vocational holiness, Wesley directs our attention to what is arguably the most neglected aspect of contemporary homiletics: the transformation of a preacher's life and speech by the living Word we confess and proclaim.

Preaching is an evangelical message *and* way of life shaped by the Word of God incarnate in Christ as mediated by Scripture within the common life of the church. Wesley's practical wisdom therefore directs our attention to the work of the living God who through the means of grace engenders the virtues of faith, hope, and love, the Spirit's gifts and fruit, and a common life of discipleship that leads to holiness and happiness. Learning to preach entails becoming a certain kind of person who knows, loves, and speaks the truth of God revealed in Christ who is apprehended within the whole of Scripture and its way of salvation. Wesley saw the existence of Christian people, including preachers, as dependent on the

> life of God in the soul of a believer [that] is . . . a continual action of God upon the soul, the reaction of the soul upon God; an unceasing presence of God, the loving, pardoning God, manifested in the heart, and perceived by faith; and an unceasing return of love, praise, and

> prayer, offering up all the thoughts of our hearts, all the words of our tongues, all the works of our hands, all our body, soul, and spirit, to be an holy sacrifice, acceptable unto God in Christ Jesus.[15]

This way of being entails a participatory way of knowing through faith in Christ by the Spirit's illumining our minds according to the parts and whole of Scripture. Here it is significant to note that Wesley does not separate learning and devotion, faith and the moral life, Scripture and theology, or grace and its fruit. Preaching is an integrative activity that springs from living faith nourished by prayerful study and loving obedience to the "oracles of God." Wesley writes of Scripture's nature,

> According to [Scripture] it lies in one single point: it is neither more nor less than love—it is love which "is the fulfilling of the law," "the end of the commandment." Religion is the love of God and our neighbor—that is, every man under heaven. This love, ruling the whole life, animating our tempers and passions, directing all our thoughts, words, and actions, is "pure religion and undefiled."[16]

Such tempers, affections, and passions constitute the content and scope of Wesley's sermons—"the essentials of true religion,"[17] which seek to communicate and nurture living faith that matures into holy love and life.[18] But God's work does not negate the importance of a preacher's work; while God and human creatures are distinct, they are not in competition. Rather, the grace of the Holy Spirit works in, with, and through a preacher's life and words to impart the gifts of faith and love that come by gladly hearing and speaking the Word as mediated by the witness of Scripture. Moreover, this freely self-giving love of Christ becomes, by the power of the Holy Spirit, the very structure of a new kind of talking, thinking, and being with one another.[19]

In a sermon prepared during the latter years of his ministry, Wesley inquires, "What is Methodism? What does this new word mean? Is it not a new religion? . . . Methodism, so called, is the old religion, the religion of the Bible, the religion of the primitive church, the religion of the Church of England." He continues,

> And this is the religion of the Church of England, as appears from all her authentic records, from the uniform tenor of her liturgy, and from numberless passages in her Homilies. . . . The scriptural primitive religion of love, . . . is beautifully summed up in that one

comprehensive petition, "Cleanse the thoughts of our hearts by the inspiration of thy Holy Spirit, that we may perfectly love thee, and worthily magnify thy holy name."[20]

Guided by such convictions, Wesley could refer to Scripture as the "oracles of God" that engender faithful preaching by the illuminative and persuasive work of the Spirit. Scripture testifies of itself and its authority for all who receive its promises and cease to rely on their own sufficiency, submitting in penitence of heart to the convicting infusion of God's prevenient grace. Justification by grace through faith in Christ—the forgiveness of sins, reconciliation to God, and a new life centered on God—becomes for receptive hearers the "Scripture way of salvation" discerned and enacted in holy living. Through the Spirit's sanctifying work, then, the knowledge of faith is evinced by a transformation of the mind and heart in love for and conformance to the image of Christ in holiness of life.

Discerning the place of Scripture in preaching will be guided by the conviction that the truth and reality of God are mediated by the testimony of the Spirit to Christ through the whole biblical canon. This calls for a participatory and transformative way of reading and speaking that includes but also exceeds the historical, cultural, and linguistic matters related to the biblical text. In other words, this theological orientation does not exclude the historical and human dimensions of study, ministry, and preaching but rather seeks their completion in God.[21] The distance between Scripture and later generations of preachers and listeners is neither historical nor cultural; it is primarily spiritual and moral and therefore overcome by conversion and transformation of life.

Accordingly, in *An Address to the Clergy*, Wesley counsels ministers to become persons of sound learning, piety, and virtue. He identifies the need for acquiring the capacities of understanding, apprehension, judgment, and reason in relation to a number of subjects: knowledge of the world and of human nature, character, dispositions, and tempers; knowledge of the sciences, natural history, metaphysics, and philosophy; competence in thinking logically and speaking clearly; and acquiring the virtue of courage to speak the truth in love. To these he adds serious engagement with the Fathers of the Church, especially their interpretation of Scripture. Wesley gives strongest emphasis to knowing Scripture, which will entail critical mastery of its original languages, its grammar and genres, as well as a grasp of its parts in relation to the whole—the analogy of faith—as the clue for unfolding its literal and spiritual senses for listeners. At the same time, only the wisdom of God the Divine Teacher is sufficient for bringing to completion these intellectual pursuits and pastoral tasks.

> [Ministers] are assured of being assisted in all their labour by Him who teacheth man knowledge. And who teacheth like Him? Who, like Him, giveth wisdom to the simple? How easy is it for Him, (if we desire it, and believe that he is both able and willing to do this,) by the powerful, though secret, influences of the Spirit, to open and enlarge our understanding; to strengthen all our faculties; to bring to our remembrance whatsoever things are needful, and to fix and sharpen our attention to them; so that we may profit above all who wholly depend upon themselves, in whatever may qualify us for our Master's work.[22]

This participatory way of knowing is evoked by God's self-gift in Christ and appropriated into human life through the Spirit's gifts, empowerments, and fruit, which are received in the worship and common life of the church. Historical interpretation, while important, will be preparation for a reading oriented to the risen Christ revealed through the words of Scripture and its place in shaping the lives of Christian people in the present and future.[23]

Geoffrey Wainwright helpfully summarizes Wesley's integrative vision of knowledge and practice,

> First, he looked to the Scriptures as the primary and abiding testimony to the redemptive work of God in Christ. Second, he was utterly committed to the ministry of evangelism, where the gospel was to be preached to every creature and needed only to be accepted in faith. Third, he valued with respect to the Christian Tradition and the doctrine of the Church a generous orthodoxy, wherein theological opinions might vary as long as they were consistent with the apostolic teaching. Fourth, he expected sanctification to show itself in the moral earnestness and loving deeds of the believers. Fifth, he manifested and encouraged a social concern that was directed toward the neediest of neighbors. Sixth, he found in the Lord's Supper a sacramental sign of the fellowship graciously bestowed by the Triune God and the responsive praise of those who will glorify God and enjoy him forever.[24]

Wesley's "family style" of practice unites theology and exegesis within the life and mission of the church.[25] And while this may not be acceptable by standards determined by specialized, modern theological disciplines, it may indeed be precisely what we need to find our way forward.

This is because Wesley's use of Scripture in preaching helps us to see that hermeneutics and homiletics have much in common. Homiletics needs to involve much more than merely practical training in the construction and delivery of sermons; it needs to be practiced as a seriously theological, exegetical, and pastoral discipline that focuses its critical attention on how the whole of faith and life of the church comes to expression in preaching. There is an intimate communion between biblical interpretation and doctrine, since authentic Christian exegesis is theological and authentic Christian theology is biblical. In addition, theology and sanctity, or spirituality, are united in a participatory way of knowing that entails commitment, love, and prayerful attention to God.

The place of Scripture in preaching is thus situated within the economy of grace, in the communion between God and God's people, with the initiative and source being God's own self-communication, which is received in the means of grace. Coming to know, trust, and love the Triune God in the present puts to rest fears about the need to prove the "contemporary relevance" of the Bible in preaching. Our primary need is for congruence between knowing God's Word in Scripture and knowing God's work in the lives of people. Here is a kind of judgment peculiar to vocational holiness, which is required and constitutive of good preaching.[26]

> Do I meditate therein day and night? Do I think (and consequently speak) thereof, "when I sit in the house, and when I walk by the way; when I lie down, and when I rise up?" By this means have I at length attained such a thorough knowledge as of the sacred text, so of its literal and spiritual meaning? Otherwise, how can I attempt to instruct others therein? Without this, I am a blind guide indeed! I am absolutely incapable of teaching my flock what I have never learned myself; no more fit to lead souls to God, than I am to govern the world.[27]

If we take seriously Wesley's conviction that preaching is bound to intimate knowledge of Scripture and the church, preachers will need to be trained in a manner that enables them to communicate the evangelical content of the Bible in sermons that allow the voices of the prophets and apostles to continue to be heard in the present. Wesley's family-style approach to ministry can assist us in the task of reuniting biblical interpretation and preaching in good working order so that the gospel will come clearly and forcefully to expression, be heard, and bear its fruit in the life of the church.[28]

William Abraham points to the way Wesley's sermons, with their aim of spiritual instruction and formation, provide an illuminating example of spiritual wisdom in homiletic form. Among Wesley's whole corpus of sermons is an initial set that deals with issues in conceptual and practical ways relevant to coming to faith for the first time: salvation, justification, repentance, the witness of the Spirit, new birth, and victory over evil. A second group describes what it is to be Christian through Wesley's use of the Sermon on the Mount. These discourses aim to share the nature of the Christian life on the way to a life of holiness. A final set of sermons addresses particular problems and challenges to the Christian life by means of the church's confession of faith as illumined by the scriptural way of salvation.[29] Abraham notes of Wesley, "In an inimitable and wonderful way he helped people find God in conversion, became a model for them of the spiritual life, and provided a network of resources to nourish genuine holiness."[30]

Shaped by an evangelical message and way of life within the catholic tradition of the church, Wesley's public witness—as preacher, evangelist, pastor, and spiritual director—was at home within the church's calling to the perfection of love for God and neighbor, or holiness of life. It is not surprising, then, that Wesley's practical wisdom was shaped not only by preaching but also by praying, reading, writing, teaching, conversing, debating, communing, presiding, singing, organizing, visiting the sick, serving the poor, and ministering to prisoners. Wesley sought to perceive the reality of God's love ruling over, in, and through all things as the source and end of faith, wisdom, virtue, and goodness.

Following Wesley's example, a capacity for discerning Scripture's place in preaching is inseparable from participating in the life of a people whose desire is to know, love, and live the truth and goodness that is proclaimed—that is, in the gospel becoming a people. If we assume this integrative vision of faith and life, preaching will presuppose the justifying and sanctifying activity of the Father that is mediated by the Son through the work of the Spirit. If we assume knowing and loving God is only personal and not relevant to public life, however, the church will be shaped by godless images, and debates about its ministry, including preaching, will be driven by utility and relevance rather than those habits of mind that dispose us toward hearing the Word and speaking the truth in love.[31]

Theological reflection is therefore intrinsic to interpreting Scripture within the practice of preaching, which becomes a matter of discerning what is perceived as true, good, and beautiful as illumined by divine revelation through participation in the means of grace. Learning to hear and speak the Word of Scripture is situated within a common life of doctrine, devotion, and discipleship handed down, sustained, and renewed in and through communities of confession and praise, with the confession of the Triune God's truth and goodness as the source and end of all things. The *Book of Common Prayer*, amended by Wesley for Methodist use, is itself pervaded by Trinitarian discourse for use in liturgical settings for the purpose of shaping a vision of God's saving activity that leads to the joy of communion with the living God.[32] In other words, by coming to know and love God within the economy of salvation, worshippers are made participants in the Triune life and mystery. Scripture thus functions "sacramentally," as a means of grace, mediating Christ and the fullness of his saving work through the "oracles of God."[33]

The Practice of Wisdom

The primary aim of preaching is assisting the Spirit's work of making and strengthening Christians through attentiveness to the Word of God in and through the words of Scripture. Practical wisdom is required for preaching that is engendered by divine grace, which heals and empowers the human capacities that enable the necessary judgment for interpreting Scripture and speaking "to the right person, to the right extent, at the right time, with the right aim, and in the right way." But, as Wesley observes, this is dependent on "the love of God and man not only filling my heart, but shining through my whole conversation."[34]

An example of Wesley's practical wisdom is evinced in a letter he wrote in December 1751, when the spread of evangelical revival was provoking both enthusiastic support and strong resistance. Wesley wrote to an inquirer on the subject of "preaching Christ" after pondering this matter for a period of three months.[35] His description of "preaching Christ" is both theological and pastoral in scope and succinctly summarizes the scriptural way of salvation—the love of God for sinners demonstrated in the life, death, resurrection, and intercession of Christ and his blessings—and the law—setting forth the commandments of Christ and, in particular, the way to holiness communicated in the Sermon on the Mount. This angle of vision was the fruit of Wesley's intimate knowledge of both the message of Scripture and the joys and struggles of the Christian life. Revealing a depth of understanding concerning the relation of law and gospel, Wesley's comments demonstrate a capacity for discernment that enabled him to address a wide range of spiritual and moral conditions, including that of sinners, the justified, the diligent, the proud, the careless, and the weak in understanding.[36]

Wesley describes this as "the Methodist manner of preaching," which construes the biblical revelation of law and gospel in light of the work of Christ by the illumination of the Spirit who instructs, challenges, forgives, and strengthens listeners. Wesley states,

> At our first beginning to preach at any place, after a general declaration of the love of God to sinners, and his willingness that they should be saved, to preach the law, in the strongest, the closest, the most searching manner possible; only intermixing the gospel here and there, and showing it, as it were, afar off. After more and more persons are convinced of sin, we may mix more and more of the gospel in order to "beget faith," to rein into spiritual life those whom the law hath slain; but is not to be done too hastily either.[37]

Wesley sketches a brief summary of the scriptural order of salvation in which we are drawn, converted, and led by the teaching of the law to living faith in the saving activity of Christ through which the Spirit bears the fruit of good works and holy love. "God loves you; therefore, love and obey him. Christ died for you; therefore, die to sin. Christ is risen; therefore, rise in the image of God. Christ liveth forevermore; therefore, live to God, till you live with him in glory."[38]

Thus, a Wesleyan "grammar" of faith will be ordered by the knowledge and love of God received through Scripture and the other means of grace.[39] Such practical wisdom entails personal knowledge of Christ's truth and goodness—having the "mind that was in

Christ" through which the Spirit transforms and guides our thinking, living, and speaking by the gospel ruling in the heart and mind.[40] As Wesley writes,

> Prudence (or practical wisdom), properly so called, is not that offspring of hell which the world calls prudence, which is mere craft, cunning dissimulation; but . . . that "wisdom from above" which our Lord peculiarly recommends to all who would promote his kingdom upon earth. . . . This wisdom will instruct you how to suit your words and whole behavior to the persons with whom you have to do, to the time, place, and all other circumstances.[41]

As a way of "knowing in action," practical wisdom, or prudence, is sustained by good character and habits that enable discernment of the good for the sake of doing good acts that are a source of joy. Joseph Dunne comments that "the good practitioner has been formed by a history of participation in the practice itself. His or her experience of serving the end or *telos* of the practice—and recurrently trying to discover what this concretely requires—has laid down certain dispositions of character which, through discipline and direction, enable and energize."[42] He continues, "For this reason, a practically wise person will possess skills of deliberation, discernment, and decisiveness that make him or her capable of transforming knowledge of reality into virtuous speech and action."[43]

Dunne's discussion challenges an instrumentalist, "cause and effect" approach to practice that frames objectives in advance, anticipates plans, controls the moves one will make, and then evaluates both the activity and results on terms defined by "effectiveness."[44] He argues persuasively that practice is irreducible to external techniques or procedures but requires a nontechnical, personal, and participatory way of knowing that cannot be framed in terms of detachment, universality, and utility.

Dunne defines this type of activity as a form of "making" that is specified by a maker who determines its end or goal in advance. In contrast to the activity of making or producing that proceeds by explanation, prediction, and control for acting externally on the raw material of one's work, Dunne discusses the social activity of practice. A practice is conducted in public places in cooperation with others and with no ulterior purpose or goals external to sharing in the truth and goodness of the practice itself, and with a view to no other end or outcome than the moral intentions, habits, and qualities exemplified by wise, experienced participants of the practice.

This definition of shared communal activity may be extended to our understanding of Christian practices, or means of grace, such as prayer and worship, the use of Scripture in preaching and teaching, evangelization, catechesis, training in discipleship, pastoral care, and works of mercy and justice. Activities of this nature are carried out to realize and demonstrate as their end those virtues, dispositions, and excellences that are valued by the church as a historical community and are constitutive of its life through faith that works through the Spirit's empowerments of love. In this alternative picture, practical knowledge is seen as a fruit that grows only in the soul of a person's experience and character. One is at the same time a feeling, expressing, and acting person; and knowing is inseparable from one's life as such.[45]

Dunne's description of these two distinct modes of activity can illumine how preaching springs from and embodies the practical wisdom that we are to love God and our neighbor as ourselves. Seen from this perspective, good preaching will be characterized by a particular kind of history, experience, judgment, and influence that, while rooted in the wisdom of Scripture and guided by the Christian tradition, remains open to the gifts, dispositions, and habits appropriate to responding to the Word and Spirit in present circumstances and situations.

As Wesleyans, we believe that what we love plays a significant role in shaping our judgments. Love moves the intellect to engage in the process of practical reasoning and focuses the intellect's attention on certain objects rather than others because of the intensity of its love.[46] Prudence is therefore akin to "love discerning well" with the power of the intellect working through practical judgment, counsel, and direction—an insightfulness that directs one's reason, desire, and actions to the end of love for God and for all things in God.[47] Because prudence is "love choosing wisely," it is in the service of human excellence—loving the truth and desiring the good—so that the person who knows, judges, speaks, and acts well is truly happy.[48]

There can be no wisdom or virtue without the Spirit's gift of love since the goal of moral discernment is dependent on knowing God through faith energized and penetrated by love. Flowing from the will to the intellect, love transforms prudence for knowing the right end and choosing the right means in conformity to that end. The wisdom of Scripture as illumined by the Spirit is a key element of the Law of the Gospel that inspired the prophets and apostles and moved the saints to act. Moreover, in addition to the union of heart and mind with God through the theological virtues of faith, hope, and love, the virtue of practical wisdom requires intellectual and moral skills that enable assessment of specific situations and the transformation of knowledge into appropriate action: speaking or doing the right thing, for the right reason, in the right manner, for the right persons, and in the right circumstances.[49]

Prudence, then, is neither a procedural method nor technical skill. Rather, it is a capacity linking the intellectual and moral virtues for choosing good ends that are well suited to particular activities such as discerning the appropriate place and use of Scripture in preaching. Seen from this perspective, "good" preaching can be understood as the practice of wisdom cultivated by receptivity to God's Word revealed in the scriptural witness to Christ; it is a nonutilitarian way of thinking, perceiving, and speaking that awakens the church to faith and love for God in ways that are timely and appropriate to its vocation as a holy people.

WESLEY ON VOCATIONAL HOLINESS

In *An Address to the Clergy*, Wesley writes of zeal for doing good and taking care in abstaining from evil. He describes the kind of pastoral wisdom which is necessary to guide and encourage others into the fullness of living faith and love, what I have called vocational holiness.

> Have I any knowledge of the world? Have I studied men (as well as books) and observed their tempers, maxims, and manners? Have I learned to beware of men; to add the wisdom of the serpent to innocence of the dove? Has God given me by nature, or have I acquired, any measure of the discernment of spirits; or of its near ally, prudence, enabling me on all occasions to consider all circumstances, and to suit and vary my behavior according to the various combinations of them? . . . And do I omit no means which is in my power, and consistent with my character, of "pleasing all men" with whom I converse, "for their good to edification?"[50]

Discerning the place of Scripture in preaching is inseparable from the preacher's vocation of making the wisdom of Scripture her own. This begins to occur when the love of God is the controlling passion of one's life and ministry—a desire that the eyes of one's heart be purified in order to see the beauty of holiness radiating in and through all things. Wesley interprets this wisdom by the light of God's self-revelation in Christ:

> Do all who have spiritual discernment take knowledge (judging of the tree by its fruits) that "the life which I now live, I live by faith in the Son of God"; and that in all "simplicity and godly sincerity I have my conversation in the world"? Am I exemplarily pure from all worldly desire, from all vile and vain affections? Is my life one continued labor of love, one tract of praising God and helping man? Do I in everything see "Him who is invisible"? and "beholding with open face the glory of the Lord," am I "changed into the same image from glory to glory, by the Spirit of the Lord"?[51]

Wesley then turns his attention to the kind of exemplary wisdom and virtue that serve as fitting instruments of the truth and goodness mediated by God's Wisdom in Christ. Theology and life are united in the work of ministry that has its basis in and springs from devotion of the heart and mind to God.

> What is a Minister of Christ, a shepherd of souls, unless he is devoted to God? Unless he abstain, with the utmost care and diligence, from every evil word and work; from all appearance of evil; yea, from the most innocent things, whereby any might be offended or made weak? Is he not called, above others, to be an example to the flock, in his private as well as public character; an example of all holy and heavenly tempers, filling the heart so as to shine through the life? . . . Do I understand my own office? Have I deeply considered before God the character which I bear? What is it to be an Ambassador of Christ, and Envoy from the King of heaven? And do I know and feel what is implied in "watching over the souls" of men "as he that must give an account"?[52]

Appropriating the knowledge of Scripture for pastoral ministry requires and leads to practical wisdom, the expression of "doctrine coming to life" in the declaration of living faith. Such "knowledge in action" is dependent on the Spirit who cleanses the eyes of the heart and understanding to "see" intimate connections between God's Word in Scripture and God's work in the lives of people.

> Consequently, is not his whole life, if he walks worthy of his calling, one incessant labor of love; one continued tract of praising God, and helping man; one series of thankfulness and beneficence? Is he not always humble, always serious, though rejoicing evermore; mild, gentle, patient, and abstinent? . . . Is he not one sent forth from God, to stand between God and man, to guard and assist the poor, helpless children of men, to supply them both with light and strength to guide them through a thousand known and unknown dangers, till at the appointed time he returns, with those committed to his charge, to his and their Father who is in heaven?[53]

Wesley encouraged pastors to immerse themselves in prayerful study of Scripture for receiving its saving wisdom and speaking its truth in love. This way of reading nurtures both knowledge of God and human excellence—the formation of a certain kind of person endued with the wisdom of love—toward God and toward the neighbor in God—that enables judgment and perception of God's work within the particular circumstances of life.

> Am I . . . such as I ought to be, with regard to my affections? I am taken from among, and ordained for, men, in things pertaining to God. I stand between God and man, by the authority of the great Mediator, in the nearest and most endearing relation both to my Creator and to my fellow creatures. Have I accordingly given my heart to God, and to my brethren for his sake? And my neighbor, every man, as myself? Does this love swallow me up, possess me whole, all my passions and tempers, and regulate all my faculties and powers? Is it the spring which gives rise to all my thoughts, and governs all my words and actions?[54]

Articulating a spiritually rich understanding of pastoral ministry, Wesley affirms the union of learning and devotion that illumines the mind in nurturing personal acquaintance with the "treasures of sacred knowledge." By following the way of holiness, the affections of the heart and mind are purified and reoriented to God—a transformation that irradiates through one's thoughts, words, and actions, or whole "conversation." The study of Scripture induces love for God and knowledge of God's saving wisdom in Christ, the true end of all aspects of preaching as an expression of theological insight and pastoral guidance.

Ought not a "steward of the mysteries of God," a shepherd of the souls for whom Christ died, to be endued with an eminent measure of love to God and love to all his brethren? A love the same in kind, but in degree far beyond that of ordinary Christians? Can he otherwise answer the high character he bears, and the relation wherein he stands? Without this, how can he go through all the toils and difficulties which necessarily attend the faithful execution of his office? Would it be possible for a parent to go through the pain and fatigue of bearing and bringing up children were it not for that vehement affection, *storge* [natural affection] which the Creator has given for that very end? How much less will it be possible for any Pastor, any spiritual parent, to go through the pain and labor of "travailing in birth for," and bringing up, many children to the measure of the full stature of Christ, without a large measure of that inexpressible affection which "a stranger intermeddleth not with"![55]

A Wesleyan understanding of the pastoral vocation will be shaped by the practical wisdom of holiness: love for God and neighbor. Discerning the place of Scripture in preaching is a way of *knowing the truth by heart*—an integrated way of thinking, feeling, and speaking in which the Holy Spirit makes receptive and responsive listeners, capable of hearing the Word and being formed by its sanctifying wisdom.

17

SCRIPTURE AND EVANGELISM

Laceye Warner

Reading Scripture within the Wesleyan tradition offers particular emphases that illuminate aspects of the biblical text for the formation and discipleship of Christian believers, particularly with regard to evangelism. Drawing on John Wesley, whose reverence for and priority of Christian Scripture is clear from his writings, provides guidance for selecting such Wesleyan emphases. In a recent essay, Randy Maddox examines Wesley's motivation, purpose and priorities related to the Bible.[1] Select themes from the essay provide a helpful framework for a Wesleyan reading of Scripture, particularly for informing a Christian understanding and practice of evangelism.

A Wesleyan reading of Scripture drawing on John Wesley and the early Wesleyan tradition includes at least three central components: (1) inspiration of the Holy Spirit, (2) reading in community, and (3) salvation. John Wesley consistently referred to and developed the significance of the inspiration of the Holy Spirit in relation to Scripture, both of the authors that composed the Bible, but also for those reading and seeking its guidance.[2] For Wesley, the inspiration of the Holy Spirit refers to the influence of the Holy Spirit that enables persons to love and serve God.[3] When reading Scripture, Wesley also emphasized the importance of reading in community, with others both past and present. Wesley desired for Methodists (and other Christians) to seek out one another for Christian conferencing or holy conversation to edify one another in the faith. He also valued the wisdom of Christian tradition embodied in the writings of those Christians who lived and practiced their faith among earlier generations.[4] Each of these components then contributes to the main purpose, or telos, of Wesley's reading of Scripture: salvation. For Wesley, salvation is a present and active reality that integrates belief, or a conceptual understanding of doctrine, with practice, or the life of faith as a disciple of Jesus Christ.[5] In his sermon "The Scripture Way of Salvation," his most mature doctrinal exposition, Wesley states, "It is easily discerned, that these two little words, I mean faith and salvation, include the substance of all the Bible, the marrow, as it were, of the whole Scripture."[6] In the pages that follow, these three components for reading Scripture in the Wesleyan tradition will frame a case study of one of the most often quoted texts related to evangelism, Matthew 28:16-20:

> Now the eleven disciples went to Galilee, to the mountain to which Jesus had directed them. When they saw him, they worshipped him; but some doubted. And Jesus came and said to them, "All authority in heaven and earth has been given to me. Go therefore and make disciples of all nations, baptizing them in the name of the Father and of the Son, and of the Holy Spirit, and teaching them to obey everything that I have commanded you. And remember, I am with you always, to the end of the age."[7]

A Wesleyan Reading of Scripture
A Case Study

The commission in Matthew is one of four commissions in the Gospels.[8] Widely known as the "Great Commission," the words of Matthew 28:16-20 comprise among the most familiar and formative biblical texts for Protestants in modernity.[9] Matthew 28 continues to rally evangelical Christians, mostly in North America and Great Britain, enthusiastically to support ministries of evangelism and mission across the world. Indeed, Matthew 28 inspired The United Methodist Church's mission statement: "To make disciples of Jesus Christ for the transformation of the world."[10]

In the early centuries of Christianity, the conviction developed that Matthew's commission and the missionary task it inspired had been accomplished by the apostles.[11] While Luther dismissed this as legend, neither Luther nor Calvin, these two leading Protestant Reformers, managed to offer a truly revised interpretation of the text.

Both continued to declare the commission binding only for the apostles.[12] Contemporary familiarity with Matt 28 dates back to William Carey and his *An Enquiry into the Obligations of Christians to Use Means for the Conversion of the Heathens* (1792). Though others reflected on and advocated for the commission's status, Carey's *Enquiry* is recognized as the turning point for the "greatness" of Matthew's commission.[13] John Wesley himself commented on Matthew 28 in his *Explanatory Notes on the New Testament* in ways that suggest an insightful perspective on the central role of God in discipling (see below under the section *Evangelism as God's "Discipling"*).[14] Indeed, the Wesleyan/Methodist movement in the U.S. emerged as a result of a missional imperative, rather than as simply a contested response to doctrinal or other polemics. The principle commission text by the late nineteenth century, Matthew's "Great Commission" assumed dominance among Protestant Christians in more conservative and premillennial circles.[15]

These words have had a disproportionate impact on Christian understandings and practices of evangelism. While Matthew 28 can urge Christians forward, these words at times also confound with misconceptions, sometimes leading to challenges for evangelism, particularly in our contemporary context among Christians in the U.S. Informed by a Wesleyan reading of Scripture, this essay acknowledges some common misconceptions and suggests related opportunities to offer a constructive theological response for faithful ecclesial practices of evangelism in and by communities of faith.

Inspiration of the Holy Spirit

John Wesley consistently emphasized the importance of seeking the Spirit's guidance when reading Scripture.[16] The inspiration of the Holy Spirit was important to Wesley for its role in bringing conceptual clarity and understanding. However, alongside this vital aspect of reading Scripture, Wesley's deepest commitment was for the personal embrace of the saving truth in Scripture, which is a gift from God.[17] While the inspiration of Scripture enables persons to love and serve God, our response to God's inspiration of Scripture enables our participation in offering salvation and forming believers as disciples in ecclesial communities. God's role in disciple making as well as Jesus' presence with the disciples in Matthew's commission demonstrate the significance of the inspiration of the Holy Spirit for reading and responding to Scripture.

Evangelism as God's "Discipling"

Evangelism is our full participation in God's reign, initiating individuals into faith and discipleship in Jesus Christ through the Holy Spirit.[18] Difficulties arise in relation to the biblical and theological integrity of evangelism when we evaluate results merely in worldly measures without recognizing the role of the Triune God in these efforts. We need a Spirit-led approach that recognizes the complexity of possibilities for the reign of God in our midst and that seeks formation through reading Scripture and responding to God's gift of salvation.

An implicit expectation in contemporary thinking about evangelism, one that is particularly addressed in Matthew 28, is that the role of making disciples is left to *human* responsibility. At times local congregations attempt to fulfill this responsibility through signage and parking, marketing strategies and programming. Who are we and what is our telos, or purpose? We are the body of Christ receiving and realizing God's reign. When we look closely at the language of Matthew 28 in light of Wesley's commentary, we learn that *the verb "discipling" identifies God as the primary actor in evangelism.* Wesley, in his *Explanatory Notes*, renders this phrase, "Go ye, and disciple all nations."[19] As Sarah Lancaster notes, in Wesley's way of salvation,

> it is God who saves, although the way in which God works is never without human responsiveness. If it is right to understand the mission of the church in light of how Wesley conceived salvation, then any discussion of "discipling" must always be mindful that it is set in the framework of God's grace, which comes to us before we can respond, enabling us to respond and bringing these efforts to fulfillment. The primary actor in discipling, then, is God.[20]

This does not mean evangelism is less significant to our ministries as baptized Christian disciples. However, it does offer a more fulsome landscape on which to see our place as baptized members of the body of Christ and the church's role in the unfolding of God's reign. God, through the Holy Spirit, inspires us to participate in the transformation of individuals and communities through God's reign most often through practices embedded in communities of faith.

According to Wesley, the Greek verb *mathēteuō* ("to disciple") suggests a collaborative relationship between God and those whom God calls to the practice of discipling, or evangelism.[21] This verb, when understood in relationship to Wesley's way of salvation, indicates that the primary actor in discipling is not human, dutiful Christians on a mission, but rather God, into whose mission we are invited.[22] Understanding our human role in discipling as invited participants adds eschatological dimensions to the commission and thus to God's reign in our midst. Matthew's imperative "to go and make disciples" is an invitation by God in Jesus Christ through the Holy Spirit to participate in sharing the message of salvation with others, inviting them into God's reign.

"Jesus Came to Them"

Another tendency related to evangelism is to focus myopically on the individual rather than acknowledging the significance of Christian community. The commission in Matthew, in Jesus' words, invites disciples "to obey all that I have commanded you," *not as a ceremonial duty, but as life in communities of faith practicing the love of God and neighbor.* Evangelism may once have been neatly identified with providing an apologetic proof of God, privately and intellectually considered, then prayerfully received, similar to individualistic practices of reading Scripture. However, ideally, the congregation is evangelistic in the totality of its corporate life together, including reading Scripture, receiving formation for discipleship, and being sent to the world.[23]

An essential characteristic of the inspiration of the Holy Spirit is God's presence in the midst of reading Scripture, enabling our living out its imperatives as Christian disciples. A related, important aspect of Jesus' appearance on the Galilean mountain is the notion that "Jesus came to them" (Matt 28:18). Jesus' presence among those on the mountain and his declaration that he is with them "always to the end of the age" in chapter 28 parallel Jesus' presence in chapter 1, in which he is referred to as Emmanuel, "God with us," a consistent theme throughout the Gospels and their commission texts. Jesus' coming to those gathered implies divine initiative to reestablish the intimate relationship shared among them prior to the betrayals and persecution of Jesus leading to his crucifixion. However, in spite of the disciples' betrayals, Jesus does not rebuke them but implicitly extends forgiveness and reconciliation.

Though not widely shared, one interpretation of Matthew's commission suggests that the eleven disciples were not alone with Jesus on the mountain in Galilee. The Matthean account of the women at the tomb suggests their inclusion in the invitation to meet on the Galilean mountain: "and indeed he is going ahead of you to Galilee; there you will see him" (Matt 28:7b). Jesus appeared following the resurrection to those who had followed him (Acts 10:41) as well as to some more skeptical (1 Cor 15:8-9; Gal 1:14-16).[24] The considerable interest of others hearing and joining the eleven in light of the significance of the event of Jesus' resurrection and the opportunity allowed by the duration of travel is also mentioned. In his *Explanatory Notes on the New Testament* (on Matt 28:16), Wesley suggests that Jesus' appearance to more than 500 (1 Cor 15:6) took place at this time.[25] If a larger crowd beyond the eleven disciples assembled to hear Jesus' commission, this is a gesture toward an ecclesial dynamic beyond the disciples' gathering related to Jesus' presence.

Reading Scripture in Community

When considering ministries of missional evangelism, Matthew 28 often inspires an emphasis on individuals *going*—usually far away.[26] While international missions are a significant aspect of our shared Christian witness, we are tempted to disproportionately emphasize the individual task, as well as glamorize those exotic locations and cultures, when similar issues and a similar need for the gospel linger just outside our doors. The church's identity is one of a baptized people going to peoples sometimes similar, sometimes not, to share and live into the message of salvation, gathering together in a variety of spaces. (Incidentally, it may be time for us to *receive* rather than to *send* ministers of the gospel.) *The Gospel of Matthew is the only Gospel explicitly to refer to the* ekklesia, *that is, the gathering of God's people.* What we need, then, are reflections on a Wesleyan ecclesial evangelism that take into account the church as a means of grace for the purpose of receiving and living into God's gift of salvation.

Emphasizing the importance of reading Scripture in community, Wesley consistently urged that authentic spiritual formation could not take place, "without society, without living and conversing with [others]."[27] His emphasis on those mature in the faith in their present context as well as the written legacy of those from Christian tradition did not favor solely the scholarly (though this was not dismissed), but rather the seasoned Christian character. Wesley acknowledged the limitations on all human understanding and the concomitant need for society, or community, to cultivate holiness.[28] Wesley consistently urged that authentic spiritual formation could not take place "without society, without living and conversing with [others]."[29] Wesley also insisted that Scripture should be read both for its understanding and its practice.[30] A Christian is not merely one who intellectually assents to specific intellectual concepts but one who lives out his or her faith in community with others.

Discipleship for Life in Community

Jesus' words in Matthew 28:16-20 give guidance for discipleship. When Jesus states that disciples should be taught "to observe all that I have commanded you," this use of language takes on a Matthean character. Matthew uses the verb *tēreō* ("to observe" or "to practice") six times, three in reference to "keeping the commandments." *Entellomai* ("to command"), used in Matthew 28:20, is the verbal form of the noun *entolē* ("commandment")—in Matthew a specific reference to the commandments of the Old Testament, or Torah.[31] Jesus commands obedience to the law but interpreted it as discipleship in God's reign.[32] Jesus' commandment is more than ceremonial moral adherence or otherworldly rule of life; it is love of God and neighbor (see Matt 19).[33] Jesus' commandment to love one's neighbor compassionately with justice (or *dikaiosynē*) in a life of righteousness includes the Torah but also extends beyond to all Jesus commanded through his words and life, which challenged the example of the Pharisees, who lacked these dimensions of love.[34]

From Going to Gathering: An Ecclesial Evangelism

When many think of God's mission and the church's participation in evangelism, the general dynamic is one of *going*. Yet we expect people to come to our churches with little reflection on what it means *to gather*. The study of evangelism needs reorientation away from the traditional notion that evangelism, particularly in the New Testament, functions mainly as a centrifugal dynamic of "going out." A centrifugal understanding of evangelism does not take full advantage of the depths and richness of biblical foundations for living out one's faith in community.[35]

Though the Old Testament often emphasizes a centripetal motion, and the New Testament a centrifugal, both Testaments hold together the centrifugal and centripetal dynamics. Richard Bauckham expresses the need to speak of these two dimensions if justice is to be done to the Bible's full witness. "The church's mission requires both the individuals and the groups who, authorized by God to communicate his message, go out from the community to others, near or far and also the community that manifests God's presence in its midst by its life together and its relationships to others."[36] In other words, a biblical view of mission (and evangelism), one that resonates with a Wesleyan reading of Scripture in community, will have to describe a way of "life together" comprising a "gathering in" as well as a "going out," with both of those directions set in complementary relation.

The dynamic of "going," though important, loses its significance and purpose when disconnected from the gathered community of faith, or *ekklēsia*, in Matthew. Those sent, to go, must be sent from some location, a community in which the commission in all its fullness is given and received. Additionally, once sent, those who go are not perpetually dislocated but rather go to bring others to gather in communities of faith, whether from the original sending congregation or in new communities from which the dynamic proceeds. Mortimer Arias addresses a truncated understanding of evangelism as merely going when he argues for a biblical emphasis on hospitality as a paradigm for evangelism, particularly as a distinctive mark of Christians and their communities in the New Testament.[37] For Arias, the characteristically Old Testament dynamic of centripetal mission changed following the resurrection and Pentecost to the traditional, centrifugal pattern. However, for Arias, even in the New Testament, the notion of centripetal mission remains—"by attraction, by incarnation, by being."[38]

Since William Carey's emphasis on Matthew's "Great Commission," the verb found at the beginning of Matthew 28:19, *poreuthentes* (the aorist participle of *poreuomai*, "to go"), has carried considerable weight in Western missionary thinking.[39] It has often been read as an imperative: "Go!"—particularly across national boundaries. As a result of this standard understanding, a misunderstanding of mission emerged, one that emphasizes "going" rather than "making disciples." This has led to an emphasis on the geography of evangelism—on the distance and location of the task—rather than an emphasis on the task itself. And this geographical emphasis has determined whether an individual indeed filled the role of a missionary, eventually resulting in a definition of mission that focused narrowly on ministry in foreign contexts.

David Bosch questions such interpretations on two points. First, Matthew frequently uses a construction that combines two actions connected to a single event by featuring the aorist participle as a preparatory action before the main verb.[40] According to some scholars, this sentence construction occurs so often in Matthew's text that it may be considered characteristic of Matthean style.[41] For Bosch, this means that, in Matt 28:19, both *poreuthentes* and *mathēteusate* ("to make disciples") refer to one event, minimizing the emphasis on a separate and distinctive action, "Go!"[42]

Second, Matthew frequently uses the verb *poreuomai* as an auxiliary verb with the imperative of another verb in a pleonastic sense. Therefore, the initial mention of "Go!" is not an event distinct from the one expressed by the main verb. Thus, "going" does not necessarily indicate traveling from one location to another. This does not mean that *poreuthentes* is redundant but rather reinforces the action of the main verb by introducing a sense of urgency.[43] According to Bosch, this is the case in Matt 28:19; "*poreuthentes* serves to underline the urgency and primacy of *mathēteusate*."[44]

Though the impetus to "Go!" remains an aspect of Matthew's commission, it has received attention disproportionate to its role and placement in the text. We may commend Carey and others with him for their courage and ambition for the gospel; their traveling to distant lands; and their risking disease, starvation, violence, as well as their lives, to dwell and minister among peoples much different than themselves. However, such travel is neither necessary nor sufficient for a faithful fulfillment of Matthew's commission. Bosch summarizes, "If, however, we translate *poreuthentes* not as a separate command, but as adding emphasis and urgency to *mathēteusate*, a different picture of mission emerges. It then refers to bringing people to Jesus as Lord, wherever they may be."[45]

Salvation: Belief and Practice in Communities of Faith

For Wesley the telos of the early Methodist movement and the church is salvation, God's gift extended to creation through Jesus Christ's universal atonement. In his sermon, "The Scripture Way of Salvation," Wesley explains salvation through an analysis of grace categorized in three ways—preventing, justifying, and sanctifying grace. An aspect of sanctification, realized through sanctifying grace, is the individual's participation in the means of grace, specifically works of piety and mercy, most often in communities of faith.[46] A Wesleyan reading of Scripture that takes seriously the centrality of salvation to Christian discipleship and evangelism emphasizes the human response to God's gift of salvation through Christian practices. Here we explore the communal practice of baptism in Matthew, followed by reflections on a Wesleyan ecclesial evangelism that understands the church as a means of grace for cultivating salvation.

From Going to Gathering: A Baptismal Community of Salvation

Language shared among international and ecumenical ecclesial communities in Christian baptismal liturgies demonstrates the integrated character of discipleship within the body of Christ, "to proclaim the gospel in one's words and in one's life."[47] All Christians are commissioned to ministry by their baptisms. As we participate in God's discipling, described by Matthew's commission, we are sent to baptize—in the name of the Trinity, Father, Son, and Holy Spirit—to invite others into God's reign, into a life of unconditional love, forgiveness, and joy in Christian community. Matthew's commission is not a simple job description for Christian disciples or strategy for church survival; rather, it is an invitation to receive, live, and participate as a witnessing church in the reign of the Triune God in response to God's salvation.[48]

The Trinitarian formula is unique to Matthew's Gospel and in this context highlights Jesus' divinity, as well as authority, by placing Jesus on the same level as the Father and Spirit.[49] In spite of the complexities related to the tradition history of the baptismal formula and its theological implications, here it underscores an ecclesial and liturgical frame for evangelism.

Baptism indicates forgiveness from sins, "justification" in Wesleyan terms, and initiation into the body of Christ, Jesus' continuing presence on earth.[50] As we have seen, Matthew's Gospel includes the only explicit mention of the gathered community of faith, the church or *ekklēsia*, which is referenced in Matt 16:17-18. Not merely an assembly, the church, or community of faith, at its fullest is a place of oneness with the risen Christ, in communion with the Triune God as well as all the saints. The community of faith when open to the Spirit's presence and guidance to faithful practices of worship and witness participates in God's reign, shares the gospel of Jesus Christ, and invites creation to receive redemption. In the context of the gathered community of faith, Christian disciples experience Jesus' authority and presence. In the gathered worshipping body, Jesus' presence is with us always, empowering the church to witness to the salvation offered by God to all in Jesus Christ through the Holy Spirit.

A Wesleyan Ecclesial Evangelism

Despite the relative lack of ecclesiological themes in traditional literature on evangelism and the ambiguity of such themes in Wesleyan theology, ecclesiology, or life in the church, is the primary means through which Christians make sense of discipleship and live into God's salvation. While the traditional emphasis of Protestant evangelicalism on personal piety is among its distinctive strengths, without a gathering of faithful Christians to worship, pray, and serve, this strength may have contributed to schism among evangelicals and an undermining of powerful witness. At the same time, while evangelistic and missional themes thread through literature on ecclesiology, such themes are often subordinated to perceived grander themes such as ecumenism, nature of ministry orders, laity, sacraments, and even the relationship between church and state.

Indeed, ecumenism often dominates conversations regarding ecclesiology, based on the assumption that until the church is one unified body its witness is compromised. While this assumption is true, perhaps a reorientation of churches' attention to our primary purpose of participating in the reign of God as witnesses to God's salvation might facilitate church renewal. According to Wesley, the nature of the church, and of the Methodist movement, is primarily evangelistic. In the "Large" *Minutes,* John Wesley summarized his understanding of Methodism's purpose: "What may we reasonably believe to be God's design in raising up the Preachers called Methodists? A. To reform the nation and, in particular, the Church; to spread scriptural holiness over the land."[51]

As scholars note, there is not one image, model, or paradigm of church sustained in biblical texts.[52] Following Scripture, the Articles of Religion offer a starting place for contemplating ecclesiology. A definitive ecclesial document dating from the Church of England in the Middle Ages, to be specific, the thirty-nine Articles of Religion still resonate through Protestant foundational documents—and for United Methodists these remain formal, recognized doctrine as a result of John Wesley's prioritization of these at the birth of the Methodist Episcopal Church in the United States. According to the Article "Of the Church," "The visible Church of Christ is a congregation of faithful [persons] in which the pure word of God is preached and the sacraments be duly ministered according to Christ's ordinance in all those things that of necessity are requisite to the same."⁵³ This statement describes both what the church is—a congregation of faithful persons (or believers)—and what the church does—preaches the word of God and administers the sacraments. This statement depends on numerous additional articles to fill out what seemed to its authors to be constitutive practices of the Christian church's faithful activity, including soteriological, eschatological, and ecclesiological components.

Some may argue that the Articles of Religion are archaic primary sources that, though possibly worthy of study, are not applicable or relevant to the embodied Christian faith today. While the Articles of Religion may be best understood from their historical context, these and other documents offer examples, even models, of attempts over the last two millennia to narrate the embodied Christian faith described in biblical texts. Maintaining connections with our biblical and theological roots is an important discipline for ecclesiological reflection to encourage the gospel's relevance to a changing and challenging world.

Yet, as many scholars argue, ecclesiology must reach beyond Reformation discussions of the marks of the true church, which were pursued during a particular time and context.⁵⁴ In addition to reaching beyond the Reformers, building on biblical and theological tradition, critical attention to the contributions and challenges of evangelicalism is needed to encourage faithful understandings of church. Ironically, those most open to the inclination of a missional evangelistic character and purpose for the church were the least able to articulate an ecclesiology or to function ecclesially in order to aid in avoiding major schisms, which would seem to enable actively pursuing evangelism.⁵⁵

Wesley's writings and ministry offer a mediating example between Reformed teaching on the church and evangelicalism. Wesley wrote and preached in the context of eighteenth-century revivalism. However, as a committed priest in the Church of England his entire life, Wesley valued the authority of the thirty-nine Articles, specifically the Article "Of the Church," mentioned above. Wesley's leadership of the Methodist renewal movement within the Church of England, his writings and example, support a Wesleyan view of church as a *means of grace*, which attempts to bring closer the dynamics of what the church "is" and what it "does," both expressed in the Article. The descriptor *means of grace* indicates both what God is doing in persons participating in the means of grace and what God does in the recipients of those means, namely, cultivating salvation.[56] A tense ambiguity remains inherent in Methodism, in both Great Britain and North America, between movement and church.

Among evangelicals, current and previous, Christian faith and identity, as well as mission, or evangelistic outreach to distant exotic lands, are primarily personal and individual. Though this emphasis has proved challenging, it is a foundational component of evangelism, a responsibility that each baptized Christian bears. However, focusing so narrowly on the individual contributes to an ecclesial identity that is merely the aggregate of these individuals' callings rather than a fuller biblical vision of the church as witness to God's reign in Jesus Christ through the Holy Spirit (e.g., Eph 2:21-22).[57]

A faithful understanding of the church will include aspects of evangelistic practice in response to the invitation of the gospel to participate in the reign of God. A biblical and theologically framed concept of evangelism is not merely a technique for new membership recruitment but rather a set of practices such as those described by the Articles of Religion: preaching the gospel, participating in the sacraments, and living lives in communities of faith shaped by these. The gathered body of Christ, and ecclesiology, at its very heart is *evangelistic*, encouraging individuals and congregations to live out their baptismal commissions to proclaim the gospel in our words and in our lives.

Conclusion
A Wesleyan Reading of Scripture

The select components of a Wesleyan reading of Scripture provide a helpful framework for discerning Christian belief and practice in communities of faith, particularly related to evangelism. These components, inspiration of the Holy Spirit, reading in community, and salvation, highlight significant emphases within Christian tradition particularly pertinent to the current challenges of the church. Though this essay focused on a reading of Matt 28:16-20, the misconceptions and opportunities for the contemporary church related to the Matthean commission text parallel those in other texts and contexts. A Wesleyan reading of Scripture that takes into account these components illuminates opportunities for the sharpening of the church's faithful witness in the world, moving beyond simple understanding or intellectual assent to an integrated communal practice of discipleship.

NOTES

INTRODUCTION

1   John Wesley, preface to *Explanatory Notes upon the Old Testament*, in *Wesley's Notes on the Bible* (Grand Rapids: Francis Asbury Press, 1987), 20.

CHAPTER 1: MADDOX

1   John Wesley, Sermon 107, "On God's Vineyard," I.1, in *Works*, 3:504. Wesley is quoting Ps 119:105.
2   See Kenneth J. Collins, "Scripture as a Means of Grace," ch. 2 of this volume.
3   See his letters to William Dodd on February 5, 1756, and March 12, 1756, in *Letters* (Telford), 3:157–58, 167.
4   Preface to *Sermons on Several Occasions* (1746), §5, in *Works*, 1:104–6.
5   1766 *Minutes*, Q. 30, in *Works*, 10:340; also as "Large Minutes," Q. 34, in *Works*, 10:887.
6   We can document Wesley's reading from his diaries, scattered lists in his manuscripts, his published *Journal*, his publication of extracts in the *Christian Library* and the *Arminian Magazine*, and the surviving volumes of his personal library. The most reliable list of Wesley's reading during his Oxford years is currently an appendix in Richard P. Heitzenrater, "John Wesley and the Oxford Methodists" (Ph.D. diss., Duke University, 1972). For Wesley's surviving library, see Randy L. Maddox, "John Wesley's Reading: Evidence in the Book Collection at Wesley's House, London," *Methodist History* 41, no. 3 (2003): 118–33. Cf. idem, "John Wesley's Reading: Evidence in the Kingswood School Archives," *Methodist History* 41, no. 2 (2003): 49–67; idem, "Remnants of John Wesley's Personal Library," *Methodist History* 42, no. 2 (2004): 122–28. Frank Baker began work

on a comprehensive list of Wesley's reading that will appear in its completeness under the auspices of the Wesley *Works* project.

7   See the reading suggested for his lay "assistants" in Minutes (August 3, 1745), Q. 13, in *Works*, 10:161–68; and similar recommendations in a letter to Margaret Lewen, June 1764, in *Letters* (Telford), 4:249, which were later published as "A Female Course of Study," *Arminian Magazine* 3 (1780): 602–4.

8   *Plain Account of Christian Perfection*, §10, in *Works* (Jackson), 11:373.

9   There are four overlapping lists in manuscript notebooks at the Methodist Archive and Research Centre, The John Rylands University Library. For a combined catalogue of these lists, see Randy L. Maddox, "Charles Wesley's Personal Library, ca. 1765," *Proceedings of the Charles Wesley Society* 14 (2010): 73–103.

10 See Maddox, "John Wesley's Reading: London," 124.

11 See Samuel Wesley, *Advice to a Young Clergyman* (London: C. Rivington & J. Roberts, [1735]), 26–28 (26). This was originally a letter Samuel wrote to a curate in his charge; John Wesley published the volume and added the preface. The specific text Samuel Wesley commended was *Biblia Sacra Polyglotta* (London, 1657).

12 See the two editions of Bengel and the editions published by Stephan and Redmayne in Maddox, "John Wesley's Reading: London," as well as the edition by John Mill (n. 13, below).

13 John Mill, *Novum Testamentum. Cum lectionibus variantibus mss. exemplarium, versionum, editionum, ss. patrum & scriptom ecclesiasticorum; & in easdem notis*, 2 vols. (Oxford: Sheldonian Theatre, 1707). Wesley records owning this work on the inside cover of his first Oxford diary.

14 Charles Le Cène, *An Essay for a New Translation of the Bible* (London: John Nutt, 1702).

15 Wesley also issued this English translation separately (without his notes) as one of his last publications: *The New Testament* (London: New Chapel, 1790). Cf. George Croft Cell, *John Wesley's New Testament Compared with the Authorized Version* (London: Lutterworth, 1938).

16 These are reproduced in *Works* (Jackson), 14:78–160.

17 See David S. Katz, "The Hutchinsonians and Hebraic Fundamentalism in Eighteenth-Century England," in *Sceptics, Millenarians and Jews*, ed. D. Katz and J. Israel (Leiden: Brill, 1990), 237–55.

18 February 13, 1770, in *Works*, 22:215–16. See also his letter to Dean D. (1785), in *Letters* (Telford), 7:251–52.

19 See, e.g., the Hebrew grammars by Bayley (1782) and Robertson (1783) in Maddox, "John Wesley's Reading: London."

20 See Justin Champion, "'Directions for the Profitable Reading of the Holy Scriptures': Biblical Criticism, Clerical Learning and Lay Readers, c. 1650–1720," in *Scripture and Scholarship in Early Modern England*, ed. A. Hessayon and N. Keene (Burlington, Vt.: Ashgate, 2006), 208–30; and Thomas R. Preston, "Biblical Criticism, Literature, and the Eighteenth-Century Reader," in *Books and Their Readers in Eighteenth-Century England*, ed. Isabel Rivers (New York: St. Martin's, 1982), 97–126.

21 *The Manners of the Ancient Christians Extracted from a French Author by John Wesley,*

M.A., *Fellow of Lincoln College, Oxford* (Bristol: Farley, 1748), an abridged translation of Claude Fleury, *Les moeurs des Chrétiens* (Paris: Clouzier, 1682).

22   See Joel B. Green, "Wesley as Interpreter of Scripture and the Emergence of 'History' in Biblical Interpretation," ch. 4 of this volume.

23   Preface to *Explanatory Notes upon the Old Testament*, §15, in *Works* (Jackson), 14:252.

24   Preface, §5, in *Works*, 1:106 (quoting 1 Cor 2:13).

25   Cf. Samuel Wesley, *Advice*, 29–30. Samuel also encouraged reading some extra-canonical works from the period of the early church.

26   The most ambitious attempt to identify instances is James H. Charlesworth, "The Wesleys and the Canon: An Unperceived Openness," *Proceedings of the Charles Wesley Society* 3 (1996): 63–88.

27   September 30, 1786, in *Works*, 23:420.

28   *Popery Calmly Considered*, I.4, in *Works* (Jackson), 10:141. Wesley is drawing on a book by John Williams for this tract, but this particular claim is in his own words.

29   See, e.g., his letter to Margaret Lewen (June 1764), in *Letters* (Telford), 4:247; and the preface to *Explanatory Notes–OT*, §18, in *Works* (Jackson), 14:253.

30   John Wesley, *Lessons for Children and Others Selected from the Holy Scriptures* (London: Henry Cock, 1746–1754). This four-part volume is simply an abridgment of the KJV OT. It is "lessons" in the sense of assigned readings, not lectures about the readings.

31   The records are not exhaustive. Even so, a list of all known sermon occasions, where we have the text, runs over 400 pages in length. This list was compiled by Wanda Willard Smith. It can be found on the website of the Center for Studies in the Wesleyan Tradition (CSWT) at Duke University: http://divinity.duke.edu/initiatives-centers/cswt/research-resources/register.

32   Cf. Matthew R. Schlimm, "Defending the Old Testament's Worth: John Wesley's Reaction to the Rebirth of Marcionism," *Wesleyan Theological Journal* 42, no. 2 (2007): 28–51.

33   See Sermon 34, "The Original, Nature, Properties, and Use of the Law," in *Works*, 2:4–19.

34   Sermon 25, "Sermon on the Mount V," II.3, in *Works*, 1:554–55; and Sermon 76, "On Perfection," II.1–8, in *Works*, 3:77–80.

35   See Sermon 67, "On Divine Providence," §4, in *Works*, 2:536; and letter to Elizabeth Hardy, April 5, 1758, in *Letters* (Telford), 4:11.

36   "Of Hell," §1, in *Works*, 3:31.

37   "Thoughts upon Methodism," §2, *Arminian Magazine* 10 (1787), in *Works*, 9:527. See also *Plain Account of Christian Perfection*, §5, in *Works* (Jackson), 11:366.

38   See particularly Sermon 16, "The Means of Grace," II.8, in *Works*, 1:388; Sermon 12, "The Witness of Our Own Spirit," §6, in *Works*, 1:302–3; and Sermon 36, "The Law Established by Faith, II," I.5, in *Works*, 2:37.

39   E.g., letter to William Law, January 6, 1756, in *Letters* (Telford), 3:345–46; letter to Bishop of Gloucester (1763), II.5, in *Works*, 11:504; and *Journal*, July 24, 1776, in *Works*, 23:25.

40   For elaboration of this point, see Randy L. Maddox, "The Rule of Christian Faith, Practice, and Hope: John Wesley on the Bible," *Methodist Review* 3 (2011): 9–13; at www.methodistreview.org.

41 Sermon 91, "On Charity," proem, in *Works*, 3:292.
42 *Journal*, July 18, 1765, in *Works*, 22:13; and *Journal*, November 9, 1772, in *Works*, 22:352.
43 For more details on this and the following paragraph, see Maddox, "Rule of Faith," 26–30.
44 Preface, §5, in *Works*, 1:106.
45 *Letter to Bishop of Gloucester* (1763), II.10, in *Works*, 11:509 (emphasis in original).
46 Sermon 18, "The Marks of the New Birth," §3, in *Works*, 1:418 (emphasis added).
47 See this image in Sermon 19, "The Great Privilege of Those That Are Born of God," III.3, in *Works*, 1:442.
48 Preface, §5, in *Works*, 1:106.
49 See respectively the preface to *Hymns and Sacred Poems* (1739), §§4–5, in *Works* (Jackson) 14:321; and Sermon 24, "Sermon on the Mount IV," §I.1, in *Works*, 1:533–34.
50 For more on this see Randy L. Maddox, "Opinion, Religion, and 'Catholic Spirit': John Wesley on Theological Integrity," *Asbury Theological Journal* 47, no. 1 (1992): 63–87.
51 Sermon 39, "Catholic Spirit," §I.4, in *Works*, 2:84.
52 Preface, §§8–9, in *Works*, 1:107.
53 Letter to the Reverend Dr. Conyers Middleton, Jan. 4–24, 1749, in *Letters* (Telford), 2:325.
54 See Augustine, *On Christian Doctrine*, trans. D. W. Robertson Jr. (Indianapolis: Bobbs-Merrill, 1958), 79 (§3.2).
55 See Robert W. Wall, "Reading Scripture, the Literal Sense, and the Analogy of Faith," ch. 3 of this volume.
56 Letter to Cradock Glascott, May 13, 1764, in *Letters* (Telford), 4:243; referring to John Pearson, *An Exposition of the Creed* (London: John Williams, 1659).
57 For more details on this and the following paragraphs, see Randy L. Maddox, "John Wesley's Precedent for Theological Engagement with the Natural Sciences," *Wesleyan Theological Journal* 44, no. 1 (2009): 23–54.
58 See Thomas Burnet, *The Theory of the Earth* (London: Walter Kettilby, 1684–90). Wesley read Burnet as early as 1734 and reread him while working on a later edition of *Survey* in 1770. See his comments in *Journal*, January 17, 1770, in *Works* 22:213–14; and Sermon 56, "God's Approbation of His Works," I.2, in *Works*, 2:389.
59 See Sermon 60, "The General Deliverance," in *Works*, 2:437–50; and Sermon 64, "The New Creation," in *Works*, 2:500–510.
60 See the discussion in Randy L. Maddox, "Anticipating the New Creation: Wesleyan Foundations for Holistic Mission," *Asbury Journal* 62 (2007): 49–66.

CHAPTER 2: COLLINS

1 "General Rules of the United Societies," in *Works*, 9:73.
2 Wilbur H. Mullen, "John Wesley's Method of Biblical Interpretation," *Religion in Life* 47 (1978): 106. Mullen maintains that the text is "simply an accommodation of Old Testament works to the sermon theme."
3 "The Means of Grace," in *Works*, 1:281.

4   *Some Late Conversations*, in *Works* (Jackson), 8:286.
5   "The Means of Grace," in *Works*, 1:381.
6   *Minutes of Several Conversations*, in *Works* (Jackson), 8:323.
7   *Minutes of Several Conversations*, in *Works* (Jackson), 8:323.
8   Henry H. Knight, *The Presence of God in the Christian Life: John Wesley and the Means of Grace* (Metuchen, N.J.: Scarecrow Press, 1992), 5.
9   January 2, 1790; *Journal and Diaries VII (1787–1791)*, ed. Richard P. Heitzenrater, vol. 24 of *Works*, 164.
10 Letter to Miss Bolton, August 1, 1789, in *Works* (Jackson), 12:487.
11 Sermon 98, "On Visiting the Sick," in *Works*, 3:385.
12 Sermon 92, "On Zeal," in *Works*, 3:313. On this topic, see also the helpful essay by Joerg Rieger, "The Means of Grace, John Wesley, and the Theological Dilemma of the Church Today," *Quarterly Review* 17 (1997): 377–93. Rieger explores the theological and practical significance of considering works of mercy, especially among the poor, as a means of grace, as a transforming activity.
13 Kenneth J. Collins, *John Wesley: A Theological Journey* (Nashville: Abingdon, 2003), 16.
14 Mack Stokes, *The Bible in the Wesleyan Heritage* (Nashville: Abingdon, 1981), 19.
15 Stokes, *Bible*, 19.
16 *Roman Catechism and Reply*, in *Works* (Jackson), 10:92.
17 "The Means of Grace," in *Works*, 1:388.
18 Matthew R. Schlimm, "Defending the Old Testament's Worth: John Wesley's Reaction to the Rebirth of Marcionism," *Wesleyan Theological Journal* 42, no. 2 (2007): 42. Moreover, Schlimm points out that more than 99 percent of Wesley's OT notes are actually an abridgement of "Matthew Poole's and Matthew Henry's commentaries on the Old Testament" (46).
19 See *Minutes of Several Conversations*, in *Works* (Jackson), 8:322–23; and "The Means of Grace," in *Works*, 1:381.
20 Ole E. Borgen, *John Wesley on the Sacraments* (Grand Rapids: Francis Asbury Press, 1985), 106.
21 See "A Clear and Concise Demonstration of the Divine Inspiration of the Holy Scriptures," in *Works* (Jackson), 11:484.
22 R. Larry Shelton, "John Wesley's Approach to Scripture in Historical Perspective," *Wesleyan Theological Journal* 16, no. 1 (1981): 37.
23 Scott Jones, *John Wesley's Concept and Use of Scripture* (Ann Arbor, Mich.: University Microfilms, 1992), 19.
24 Lycurgus M. Starkey, *The Work of the Holy Spirit: A Study in Wesleyan Theology* (Nashville: Abingdon, 1962), 90.
25 John Wesley, *Explanatory Notes upon the New Testament* (Salem, Ohio: Schmul, 1975), 554 (on 2 Tim 3:16); cf. Gayle C. Felton, ed., *How United Methodists Study Scripture* (Nashville: Abingdon, 1999), 43.
26 Letter to the Bishop of Gloucester, November 26, 1762, in *Works*, 11:509. Gerald R. Cragg indicates that the exact language here was drawn from the medieval classic *The Imitation of Christ*, then translated by Wesley, *Omnis scriptura sacra eo spiritu debet legi, quo facta est* (in *Works*, 11:509n2).

27   *Works*, 1:105–6. Wesley does not mean in this context that he read only the Bible. Instead, he is affirming by means of such an expression that Scripture was at the center of all his reading, which was actually quite broad.
28   *Works*, 1:105.
29   Jones, *Scripture*, 32.
30   Sermon 106, "On Faith (Heb. 11:6)," in *Works*, 3:496.
31   *The Advantage of the Members of the Church of England*, in *Works* (Jackson), 10:134. For a much different view and one that fails to properly assess and appreciate the *preeminent* role of Scripture so clearly articulated by Wesley, see William J. Abraham, *Canon and Criterion in Christian Theology* (New York: Oxford University Press, 1998). Indeed, the understanding of the canon of Scripture articulated in this work is more expressive of that held by Eastern Orthodoxy rather than that of historic Methodism.
32   "On Faith," in *Works*, 3:496.
33   Championing his canonical theism project (which is problematic on a number of levels, especially as it faces Protestantism in general and evangelicalism in particular), William J. Abraham misconstrues my own understanding of Scripture. Oddly enough, Abraham now considers my work in Wesley studies as being done in "the spirit of liberal Protestantism," an observation that may be his own faint attempt at humor. To be sure, one can disagree with the project of canonical theism, given its missteps, and yet remain a Wesleyan evangelical. See William J. Abraham, "The Future of Scripture: In Search of a Theology of Scripture," *Wesleyan Theological Journal* 46, no. 1 (2011): 14. See also Kenneth J. Collins, "Is 'Canonical Theism' a Viable Option for Wesleyans?" *Wesleyan Theological Journal* 45, no. 2 (2010): 82–107.
34   "The Witness of Our Own Spirit," in *Works*, 1:302–3.
35   *Advice to Methodists with Regard to Dress*, in *Works* (Jackson), 11:472.
36   *Popery Calmly Considered*, in *Works* (Jackson), 10:142. Here is the strong normative role of Scripture *advocated by John Wesley* that is set aside in canonical theism as epistemic error (see Abraham, *Canon and Criterion*, 416).
37   Letter to William Dodd, March 12, 1756, in *Letters* (Telford), 3:172.
38   Preface to *Explanatory Notes–NT*, 5. The practical normative power of the Bible for Wesley is revealed in Stephen Gunter's observation that "Wesley quotes Scripture far more times than anything else. In one representative sample of his writings, he quoted Scripture 2,181 times. In the same writings, he referred to early church sources only fourteen times." Stephen Gunter, Scott J. Jones, Ted A. Campbell, Rebekah L. Miles, and Randy L. Maddox, *Wesley and the Quadrilateral: Renewing the Conversation* (Nashville: Abingdon, 1997), 42–43.
39   "A Letter to a Person Lately Joined with the People Called Quakers," in *Works* (Jackson), 10:178. See also "Extract of a Letter to the Rev. Mr. Law," in *Works* (Jackson), 9:503.
40   *Journal*, June 2, 1766, in *Works*, 22:42.
41   "The Original, Nature, Properties and Use of the Law," in *Works*, 2:9–10.
42   "The Original, Nature, Properties and Use of the Law," in *Works*, 2:9. Since the moral law is expressive of the divine being, it is also an apt portrayal of the love of God, the principal divine attribute. Charles Wilson explores the relations

43 "The Original, Nature, Properties and Use of the Law," in *Works*, 2:10. See also John Deschner, *Wesley's Christology: An Interpretation* (Dallas: Southern Methodist University Press, 1985), 107–8, in which the late scholar raised the question, "Is Christ the only-begotten of the Father?"

between love and law in terms of this significant "conjunction" in his work, *The Correlation of Love and Law in the Theology of John Wesley* (Ann Arbor, Mich.: University Microfilms, 1959), 99–115.

44 For an exploration of the conjunctive style of Wesley's theology, see Kenneth J. Collins, *The Theology of John Wesley: Holy Love and the Shape of Grace* (Nashville: Abingdon, 2007), 3–5.
45 "The Original, Nature, Properties and Use of the Law," in *Works*, 2:16 (emphasis added).
46 Joel B. Green, *Reading Scripture as Wesleyans* (Nashville: Abingdon, 2010), 38. Green's view obviously differs from this approach.
47 Joel B. Green, *Seized by Truth* (Nashville: Abingdon, 2007), 14.
48 Cited in Green, *Seized by Truth*, 14.
49 Green, *Seized by Truth*, 75.
50 Green, *Seized by Truth*, 5.
51 Sermon 37, "The Nature of Enthusiasm," in *Works*, 2:44–45. See the introduction. Wesley engaged in a practice, from time to time, known as bibliomancy or Bible-dipping. After exhausting other means of making a decision, Wesley on occasion resorted to the lot or opening up the Bible in a random place to seek its counsel. Edward H. Sugden traces this practice back to "the old Greek and Roman practice of divination." *Wesley's Standard Sermons*, 2 vols. (London: Epworth, 1951), 2:97. For Wesley's defense of the practice, see *Principles of a Methodist Farther Explained*, in *Works*, 9:201–4.
52 "The Nature of Enthusiasm," in *Works*, 2:45. Outler indicates that the sermon "The Nature of Enthusiasm" is an "exercise in irony" since Wesley turns the tables on his detractors by suggesting that real enthusiasm is to assume one has the grace that one so obviously lacks; in other words, here as elsewhere Wesley is targeting the nominal Christianity that he repeatedly criticized.
53 Wesley was dependent on Matthew Henry (1662–1714) for so many of his observations on the biblical text. Henry had published his *Exposition of the Old and New Testaments* in 1706, which treated the entirety of the OT as well as the Gospels and the Book of Acts in the New.
54 *Works Abridged from Various Authors*, in *Works* (Jackson), 14:253.
55 Letter to Samuel Furly, May 10, 1755, in *Works*, 26:557.
56 *A Plain Account of Christian Perfection*, in *Works* (Jackson), 11:429.
57 Donald A. Bullen accuses Wesley of engaging in eisegesis in that he failed to acknowledge how he "brought to the text the ideas and beliefs that were consistent with his Arminian Anglican theology." *A Man of One Book? John Wesley's Interpretation and Use of the Bible* (Waynesboro, Ga.: Paternoster, 2007), 206. It is not all clear, however, that Wesley was, especially later in his career, the High Church Arminian that Bullen has imagined.
58 Sermon 74, "Of the Church," in *Works*, 3:50 (emphasis added).
59 *Works Abridged; Preface to the Explanatory Notes–OT*, in *Works* (Jackson), 14:252–53.

60 *Works Abridged; Preface to the Explanatory Notes–OT*, in *Works* (Jackson), 14:252–53.
61 *Works Abridged; Preface to the Explanatory Notes–OT*, in *Works* (Jackson), 14:252–53. Matthew Henry, in commenting on Rom 12:1-21, explored the analogy of faith along the following lines: "Truths that are more dark must be examined by those that are more clear; and then entertained when they are found to agree and comport with the analogy of faith; for it is certain one truth can never contradict another." *Matthew Henry's Commentary on the Whole Bible: Complete and Unabridged in One Volume* (Peabody, Mass.: Hendrickson, 1996).
62 J. J. Pelikan, H. C. Oswald, and H. T. Lehmann, eds., *Luther's Works*, vol. 2: *Lectures on Genesis: Chapters 6–14* (Saint Louis, Mo.: Concordia, 1999), 16 (on Gen 6:3). Luther writes, "And so we do not invent any new understanding, but we adhere to the analogy both of Holy Scripture and of the faith."
63 *Address to the Clergy*, in *Works* (Jackson), 10:490–91 (emphasis added).
64 Sermon 17, "The Circumcision of the Heart," in *Works*, 1:402.
65 *An Earnest Appeal to Men of Reason and Religion*, in *Works*, 11:56 (emphasis added).
66 See *Works* (Jackson), 14:253.
67 *Works Abridged*, in *Works* (Jackson), 14:267–68.
68 November 24, 1739, in *Works*, 19:123–24.
69 February 1, 1738, in *Works*, 18:214.
70 Sermon 22, "Sermon on the Mount II," in *Works*, 1:496–97.
71 "Letter to the Bishop of Gloucester," in *Works* (Jackson), 9:136.
72 "The Means of Grace," in *Works*, 1:382.
73 *A Short Address to the Inhabitants of Ireland*, in *Works* (Jackson), 9:174.
74 "Means of Grace," in *Works*, 1:383.
75 "Letters to Mr. John Smith," in *Works* (Jackson), 12:71.
76 "The Means of Grace," in *Works*, 1:381.
77 "The Means of Grace," in *Works*, 1:378.
78 Saint Augustine, *On Christian Doctrine*, trans. D. W. Robertson Jr. (Indianapolis: Bobbs-Merrill, 1985), 30. Joel B. Green's work expresses this emphasis in a similar way by pointing out that the first questions of the biblical narrative are "not about historical veracity ('Did this really happen this way?'), but about signification ('What does this mean?') and invitation ('What does this call me to be and do?')." *Seized by Truth*, 168.

CHAPTER 3: WALL

1 The literature on this question is sparse. The most comprehensive treatment of the topic is by Jones, *Scripture*. More recently, S. J. Koskie has offered a significant study of Wesleyan hermeneutics, the predicate of which is a discussion of Wesley's account of Scripture, in his unpublished Ph.D. thesis, "Reading the Way to Heaven: A Wesleyan Theological Hermeneutic of Scripture" (Ph.D. diss., Brunel University, 2009).
2 Albert Outler, "The Wesleyan Quadrilateral—in John Wesley," in *The Wesleyan Theological Heritage: Essays of Albert C. Outler*, ed. T. C. Oden and L. R. Longden (Grand Rapids: Zondervan, 1991), 31.
3 I have tried to develop this point more fully in my essay, "Wesley as Biblical Interpreter," in *The Cambridge Companion to John Wesley*, ed. Randy L. Maddox and Jason E. Vickers (Cambridge: Cambridge University Press, 2010), 113–28.

4   For example, Luther writes, "Apart from Christ, all men are everlastingly subjects and captives in the power of the devil, of sin, and of death; but He rescues them for an eternal, divine freedom, righteousness, and life. This great and marvelous thing is accomplished entirely through the office of preaching the Gospel." *Luther's Works*, 13:291.
5   Preface to *Explanatory Notes–NT*, §10, in *Works* (Jackson), 14:238.
6   *Explanatory Notes–NT*, §12, in *Works* (Jackson), 14:239.
7   Preface to *Explanatory Notes–OT*, §15, in *Works* (Jackson), 14:252.
8   For a list of five interpretive rules that follow from this conception of Scripture, see A. C. Outler, introduction to *Works*, 1:57–59. What is lacking from his list is a sixth interpretive rule supplied in "The Nature of Enthusiasm," in *Works*, 2:54–55. According to Wesley, the target of Scripture's interpretation is to know the will of God, "which is our sanctification." Below I seek to apply this general rule to define, in Wesley's implied terms, Scripture's "literal sense."
9   See Jones, *Scripture*; and esp. Koskie, "Wesleyan Theological Hermeneutic."
10 Found in Albert Outler, ed., *John Wesley* (Oxford: Oxford University Press, 1964), 123. Wesley's nod to Romans and Galatians reflects his formal dependence on the Reformation's Pauline canon within the canon; I have argued, however, that Wesley's true home is 1 John—by which the rest of Scripture, including Paul, is glossed. Wall, "Wesley as Biblical Interpreter," 118–22.
11 For Wesley's routine use of a scholar's tools, see Maddox, "Rule of Faith," 3–7; in responding to the anachronistic use of Wesley by Protestant fundamentalists, note especially Maddox's helpful "excursus on inerrancy" (9–13).
12 See esp. K. G. Howcroft, "Reason, Interpretation and Postmodernism—Is There a Methodist Way of Reading the Bible?" *Epworth Review* 25 (1998): 28–42.
13 Outler puts it this way: "We can see in Wesley a distinctive theological method, with Scripture as its preeminent norm but interfaced with tradition, reason and Christian experience as dynamic and interactive aids in the interpretation of the Word of God in Scripture." "Wesleyan Quadrilateral," 77.
14 Letter to Dr. Rutherforth, March 28, 1768, in *Letters* (Telford), 5:164. On this point, see Maddox, "Rule of Faith," 5–7.
15 E.g., S. B. Dawes, "John Wesley and the Bible," *Proceedings of the Wesley Historical Society* 54, no. 1 (2003): 1–10.
16 D. Bebbington, *Evangelicalism in Modern Britain: A History from the 1730's to the 1980's* (London: Unwin Hyman, 1989), 50–66.
17 Preston, "Biblical Criticism, Literature," 98–102.
18 *Explanatory Notes–NT*, §9, in *Works* (Jackson), 14:238.
19 Letter to John Newton, April 1, 1766, in *Letters* (Telford), 5:8.
20 "An Address to the Clergy," in *Works*, 10:482.
21 "An Address to the Clergy," in *Works*, 10:482.
22 S. E. Fowl, "The Importance of a Multivoiced Literal Sense of Scripture," in *Reading Scripture with the Church: Toward a Hermeneutic for Theological Interpretation*, by A. K. M. Adam, S. E. Fowl, K. J. Vanhoozer, and F. Watson (Grand Rapids: Baker, 2006), 35–50. On this point, Fowl would distinguish Aquinas from the Reformers who were more keen to pursue a single literal sense, even if this sense is believed to be God's (rather than the author's) intended meaning.

23 Cf. F. M. Young, *Biblical Exegesis and the Formation of Christian Culture* (Cambridge: Cambridge University Press, 1997).
24 Fowl, "Multivoiced Literal Sense," 49–50.
25 B. S. Childs, "The *Sensus Literalis* of Scripture: An Ancient and Modern Problem," in *Beiträge zur Alttestamentttlichen Theologie: Festschrift für Walther Zimmerli zum 70. Geburtstag*, ed. H. Donner, R. Hanhart, and R. Smend (Göttingen: Vandenhoeck & Ruprecht, 1977), 80–95. Of course, the reception of Scripture in the academy is also multifaceted, but it is based on either new interpretive methods or new historical evidence about the author, the author's social world, and a more precise portrait of his first readers and auditors. Modern criticism's conception of a "multifaceted literal sense," then, is very different than what Fowl has in mind for Aquinas and I for Wesley.
26 Although well beyond the scope of this chapter, let me simply observe that a comparison of Jonathan Edwards' explanatory notes on a sample of set texts in his *Blank Bible* and those in Wesley's *Explanatory Notes*—along with the notes of other contemporary interpreters—will reflect their different readings of these texts and help secure this point, which otherwise is made with common sense.
27 Wall, "Wesley as Biblical Interpreter," 123–24. See Jones, *Scripture*, who stipulates that Wesley's use of Scripture was regulated by this rule: "use the literal sense unless it contradicts another Scripture or implies an Absurdity" (114) and then examines examples of his appeal to literal sense in his sermons (114–21).
28 "The Nature of Enthusiasm," in *Works*, 2:54.
29 "The Nature of Enthusiasm," in *Works*, 2:55.
30 This conclusion is not very different from Koskie's fluent description of a literal sense in that he also defines Wesley's conception as including its Christian rather than merely its verbal sense. "Wesleyan Theological Hermeneutic," 88–119. However, my definition assumes that the nature of God who addresses readers in Scripture is living and present (Deut 5:26; Matt 16:16; 1 Tim 3:15) and whose self-communication via Scripture's "literal sense" is therefore more particular to the audience and so dynamic and multivoiced in substance and effect. The better way of testing this thesis is to compare different Wesley sermons based on the same set text but preached or written for different audiences and at different stages of his life—a set text such as Eph 2:8-10 or John 3:8, among Wesley's most strategic. My findings from a cursory analysis are more in line with Fowl's idea of a "multivoiced literal sense" for ever-changing audiences than a more static meaning based on an unchanging theological grammar.
31 The "general tenor" of Scripture refers to its simultaneity. In Wesley's reading, every Scripture agreed with the literal sense of every other Scripture, since the literal sense of any biblical text, properly understood, testifies to God's way of salvation.
32 Wesley, *Explanatory Notes–NT*, Rom 12:6.
33 N. T. Wright, "Romans," in *New Interpreter's Bible*, ed. Leander E. Keck (Nashville: Abingdon, 2003), 10:709.
34 Maddox, "Rule of Faith," 22.

35   "Great Privilege," in *Works*, 1:279.
36   Sermon 45, "The New Birth," in *Works*, 2:193.
37   *Works*, 1:105.

CHAPTER 4: GREEN

1   E.g., Mullen: "In a brief summary reaction to his method I would conclude that Wesley is not critical." "Wesley's Method of Interpretation," 106–7. See also Duncan S. Ferguson, "John Wesley on Scripture: The Hermeneutics of Pietism," *Methodist History* 22 (1984): 234–45, esp. 244; George A. Turner, "John Wesley as an Interpreter of Scripture," in *Inspiration and Interpretation*, ed. John F. Walvoord (Grand Rapids: Eerdmans, 1957), 156–78, esp. 165–66.
2   John Barton, *The Nature of Biblical Criticism* (Louisville, Ky.: Westminster John Knox, 2007), 31.
3   John Sandys-Wunsch and Laurence Eldredge, "J. P. Gabler and the Distinction between Biblical and Dogmatic Theology: Translation, Commentary, and Discussion of His Originality," *Scottish Journal of Theology* 33 (1980): 133–58 (137).
4   Krister Stendahl, "Biblical Theology, Contemporary," in *Interpreter's Dictionary of the Bible*, 4 vols., ed. George A. Buttrick (Nashville: Abingdon, 1962), 1:418–32. For a comparison of Gabler's and Stendahl's proposals, see Loren T. Stuckenbruck, "Johann Philipp Gabler and the Delineation of Biblical Theology," *Scottish Journal of Theology* 52 (1999): 139–57 (154–57). Gordon D. Fee speaks for many when he describes the move from historical exegesis to contemporary meaning as "the core of the hermeneutical problem today." *Gospel and Spirit: Issues in New Testament Hermeneutics* (Peabody, Mass.: Hendrickson, 1991), 2–3.
5   Heikki Räisänen, *Beyond New Testament Theology: A Story and a Programme*, 2nd ed. (London: SCM Press, 2000); Peter Balla, *Challenges to New Testament Theology: An Attempt to Justify the Enterprise*, Wissenschaftliche Untersuchungen zum Neuen Testament 2 (Tübingen: Mohr Siebeck, 1997), 95.
6   Stendahl, "Biblical Theology," 422.
7   John J. Collins, "The Politics of Biblical Interpretation," in *Encounters with Biblical Theology* (Minneapolis: Fortress, 2005), 34–44; cf., idem, "Is a Critical Biblical Theology Possible?" in *The Hebrew Bible and Its Interpreters*, ed. William Henry Propp et al. (Winona Lake, Ind.: Eisenbrauns, 1990), 1–17 (reprinted in *Encounters with Biblical Theology*, 11–23; citations are from the reprint edition); idem, "Is a Postmodern Biblical Theology Possible?" in *The Bible after Babel: Historical Criticism in a Postmodern Age* (Grand Rapids: Eerdmans, 2005), 131–61.
8   Collins, "Politics," 35.
9   Collins refers to Ernst Troeltsch, "Über historische und dogmatische Methode in der Theologie," in *Gesammelte Schriften*, 4 vols. (Tübingen: Mohr Siebeck, 1913), 2:729–53; idem, "Historiography," in *Encyclopedia of Religion and Ethics*, ed. J. Hasting, 13 vols. (New York: Charles Scribner's Sons, 1914), 6:716–23; Van A. Harvey, *The Historian and the Believer* (New York: Macmillan, 1966). Troeltsch's seminal essay is available in English in Ernst Troeltsch, "Historical and Dogmatic Method in Theology," in *Religion in History*, Fortress Texts in Modern Theology (Minneapolis: Fortress, 1991), 11–32.

10   Collins, "Politics," 35. See Harvey, *Historian*, 39–42.
11   Collins, "Critical Biblical Theology," 22.
12   Collins, "Politics," 36. Thus, Collins understands *criticism* more along the lines of what we find in Harvey's work than in Troeltsch's, and he neglects to develop here Troeltsch's third principle of *correlation*.
13   "Literary simultaneity" emphasizes Scripture's self-referentiality, the mutual implication of all its parts, rather than the historical succession of its ingredients. Speaking of the Tanak, Jon D. Levinson describes literary simultaneity thus: "What is most important is not the empirical issue of how the several parts of the Torah came to assume their present shape but, rather, the affirmation that they now form an indissoluble unity and a revelation from God." "The Eighth Principle of Judaism and the Literary Simultaneity of Scripture," in *The Hebrew Bible, the Old Testament, and Historical Criticism* (Louisville, Ky.: Westminster John Knox, 1993), 62–81.
14   See Joel B. Green, "Rethinking 'History' for Theological Interpretation," *Journal of Theological Interpretation* 5, no. 2 (2011): 159–74.
15   See M. H. Abrams, *The Mirror and the Lamp: Romantic Theory and the Critical Tradition* (Oxford: Oxford University Press, 1953); cf. Hazard Adams, ed., *Critical Theory since Plato*, rev. ed. (Fort Worth: Harcourt Brace Jovanovich, 1992).
16   Werner Georg Kümmel, *The New Testament: The History of the Investigation of Its Problems* (Nashville: Abingdon, 1972), 40 (original emphasis removed).
17   John Wesley, preface to *Explanatory Notes–NT* (London: Epworth, 1876 [1754]), §7, p. 7: "Many of his excellent notes I have therefore translated; many more I have abridged, omitting that part which was purely critical, and giving the substance of the rest. Those various readings, likewise, which he has showed to have a vast majority of ancient copies and translations on their side, I have without scruple incorporated with the text; which, after his manner, I have divided all along . . . according to the matter it contains, making a larger or smaller pause, just as the sense requires." Elsewhere, Wesley refers to Bengel (i.e., to Bengelius) as "the most pious, the most judicious, and the most laborious, of all the modern Commentators on the New Testament." "On the Trinity," §5 in *Works* (Jackson), 6:201.
18   Bruce M. Metzger, *The Text of the New Testament: Its Transmission, Corruption, and Restoration* (New York: Oxford University Press, 1968), 112.
19   Johann Albrecht Bengel, "Essay on the Right Way of Handling Divine Subjects," excerpted from A. R. Fausset, "Sketch of the Life and Writings of J. A. Bengel," in *Gnomon of the New Testament*, by John Albert Bengel (Edinburgh: T&T Clark, 1858), 5:xvii (emphasis in original).
20   Augustus Herman Francke, *A Guide to the Reading and Study of the Holy Scriptures*, 3rd ed. (London: D. Jaques, 1819).
21   Francke, *Reading and Study*, 1–2.
22   Francke, *Reading and Study*, 38.
23   Francke, *Reading and Study*, 99.
24   Francke, *Reading and Study*, 106.
25   Lest someone assume that this was true only of the Pietist strand of biblical interpretation represented by Bengal and Francke (and, indeed, by Wesley), we

might draw attention to other interpreters of the period, who similarly drew attention to the importance of, for example, textual criticism, Palestinian geography, and the rabbinical literature, sans the historical consciousness that would lead to the view that the biblical writings were witnesses primarily for their own time. See the discussion in Kümmel, *New Testament*, 40–73; William Baird, *History of New Testament Research*, vol. 1: *From Deism to Tübingen* (Minneapolis: Fortress, 1992), 3–154.

26   Preface to *Explanatory Notes–OT*, §18, in *Works* (Jackson), 14:252–53.
27   Preface to *Sermons on Several Occasions*, §5, in *Works* (Jackson), 5:3.
28   *Explanatory Notes–NT*, 53.
29   "An Address to the Clergy," II.1.2–6, in *Works* (Jackson), 10:491–92.
30   "An Address to the Clergy," II.1.1, in *Works* (Jackson), 10:490–91.
31   *Explanatory Notes–NT*, 11.
32   *Explanatory Notes–NT*, 808.
33   Kümmel identifies the inauguration of "the science of New Testament introduction" with the publication in 1788 of Johann David Michaelis' two-volume *Introduction to the Divine Scriptures of the New Covenant. New Testament*, 69.
34   *Explanatory Notes–NT*, 200.
35   *Explanatory Notes–NT*, 202.
36   *Explanatory Notes–NT*, 240.
37   *Explanatory Notes–NT*, 288.
38   Baird, *History*, 89.
39   On this last point, see, e.g., preface to *Explanatory Notes–OT*, §§4, 9, in *Works* (Jackson), 14:247, 249; *Explanatory Notes–NT*, 872–73 (on 1 Pet 1:2). On Wesley's anthropology and Christology, as found in his *Explanatory Notes upon the New Testament*, cf. Robin Scroggs, "John Wesley as Bible Scholar," *Journal of Bible and Religion* 28 (1960): 415–22 (419–22).

CHAPTER 5: BROADNAX

1   Johnson is now deceased.
2   Joseph A. Johnson, *Proclamation Theology* (Shreveport, La.: Fourth Episcopal District Press, 1977), 43–44 (emphasis in original).
3   African American idiom.
4   Mack B. Stokes, *Theology for Preaching* (Anderson, Ind.: Bristol, 1994), 28.
5   Albert J. Raboteau, *Slave Religion: The "Invisible Institution" in the Antebellum South* (Oxford: Oxford University Press, 1980), 213.
6   Richard Allen, *The Life Experience and Gospel Labors of the Rt. Rev. Richard Allen* (Nashville: Abingdon, 1983), 15–16.
7   Dennis C. Dickerson, *African Methodism and Its Wesleyan Heritage: Reflections on AME Church History* (Nashville: Dennis C. Dickerson, 2009), 15.
8   Dickerson, *African Methodism*, 16.
9   Dale Andrews, *Practical Theology for Black Churches: Bridging Black Theology and African American Folk Religion* (Louisville, Ky.: Westminster John Knox, 2002), 17. For a full discussion of the role of the black preacher, see Henry H. Mitchell, *Black Preaching* (San Francisco: Harper & Row, 1970).

10   Harry V. Richardson, *Dark Salvation: The Story of Methodism as It Developed among Blacks in America* (Garden City, N.Y.: Doubleday, 1976), 28.
11   Ira Berlin, Marc Favreau, and Steven F. Miller, eds., *Remembering Slavery* (New York: Free Press, 1998), xli.
12   "The Character of a Methodist," in *Works* (Jackson), 8:340.
13   Randy L. Maddox, *Responsible Grace: John Wesley's Practical Theology* (KB; Nashville: Abingdon, 1994), 37.
14   Ted A. Campbell, "Authority and the 'Wesleyan Quadrilateral' in *T&T Clark Companion to Methodism*, ed. Charles Yrigoyen Jr. (London: Continuum, 2010), 61; with reference to Colin W. Williams, *John Wesley's Theology Today* (Nashville: Abingdon, 1960). See also idem, "The 'Wesleyan Quadrilateral': The Story of a Modern Methodist Myth," in *Doctrine and Theology in The United Methodist Church*, ed. Thomas A. Langford (KB; Nashville: Abingdon, 1991).
15   Campbell, "Authority," 62.
16   Albert C. Outler, "Introduction of the Disciplinary Statement," in *Wesleyan Theology: A Sourcebook*, ed. Thomas A. Langford (Durham, N.C.: Labyrinth, 1984), 274.
17   Outler, "Disciplinary Statement," 278.
18   Campbell, "Authority," 62.
19   *The Book of Discipline of The United Methodist Church, 1988* (Nashville: United Methodist Publishing House, 1988), 81.
20   *1988 Book of Discipline*, 82.
21   Maddox, *Responsible Grace*, 36.
22   Jones, *Scripture*, 63.
23   Jones, *Scripture*, 117.
24   Jones, *Scripture*, 80.
25   Sermon 144, "The Love of God," II.5, in *Works*, 4:337. See also Sermon 21, "Sermon on the Mount I," in *Works*, 1:473n22.
26   Sermon 139, "On the Sabbath," in *Works*, 4:273.
27   *Explanatory Notes–NT*.
28   Jones, *Scripture*, 211.
29   Jones, *Scripture*, 209, 213.
30   Karl Heinrich Rengstorf, "δοῦλος, κτλ," *Theological Dictionary of the New Testament*, ed. Gerhard Kittel and Gerhard Friederich, 10 vols. (Grand Rapids: Eerdmans, 1964–1976), 2:261–80 (261).
31   Now deceased.
32   Alfred G. Dunston Jr., *The Black Man in the Old Testament and Its World* (Philadelphia: Dorrance, 1974), 18–21. Dunston refers in particular to translations regarding the geography of both Egypt and Ethiopia.
33   *Explanatory Notes–NT*, 772.
34   *Explanatory Notes–NT*, 720 (emphasis in original).
35   *Explanatory Notes–NT*, 750 (emphasis in original).
36   *Explanatory Notes–NT*, 750 (emphasis in original).
37   *Explanatory Notes–NT*, 879 (emphasis in original).
38   Pheme Perkins, *First and Second Peter, James, and Jude* (Interpretation; Louisville, Ky.: Westminster John Knox, 1995), 52.

39 *Works* (Jackson), 1:49. See also Warren Thomas Smith, *John Wesley and Slavery* (Nashville: Abingdon, 1986), 50.
40 *Works* (Jackson), 9:59.
41 William B. McClain, *Black People in the Methodist Church* (Nashville: Abingdon, 1984), 12. See David N. Hempton, "Wesley in Context," in *Cambridge Companion to John Wesley*, 70; Donald G. Mathews, *Slavery and Methodism: A Chapter in American Morality 1780–1845* (Princeton, N.J.: Princeton University Press, 1965), 6.
42 Smith, *Slavery*, 91.
43 Jason E. Vickers, *Wesley: A Guide for the Perplexed* (London: T&T Clark, 2009), 68.
44 *Thoughts upon Slavery*, in *Works* (Jackson), 11:59.
45 *Thoughts upon Slavery*, in *Works* (Jackson), 11:60.
46 Smith, *Slavery*, 84–85.
47 *Thoughts upon Slavery*, in *Works* (Jackson), 11:61.
48 *Thoughts upon Slavery*, in *Works* (Jackson), 11:62.
49 *Thoughts upon Slavery*, in *Works* (Jackson), 11:64.
50 *Thoughts upon Slavery*, in *Works* (Jackson), 11:70.
51 *Thoughts upon Slavery*, in *Works* (Jackson), 11:70.
52 *Thoughts upon Slavery*, in *Works* (Jackson), 11:71.
53 *Thoughts upon Slavery*, in *Works* (Jackson), 11:79.
54 Smith, *Slavery*, 96. See also Barry E. Bryant, "Original Sin," in *The Oxford Handbook of Methodist Studies*, ed. William J. Abraham and James E. Kirby (Oxford: Oxford University Press, 2009), 527.
55 *Thoughts upon Slavery*, in *Works* (Jackson), 11:79.
56 Maddox, *Responsible Grace*, 37.
57 Vickers, *Guide for the Perplexed*, 68.
58 *Thoughts upon Slavery*, in *Works* (Jackson), 11:76.
59 *Thoughts upon Slavery*, in *Works* (Jackson), 11:70 (emphasis added).
60 Jones, *Scripture*, 80.
61 See Anthony B. Pinn, *Why, Lord? Suffering and Evil in Black Theology* (London: Continuum, 1999).
62 James Evans, "Black Theology and Black Feminism," in *Journal of Religious Thought* 38 (1981): 46–47. See also Cain Hope Felder, *Troubling Biblical Waters: Race, Class and Family* (Maryknoll, N.Y.: Orbis, 1989), 104–5.
63 Thomas Hoyt Jr., "Interpreting Biblical Scholarship for the Black Church Tradition," in *Stony the Road We Trod: African American Biblical Interpretation*, ed. Cain Hope Felder (Minneapolis: Fortress, 1991), 24.
64 Hoyt, "Interpreting Biblical Scholarship," 25.
65 Hoyt, "Interpreting Biblical Scholarship," 33.
66 Hoyt, "Interpreting Biblical Scholarship," 33.
67 See Richardson, *Dark Salvation*.
68 This follows the two principles of a black hermeneutic as outlined by Henry Mitchell: (1) that one must speak in the language (vernacular) of the people and (2) that the gospel must speak to contemporary needs. *Black Preaching: The Recovery of a Powerful Art* (Nashville: Abingdon, 1990), 29.

Chapter 6: González

1. There has been and still is much debate about the use of the term "Hispanic." The first to call themselves *hispanos* were some of the ancient families who lived and owned land in the Southwest before the Mexican-American War. As the Mexican Revolution produced a large influx of Mexicans into the United States, the term *hispano* was used by those who sought to differentiate themselves from the more recently arrived *mexicanos*. When the U.S. Bureau of the Census began referring to people of Hispanic heritage and culture as "Hispanics," many rejected this term as an imposition from outside. As a result, the term "Latino" came to the foreground. But this term had also been used by some Latin American immigrants in the Northeast to distinguish themselves from Puerto Ricans. Therefore the term "Latino" was not always to the liking of some native born. In this article, while taking cognizance of the ongoing debate, I have simply used the term "Hispanic" as a synonym of "Latino."
2. For instance, when the General Conference of the Methodist Episcopal Church, South, gave approval to the creation of a Mexican Border Conference, this was divided into four districts, two headquartered in Texas and two in Mexico. See Joel N. Martínez, "The South Central Jurisdiction," in *Each in Our Own Tongue: A History of Hispanic United Methodism*, ed. Justo L. González (Nashville: Abingdon, 1991), 44–45.
3. On the origins of Hispanic Methodist work in this area, see Alfredo Cotto-Thorner, "The Northeastern Jurisdiction," in *Each in Our Own Tongue*, 106–22; and Gildo Sánchez, "Puerto Rico," in *Each in Our Own Tongue*, 131–51.
4. See Justo L. González and Carlos F. Cardoza, *Historia general de las misiones* (Barcelona: CLIE, 2008), 299–300.
5. A fact amply attested by the far-ranging work of Clifton L. Holland and others who have been working on a compilation of data on Hispanic churches. See www.hispanicchurches.net.
6. While in common North American usage "evangelicalism" is often defined in terms of contrast with liberalism, the Spanish term *evangélico* is usually understood in terms of a contrast with Roman Catholicism.
7. For Hispanic use of the Bible prior to that date, see the unpublished doctoral dissertation by Jorge Nehemías Cintrón-Figueroa, "The Use of the Bible in Selected Materials of the Hispanic-American Evangelical Curriculum" (Boston University, 1969).
8. Among the many articles in *Apuntes* on biblical interpretation, the following deserve particular attention as examples of ways in which Methodist Hispanics bring new insights into the subject: Minerva Carcaño Garza, "Una perspectiva bíblico-teológica sobre la mujer en el ministerio ordenado," *Apuntes* 10 (1990): 27–35; Aquiles E. Martínez, "Jesus, the Immigrant Child: A Diasporic Reading of Matthew 2:1-23," *Apuntes* 26 (2006): 84–114; idem, "El apóstol Pablo y la comunidad de Tesalónica: Lecciones sobre el uso del poder," *Apuntes* 15 (1995): 3–13; idem, "The Immigration Controversy and Romans 13:1-7," *Apuntes* 27 (2007): 124–44; Jorge E. Sánchez, "La educación bíblica en nuestra iglesia hispana," *Apuntes* 9 (1989): 35–38.

9   See, for instance, the articles by Aquiles E. Martínez, "Mordecai and Esther: Lessons from Persian Soil," *Journal of Latin American Theology* 4 (2009): 16–50; idem, "On Sheep and Goats: The Treatment of Foreigners According to Jesus (Matthew 25:31-46)," *Journal of Hispanic/Latino Theology* (2007): 17–29.
10 Jorge A. González, *Daniel: A Tract for Troubled Times* (New York: General Board of Global Ministries, The United Methodist Church, 1985); Aquiles E. Martínez, *Después de Damasco: El apóstol Pablo desde una perspectiva latina* (Nashville: Abingdon, 2004); Justo L. González, *For the Healing of the Nations: The Book of Revelation in an Age of Cultural Conflict* (Maryknoll, N.Y.: Orbis, 1999); idem, *Acts: The Gospel of the Spirit* (Maryknoll, N.Y.: Orbis, 2001); idem, *Luke* (Belief: A Theological Commentary on the Bible; Louisville, Ky.: Westminster John Knox, 2010).
11 Justo L. González, *Santa Biblia: The Bible through Hispanic Eyes* (Nashville: Abingdon, 1996).
12 See Virgilio Elizondo, *Galilean Journey: The Mexican American Promise* (Maryknoll, N.Y.: Orbis, 1985); idem, *The Future Is Mestizo: Life Where Cultures Meet* (Boulder: University of Colorado Press, 2000); idem, *A God of Incredible Surprises: Jesus of Galilee* (Lanham, Md.: Rowman & Littlefield, 2003).
13 See Daisy L. Machado, "Voices from *Nepantla*: Latinas in U.S. Religious History," in *Feminist Intercultural Theology: Latina Explorations for a Just World*, ed. María Pilar Aquino and María José Rosado-Nunes (Maryknoll, N.Y.: Orbis, 2007).
14 See Michelle A. González, "What about *mulatez*?" in *Futuring Our Past: Explorations in the Theology of Tradition*, ed. Orlando O. Espín and Gary Macy (Maryknoll, N.Y.: Orbis), 180–203.
15 Jorge A. González, forthcoming in a commentary on Jeremiah to be published in Buenos Aires.
16 Justo L. González, "Prophets in the King's Sanctuary," *Apuntes* 1 (1981): 3–6.
17 The examples from Acts given here, and many others, may be found in Justo L. González, *Acts*.

CHAPTER 7: CHOI AND CHOI

1   Samuel Hugh Moffett, *A History of Christianity in Asia*, vol. 2: *1500–1900* (Maryknoll, N.Y.: Orbis, 2005), 143–49.
2   Moffett, *History*, 309–21.
3   Moffett, *History*, 317. See Meesaeng Lee Choi, *The Rise of the Korea Holiness Church in Relation to American Holiness Movement: Wesley's "Scriptural Holiness" and the "Fourfold Gospel"* (Lanham, Md.: Scarecrow, 2008), 88–89.
4   Sebastian C. H. Kim, "Henry Martyn, the Bible, and the Christianity in Asia," The Henry Martyn Center, ¶21, accessed August 5, 2011, http://131.111.227.198/CSKim.htm.
5   The British and Foreign Bible Society, *The Ninety-Second Report of the British and Foreign Bible Society* (London: Richard Clay & Sons, 1896), 242.
6   Man-Yeol Yi, "Study on Colporteur," in *Korean Christianity and National Consciousness* (Seoul: Chisik sanOpsa, 1991), 152.
7   Yi, "Study on Colporteur," 156.
8   Man-Yeol Yi, "한글 성경 완역 출판과 한국 사회 (The Publication of the

Korean Bible and Korean Society)," 7, accessed March 3, 2011, http://www.koreanbible.or.kr/100th_anniversary/download/100-01%20이만열.pdf.

9   Arthur Judson Brown, *Report on a Second Visit to China, Japan and Korea, 1909, with a Discussion of Some Problems of Mission Work* (New York: The Board of Foreign Mission of the Presbyterian Church in the U.S.A., n.d.), 91–92; quoted in Lak-Geoon George Paik, *The History of Protestant Missions in Korea 1832–1910* (Seoul: Yonsei University Press, 1970), 448.

10 Sebastian Kim, "The Word and the Spirit: Overcoming Injustice and Division in Korea," in *Christian Theology in Asia*, ed. Sebastian Kim (Cambridge: Cambridge University Press, 2008), 10.

11 William N. Blair and Bruce Hunt, *The Korean Pentecost and the Sufferings Which Followed* (Edinburgh: The Banner of Truth Trust, 1977), 67.

12 Jonathan Park, "Thousands of Korean Missionaries Lauded at Major Conference," *Christian Post*, July 29, 2008, accessed in August 10, 2011, http://www.christianpost.com/news/thousands-of-korean-missionaries-lauded-at-major-conference-33549. From the report at the sixth quadrennial Korean World Mission Conference on July 28, 2008, in Wheaton, Illinois. South Korea has now become the number one diaspora country, with emigrants scattered in around 180 countries. See Meesaeng Lee Choi, "A Brief History of the Korean United Methodist Church," *United Methodists in Service* 13, no. 1 (2010): 24–25, http://www.nxtbook.com/nxtbooks/unitedmethodist/inservice_20100102/#/24.

13 Eui Hang Shin, "Religion and Adaptation of Immigrants: The Case of Revival Meeting in Korean-American Churches," *Development and Society* 31, no. 1 (2002): 128.

14 R. Stephen Warner, "Korean Americans Reshape Their Churches: Second Generation," *Christian Century*, November 13, 2007, 30. Korean immigrants have humorously distinguished themselves from Chinese and Japanese arrivals by saying, "Chinese build restaurants, Japanese start electronic goods shops, and Koreans build churches."

15 For the exact distribution of the churches throughout the United States, see *Korean Churches Yellow Pages* (http://www.koreanchurchyp.com). According to the Ministry of Foreign Affairs and Trade, South Korea, as of May 21, 2009, 2.1 million Koreans are residing in the U.S.

16 Warner, "Korean Americans Reshape Their Churches," 30. He states that though others argue otherwise, about 70 percent Koreans in America are church members. Depending on location, church attendance fluctuates from 45 to 75 percent.

17 Attending ethnic churches has shown to have positive social functions. It not only means being religious but also mean an access to a storehouse of coethnic social support and tremendous benefits from that social support.

18 David K. Yoo, *Contentious Spirits: Religion in Korean American History, 1903–1945* (Stanford, Calif.: Stanford University Press, 2010), 7.

19 Green, *Reading Scripture*, 104.

20 Green, *Reading Scripture*, ix.

21 Cf. Fernando F. Segovia, "'And They Began to Speak in Other Tongues': Competing Modes of Discourse in Contemporary Biblical Criticism," in *Reading from*

This Place, vol. 1: *Social Location and Biblical Interpretation in the United States*, ed. Fernando F. Segovia and Mary Ann Tolbert (Minneapolis: Fortress, 1995), 32.

22   Steve Kang, "The Bible and the Communion of Saints: A Churchly Plural Reading of Scripture," in *This Side of Heaven: Race, Ethnicity, and Christian Faith*, ed. Robert J. Priest and Alvaro L. Nieves (Oxford: Oxford University Press, 2007), 234.

23   Sang-Taek Yi, *Religion and Social Formation in Korea: Minjung and Millenarianism* (Berlin: de Gruyter, 1996), 136.

24   Soo-Young Lee, "God's Chosen People: Protestant Narratives of Korean Americans and American National Identity" (Ph.D. diss., University of Texas at Austin, 2007), 74.

25   The term *minjung* was first used in academic discourse by two scholars Byung-Mu Ahn and Nam-Dong Suh in 1975.

26   See Seyoon Kim, "Is 'Minjung Theology' a Christian Theology?" *Calvin Theological Journal* 22, no. 2 (1987): 251–74.

27   Sharon Kim, "Hybrid Spiritualities: The Development of Second Generation Korean American Spirituality," *Human Architecture: Journal of the Sociology of Self-Knowledge* 4 (2006): 225–38. Kim explains the hybrid spirituality of second-generation Korean Americans, who, situated on the margins of multiple cultures, are engaged in a struggle to articulate a hybrid spirituality by appropriating elements of Confucianism, Korean Christianity, and various expressions of American Evangelicalism.

28   Yoka van Dyk, "Hyphenated—Living: Between Longing and Belonging: An Exposition of Displacement as Liminality in the Transnational Condition" (M.A. thesis, Auckland University of Technology, 2005), 27, accessed August 10, 2011, http://aut.researchgateway.ac.nz/bitstream/10292/273/1/van DykY.pdf.

29   Kate Bowler, "Generation K: Korean American Evangelicals," *Books & Culture* 15 (2009): 16.

30   Nadia Y. Kim, *Imperial Citizens: Koreans and Race from Seoul to LA* (Stanford, Calif.: Stanford University Press, 2008), 197.

31   N. Y. Kim, *Imperial Citizens*, 197 (emphasis added). In many ways, the American dream of getting a good education, working at a good job, and earning a good living is an achievable reality for Korean Americans. This is not to say that they no longer experience discrimination even when highly successful, however, because of their Asian ethnicity. The process of achieving socioeconomic success among Asian Americans is complex. There are many examples of affluence and prosperity among Asian Americans, but they still face the same types of racism, social inequality, and institutional discrimination that other groups of color face. Therefore, the image that the entire Asian American community is the "model minority" is a myth (cf. C. N. Le, "The Model Minority Image," *Asian-Nation: The Landscape of Asian America*, accessed August 12, 2011, www .asian-nation.org/model-minority.shtml).

32   Jung Young Lee, *Marginality: The Key to a Multicultural Theology* (Minneapolis: Fortress, 1995).

33   Sang Hyun Lee, "Pilgrimage and Home in the Wilderness of Marginality:

Symbols and Context in Asian American Theology," in *Korean Americans and Their Religions: Pilgrims and Missionaries from a Different Shore*, ed. Hoyoun Kwon, Kwang Chung Kim, and R. Stephen Warner (University Park: Pennsylvania State University Press, 2001), 55–69.

34 R. Stephen Warner, "Religion and New (Post-1965) Immigrants: Some Principles Drawn from Field Research," *American Studies* 41, nos. 2–3 (2000): 271.
35 Sinyil Kim, "Korean Immigrants and Their Mission: Exploring the Missional Identity of Korean Immigrant Churches in North America" (D.Miss., Asbury Theological Seminary, 2008), 7.
36 Kang, "Bible and Communion of Saints," 234.
37 J. Y. Lee, *Marginality*, 4.
38 J. Y. Lee, *Marginality*, 71.
39 Harvey J. Sindiman, *The Gospel According to the Marginalized* (New York: Peter Lang, 2008), 117.
40 Ig-Jin Kim, *History and Theology of Korean Pentecostalism: Sunbogeum (Pure Gospel) Pentecostalism* (Zoetermeer: Uitgeverij Boekencentrum, 2003), 227.
41 Sindiman, *Gospel*, 117.
42 Sebastian Kim, "Word and Spirit," 137.
43 Bruce Cumings, *Korea's Place in the Sun: A Modern History* (New York: Norton, 1997), 10.
44 Sebastian Kim, "Word and Spirit," 137.
45 Sebastian Kim, "Word and Spirit," 138.
46 Sharon Kim, "Hybrid Spiritualities," 235.
47 Eunjoo Mary Kim, "Hermeneutics and Asian American Preaching," *Semeia* 90–91 (2002): 277.
48 Steve Ybarrola, "An Anthropological Approach to Diaspora Missiology" (unpublished paper), 8, accessed September 11, 2011, http://ureachtoronto.com/sites/default/files/resources/An%20Anthropological%2Approach%20to%20Diaspora%20Missiology%20S11%20Final.pdf.
49 James Sunghoon Myung, "Spiritual Dimension of Church Growth: As Applied in Yoido Full Gospel Church" (Ph.D. diss., Fuller Theological Seminary, 1990), 258–60.
50 Hwa Yung, "The Missiological Challenge of David Yonggi Cho's Theology," *Asian Journal of Pentecostal Studies* 7, no. 1 (2004): 77.
51 Soong-Chan Rah, *The Next Evangelicalism: Freeing the Church from Western Cultural Captivity* (Downers Grove, Ill.: InterVarsity, 2009), 46–63.
52 Joseph Chang-Hyung Yoo, "A Reformed Doctrine of Sanctification for the Korean Context" (Ph.D. diss., University of Pretoria, 2007), 228.
53 Quoted in John Telford, *The Life of John Wesley* (London: Kelley, 1910), 229.
54 Sermon 50, "The Use of Money," in *Works*, 2:266–80.
55 "The Use of Money," in *Works*, 2:268.
56 Maddox, *Responsible Grace*.
57 Ybarrola, "Diaspora Missiology," 8.
58 Daniel S. Schipani, "Transformation in the Borderlands: A Study of Matthew 15:21-28," *Vision* 2, no. 2 (2001): 18.
59 Schipani, "Transformation in the Borderlands," 19.

60 Schipani, "Transformation in the Borderlands," 20.
61 Sinyil Kim, "Korean Immigrants," 7–8.
62 "Minutes of Several Conversations," Q.3, in *Works* (Jackson), 8:299.
63 Sang Hyun Lee, *From a Liminal Place: An Asian American Theology* (Minneapolis: Fortress, 2010), 122.
64 Quoted in Eddie Arthur, "Reading the Bible on Behalf of the World," *Kouya Chronicle*, accessed June 10, 2011, http://www.kouya.net/?p=1232.
65 Michael W. Goheen, "A Critical Examination of David Bosch's Missional Reading of Luke," in *Reading Luke: Interpretation, Reflection, Formation*, ed. Craig G. Bartholomew, Joel B. Green, and Anthony C. Thiselton (Grand Rapids: Zondervan, 2005), 229.
66 Sharon Kim, "Shifting Boundaries within Second-Generation Korean American Churches," *Sociology of Religion* 71, no. 1 (2010): 107; idem, "Replanting Sacred Spaces: The Emergence of Second-Generation Korean American Churches," in *Religion and Spirituality in Korean America*, ed. David K. Yoo and Ruth H. Chung (Chicago: University of Illinois Press, 2008), 169.
67 J. Y. Lee, *Marginality*, 62.
68 Ybarrola, "Diaspora Missiology," 8.
69 Ybarrola, "Diaspora Missiology," 8–9.
70 "With Arms Open Wide," *The Ooze*, accessed June 11, 2011, http://theooze.com/family/with-arms-wide-open/.
71 Su Yon Pak, Unzu Lee, Jung Ha Kim, and Myungji Cho, *Singing the Lord's Song in a New Land: Korean American Practices of Faith* (Louisville, Ky.: Westminster John Knox, 2005), 88.
72 S.Y. Pak et al., *Singing the Lord's Song*, 91.
73 Soong-Chan Rah, *Many Colors: Cultural Intelligence for a Changing Church* (Chicago: Moody, 2010), 175.
74 S. H. Lee, *From a Liminal Place*, 123 (emphasis in original).
75 Walter Brueggemann, "Rethinking Church Models through Scripture," *Theology Today* 48 (1991): 135.
76 Christaan Mostert, "The Church as a Textual Community," *Conversations* 1 (2011): 4, accessed October 21, 2011, http://ctm.uca.edu.au/sites/default/files/the_church_aas_a_textual_community_-_christiaan_mostert_0.pdf.
77 Martin Copenhaver, Anthony Robinson, and William Willimon, *Good News in Exile: Three Pastors Offer a Hopeful Vision for the Church* (Grand Rapids: Eerdmans, 1999), 34.
78 "On Perfection," in *Works*, 3:74.
79 Michael A. Rynkiewich, "The World in My Parish: Rethinking the Standard Missiological Model," *Missiology* 30, no. 3 (2002): 301–21. Apparently, Rynkiewich coined the phrase, "the world in my parish."

CHAPTER 8: ABRAHAM

1 Even though the convention of this volume is to use Scripture with a capital "S," the author of this article intentionally chose to use scripture with a lower-case "s," reflecting a move to develop a deflationary view of scripture.

2   See the fine discussion by James L. Kugel in *Traditions of the Bible* (Cambridge, Mass.: Harvard University Press, 1988), 14–19.

3   Jones, *Scripture*, remains the most comprehensive study of Wesley's theology of scripture.

4   The point is well made by Walter Klaiber and Manfred Marquardt, *Living Grace: An Outline of United Methodist Theology*, trans. and adapted J. Stephen O'Malley and Ulrike R. M. Guthrie (Nashville: Abingdon, 2001), 54.

5   It is no accident that Wesleyans took up and developed an inductive approach to hermeneutics. They recognized how easy it is to read our own theological commitments into the scriptures. See David A. Bauer and Robert A. Traina, *Inductive Bible Study: A Comprehensive Guide to the Practice of Hermeneutics* (Grand Rapids: Baker Academic, 2011).

6   John Wesley, preface to *Sermons on Several Occasions* (London: Epworth, 1944). He is equally willing to receive instruction from others: "I trust, whereinsoever I have mistaken, my mind is open to instruction. I sincerely desire to be better informed. I say to God and man, 'What I know not, teach thou me!'" (vii).

7   See, e.g., Scroggs, "Wesley as Biblical Scholar."

8   See, e.g., Justo L. González, "Reading the Bible in Spanish," in *Mañana: Christian Theology from a Hispanic Perspective* (Nashville: Abingdon, 1990), ch. 5. For a more vigorous statement of a similar position, see James H. Cone, *A Black Theology of Liberation: Twentieth Anniversary Edition* (Maryknoll, N.Y.: Orbis, 2010), ch. 4.

9   Ellen Charry, "Experience," in *The Oxford Handbook of Systematic Theology*, ed. John Webster, Kathryn Tanner, and Iain Torrance (Oxford: Oxford University Press, 2007), 415.

10 The point is well made in the preface to *Sermons on Several Occasions*, §6, vi.

11 The use of these theological designations is not casual. The move to refer to the OT as "Hebrew Bible," aside from making no real sense to our Jewish neighbors, represents a reading of the material that already presupposes a pious and moralistic form of functional atheism.

12 One besetting drawback of construing scripture as the Word of God is that it invites theologians to think of scripture as analogous to the incarnation. One can understand the motives for this move; it is intended to allow theologians to think of scripture as human and also beyond what is human. However, once the analogy is pressed, it readily spills over into doctrines of the divinity of scripture, and it lands us right back in the problems of inerrancy that motivated the move in the first place when scholars sought to insist on the full humanity of scripture as written by human agents.

13 I argue the case for this in *Aldersgate and Athens: John Wesley and the Foundations of Christian Belief* (Waco, Tex.: Baylor University Press, 2010). For my own full-dress exposition of this move in the epistemology of theology, see *Crossing the Threshold of Divine Revelation* (Grand Rapids: Eerdmans, 2006).

14 John Paul II, *Fides et Ratio* (Washington, D.C.: United States Catholic Conference, 1998), 75.

15 John Paul II, *Fides et Ratio*, 76.

16 John Paul II, *Fides et Ratio*, 114.

17 Happily, the move to canonize the so-called Wesleyan quadrilateral failed in the

    General Conference of The United Methodist Church in that its adoption was merely a legislative change rather than a constitutional amendment.
18 Paul takes this line in the case of excommunication for very serious moral failure in 1 Cor 5:3-6.
19 See Albert C. Outler and Richard P. Heitzenrater, eds., *John Wesley's Sermons: An Anthology* (Nashville: Abingdon, 1991).
20 For the former see Theodore W. Jennings Jr., *Good News to the Poor: John Wesley's Evangelical Economics* (Nashville: Abingdon, 1990); for the latter see the widely used Maddox, *Responsible Grace*. I take notice here of only two highly influential examples.
21 In this I follow the British and Irish tradition of limiting Wesley's canonical sermons to the forty-four to be found in his *Sermons on Several Occasions*. Not much hangs on our preferring the longer edition generally used in North America and edited by Edward H. Sugden: *John Wesley's Fifty-Three Sermons* (Nashville: Abingdon, 1983).
22 For a recent articulation of these options see David A. Hollinger, "After Cloven Tongues of Fire: Ecumenical Protestantism and the Modern America Encounter," *Journal of American History* 98, no. 1 (2011): 21–48, http://history.berkeley.edu/faculty/Hollinger/cloventongues.pdf. Hollinger's comments on Methodism are especially worth pondering. The paper as a whole is a brilliant tour de force despite the inadequacy of Hollinger's all too sharp distinction between mainline and evangelical Protestantism.
23 David A. Hollinger, a secularist who wants to make political allies of liberal and progressive Christians, readily opts for the first of these two possibilities. See his "Religious Ideas: Should They Be Critically Engaged or Given a Pass?" *Representations* 101 (2008): 144–54; accessed September 14, 2011, http://history.berkeley.edu/faculty/Hollinger/articles/religideas-final.pdf.

CHAPTER 9: KOSKELA

1 While I use the terms "Scripture" and "the Bible" (or "biblical") interchangeably in this essay, I want to make it clear at the outset that this is a stylistic choice and not an implicit suggestion that I regard the terms as theologically equivalent. In particular, the former term carries confessional and devotional weight that the latter does not. Thus when I regard the Bible as Scripture, I affirm that there is confessional significance in doing so.
2 "On God's Vineyard," in *Works*, 3:504 (emphasis in original).
3 For more on Wesley's own approach to Scripture, see the essays in the first section of this volume (chs. 1–4). A detailed exploration of Wesley's view of Scripture and his actual engagement of the biblical texts is offered by Jones in *Scripture*.
4 Douglas M. Koskela, "The Authority of Scripture in Its Ecclesial Context," in *Canonical Theism: A Proposal for Theology and the Church*, ed. William J. Abraham, Jason E. Vickers, and Natalie B. Van Kirk (Grand Rapids: Eerdmans, 2008), 210–23.
5 A very helpful treatment of this issue is offered in Hugh Heclo, *On Thinking Institutionally* (Boulder, Colo.: Paradigm, 2008).

6   An academic conference on climate change, however, might represent an interesting exception. Indeed, the politically charged atmosphere of that discussion is a good indication that the relationship between expert knowledge and power is not so easily separated.

7   I avoid the language of "person" here in recognition of the fact that the concept is not limited to human beings. Authority is clearly present in the animal kingdom, for example, and of course we want to create space theologically to talk about God's authority.

8   I find the distinction between "personal" and "impersonal" authority to be a useful one, particularly in setting the stage for a discussion of biblical authority. For one helpful discussion, see Joseph T. Lienhard, *The Bible, the Church, and Authority: The Canon of the Christian Bible in History and Theology* (Collegeville, Minn.: Liturgical Press, 1995), 75–76.

9   Lienhard makes a similar point when he suggests that "real authority is not arbitrary, because the final authority is the truth" (*Bible, the Church, and Authority*, 75).

10 It is necessary to make two qualifications at this point. First, we occasionally use the term "authority" in cases where those subject to power do not have the capacity to recognize it—a parent's "authority" over a newborn baby is a clear example. While the exercise of power is legally and morally appropriate in such cases, "authority" as I am using the term does not emerge until the capacity is present to recognize it. Second, in some circumstances authority can be present when reception is offered by a critical mass of people rather than by everyone. Thus, a small number of citizens who do not recognize the authority of a national government do not necessarily nullify its authority.

11 Lienhard, *Bible, the Church, and Authority*, 75.

12 This is not to suggest that ignoring a traffic citation would render it ineffective. Society's recognition of the authority of official traffic citations means that the violator would be subject to all due penalties.

13 John Webster, *Holy Scripture: A Dogmatic Sketch* (Cambridge: Cambridge University Press, 2003), 56.

14 For illuminating discussions of intrinsic and extrinsic authority, see Richard Bauckham, "Scripture and Authority," *Transformation* 15 (1998): 5–11; and Green, *Seized by Truth*, 162–64.

15 Green, *Seized by Truth*, 163.

16 N. T. Wright, *The Last Word: Beyond the Bible Wars to a New Understanding of the Authority of Scripture* (San Francisco: Harper, 2005), 23 (emphasis in original).

17 A crucial patristic account of the person and work of the Spirit along these lines is St. Basil the Great's *On the Holy Spirit*. In ch. 19, for example, Basil argues for the appropriateness of glorifying the Holy Spirit on the basis of the transformative work of the Spirit in the lives of God's creatures.

18 For a representative example, see John Wesley, Sermon 9, "The Spirit of Bondage and of Adoption," in *Works*, 1:248–66. For helpful secondary treatments of Wesley's pneumatology, see Maddox, *Responsible Grace*, 119–40; and Collins, *Theology of John Wesley*, 121–53.

19 Charles Wesley, Hymn 16, "Come, Thou Everlasting Spirit," in *Hymns on the Lord's Supper*, John Wesley and Charles Wesley (Bristol: Felix Farley, 1745),

reprinted with an introduction by Geoffrey Wainwright (Madison, N.J.: Charles Wesley Society, 1995), 13.
20   Wright, *Last Word*, 116 (emphasis in original).
21   Consider the following definition of inerrancy from Paul D. Feinberg: "Inerrancy means that when all facts are known, the Scriptures in their original autographs and properly interpreted will be shown to be wholly true in everything that they affirm, whether that has to do with doctrine or morality or with the social, physical, or life sciences." Paul D. Feinberg, "The Meaning of Inerrancy," in *Inerrancy*, ed. Norman L. Geisler (Grand Rapids: Zondervan, 1979), 294. While Feinberg (who defends this view) leaves plenty of hermeneutical space to deal with tensions that will arise, it is striking that he includes the natural sciences in his definition.
22   Donald W. Dayton explores a whole host of other reasons—many of them soteriological—why the Pietist movement rejected such a vision in his illuminating essay, "The Pietist Theological Critique of Biblical Inerrancy," in *Evangelicals and Scripture: Tradition, Authority and Hermeneutics*, ed. Vincent Bacote, Laura C. Miguélez, and Dennis L. Okholm (Downers Grove, Ill.: InterVarsity, 2004), 76–89.
23   Carl F. H. Henry offers perhaps the clearest articulation of this position: "The Bible depicts God's very revelation as meaningful, objectively intelligible disclosure. We mean by propositional revelation that God supernaturally communicated his revelation to chosen spokesmen in the express form of cognitive truths, and that the inspired prophetic-apostolic proclamation reliably articulates these truths in sentences that are not internally contradictory." Carl F. H. Henry, *God, Revelation and Authority*, 5 vols. (Waco, Tex.: Word, 1979), 3:456–57.
24   Webster, *Holy Scripture*, 52.
25   Telford Work, *Living and Active: Scripture in the Economy of Salvation* (Grand Rapids: Eerdmans, 2002), 129–30.
26   Green nicely captures this formative task: "Christian formation relates to the whole of who we are, our embodied lives, with Scripture taking on the role of sculptor, shaping our patterns of thinking, feeling, believing, and acting" (*Seized by Truth*, 24).
27   Granted, one could certainly argue that the purpose of the written prescription on its own is to convey information. But the analogy extends to the medicine itself precisely because that information is in service of a deeper purpose, namely, to heal the patient. No physician would write a prescription simply to give instructions to a pharmacist. In this light, the appropriate analogy for Scripture is the entire process of prescribing medicine for the purpose of healing.
28   My use of this particular analogy draws on a deep conviction about how Scripture and the other gifts of the Holy Spirit to the church should be conceived. Consider the following use of the image from Jason E. Vickers: "canonical theists believe that ecclesial canons [among which he includes the canon of Scripture] are first and foremost gifts of the Holy Spirit in and through which the Holy Spirit is present and at work in the life of the church. More specifically, we believe that the canonical heritage of the church is like a grand medicine

chest, the contents of which the Holy Spirit uses to bring about the healing of the world." Jason E. Vickers, "Medicine of the Holy Spirit: The Canonical Heritage of the Church," in *Canonical Theism*, 11.

29 Two important pneumatological qualifications are in order here: (1) the fact that the church did not ultimately receive *The Shepherd* as part of its canon does not preclude the Holy Spirit's use of that or any other means in the lives of God's people. The Spirit is free to use whatever the Spirit will. What is implied, though, is the recognized legitimacy of the power of those texts that were received into the canon (and thus their authority); (2) my emphasis on the church's process of discerning the canon over time does not at all limit this process to the creaturely plane. It can and should be said that the Holy Spirit worked in and through the church as the canon of Scripture took shape.

30 Part 1 of Work's *Living and Active* offers a thorough treatment of the respective ontologies of Scripture offered by Athanasius, Augustine, Karl Barth, and Hans Urs von Balthasar.

31 Here I am following Work's suggestion that these dimensions must be held together. An exclusively word-centered ontology of Scripture can tend to neglect the role of the Holy Spirit in the economy of salvation, while an exclusively Spirit-centered account of Scripture might undermine the uniqueness of the incarnation of the Son in Jesus. See Work, *Living and Active*, 122–23.

32 Athanasius makes this move in *On the Incarnation of the Word*, §12, though he clearly subordinates this manifestation (in the law and the prophets) to the incarnation in Jesus.

33 Significant reflection on these materials and practices is offered throughout William J. Abraham, Jason E. Vickers, and Natalie B. Van Kirk, eds., *Canonical Theism: A Proposal for Theology and the Church* (Grand Rapids: Eerdmans, 2008).

34 This claim need not necessarily rule out the possibility of God occasionally working in a monergistic fashion through Scripture, as in the case of a skeptic approaching the Bible arrogantly and then being reluctantly converted in the act of actually reading it. If such a case were to occur, it would be appropriate to say that *in that particular instance* Scripture was not functioning as an auxiliary authority so much as a direct means of divine sovereignty.

35 Webster, *Holy Scripture*, 55.

36 Work, *Living and Active*, 216.

37 See the thorough discussion of these in Jones, *Scripture*, 23–31, 41–43, 147–49, 150–51.

38 See, e.g., Jones, *Scripture*, 25–26, 43.

39 Maddox's language of Wesley's "orienting concern" of "responsible grace" is quite helpful in this regard (*Responsible Grace*, 18–19).

40 "The Means of Grace," in *Works*, 1:381 (emphasis in original).

41 Maddox's *Responsible Grace* represents a rich and thorough exploration of this divine-human interaction in Wesley's theology.

42 "Large *Minutes*" (1763), in *Works*, 10:845.

43 "Large *Minutes*" (1763), in *Works*, 10:856.

CHAPTER 10: VICKERS

1   For recent examples, see Donald Dayton, "The Pietist Theological Critique of Biblical Inerrancy," in *From the Margins: A Celebration of the Theological Work of Donald W. Dayton*, ed. Christian T. Collins Winn (Eugene, Ore.: Wipf & Stock, 2007), 193–205; Green, *Seized by Truth*; Jones, *Scripture*; and Michael Lodahl, *All Things Necessary to Our Salvation: The Hermeneutical and Theological Implications of the Article on the Holy Scriptures in the Manual of the Church of the Nazarene* (San Diego Calif.: Point Loma Press, 2005).
2   E.g., see Abraham, *Canon and Criterion*. Also see the chapter by David F. Watson in this volume.
3   See Gunter et al., *Wesley and the Quadrilateral*; William J. Abraham, "The Wesleyan Quadrilateral," in *Wesleyan Theology Today*, ed. Theodore Runyon (KB; Nashville: Abingdon, 1985), 119–26; Albert Cook Outler, "The Wesleyan Quadrilateral in Wesley," *Wesleyan Theological Journal* 20, no. 1 (1985): 7–18; Donald Thorsen, *The Wesleyan Quadrilateral: Scripture, Tradition, Reason and Experience as a Model of Evangelical Theology* (Grand Rapids: Zondervan, 1990).
4   For example, in a recent volume on holiness by Wesleyan scholars, Kevin W. Mannoia and Don Thorsen, eds., *The Holiness Manifesto* (Grand Rapids: Eerdmans, 2008), an entire section is devoted to holiness *in* the Old and New Testaments, but there is no discussion of the holiness of Scripture itself. An exception to this is Daniel Castelo and Robert W. Wall, "Scripture and the Church: A Precis for an Alternative Analogy," *Journal of Theological Interpretation* 5, no. 2 (2011): 197–210.
5   Webster, *Holy Scripture*. For a discussion of Webster's proposal from a Wesleyan perspective, see Castelo and Wall, "Scripture and the Church," 203–5.
6   In my contention that Wesleyans should conceive of holiness first and foremost as a matter of theology proper, I am in fundamental agreement with John Webster. For more on this, see John Webster, *Holiness* (Grand Rapids: Eerdmans, 2003). With respect to the attribution of holiness to creaturely realities such as the church, the sacraments, and Scripture, I part ways with Webster insofar as I understand creaturely holiness as a function of sacramental presence and Spirit-enabled participation rather than election.
7   The classic work on the long eighteenth century is J. C. D. Clark, *English Society 1660–1832* (Cambridge: Cambridge University Press, 2000). For a shorter account of the long eighteenth century written with the rise of Methodism in mind, see J. C. D. Clark, "The Eighteenth Century," in *Oxford Handbook of Methodist Studies*, 3–29.
8   I discuss this more fully in my *Guide for the Perplexed*. Also see Hempton, "Wesley in Context," 60–79.
9   For the return of Arianism and the rise of deism and Unitarianism in seventeenth- and eighteenth-century England, see Maurice Wiles, *Archetypal Heresy: Arianism through the Centuries* (Oxford: Oxford University Press, 2001). Also see Peter Harrison, *"Religion" and the Religions in the English Enlightenment* (Cambridge: Cambridge University Press, 1990); Gerard Reedy, *The Bible and Reason: Anglicans and Scripture in Late Seventeenth-Century England* (Philadelphia: University of Pennsylvania Press, 1985).

10 For examples of how particular thinkers such as Joseph Butler, Herbert of Cherbury, Thomas Hobbes, John Locke, Benedict Spinoza, and others were beginning to read the Bible in the light of emerging natural sciences and biblical criticism, see Reedy, *Bible and Reason*. Also see Henning Graf Reventlow, *The Authority of the Bible and the Rise of the Modern World* (Philadelphia: Fortress, 1985). What is often overlooked today is the extent to which Protestant approaches to texts—approaches that stressed rationality and literal meaning over the fast-fading medieval approach of symbolic reading—helped to contribute to the development of the natural sciences. For more on this, see Peter Harrison, *The Bible, Protestantism, and the Rise of Natural Science* (Cambridge: Cambridge University Press, 2001).

11 I traced these developments in detail in my *Invocation and Assent: The Making and Remaking of Trinitarian Theology* (Grand Rapids: Eerdmans, 2008).

12 I will say more about what I take to be "theology proper" later in the chapter.

13 Letter to James Clark, July 3, 1756, in *Letters* (Telford), 3:182.

14 For more on this, see Jason E. Vickers, "Christology," in *Oxford Handbook of Methodist Studies*, 554–72.

15 See Ted A. Campbell, *Wesleyan Beliefs: Formal and Popular Expressions of the Core Beliefs of Wesleyan Communities* (KB; Nashville: Abingdon, 2010), ch. 1. Also see Geoffrey Wainwright, "Why Wesley Was a Trinitarian," in *Methodists in Dialog* (KB; Nashville: Abingdon, 1995), 261–76; and Elmer M. Colyer, "Trinity," in *Oxford Handbook of Methodist Studies*, 505–21.

16 See Jason E. Vickers, "Charles Wesley and the Revival of the Doctrine of the Trinity: A Methodist Contribution to Modern Theology," in *Charles Wesley: Life, Literature and Legacy*, ed. Kenneth G. C. Newport and Ted A. Campbell (Peterborough: Epworth), 278–98.

17 Thomas Coke, *The Substance of a Sermon on the Godhead of Christ, Preached at Baltimore, in the State of Maryland, on the 26th Day of December, 1784, before the General Conference of the Methodist Episcopal Church* (London: J. Passmore, 1785).

18 For the best-known instance of this, see Sermon 7, "The Way to the Kingdom," 1.5–6, in *Works*, 1:220–21.

19 Sermon 62, "The End of Christ's Coming," 3.5–6, in *Works*, 2:483.

20 Letter to William Law, January 6, 1756, in *Letters* (Telford), 3:345–46.

21 *Letter to Bishop of Gloucester* (1763), II.5, in *Works*, 11:504.

22 "Thoughts upon Methodism," §2, in *Works*, 9:527.

23 Asa Shinn, *An Essay on the Plan of Salvation* (Baltimore: Neal, Wills & Cole, 1813), 230.

24 While this may appear to be a portrait of a conservative evangelical or even fundamentalist way of thinking about Scripture, it applies equally to liberal Protestant ways of thinking about Scripture. Liberal Protestants simply locate the meaning of the propositions contained in Scripture in the prior religious experiences of early Christians and Christian communities. This approach is no less susceptible to the logic of deism. Scripture can be said to originate with God insofar as it is a record of religious experiences set forth in speech, but this says nothing about the relationship between Scripture and the ongoing Trinitarian life of God.

25 Some Wesleyans are more favorably disposed to process theology. For more on this, see Bryan P. Stone and Thomas Jay Oord, eds., *Thy Nature and Thy Name Is Love: Wesleyan and Process Theologies in Dialogue* (KB; Nashville: Abingdon, 2001).
26 While we can observe the problem of functional deism throughout the pan-Wesleyan communion of churches, it is especially acute in The United Methodist Church in North America.
27 In Trinitarian theology, this is known as Rahner's rule, the original statement of which can be found in Karl Rahner, *The Trinity* (New York: Crossroad, 1999), 21–23. For more on this, see Catherine Mowry LaCugna, *God for Us: The Trinity and Christian Life* (San Francisco: HarperCollins, 1991).
28 The really deep issues here have to do with divine *aseity* and divine attributes. For more on these issues, see Webster, *Holiness*, ch. 2; also see Stephen R. Holmes, "The Attributes of God," in *The Oxford Handbook of Systematic Theology*, ed. John B. Webster, Kathryn Tanner, and Iain Torrance (Oxford: Oxford University Press, 2007), 54–71.
29 Webster, *Holiness*, 36.
30 Webster, *Holiness*, 41–42.
31 Webster, *Holiness*, 43 (emphasis in original).
32 As I said near the beginning, the account of Scripture's holiness on offer here in no way prohibits Wesleyans from turning to Scripture in the epistemology of theology. If anything, attending to the holiness of Scripture may open up a different way of thinking about the relationship between Scripture and the epistemology of theology. Insofar as Scripture's holiness has to do with God's transformative presence in our midst, Scripture's reliability or truthfulness will be made manifest through the conspicuous sanctity that follows faithful attendance to its pages.
33 Castelo and Wall's proposal that the proper analogy for Scripture is the church rather than Christ mandates a consideration of the holiness of Scripture. Unfortunately, this particular part of their proposal is underdeveloped, focusing as it does in a helpful but limited way on Scripture's "holy effect on readers" ("Scripture and the Church," 208). What is missing from their account of Scripture's holiness is a sacramental vision of the real presence of Christ in the life of the church. Indeed, this omission is glaring, even jarring, when Castelo and Wall speak of Scripture as a Spirit-given substitute that is necessary because of "the absence of the incarnate One" ("Scripture and the Church," 206). I think it is much better to see the Spirit at work in and through Scripture attuning us to the *presence* of the resurrected Lord in the life of the church.
34 When I suggest that Wesleyans conceive of Scripture's holiness on analogy with Holy Eucharist or with iconography, I do not have in mind something like transubstantiation. I do not mean to suggest that we conceive of Scripture as something by which the ordained among us summon God to their service. God's presence and work in and through Scripture is always a matter of divine gratuity and generosity. It is a gift that God gives freely. At the same time, I think Wesleyans will want to say that it is gift that God gives faithfully.
35 I am not suggesting that Scripture does not contain true propositions or that scriptural propositions are not important for matters like doctrine. I am simply

saying that the attribution of holiness to Scripture means that Scripture is more than a repository of true propositions or a source for Christian doctrine.
36. For more on this, see Jason E. Vickers, *Minding the Good Ground: A Theology for Church Renewal* (Waco, Tex.: Baylor University Press, 2011), ch. 3.

Chapter 11: Watson

1. John Wesley, *The Complete English Dictionary, Explaining Most of Those Hard Words That Are Found in the Best English Writers*, 2nd ed. (Bristol: William Pine, 1764), s.v. "Methodist."
2. *Explanatory Notes–NT*, 9.
3. See Maddox, "Rule of Faith," 3–5.
4. See Wall, "Wesley as Biblical Interpreter," 117.
5. See Koskie, "Wesleyan Theological Hermeneutic," 117.
6. F. L. Cross and E. A. Livingstone, eds., *The Oxford Dictionary of the Christian Church*, 3rd ed. (Oxford: Oxford University Press, 1997).
7. Bruce M. Metzger, *The Canon of the New Testament: Its Origin, Development, and Significance* (Oxford: Clarendon, 1987), 293.
8. Wall, "Wesley as Biblical Interpreter," 117.
9. See Abraham, *Canon and Criterion*, ch. 2: "The Emergence of the Canonical Heritage of the Church."
10. See Jones, *Scripture*, 169–76.
11. "Methodism, Wesley claimed, was in continuity with 'the religion of the Bible, the religion of the primitive church, [and] the religion of the Church of England.'" Ted A. Campbell, "The Interpretive Role of Tradition," in *Wesley and the Quadrilateral*, 68; see also 72.
12. See Jones, *Scripture*, 176.
13. Robert W. Jenson, *Canon and Creed* (Louisville, Ky.: Westminster John Knox, 2010), 40.
14. Wall, "Wesley as Biblical Interpreter," 116.
15. "The Witness of the Spirit," 8, in *Wesley's Standard Sermons*, 5th ed., 2 vols., ed. Edward H. Sugden (London: Epworth, 1961), 1:208.
16. See Maddox, "Rule of Faith," 17–19.
17. "The Catholic Spirit," in *Standard Sermons*, 2:134–35.
18. See Nicholas Wolterstorff, "The Unity behind the Canon," in *One Scripture or Many?* ed. Christine Helmer and Christof Landmesser (Oxford: Oxford University Press, 2004), 217–32.
19. Wall, "Wesley as Biblical Interpreter," 124–25.
20. "The Catholic Spirit," 3.1, in *Standard Sermons*, 2:142.
21. "The Catholic Spirit," 3.1, in *Standard Sermons*, 2:143.
22. See Lee Martin McDonald, "Identifying Scripture and Canon in the Early Church: The Criteria Question," in *The Canon Debate*, ed. Lee Martin McDonald and James A. Sanders (Peabody, Mass.: Hendrickson, 2002), 428–30.
23. Abraham et al., eds., *Canonical Theism*, 2.
24. "The Scripture Way of Salvation," 1.1, in *Standard Sermons*, 2:444–45 (emphasis in original).

25 "The Scripture Way of Salvation," 2, in *Standard Sermons*, 2:444.
26 Webster, *Holy Scripture*, 44. Clearly Webster does not mean to exclude people who are hearing impaired; rather, "hearing" in this case refers to our collective encounter with the gospel.
27 In fact, as David C. Steinmetz notes, "*Sola Scriptura* generally meant *prima Scriptura*. Scripture as the final source and norm by which all theological sources and arguments were to be judged, not Scripture as the sole source of theological wisdom." David C. Steinmetz, *Luther in Context*, 2nd ed. (Grand Rapids: Baker Academic, 2002), 129.
28 In general, he seems to regard biblical slavery as something akin to indentured servitude. Yet he must also see some differences, given passages such as Luke 12:45-48, which speaks of "manservants" and "maidens" as being beaten, the lord coming to his servant to "cut him in sunder," and the servant's being beaten with many "stripes" (*Explanatory Notes–NT*, 251). Wesley does not comment on these references to violence inflicted by the lord on the servant.
29 *Thoughts upon Slavery*, 5.3, in *Works* (Jackson), 11:77.
30 *Thoughts upon Slavery*, 5.5, in *Works* (Jackson), 11:78.
31 *Thoughts upon Slavery*, 5.3, in *Works* (Jackson), 11:76.
32 See Maddox, "Rule of Faith," 16–17.
33 Jones, *Scripture*, 49.
34 See Baird, *History*, ch. 5: "Refining Historical Research: Canon and Higher Criticism," 116–54.
35 Baird, *History*, 154.
36 On the historical-critical method, see the essay by Joel B. Green in this volume.
37 James A. Sanders, *Canon and Community: A Guide to Canonical Criticism* (Philadelphia: Fortress, 1984), 37 (emphasis in original).
38 Sanders, *Canon and Community*, 46.
39 James Barr, "Unity: Within the Canon or after the Canon," in *One Scripture or Many? Canon from Biblical, Theological, and Philosophical Perspectives*, ed. Christine Helmer and Christof Landmesser (New York, Oxford University Press, 2004), 152.
40 Barr, "Unity," 153.

CHAPTER 12: LAYTHAM

1 E.g., Don Thorsen, "The Wesleyan Quadrilateral in Contemporary American Evangelical Theology," in *Holiness as a Root of Morality: Essays on Wesleyan Ethics in Honor of Lane A. Scott*, ed. John Sungmin Park (Lewiston, N.Y.: Mellen, 2006), 47–77.
2 United Methodism's Bicentennial Theological Consultation published three articles that display the variety of this approach in the section "Wesleyan Thought and Christian Social Ethics": James C. Logan, "Toward a Wesleyan Social Ethic" (361–72), Leon O. Hynson, "Implications of Wesley's Ethical Method and Political Thought" (373–88), and J. Philip Wogaman, "The Wesleyan Tradition and the Social Challenges of the Next Century" (389–99), in *Wesleyan Theology Today*, ed. Theodore Runyon (KB; Nashville: Abingdon, 1985).

3   Preface to "List of Poetical Works," in *Works* (Jackson), 14:321.
4   See Joel B. Green's fourth thesis in his essay, "Is There a Contemporary Wesleyan Hermeneutic," in *Reading the Bible in Wesleyan Ways: Some Constructive Proposals*, ed. Barry Callen and Richard Thompson (Kansas City, Mo.: Beacon Hill, 2004), 123–34 (132–33).
5   Bob Terry gets at this in his essay, "If Only the Bible Said . . . ," in *The Gambling Culture*, ed. Robert B. Kruschwitz, Christian Reflection 40 (Waco, Tex.: The Center for Christian Ethics at Baylor University, 2011), 78–81: "If only the Bible said, 'Thou shalt not gamble,' then life would be simpler" (78).
6   In response to social, economic, and cultural trends, British Methodists have considerably relaxed Wesleyanism's traditional stance against gambling but have done so with a utilitarian calculus at significant remove from Scripture. In response to similar trends in the U.S., United Methodists have preserved the traditional Wesleyan embargo on gambling but have done so with a sweeping deontology at significant remove from the prevailing cultural ethos.
7   *Works*, 11:232 (emphasis in original).
8   "The Reformation of Manners," I.7, in *Works*, 2:306; quoting 2 Thess 2:7.
9   "The Nature, Design, and General Rules of the United Societies," in *Works*, 9:71.
10 This description is from Richard M. Cameron, *Methodism and Society in Historical Perspective* (New York: Abingdon, 1961), 218. Cf. Georgia Elma Harkness, *The Methodist Church in Social Thought and Action* (New York: Abingdon, 1964), 40. Similarly, British Methodism's 1936 statement unreservedly condemned gambling as producing social evil and moral corruption.
11 Quoting Stanley Hauerwas, "Characterizing Perfection: Second Thoughts on Character and Sanctification," in *Sanctify Them in Truth: Holiness Exemplified* (Nashville: Abingdon, 1998), 123–42 (125).
12 E.g., The United Methodist Church, the Salvation Army, the Church of the Nazarene, and the Wesleyan Church all condemn gambling.
13 "A Methodist Statement on Gambling" (adopted by the Methodist Conference of 1992), 55.d.
14 *Catechism of the Catholic Church* (New York: Doubleday, 1995), §2413.
15 Wesley also sees gambling (in the context of horse racing) as exercising and increasing covetousness. "Public Diversions Denounced," IV.2, in *Works*, 4:325. The Wesleyan Church follows his lead in its statement: "Gambling violates the principle of Christian stewardship and the tenth commandment." Task Force on Public Morals and Social Concerns, *Standing Firm: The Wesleyan Church Speaks on Contemporary Issues* (Indianapolis: Wesleyan Publishing House, 2000), 4; accessed September 22, 2011, at http://www.wesleyan.org/bgs/assets/downloads/down.php?dfile=Standing%20Firm.pdf.
16 Tim Stafford, "None Dare Call It Sin," *Christianity Today*, May 18, 1998, 37. Similarly, midcentury Methodist parenting literature on gambling makes much of the moral arguments against "something for nothing" and for the work ethic. Unfortunately, four double-sided pages contained only one explicit mention of Scripture. Methodist Board of Temperance, *Parents' Packet on Gambling* (Washington, D.C.: Methodist Board of Temperance, n.d.).

17 *The Book of Resolutions of The United Methodist Church* (Nashville: Abingdon, 2008), §4041.
18 For an overview, see Alan Wolfe and Erik C. Owens, eds., *Gambling: Mapping the American Moral Landscape* (Waco, Tex.: Baylor University Press, 2009).
19 Both *Christian Century* (April 22, 2008) and *Christianity Today* (March 2008; http://www.christianitytoday.com/ct/2008/marchweb-only/112-22.0.html) reported on the Ellison Research study (http://greymatterresearch.com/index_files/Sin.htm, accessed 10/10/2011), which showed that 70 percent of Americans did not consider gambling to be a sin.
20 "An Earnest Appeal to Men of Reason and Religion," in *Works*, 11:60. See Wesley's similar discussion in "A Farther Appeal to Men of Reason and Religion, Part II," III.15–17, in *Works*, 11:263–65, where Wesley answers the time bind with the cultivation of virtue.
21 Sermon 89, "The More Excellent Way," V.1, in *Works*, 3:272. Wesley then catalogues diversions along a spectrum from unacceptable to possibly innocent but unacceptable for Wesley to "more excellent ways." These latter are gardening; serious conversation; visiting the sick, poor, widows, afflicted; and reading history, pious poetry, and natural philosophy. Notice that Wesley's standard of judgment here is outcome—the positive improvement each makes on one's character.
22 Wesley substitutes "hath" for "gathered" and transposes the tense from past to present.
23 This quotation and the approach I am following here owe much to Richard B. Hays' exposition of 2 Cor 8:15 in *Echoes of Scripture in the Letters of Paul* (New Haven, Conn.: Yale University Press, 1989), 88–91. Metalepsis here means a quotation's carrying theological resonances of its original context.
24 I owe this quip to Jake Wilson, along with gratitude for enriching critiques of an earlier draft of the paper.
25 In the OT, God's "testing" is intended to be transformative, not evaluative. See Deut 8; and R. W. L. Moberly's elaboration in "Living Dangerously: Genesis 22 and the Quest for Good Biblical Interpretation," in *The Art of Reading Scripture*, ed. Ellen Davis and Richard B. Hays (Grand Rapids: Eerdmans, 2003), 181–97 (191–92).
26 Notice how the petition "give us this day our daily bread" asks "Our Father" to draw us into that same temporally extended rhythm of trust.
27 Wesley's sermon "On Redeeming the Time" argues that sleeping in "is a sin against God" (Sermon 93, II.7, in *Works*, 3:327) that makes "it impossible for you to get one step forward in vital holiness" (III.7, in *Works*, 3:332)
28 Sermon 148, "A Single Intention," in *Works*, 4:375
29 Lest the early date of "A Single Intention" (1736) suggest that perhaps the mature Wesley thought differently, note that his late sermon "The More Excellent Way" maintains a hierarchy of diversions that are clearly ordered according to their extrinsic impact on us.
30 The verbal echo of Gen 1:29 "See, I have given you every plant" emphasizes that Sabbath means providence.
31 Brevard Childs, *The Book of Exodus* (OTL; Philadelphia: Westminster, 1974), 290.

32 In the General Rules, recreational activity only appears in the first rule to do no harm, making it continually suspect of diverting us from holiness. The rule implicitly acknowledges that there are songs and books that do "tend to the knowledge or love of God" but with the inference that these activities can only tend thusly when their subject matter is explicitly theological (*Works*, 9:71).

33 A canonical exploration of Sabbath is far beyond the scope of this essay, especially given the distorting traditions of sabbatarianism.

34 The positive place for entertainment I am developing integrates well with Wesley the virtue ethicist. See Richard Heitzenrater, "The *Imitatio Christi* and the Great Commandment: Virtue and Obligation in Wesley's Ministry with the Poor," in *The Portion of the Poor: Good News to the Poor in the Wesleyan Tradition*, ed. M. Douglas Meeks (KB; Nashville: Abingdon, 1995), 49–63, 177–78. The Oxford Methodists' weekly cycle of self-examination, with Saturday given for "thankfulness," could be expanded to include joy, with the recognition that faithful recreations will inculcate both gratitude and joy.

35 Wesley, "The New Creation," in *Works*, 2:510.

36 My use of Wesley's second and third rules on "The Use of Money" (in *Works*, 2:273–80) is not to imply that his scriptural engagement is "wooden," only that if my corrective of Wesley on recreative amusements is accepted, then money spent on them may not count as "needless expense."

37 It "began last year" (2 Cor 8:10) with a Lord's day putting aside and saving "whatever extra you earn."

38 At the conclusion of the General Rules, Wesley wrote, "These are the General Rules of our societies; all of which we are *taught of God to observe, even in his written Word*, which is the only rule, and the sufficient rule, both of our faith and practice. And all these we know *his Spirit writes on truly awakened hearts*" (*Works*, 9:73, emphasis added). In this claim, Wesley implies that observing the General Rules is a *practice of Scripture* through which the Holy Spirit transforms us *affectively*.

39 Joel B. Green, "Scripture and Theology: Failed Experiments, Fresh Perspectives," *Interpretation* 56, no. 1 (2001): 5–20 (6). See also his *Seized by Truth*, 50–56.

40 Here I extrapolate from the question of Paul's apostleship, at issue in 2 Corinthians, to its consequence for the apostolicity of churches arising from the Gentile mission, the very churches to which most Wesleyans belong. As the collection was to be a sign of the validity of Paul's apostleship to the Gentiles, so today its continuance can be a sign of the church's apostolicity.

41 Or perhaps we confuse giving to the church's operational budget with giving to the poor. Cf. Theodore W. Jennings Jr., *Good News to the Poor: John Wesley's Evangelical Economics* (Nashville: Abingdon, 1990), 190.

42 Beverly Roberts Gaventa, "The Economy of Grace: Reflections on 2 Corinthians 8 and 9," in *Grace upon Grace: Essays in Honor of Thomas A. Langford*, ed. Robert K. Johnston, L. Gregory Jones, and Jonathan R. Wilson (Nashville: Abingdon, 1999), 51–62 (53). Only in Romans does Paul have more to say about grace.

43 Note that "the *privilege* of *sharing*" is *charis* and *koinonia*, respectively, which at 2 Cor 13:13 appears in the benedictory "the *charis* of the Lord Jesus Christ, the love of God, and the *koinonia* of the Holy Spirit."

44 See Gaventa, "Economy of Grace," 58; and Frank J. Matera, *II Corinthians: A Commentary* (Louisville, Ky.: Westminster John Knox, 2003), 190.
45 For this term and an extensive discussion of such passages in Paul, see Morna Hooker, "Interchange in Christ and Ethics," *Journal for the Study of the New Testament* 25 (1985): 3–17.
46 Hooker notes that "the behaviour which is required of those who are in Christ . . . conforms to the attitude which *he* showed in becoming like us" ("Interchange," 10); moreover, "being in Christ means sharing in the dying as well as the living, in the giving as well as the receiving, in the poverty as well as the riches" (14).
47 I cannot develop here my argument with commentators who take the primary referent of "he" in 9:9 to be either God or the Corinthians, never considering this as a christologically rendered restatement of 8:9.
48 Nigel E. Turner, "Games, Gambling, and Gambling Problems," in *In the Pursuit of Winning: Problem Gambling Theory, Research and Treatment*, ed. Masood Zangeneh, Alex Blaszczynski, and Nigel E. Turner (New York: Springer, 2008), 34.
49 "Our identity in Christ is not a foundation but a risk." John L. Meech, *Paul in Israel's Story: Self and Community at the Cross* (Oxford: Oxford University Press, 2006), 3.
50 Turner, "Games," 35.
51 Turner, "Games," 49.
52 Turner, "Games," 51.
53 T. J. Jackson Lears, "Beyond Pathology: The Cultural Meaning of Gambling," in *Gambling: Mapping the American Moral Terrain*, ed. Alan Wolfe and Erik C. Owens (Waco, Tex.: Baylor University Press, 2009), 321.
54 See the argument of Ched Myers, *Binding the Strong Man: A Political Reading of Mark's Story of Jesus* (Maryknoll, N.Y.: Orbis, 1988), 320–22.
55 Lears, "Beyond Pathology," 302.
56 Rereading is not an accommodation to our human limitations or interpretative deficiencies but is integral to Scripture's identity as the text through which God faithfully speaks, in which Christ faithfully appears, and by which the Spirit renews our minds.
57 "Every part thereof is worthy of God; and all together are one entire body." Preface to *Explanatory Notes–NT,* §10, 9.
58 "Scripture is the story in which we live." Richard B. Hays, "The Future of Scripture," *Wesleyan Theological Journal* 46, no. 1 (2011): 24–38 (26).
59 "The written Word is the whole and sole rule of . . . *faith*, as well as *practice.*" Wesley, "On Faith," in *Works*, 3:496.
60 Preface to *Explanatory Notes OT,* §10 (Salem, Ohio: Schmul, 1975), 1:ix.
61 Stanley Hauerwas and D. Stephen Long, "Methodist Theological Ethics," in *Working with Words: On Learning to Speak Christian*, by Stanley Hauerwas (Eugene, Ore.: Wipf & Stock, 2011), 257.
62 Preface to the "Standard Sermons," §5, in *Works*, 1:105.

Chapter 13: Koskie

1. In 2009 the Board of General Superintendents of the Wesleyan Church sponsored a symposium on Wesleyan hermeneutics, and in 2010 the Wesleyan Theological Society took up "The Future of Scripture" in Wesleyan theology. Recent publications contributing to the discussion are William H. Willimon and Joel B. Green, eds., *The Wesley Study Bible* (Nashville: Abingdon, 2009); and Green, *Reading Scripture*.
2. Robert W. Wall, "Toward a Wesleyan Hermeneutic of Scripture," in *Reading the Bible in Wesleyan Ways*, 43.
3. Robert W. Wall, "Facilitating Scripture's Future Role among Wesleyans," in *Reading the Bible in Wesleyan Ways*, 119.
4. Wall, "Wesleyan Hermeneutic," 55.
5. See Oden and Longden's remarks in their introduction to *The Wesleyan Theological Heritage*, 11.
6. William J. Abraham, "The End of Wesleyan Theology," *Wesleyan Theological Journal* 40 (2005): 7–25; Jason E. Vickers, "Albert Outler and the Future of Wesleyan Theology: Retrospect and Prospect," *Wesleyan Theological Journal* 43 (2008): 56–67. Of the two, Abraham is far more critical.
7. Abraham, "End of Wesleyan Theology," 8–13. See also Randy L. Maddox, "Respected Founder/Neglected Guide: The Role of Wesley in American Methodist Theology," *Methodist History* 37 (1999): 71–88. See Outler's programmatic statement in Albert C. Outler, *Theology in the Wesleyan Spirit* (Nashville: Discipleship Resources, 1975), 1–2.
8. "Folk theologian" is, of course, Outler's term. Albert Outler, "John Wesley: Folk Theologian," in *Wesleyan Theological Heritage*, 111–24.
9. A good example of systematizing Wesley's doctrines is Thomas C. Oden, *John Wesley's Scriptural Christianity: A Plain Exposition of His Teaching on Christian Doctrine* (Grand Rapids: Zondervan, 1994). On the quadrilateral, see Outler, "Wesleyan Quadrilateral," 21–37; see also Thorsen, *Wesleyan Quadrilateral*.
10. Thorsen, *Wesleyan Quadrilateral*.
11. William J. Abraham, *Waking from Doctrinal Amnesia: The Healing of Doctrine in the United Methodist Church* (Nashville: Abingdon, 1995). He reiterates his criticism in Abraham, "End of Wesleyan Theology," 12n18. See also Philip R. Meadows, "The 'Discipline' of Theology: Making Methodism Less Methodological," *Wesleyan Theological Journal* 36 (2001): 50–87.
12. Gunter et al., *Wesley and the Quadrilateral*.
13. Outler, introduction to *Works*, 1:xi.
14. Of course, theologically and morally formative readings can also be historically informed. The point is that a historical reading is neither the only nor necessarily the most important or appropriate reading of a text, depending largely on the situation.
15. Abraham would seem to concur when he observes that scholarly versions of the standard sermons, at home in the seminary or university, are inadequate as "spiritual nourishment" in the church. "End of Wesleyan Theology," 24n45.

16 Alasdair C. MacIntyre, *Whose Justice? Which Rationality?* (Notre Dame, Ind.: University of Notre Dame Press, 1988), 356.
17 MacIntyre, *Whose Justice*, 362.
18 By offering a revised agenda for the future, Vickers appears to come to the same conclusion without recourse to MacIntyre. Vickers, "Outler," 62–65.
19 See Abraham, "End of Wesleyan Theology," 24–25. Abraham argues that the move from source to veneration is necessary because appealing to Wesley as an authority in theology is a category mistake: Wesley himself only ever appealed to Scripture in the final balance of things. A MacIntyrean response is that this is irrelevant, since the tradition issuing from Wesley has moved into territory he could not have imagined. Abraham's own critique of Protestant biblicism is a case in point. If *sola Scriptura* as Wesley practiced it is no longer viable, adherents to the Wesleyan tradition must find the resources to innovate in the face of these new challenges. In fact, this is exactly what Abraham is doing in his work.
20 Alasdair C. MacIntyre, *Three Rival Versions of Moral Enquiry: Encyclopaedia, Genealogy, and Tradition* (Notre Dame, Ind.: University of Notre Dame Press, 1989), 65–66.
21 MacIntyre, *Rival Versions*, 63.
22 Hans W. Frei, *The Eclipse of Biblical Narrative: A Study in Eighteenth and Nineteenth Century Hermeneutics* (New Haven, Conn.: Yale University Press, 1974).
23 Frei reads Wesley differently, believing Wesley locates meaning in the soul's journey from sin to salvation (*Eclipse*, 153). It is intriguing to wonder whether Frei's reading of Wesley might have changed after he critiqued his own idea of "realistic narrative" and permitted the role of the community in interpretation as the "literal reading" of the Bible.
24 "Of the Church," I.12, in *Works*, 3:50.
25 "The Love of God," II.5, in *Works*, 4:337.
26 Charles M. Wood, *The Formation of Christian Understanding: Theological Hermeneutics*, 2nd ed. (Valley Forge, Pa.: Trinity Press International, 1993), 40.
27 David H. Kelsey, *Proving Doctrine: The Uses of Scripture in Modern Theology* (Harrisburg, Pa.: Trinity Press International, 1999), 92.
28 Paul L. Holmer, *The Grammar of Faith* (San Francisco: Harper & Row, 1978), 20 (emphasis in original).
29 Hans W. Frei, "The 'Literal Reading' of Biblical Narrative in the Christian Tradition: Does It Stretch or Will It Break?" in *Theology and Narrative: Selected Essays*, ed. George Hunsinger and William C. Placher (New York: Oxford University Press, 1993), 122.
30 John Behr, *The Way to Nicaea*, vol. 1: *Formation of Christian Theology* (Crestwood, N.Y.: St. Vladimir's Seminary Press, 2001), 32–33.
31 *Explanatory Notes–NT*, 397n6. Although Wesley is commenting on a Pauline verse, note that he immediately links it to 1 Pet 4:11 (hence his mention of Peter at the comment's opening).
32 For other examples, see "The Causes of the Inefficacy of Christianity," §6, in *Works*, 4:89; *Principles of a Methodist Farther Explained*, §VI.4, in *Works*, 9:226–27.
33 "On Divine Providence," §4, in *Works*, 2:536.

34 Richard B. Hays, "Can Narrative Criticism Recover the Theological Unity of Scripture?" *Journal of Theological Interpretation* 2 (2008): 193–211 (203).
35 I therefore disagree with both Robert W. Wall and Randy L. Maddox in their contentions that Wesley prefers 1 John as his "canon within the canon." Maddox enumerates both the number of times Wesley cites certain NT books plus "the ratio of citations per length of the biblical book" to make the point. Wall's argument is more extensive, pointing to Wesley's appeal to 1 John to support his expectation for present perfection, though he concedes the primacy of the Pauline doctrine of justification. Both rehearse well-known superlatives Wesley grants 1 John (Wall, "Wesley as Biblical Interpreter," 113–28; Maddox, "Rule of Faith"; I am grateful to Professor Maddox for making a copy of his paper available to me ahead of publication).
My point has nothing to do with quantities, ratios, or superlatives (though 1 John is not alone in receiving superlatives from Wesley). It is rather that the grammar that governs Wesley's reading comes out of a certain tradition—the Protestant reading of Augustine reading Paul. Wesley's welcome insistence on perfect love was out of step with some in his day, but was by no means unique in Augustinian-dominated Western Christianity.
36 A recent and accessible discussion of the issues from a Wesleyan biblical scholar is Michael J. Gorman, *Apostle of the Crucified Lord: A Theological Introduction to Paul and His Letters* (Grand Rapids: Eerdmans, 2004).
37 Given that an altered hermeneutical landscape changes the questions and assumptions we bring to Scripture, it should be clear I am not claiming that Wesley erroneously diverged from the "true" or "original meaning" of justification in Romans. Interestingly, Wesley's covenantal reading of Rom 9 in his *Explanatory Notes–NT* seems quite friendly to new perspective scholarship (see esp. *Notes*, 387–91).
38 Green, "Contemporary Wesleyan Hermeneutic," 124.
39 "Sermon on the Mount I," §I.1, in *Works*, 1:475. See Wesley's summary remarks in Sermon 30, "Sermon on the Mount X," §§1–3, in *Works*, 1:650–51.
40 "Sermon on the Mount II," §II.6, in *Works*, 1:498.
41 Sermon 33, "Sermon on the Mount XIII," §II.2, in *Works*, 1:692; cf. "Sermon on the Mount XIII," §III.11, in *Works*, 1:698; also Sermon 23, "Sermon on the Mount III," §I.2, in *Works*, 1:511; Sermon 28, "Sermon on the Mount VIII," §§6, 21, in *Works*, 1:615, 626; Sermon 29, "Sermon on the Mount IX," §§5, 15, in *Works*, 1:635, 639; "Sermon on the Mount X," §7, in *Works*, 1:653.
42 "Sermon on the Mount III," §IV, in *Works*, 1:530.
43 See esp. "Sermon on the Mount, IV," §1, in *Works*, 1:531–32.
44 *The Character of a Methodist*, §2, in *Works*, 9:32 (emphasis in original).
45 *The Character of a Methodist*, §§1–4, in *Works*, 9:33–35 (emphasis in original).
46 *The Character of a Methodist*, §5, in *Works*, 9:35.
47 *The Character of a Methodist*, §§6–8, in *Works*, 9:35–37.
48 *The Character of a Methodist*, §10, in *Works*, 9:38. Wesley quotes here from Col 3:12.
49 *The Character of a Methodist*, §14, in *Works*, 9:39 (emphasis in original).
50 Cf. *The Character of a Methodist*, §18, in *Works*, 9:42.

51 Preface to *Sermons*, §5, in *Works*, 1:105.
52 As he writes in his sermon "On the Trinity," "The knowledge of the Three-One God is interwoven with all true Christian faith." §17, in *Works*, 2:385.
53 Frances M. Young, *Brokenness and Blessing: Towards a Biblical Spirituality* (Grand Rapids: Baker Academic, 2007), 20.
54 John David Dawson, *Christian Figural Reading and the Fashioning of Identity* (Berkeley: University of California Press, 2002), 216.
55 "The Unity of the Divine Being," §17, in *Works*, 4:67.
56 See, e.g., "Sermon on the Mount III," §IV, in *Works*, 1:530.

CHAPTER 14: HEATH

1 Scott J. Jones, *United Methodist Doctrine: The Extreme Center* (Nashville: Abingdon, 2002), 130.
2 Quoted in Jones, *Doctrine*, 130.
3 Maddox, *Responsible Grace*, 38.
4 Wall, "Wesley as Biblical Interpreter," 116.
5 Wall, "Wesley as Biblical Interpreter," 123–28.
6 Some people prefer the phrase "Christian formation" to "spiritual formation," wanting to emphasize that for Christians spiritual formation has to do with being formed in Christ rather than with individualistic spirituality, and that being formed as a Christian is about justice and moral formation as well as formation in prayer and other individual spiritual practices.
7 "The General Rules of the Methodist Church," in *The Book of Discipline of The United Methodist Church* (Nashville: The United Methodist Publishing House, 2008), ¶103. For an excellent recent study on the use of the General Rules for contemporary Christian formation, see Kevin M. Watson, *A Blueprint for Discipleship: Wesley's General Rules as a Guide for Christian Living* (Nashville: Discipleship Resources, 2009).
8 Campbell, *Wesleyan Beliefs*, 31.
9 Albert C. Outler and Richard P. Heitzenrater, introduction to "The Means of Grace," *John Wesley's Sermons: An Anthology* (Nashville: Abingdon, 1987), 160.
10 "The Means of Grace," 170.
11 "The Means of Grace," 161.
12 Preface to *Explanatory Notes–OT*.
13 Preface to *Explanatory Notes–NT*.
14 For an in-depth treatment of *lectio divina*, including 500 passages of Scripture with which to pray using *lectio*, see Thelma Hall, *Too Deep for Words: Rediscovering Lectio Divina* (Mahwah, N.J.: Paulist Press, 1988).
15 Hall, *Lectio Divina*, 37.
16 Hall, *Lectio Divina*, 42–43.
17 Jean Orcibal, "The Theological Originality of John Wesley and Continental Spirituality," in *A History of the Methodist Church in Great Britain*, ed. Rupert Davies and Gordon Rupp (London: Epworth, 1965), 95.
18 Orcibal, "Theological Originality," 94.
19 This classic text in Christian spirituality has been published under various titles.

For an accessible translation see *Experiencing the Depths of Jesus Christ* (Gardiner, Maine: Christian Books, 1975).

20   Richard P. Heitzenrater, "The Founding Brothers," in *Oxford Handbook of Methodist Studies*, 36–37.
21   *MS Scriptural Hymns* (1783), edited by Randy Maddox. In the Methodist Archive and Research Centre, accession number MA 1977/576 (Charles Wesley Notebooks Box 3), public domain, http://divinity.duke.edu/sites/default/files/documents/cswt/83_MS_Scriptural_Hymns_NT.pdf.
22   Charles Wesley (1762), public domain, http://en.wikisource.org/wiki/Come,_Divine_Interpreter.
23   For a detailed study of the life and thought of Phoebe Palmer, including her teaching on being a Bible Christian, see Elaine A. Heath, *Naked Faith: The Mystical Theology of Phoebe Palmer* (Eugene, Ore.: Pickwick, 2009).
24   Heath, *Naked Faith*, 10–13.
25   Heath, *Naked Faith*, 21.
26   For a short history of the *Disciple Bible Study* series and related curricula, and information on ordering the materials see http://www.cokesbury.com/forms/DynamicContent.aspx?id=17&pageid=50, accessed September 7, 2011.
27   *United Methodist Hymnal*, 876–79.
28   Ruben P. Job and Norman Shawchuck, eds., *A Guide to Prayer for Ministers and Other Servants* (Nashville: The Upper Room), 1983.
29   Laurence Hull Stookey, *This Day: A Wesleyan Way of Prayer* (Nashville: Abingdon, 2004).
30   For examples of communities of interpretation among those who are incarcerated and among survivors of sexual abuse, see Bob Eckblad, *Reading the Bible with the Damned* (Louisville, Ky.: Westminster John Knox, 2005); and Elaine A. Heath, *We Were the Least of These: Reading the Bible with Survivors of Sexual Abuse* (Grand Rapids: Brazos, 2011). These books can help the whole church gain insights and wisdom often missing from dominant readings of the text.
31   M. Robert Mulholland Jr., *Shaped by the Word: The Power of Scripture in Spiritual Formation* (Nashville: Upper Room, 2001).

Chapter 15: Westerfield Tucker

1   In "Farther Thoughts on Separation from the Church" written late in his life, John Wesley noted that "from a child I was taught to love and reverence the Scripture, the oracles of God." §1, in *Works*, 9:538.
2   Pr Azar 35–66a; also known as the Song of the Three Children or a Song of Creation.
3   Luke 1:68-79; also known as the Song of Zechariah.
4   Luke 1:46-55; also known as the Song of Mary.
5   The Wesleys knew the 1662 version of the *Book of Common Prayer*—which is still the official (Parliament-approved) prayer book of the Church of England.
6   Cf. John Wesley's sermon "On the Sabbath," in *Works*, 4:268–78.
7   *The Book of Common Prayer* (London: John Baskett, 1717), 96.
8   See Geoffrey Wainwright, "Wesley's Trinitarian Hermeneutics," *Wesleyan*

Theological Journal 36 (2001): 7–30; reprinted as "The Trinitarian Hermeneutic of John Wesley," in *Reading the Bible in Wesleyan Ways*, 17–37.
9   Journal, April 12, 1789, in *Works*, 24:128.
10 Charles Wesley, Sermon on Rom 3:23-25, in *The Sermons of Charles Wesley*, ed. Kenneth G. C. Newport (Oxford: Oxford University Press, 2001), 192.
11 "Sermon on the Mount IV," III.4, in *Works*, 1:544; cf. Hab 1:13; Eph 1:6; Mark 12:30/Luke 10:27; 1 John 3:3; 1 Cor 10:31.
12 Letter "To a Friend," September 20, 1757, in *Letters* (Telford), 3:227.
13 Journal, May 5, 1766, in *Works*, 22:42–43 (emphasis in original).
14 Cf. Journal, September 13, 1736, in *Works*, 18:171.
15 "Nature, Design, and General Rules," and "Directions Given to the Band Societies," in *Works*, 9:73, 79. Later these "ordinances" would figure as "instituted" means of grace; see "The Means of Grace," in *Works*, 1:376–97.
16 Charles Wesley, Hymn 973, *Short Hymns on Select Passages of the Holy Scriptures* (Bristol: E. Farley, 1762), 1:310.
17 E.g., Letter to Samuel Walker, September 24, 1755, in *Letters* (Telford), 3:145.
18 From a statement dated September 9, 1784, and found as a preface in most extant copies of *The Sunday Service of the Methodists in North America. With Other Occasional Services* (London: [William Strahan], 1784); cited elsewhere as "Statement of September 9, 1784." A modern reprint (with the statement) is *John Wesley's Prayer Book: The Sunday Service of the Methodists in North America* (Akron, Ohio: OSL, 1991).
19 *Explanatory Notes–NT*, 194; cf. Sermon 115, "Dives and Lazarus," II.6, in *Works*, 4:14.
20 Letter to Dr. Conyers Middleton, January 4, 1749, in *Letters* (Telford), 2:320; and "A Second Letter to the Author of the Enthusiasm of Methodists and Papists Compar'd," §44, in *Works*, 11:423. See also Letter to James Hutton, November 27, 1738, in *Works*, 25:593.
21 In his September 10, 1784, letter to the Methodist leaders in America, John Wesley advised the recipients that they were "now at full liberty simply to follow the Scriptures and the Primitive Church," in *Letters* (Telford), 7:239. On vigils, see his letter to John Baily, June 8, 1750, in *Letters* (Telford), 3:287.
22 "Ought We to Separate from the Church of England?" [III].2, in *Works*, 9:570.
23 Cf. "Catholic Spirit," III.2, in *Works*, 2:93.
24 Methodist worship's "defectiveness" lay in that "it seldom has the four grand parts of public prayer: deprecation, petition, intercession and thanksgiving." Minutes from August 12, 1766, in *Minutes of the Methodist Conference* (London: Conference Office, Thomas Cordeux, 1812), 1:58.
25 Journal, August 1, 1742, in *Works*, 19:290. Cf. Question 48 of the "Large Minutes" regarding the reading of Scriptures in *Minutes of Several Conversations between the Rev. Mr. Wesley and Others; from the Year 1744 to the Year 1789* (London: Conference Office, Thomas Cordeux, 1811), 30.
26 Preface to *Explanatory Notes–NT*, 1:ix. John had written similar words drawn from Thomas à Kempis' *Imitation of Christ* (I.5) in an extended letter to William Warburton, Bishop of Gloucester: "we need the same Spirit to *understand* the Scripture which enabled the holy men of old to *write it*" (1763), in *Works*, 11:509.

27   Cf. Journal, March 26, 1738, in *Works*, 18:232.
28   John Wesley notes in his sermon "On Knowing Christ after the Flesh" that when he translated the German hymns of the Moravians, he chose those which he judged to be "most scriptural" and "most suitable to sound experience." Sermon 123, §8, in *Works*, 4:101.
29   Charles Wesley, Hymn 9, *Hymns for Those That Seek, and Those That Have Redemption, in the Blood of Jesus Christ*, 2nd ed. (Bristol: Felix Farley, 1747), 13, stanza 1.
30   John Wesley and Charles Wesley, Hymn 29, *Hymns on the Lord's Supper* (Bristol: Felix Farley, 1745), 22–23.
31   Charles Wesley, *Short Hymns*, 1:n.p.
32   See Journal, July 12, 1778, in *Works*, 23:99.
33   Charles Wesley, Hymn 1242, in *Short Hymns*, 2:36–37, stanzas 1–2.
34   The statement of the function of the hymns paraphrases Wesley's language in his preface to the 1780 *A Collection of Hymns, for the Use of the People called Methodists*, in *Works*, 7:75.
35   The "Statement of September 9, 1784," noted that "most of the holy-days (so-called) are omitted, as at present answering no valuable end." Many of these holy days and, of course, the saints days, had no precedent in Scripture.
36   Wesley, Article V, in *John Wesley's Prayer Book*. See, e.g., his comments in *Popery Calmly Considered* (Edinburgh, 1779), 4, §4.
37   Compare Article VI of the 1662 *Book of Common Prayer* with John Wesley's Article V.
38   "Statement of September 9, 1784."
39   See Journal, August 15, 1750, in *Works*, 20:357.
40   John Jones, *Free and Candid Disquisitions Relating to the Church of England, and the Means of Advancing Religion Therein* (London: A. Millar, 1749), 64–66. Other Prayer Book revisions of the eighteenth century made similar adjustments to the Psalms, including Benjamin Franklin's *Abridgement of the Book of Common Prayer* (London, 1773).
41   Charles Wesley, Sermon on 1 Kgs 18:21 in Newport, in *Sermons of Charles Wesley*, 121.
42   From the collect for the Second Sunday in Advent in the 1662 *Book of Common Prayer* and in Wesley's *Sunday Service*. John recommended this collect as a model prayer for use prior to the reading of the Scripture; see John Wesley, "To the Reader," in *The New Testament with an Analysis of the Several Books and Chapters* (London: Printed at the New Chapel, City-Road, 1790), ii.
43   "The New Creation," §18, in *Works*, 2:510.
44   In 1891 Charles S. Harrower published *Select Psalms* (New York: Eaton & Mains; Cincinnati: Jennings & Pye), which was inspired by and borrowed from Wesley's text of that name.
45   *The Doctrines and Discipline of the Methodist Episcopal Church in America*, §23, 8th ed. (Philadelphia: Parry Hall, 1792), 40–41.
46   Notes for §24 "Of Public Worship," in *The Doctrines and Discipline of the Methodist Episcopal Church in America*, with explanatory notes by Thomas Coke and Francis Asbury, 10th ed. (Philadelphia: Henry Tuckniss, 1798); facsimile ed., ed. Frederick A. Norwood (Rutland, Vt.: Academy, 1979), 121.

47 See, e.g., §43 in *The Doctrines and Discipline of the Methodist Episcopal Church* (Cincinnati: Cranston & Stowe; New York: Hunt & Eaton, 1888), 38. This paragraph also stipulated the reading of a "lesson" at the evening service.
48 For a study of worship and its changes, see my *American Methodist Worship* (New York: Oxford University Press, 2001), 8–25, 31–39.
49 The Revised Common Lectionary for Sundays and holidays, with readings from OT, Psalm, Epistle, and Gospel organized according to a three-year cycle, was produced by the North American Consultation on Common Texts (CCT) and the International English Language Liturgical Consultation (ELLC) and released to the churches in 1992.
50 *The Bicentennial Book of Worship of the African Methodist Episcopal Zion Church* (Charlotte, N.C.: A.M.E. Zion Church, 1996), 10.
51 The Revised Common Lectionary, with some United Methodist peculiarities, is included in *The United Methodist Book of Worship* (Nashville: United Methodist Publishing House, 1992), 227–37.
52 See, e.g., *The Book of Worship of the African Methodist Episcopal Church* (Nashville: The A.M.E. Sunday School Union, 1984), 212–20.
53 E.g., *Bicentennial Book of Worship*, 55–57.
54 The prayers authorized by The United Methodist Church's General Conference are in *The United Methodist Book of Worship*, 36–38, 54–80.
55 See n. 21, above.

CHAPTER 16: PASQUARELLO

1 Carl Trueman, "The Impact of the Reformation and Emerging Modernism," in *The Bible in Pastoral Practice: Readings in the Place and Function of Scripture in the Church*, ed. Paul Ballard and Stephen R. Holmes (Grand Rapids: Eerdmans, 2005), 93.
2 E. Brooks Holifield, *Theology in America: Christian Thought from the Age of the Puritans to the Civil War* (New Haven, Conn.: Yale University Press, 2003), 260; cf., idem, *God's Ambassadors: A History of the Christian Clergy in America* (Grand Rapids: Eerdmans, 2007), chs. 3–4.
3 D. Stephen Long, *John Wesley's Moral Theology: The Quest for God and Goodness* (Nashville: Abingdon, 2005), 118–19.
4 Horton Davies, *Worship and Theology in England: From Watts and Wesley to Martineau, 1690–1900* (Grand Rapids: Eerdmans, 1996), 143–83.
5 Holmer, *Grammar of Faith*, 203–4.
6 Nicholas Tyacke, "The Making of a Protestant Nation: 'Success' and 'Failure' in England's Long Reformation," in *England's Long Reformation: 1500–1800*, ed. Nicholas Tyacke (London: UCL, 1998), 124.
7 Outler, *Wesleyan Theological Heritage*, 101.
8 Mark McIntosh, "Faith, Reason, and the Mind of Christ," in *Reason and the Reasons of Faith*, ed. Paul J. Griffiths and Reinhard Hutter (New York: T&T Clark, 2005), 137. I am indebted to McIntosh's discussion of the "mind of Christ."
9 On the centrality of worship for Wesley, see Karen Westerfield Tucker, "Wesley's Emphasis on Worship and the Means of Grace," in *Cambridge Companion to John Wesley*, 225–44.

10   Sermon 122, "Causes of the Inefficacy of Christianity," in *Works*, 4:86–89.
11   Sermon 77, "Spiritual Worship," in *Works*, 3:99.
12   Jones, *Scripture*, 48.
13   *Explanatory Notes–NT*, 569–70.
14   For my understanding of vocational holiness, I am indebted to Eugene H. Peterson, *Under the Unpredictable Plant: An Exploration in Vocational Holiness* (Grand Rapids: Eerdmans, 1992), 21: "The congregation is the pastor's place for developing vocational holiness. . . . We preach the word and administer the sacraments, we give pastoral care and administer the community life, we teach and we give spiritual direction. But it is also the place in which we develop virtue, learn to love, advance in hope—*become* what we preach" (emphasis in original).
15   Sermon 19, "The Great Privilege of Those That Are Born of God," in *Works*, 1:442.
16   Sermon 84, "The Important Question," in *Works*, 3:189.
17   "Preface," in *Works*, 1:103
18   "Introduction," in *Works*, 1:14–15.
19   McIntosh, "Faith, Reason, and the Mind of Christ," 139.
20   Sermon 112, "On Laying the Foundation of the New Chapel," in *Works*, 3:586.
21   Here I would recommend the essays in *Reading the Bible in Wesleyan Ways*.
22   "An Address to the Clergy," in *Works*, 10:485–86.
23   See Matthew Levering, *Participatory Exegesis: A Theology of Biblical Interpretation* (Notre Dame, Ind.: University of Notre Dame Press, 2008).
24   Wainwright, *Methodists in Dialog*, 283–84.
25   Here I am indebted to the work of William M. Thompson, *The Struggle for Theology's Soul: Contesting Scripture in Christology* (New York: Crossroad, 1996), 15–21.
26   See Jones, *Scripture*.
27   "An Address to the Clergy," in *Works*, 10:493.
28   On Wesleyan spirituality, see Geoffrey Wainwright, "Trinitarian Theology and Wesleyan Holiness," in *Orthodox and Wesleyan Spirituality*, ed. S. T. Kimbrough (Crestwood, N.Y.: St. Vladimir's Seminary Press, 2002), 59–80.
29   William J. Abraham, "Wesley as Preacher," in *Cambridge Companion to John Wesley*, 110–11.
30   Abraham, "End of Wesleyan Theology," 22.
31   See Kenneth L. Carder, "Proclaiming the Gospel of Grace," in *Theology and Evangelism in the Wesleyan Heritage*, ed. James C. Logan (Nashville: Abingdon, 1994), 88–89: "The sociology of church growth has replaced the theology of personal and social transformation. It is indeed a sad commentary that United Methodist preachers are more familiar with pop sociology than with the theology of John Wesley. This preoccupation with institutional power and statistics contributes to preaching that is heavy on institutional promotion and narcissistic self-help and light on individual and communal salvation."
32   Vickers, *Invocation and Assent*, 37–38.
33   Gary Dorrien, *The Remaking of Evangelical Theology* (Louisville, Ky.: Westminster John Knox, 1998) 165–67.
34   "An Address to the Clergy," in *Works*, 10:485, 499.

35 For the following description I am drawing from "Letter on Preaching Christ," in *Works* (Jackson), 11:486–92.
36 "Letter on Preaching Christ," December 20, 1751, in *Works* (Jackson), 11:488–90.
37 "Letter on Preaching Christ," in *Works* (Jackson), 11:491.
38 "Letter on Preaching Christ," in *Works* (Jackson), 11:486, 492.
39 Maddox, *Responsible Grace*, 26–47.
40 Long, *John Wesley's Moral Theology*, 171–202.
41 Sermon 52, "The Reformation of Manners," in *Works*, 2:318.
42 Joseph Dunne, *Back to the Rough Ground: Practical Judgment and the Lure of Technique* (Notre Dame, Ind.: University of Notre Dame Press, 1993), 378.
43 Dunne, *Practical Judgment*, 378. See also the discussion in Michael Dauphinias and Matthew Levering, *Knowing the Love of Christ: An Introduction to the Theology of St. Thomas Aquinas* (Notre Dame, Ind.: University of Notre Dame Press, 2002): "Prudence not only includes making the right decision, but also demands we carry out the decision. In this way prudence links the intellectual and moral virtues (knowing and doing). Moreover, prudence shapes the other moral virtues insofar as it enables the just person to act justly, the courageous person to act bravely, and the temperate person to act with self-control" (57).
44 Dunne, *Practical Judgment*, 235.
45 Dunne, *Practical Judgment*, 358.
46 Michael S. Sherwin, *By Knowledge and by Love: Charity and Morality in the Moral Theology of Thomas Aquinas* (Washington, D.C.: Catholic University of America, 2005), 102.
47 Sherwin, *Knowledge*, 106–18.
48 Sherwin, *Knowledge*, 120.
49 John Mahoney, *Seeking the Spirit: Essays in Moral and Pastoral Theology* (London: Sheed & Ward, 1982), 67–69.
50 "An Address to the Clergy," in *Works*, 10:484.
51 "An Address to the Clergy," in *Works*, 10:499.
52 "An Address to the Clergy," in *Works*, 10:487–78, 491.
53 "An Address to the Clergy," in *Works*, 10:488–89.
54 "An Address to the Clergy," in *Works*, 10:498.
55 "An Address to the Clergy," in *Works*, 10:486–87.

CHAPTER 17: WARNER

1 Maddox, "Rule of Faith."
2 Maddox, "Rule of Faith," 13–14.
3 Maddox, "Rule of Faith," 13.
4 Maddox, "Rule of Faith," 17–19.
5 Maddox, "Rule of Faith," 2, 31. See also introduction to Sermon 43, "The Scripture Way of Salvation," in *Works*, 1:153–69.
6 "Scripture Way of Salvation," in *Works*, 1:156.
7 All Scripture citations are from the NRSV.
8 Matt 28:16-20; Mark 16:1-8; Luke 24:44-49; John 20:19-23; though Acts 1:8 is sometimes included as a commission text as well.

9   Matthew 28:16-20 appears in the Revised Common Lectionary only once in a three-year cycle, among the texts for Trinity Sunday (Year A). See J. Daniel Day, "A Fresh Reading of Jesus' Last Words: Matthew 28:16-20," *Review and Expositor* 104 (2007): 375–76.
10 *2008 Book of Discipline*, §§120–42.
11 David Bosch, "The Structure of Mission: An Exposition of Matthew 28:16-20," in *The Study of Evangelism*, ed. Paul W. Chilcote and Laceye C. Warner (Grand Rapids: Eerdmans, 2008), 73. See also Ulrich Luz, *Matthew 21–28: A Commentary* (Minneapolis: Fortress, 2005), 626–28, for a helpful and detailed history of interpretation of Matt 28:16-20.
12 Bosch, "Structure," 73. See also Luz, *Matthew 21–28*, 626.
13 Bosch, "Structure," 73–74. Bosch describes Philip Nicolai's (d. 1607) relative success in proving the Great Commission had been accomplished, as well as Justinian von Welz's published plea advocating for Matt 28:16-20 as an impetus for worldwide mission and Johann H. Ursinus' dismissal of von Welz. Interestingly, while Carey focuses on the commission in Matthew, he also refers to commission language in the longer ending of Mark, "Go into all the world, and preach the gospel to every creature" (16:15).
14 Sarah Heaner Lancaster, "Our Mission Reconsidered: Do We Really 'Make' Disciples?" *Quarterly Review* 23, no. 2 (2003): 117–30.
15 David J. Bosch, *Transforming Mission: Paradigm Shifts in Theology of Mission* (Maryknoll, N.Y.: Orbis, 1991), 340–41.
16 Maddox, "Rule of Faith," 14.
17 Maddox, "Rule of Faith," 14–15.
18 Scott J. Jones, *The Evangelistic Love of God and Neighbor: A Theology of Witness and Discipleship* (Nashville: Abingdon, 2003), 65, 65–98. Jones argues for evangelism as initiation into Christian discipleship without equating the reign of God with the church.
19 *Explanatory Notes–NT*, 138.
20 Lancaster, "Our Mission Reconsidered," 120.
21 Lancaster, "Our Mission Reconsidered," 120.
22 Lancaster, "Our Mission Reconsidered," 120.
23 Jones, *Evangelistic Love*, 139–40. A related tendency is the relinquishing of evangelistic ministry by congregations to parachurch organizations. Over the last two centuries, evangelism has largely been undertaken by mission societies and parachurch organizations rather than by congregations, most likely as a result of the local church's unwillingness to evangelize, particularly to specific groups historically marginalized from mainstream Christianity—traditionally the groups most open to the gospel.
24 Craig S. Keener, *A Commentary on the Gospel of Matthew* (Grand Rapids: Eerdmans, 1999), 716. "Signs are just as likely to create doubt and opposition as they are to make believers." Stanley Hauerwas, "Believing Is Seeing," Sermon, Duke Chapel, March 30, 2008.
25 Wesley, *Explanatory Notes–NT*, 138. See D. Edmond Hiebert, "An Expository Study of Matthew 28:16-20," *Bibliotheca Sacra* 149, no. 595 (1992): 342; Luz, *Matthew 21–28*, 622.

26 See Musa W. Dube, *Postcolonial Feminist Interpretation of the Bible* (St. Louis, Mo.: Chalice, 2000), for a poignant critique of the Great Commission and its use historically to validate a less than "liberating interdependence" method of mission (136–38).
27 "Sermon on the Mount IV," in *Works*, 1:533–34.
28 Maddox, "Rule of Faith," 18.
29 "Sermon on the Mount IV," in *Works*, 1:533–34.
30 Maddox, "Rule of Faith," 31.
31 Bosch, "Structure," 82. According to Bosch, references to Torah in Matthew include 5:19; 15:3; 19:17; 22:36.
32 Bosch, "Structure," 83.
33 Bosch, "Structure," 83. Jones argues for love of God and neighbor as the starting point for understanding and practicing evangelism since God's evangelistic love of the world is the central message of Scripture (*Evangelistic Love*, 33).
34 Bosch, "Structure," 83. See Matt 25:31-46.
35 See Mortimer Arias, "Centripetal Mission, or Evangelism by Hospitality," in *Study of Evangelism*, 424–35; Brad J. Kallenberg, *Live to Tell: Evangelism in a Postmodern World* (Grand Rapids: Brazos, 2002). "The church of Jesus Christ lives in gathering and scattering, in being called together and in being set forth. This dual motion is as necessary for her life as breathing in and breathing out is for human life." Walter Klaiber, *Call and Response: Biblical Foundations of a Theology of Evangelism*, trans. Howard Perry-Trauthig and James A. Dwyer (Nashville: Abingdon, 1997), 199. Klaiber offers a few pages of reflection on "The Praxis of Evangelism" at the conclusion of his biblical theology of evangelism.
36 Richard Bauckham, *Bible and Mission: Christian Witness in a Postmodern World* (Grand Rapids: Baker, 2003), 77; see esp. 72–80. See also Stephen B. Chapman and Laceye C. Warner, "Rethinking Evangelism and the Old Testament: Jonah and the Imitation of God," *Journal of Theological Interpretation* 2, no. 1 (2008): 43–69.
37 Arias, "Centripetal Mission," 424–26.
38 Arias, "Centripetal Mission," 429.
39 Bosch, "Structure," 76–77.
40 Bosch, "Structure," 77. In his commentary on Matt 28:16-20, Keener concurs with Bosch's and Schlatter's readings: "Because 'going' is a participle, we could read, 'as you go,' essentially 'on your way,' implying that one need not cross cultural boundaries to fulfill this commission" (Matthew, 718).
41 Bosch, "Structure," 77; citing Adolf Schlatter, *Der Evangelist Matthaus* (Stuttgart: Calwer, 1948), 23.
42 Bosch, "Structure," 77.
43 Bosch, "Structure," 77.
44 Bosch, "Structure," 78.
45 Bosch, "Structure," 78.
46 "Scripture Way of Salvation," in *Works*, 1:166.
47 *United Methodist Hymnal*, 35, 40; see also *Baptism, Eucharist, and Ministry* (Geneva: World Council of Churches, 1982).
48 According to Wilbert R. Shenk, "Since the 1940s certain biblical scholars have

argued that the Great Commission that Jesus gave to his disciples following the resurrection is essentially an ecclesiological statement." "New Wineskins for New Wine: Toward a Post-Christendom Ecclesiology," *International Bulletin of Missionary Research* 29, no. 2 (2005): 73, 79n6.

49 Keener, *Matthew*, 716–17.
50 See also "A Treatise on Baptism," in *Works* (Jackson), 10:188.
51 *Works*, 10:845.
52 See, e.g., Paul Minear, *Images of the Church in the New Testament* (Cambridge: Clarke, 2007); Michael Jinkins, *The Church Faces Death* (Oxford: Oxford University Press, 1999); Richard R. Gaillardetz, *Ecclesiology for a Global Church: A People Called and Sent* (Maryknoll, N.Y.: Orbis, 2008).
53 *2008 Book of Discipline*, 62.
54 George Hunsberger, "Evangelical Conversion toward a Missional Ecclesiology," in *Evangelical Ecclesiology: Reality or Illusion?* ed. John Stackhouse (Grand Rapids: Baker Academic, 2003), 107.
55 This is a broad statement, though instructive. Other groups such as Anabaptists seem more effective at both. See, e.g., John Howard Yoder, *Body Politics: Five Practices of the Christian Community before the Watching World* (Scottdale, Pa.: Herald, 1992).
56 For a fuller discussion of practices included among Wesley's means of grace, see his sermon, "Means of Grace," in *Works*, 1:378–97; see also Knight, *Presence of God*.
57 Hunsberger, "Evangelical Conversion," 119.

LIST OF CONTRIBUTORS

WILLIAM J. ABRAHAM, Albert Cook Outler Professor of Wesley Studies, Altshuler Distinguished Teaching Professor, Perkins School of Theology, Southern Methodist University

REGINALD BROADNAX, associate professor of philosophical theology, Hood Theological Seminary; and pastor, Trinity A.M.E. Zion Church, Woodruff, South Carolina

HUNN CHOI, senior pastor, Lexington United Methodist Church, Nicholasville, Kentucky

MEESAENG LEE CHOI, professor of church history and historical theology, Asbury Theological Seminary

KENNETH J. COLLINS, professor of historical theology and Wesley studies and director of the Wesleyan Studies Summer Seminar, Asbury Theological Seminary

JUSTO L. GONZÁLEZ, United Methodist pastor and theologian

JOEL B. GREEN, professor of New Testament interpretation and associate dean for the Center for Advanced Theological Studies, Fuller Theological Seminary

ELAINE A. HEATH, McCreless Associate Professor of Evangelism, Perkins School of Theology, Southern Methodist University

DOUGLAS M. KOSKELA, associate professor of theology, School of Theology, Seattle Pacific University

STEVEN J. KOSKIE, pastor, Antioch United Methodist Church, Simsboro, Louisiana

D. BRENT LAYTHAM, professor of theology and ethics, North Park Theological Seminary

RANDY L. MADDOX, William Kellon Quick Professor of Theology and Methodist Studies, Duke University Divinity School

MICHAEL PASQUARELLO III, Granger E. and Anna A. Fisher Professor of Preaching, Asbury Theological Seminary

JASON E. VICKERS, associate professor of theology and Wesleyan studies and director of the Center for Evangelical United Brethren Heritage, United Theological Seminary

ROBERT W. WALL, Paul T. Walls Professor of Scripture and Wesleyan Studies, School of Theology, Seattle Pacific University

LACEYE WARNER, associate dean for academic formation and programs, associate professor of the practice of evangelism and Methodist studies, and Royce and Jane Reynolds Teaching Fellow, Duke University Divinity School

DAVID F. WATSON, academic dean, vice president for academic affairs, and associate professor of New Testament, United Theological Seminary

KAREN B. WESTERFIELD TUCKER, professor of worship, Boston University School of Theology

INDEX OF NAMES

Abraham, W. J., 163, 197, 199–200, 254, 282n31, 282n33, 282n36, 291n54, 298n13, 299n4, 302n33, 303nn2–3, 306n9, 306n23, 312nn6–7, 312n11, 312n15, 313n19, 320nn29–30
Abrams, M. H., 288n15
Adam, A. K. M., 285n22
Adams, H., 288n15
Ahn, B.-M., 295n25
Albright, J., 69
Allen, R., 66, 289n6
Ambrose, 40
Andrews, D., 289n9
Aquino, M. P., 293n13
Arias, M., 270, 323n35, 323nn37–38
Aristotle, 53
Arthur, E., 296n54
Asbury, F., 79, 318n46
Astruc, J., 26
Athanasius, 302n30, 302n32
Augustine, 32, 40, 168, 204–5, 280n54, 284n78, 302n30, 314n35

Bacote, V., 301n22
Baily, J., 317n21
Baird, W., 59, 173, 288–89n25, 289n38, 307nn34–35
Baker, F., 277–78n6
Balla, P., 48, 287n5
Ballard, P., 319n1
Balthasar, H. U. von, 302n30
Barr, J., 174–75, 307nn39–40
Barth, K., 129, 302n30
Bartholomew, C. G., 297n65
Barton, J., 48, 287n2
Basil of Caesarea, 300n17
Bauckham, R., 269, 300n14, 323n36
Bauer, D. A., 298n5
Bayley, C., 278n19
Bebbington, D., 37, 285n16
Behr, J., 313n30
Benezet, A., 74–75
Bengel, J. A., 6, 52, 54–56, 59, 198, 278n12, 288n17, 288n19
Benson, J., 150
Berlin, I., 290n11
Beza, T., 5
Blair, W. N., 100, 294n11
Blaszczynski, A., 311n48
Booth, C., 222
Booth, W., 222

327

Borgen, O., 22, 281n20
Bosch, D., 270–71, 297n65, 322nn11–13, 322n15, 323nn31–34, 323nn39–45
Bowler, K., 295n29
Bray, J., 31
Brown, A. J., 294n9
Brueggemann, W., 114, 297n75
Bryant, B. E., 291n54
Bullen, D. A., 283n57
Burnet, T., 16, 280n58
Busby, R., 6
Butler, J., 27, 304n10
Buttrick, G. A., 287n4
Buxtorf, J., 6

Callen, B., 308n4
Calvin, J., 264
Cameron, R. M., 308n10
Campbell, T. A., 68, 282n38, 290nn14–15, 290n18, 303n3, 304nn15–16, 306n11, 312n12, 315n8
Carder, K. L., 320n31
Cardoza, C. F., 292n4
Carey, W., 265, 270–71, 322n13
Castelo, D., 303nn4–5, 305n33
Catherine of Genoa, 220
Cell, G. C., 278n15
Champion, J., 278n20
Chapman, S. B., 323n36
Charlesworth, J. H., 279n26
Charry, E., 120–21, 298n9
Chilcote, P. W., 322n11
Childs, B. S., 41, 185, 286n25, 309n31
Cho, M., 297n71
Choi, M. L., 293n3, 294n12
Chung, R. H., 297n66
Cintrón-Figueroa, J. N., 292n7
Clark, J. C. D., 303n7
Coke, T., 79, 150, 304n17, 318n46
Collins, J. J., 49–50, 54, 287nn7–9, 288nn10–12
Collins, K. J., 277n2, 281n13, 282n33, 283n44, 300n18

Collins Winn, C. T., 303n1
Colyer, E. M., 304n15
Cone, J. H., 298n8
Copenhaver, M., 297n77
Cotto-Thorner, A., 292n3
Coverdale, M., 5
Cragg, G. R., 281n26
Cranmer, T., 35
Cross, F. L., 306n6

Davies, H., 319n4
Davies, R., 315n17
Davis, E., 309n25
Dawes, S. B., 285n15
Dawson, J. D., 208, 315n54
Day, J. D., 322n9
Dayton, D. W., 301n22, 303n1
Deschner, J., 283n43
Dickerson, D. C., 66, 289nn7–8
Dodd, W., 24, 277n3, 282n37
Donner, H., 286n25
Dorrien, G., 320n33
Dube, M. W., 323n26
Dunne, J., 257–58, 321nn42–45
Dunston, A. G., Jr., 72, 290n32
Dwyer, J. A., 323n35
Dyk, Y. van, 295n28

Eckblad, B., 316n30
Edwards, J., 286n26
Eichhorn, J. G., 26, 173
Eldredge, L., 287n3
Elizondo, V., 89–90, 293n12
Espín, O. O., 293n14
Evans, J., 77, 291n62

Fausset, A. R., 288n19
Favreau, M., 290n11
Fee, G. D., 287n4
Feinberg, P. D., 301n21
Felder, C. H., 291nn62–63
Felton, G. C., 22, 281n25
Ferguson, D. S., 287n1
Fletcher, J., 150
Fleury, C., 278–79n21

Fowl, S. E., 40–41, 285–86n22, 286n24
Fox, M., 26
Francke, A. H., 52–55, 57, 59, 288nn20–25
Franklin, B., 318n40
Frei, H. W., 200–202, 313nn22–23, 313n9
Friederich, G., 290n30
Furly, S., 28, 283n55

Gabler, J. P., 48, 287nn3–4
Gaillardetz, R. R., 324n52
Garza, M. C., 292n8
Gaventa, B. R., 310n42, 311n44
Geisler, N. L., 301n21
Glascott, C., 280n56
Goheen, M. W., 297n65
González, J. A., 85, 293n10, 293n15
González, J. L., 85, 292n2, 292n4, 293nn10–11, 293nn16–17, 298n8
González, M. A., 293n14
Gorman, M. J., 314n36
Green, J. B., 26–27, 140, 206, 279n22, 283nn46–50, 284n78, 288n14, 294nn19–20, 297n65, 300nn14–15, 301n26, 303n1, 307n36, 308n4, 310n39, 312n1, 314n38
Griesbach, J. J., 173
Griffiths, P. J., 319n8
Grotius, H., 36
Gunter, S., 282n38, 303n3, 312n12
Guthrie, U. R. M., 298n4
Guyon, J.-M. B., 217, 315n19

Hall, T., 215–16, 315nn14–16
Hanhart, R., 286n25
Hardy, E., 279n35
Harkness, G. E., 308n10
Harrison, P., 303n9, 304n10
Harrower, C. S., 318n44
Harvey, V. A., 49, 287n9, 288n10, 288n12
Hasting, J., 287n9

Hauerwas, S., 308n11, 311n61, 322n24
Hays, R. B., 204, 309n23, 309n25, 311n58, 314n34
Heath, E. A., 316nn23–25, 316n30
Heber, R., 219
Heclo, H., 299n5
Heitzenrater, R. P., 277n6, 281n9, 299n19, 310n34, 315n9, 316n20
Helmer, C., 306n18, 307n39
Hempton, D. N., 291n41, 303n8
Henry VIII, 5
Henry, C. F. H., 301n23
Henry, M., 28, 281n18, 283n53, 284n61
Herbert of Cherbury, 304n10
Hessayon, A., 278n20
Hiebert, D. E., 322n25
Hobbes, T., 7, 26, 304n10
Holifield, E. B., 245, 319n2
Holland, C. L., 292n5
Hollinger, D. A., 299nn22–23
Holmer, P. L., 202–3, 313n28, 319n5
Holmes, S. R., 305n28, 319n1
Hooker, M., 311nn45–46
Howcroft, K. G., 285n12
Hoyt, T., Jr., 78, 291nn63–66
Hume, D., 33, 37
Hunsberger, G. R., 324n54, 324n57
Hunsinger, G., 313n29
Hunt, B., 100, 294n11
Hutchinson, J., 6–7, 16, 278n17
Hutter, R., 319n8
Hutton, J., 317n20
Hynson, L. O., 307n2

Irenaeus, 40

Jackson, T., 278n7 et passim
Jennings, T. W., Jr., 299n20, 310n41
Jenson, R. W., 164, 306n13
Jinkins, M., 324n52
Job, R. P., 316n28
John Paul II, 127, 298nn14–16
Johnson, J. A., 65, 289nn1–2

Johnston, R. K., 310n42
Jones, J., 237, 318n40
Jones, L. G., 310n42
Jones, S. J., 70, 77, 79, 173, 281n23, 282n29, 282n38, 284n1, 285n9, 286n27, 290nn22–24, 290nn28–29, 291n60, 298n3, 299n3, 302n37, 302n38, 303n1, 303n3, 306n10, 306n12, 307n33, 312n12, 315nn1–2, 320n12, 320n26, 322n18, 322n23, 323n33
Josephus, T. F., 56
Julian of Norwich, 168

Kallenberg, B. J., 323n35
Kang, S., 102, 105, 295n22, 296n36
Kant, I., 33, 150
Katz, D. S., 278n17
Keck, L. E., 286n33
Keene, N., 278n20
Keener, C. S., 322n24, 323n40, 324n49
Kelsey, D. H., 202, 313n27
Kim, E. M., 296n47
Kim, I.-J., 106, 296n40
Kim, J. H., 297n71
Kim, K. C., 295–96n33
Kim, N. Y., 104, 295nn30–31
Kim, S. C. H., 106, 293n4, 294n10, 296n42, 296nn44–45
Kim, Seyoon, 295n26
Kim, Sharon, 107, 295n27, 296n46, 297n66
Kim, Sinyil, 111, 296n35, 297n61
Kimbrough, S. T., 320n28
Kirby, J. E., 291n54
Kittel, G., 290n30
Klaiber, W., 298n4, 323n35
Knight, H. H., 281n8, 324n56
Koskela, D. M., 299n4
Koskie, S. J., 162, 284n1, 285n9, 286n30, 306n5
Kruschwitz, R. B., 308n5
Kugel, J. L., 298n2
Kümmel, W. G., 51–52, 288n16, 288–89n25, 289n33

Kwon, H., 295–96n33

LaCugna, C. M., 305n27
Lancaster, S. H., 266, 322n14, 322nn20–22
Landmesser, C., 306n18, 307n39
Langford, T. A., 290n14, 290n16, 310n42
Lankford, S., 220
Lavington, G., 27
Law, W., 151, 217, 279n39, 282n39, 304n20
Le, C. N., 295n31
Le Cène, C., 278n14
Le Clerc, J., 7
Lears, T. J. J., 192, 311n53, 311n55
Lee, J. Y., 104, 295n32, 296nn37–38, 297n67
Lee, S. H., 104, 112, 295–96n33, 297n63, 297n74
Lee, S.-Y., 295n24
Lee, U., 297n71
Lehmann, H. T., 284n62
Levering, M., 320n23, 321n43
Levinson, J. D., 288n13
Lewen, M., 278n7, 279n29
Lienhard, J. T., 138, 300nn8–9, 300n11
Livingstone, E. A., 306n6
Locke, J., 36–37, 43, 304n10
Lodahl, M., 303n1
Logan, J. C., 307n2, 320n31
Long, D. S., 311n61, 319n3, 321n40
Longden, L. R., 284n2, 312n5
Luther, M., 5, 29, 34–35, 264, 284n62, 285n4, 307n27
Luz, U., 322nn11–12, 322n25

Machado, D. L., 293n13
MacIntyre, A., 196, 198–200, 206, 313nn16–21
Macy, G., 293n14
Maddox, R. L., 43, 68–70, 76, 162, 165, 212, 263, 277n6, 278nn9–10, 278n12, 278n19, 279n40, 280n43, 282n38, 284–85n3, 285n11,

285n14, 286n34, 290n13, 291n56, 296n56, 299n20, 300n18, 302n39, 303n3, 306n3, 307n32, 312n7, 312n12, 314n35, 315n3, 316n21, 321n39, 321nn1–5, 322nn16–17, 323n28, 323n30
Mahoney, J., 321n49
Mannoia, K. W., 303n4
Marcion, 9, 279n32, 281n18
Marquardt, M., 298n4
Martínez, A. E., 85, 292n8, 293nn9–10
Martínez, J. N., 292n2
Martyn, H., 293n4
Matera, F. J., 311n44
Mathews, D. G., 291n41
McClain, W. B., 291n41
McDonald, L. M., 306n22
McIntosh, M., 319n8, 320n19
Meadows, P. R., 312n11
Meech, J. L., 311n49
Meeks, M. D., 310n34
Metzger, B. M., 163, 288n18, 306n7
Michaelis, J. D., 173, 289n33
Middleton, C., 15, 280n53, 317n20
Miguélez, L. C., 301n22
Miles, R. L., 282n38, 303n3, 312n12
Mill, J., 5, 278nn12–13
Miller, S. F., 290n11
Minear, P., 324n52
Mitchell, H. H., 289n9, 291n68
Moberly, R. W. L., 309n25
Moffett, S. H., 99, 293nn1–3
Molther, P. H., 31
Mostert, C., 297n76
Mulholland, M. R., Jr., 225, 316n31
Mullen, W. H., 280n2, 287n1
Myers, C., 311n54
Myung, J. S., 108, 296n49

Newport, K. G. C., 304n16, 317n10, 318n41
Newton, I., 7, 41
Newton, J., 38, 285n19
Nicolai, P., 322n13
Nieves, A. L., 295n22

Norwood, F. A., 318n46

Oden, T. C., 284n2, 312n5, 312n9
Okholm, D. L., 301n22
O'Malley, J. S., 298n4
Oord, T. J., 305n25
Orcibal, J., 217, 315nn17–18
Origen, 40
Oswald, H. C., 284n62
Otterbein, P. W., 69
Outler, A. C., 69, 196–200, 246, 283n52, 284n2, 285n8, 285n10, 285n13, 290nn16–17, 299n19, 303n3, 312nn6–9, 312n13, 313n18, 315n9, 319n7
Owens, E. C., 309n18, 311n53

Paik, L.-G., 294n9
Pak, S. Y., 113, 297nn71–72
Palmer, P., 220–22, 224, 316n23
Park, C., 102
Park, J., 294n12
Park, J. S., 307n1
Paul, Apostle, 4, 36, 42–43, 50, 56–57, 60, 67, 91, 105, 121, 124, 162, 173, 184, 187–92, 204–5, 228, 233, 285n10, 299n18, 310n40, 310n42, 311n45, 313n31, 314n35
Pearson, J., 16, 280n56
Pelikan, J. J., 284n62
Perkins, P., 290n38
Perry-Trauthig, H., 323n35
Peterson, E. H., 320n14
Philo, 56
Pinn, A. B., 77, 291n61
Pius XII, 127
Placher, W. C., 313n29
Poole, M., 281n18
Preston, T. R., 278n20, 285n17
Priest, R. J., 295n22
Priestley, J., 150
Propp, W. H., 287n7

Raboteau, A. J., 289n5
Rah, S.-C., 108, 114, 296n51, 297n73

Rahner, K., 305n27
Räisänen, H., 48, 287n5
Reedy, G., 303n9, 304n10
Rengstorf, K. H., 290n30
Reventlow, H. G., 304n10
Rhee, S., 102
Richardson, H. V., 67, 290n10, 291n67
Rieger, J., 281n12
Rivers, I., 278n20
Robertson, D. W., Jr., 280n54, 284n78
Robertson, J., 278n19
Robinson, A., 297n77
Rosado-Nunes, M. J., 293n13
Runyon, T., 303n3, 307n2
Rupp, G., 315n17
Russell, B. D., 113, 297n64
Rynkiewich, M. A., 297n79

Sánchez, G., 292n3
Sánchez, J. E., 292n8
Sanders, J. A., 174, 306n22, 307nn37–38
Sandys-Wunsch, J., 287n3
Schipani, D. S., 110, 296nn58–59, 297n60
Schlatter, A., 323nn40–41
Schlimm, M., 21, 279n32, 281n18
Scroggs, R., 289n39, 298n7
Segovia, F. F., 294–95n21
Semler, J. S., 173
Shawchuck, N., 316n28
Shelton, R. L., 281n22
Shenk, W. R., 323n48
Sherwin, M. S., 321nn46–48
Shin, E. H., 294n13
Shinn, A., 151, 304n23
Simon, R., 7
Sindiman, H. J., 296n39, 296n41
Smend, R., 286n25
Smith, W. T., 74, 76, 291n39, 291n42, 291n46, 291n54
Smith, W. W., 279n31
Spinoza, B., 7, 26, 304n10
Stackhouse, J., 324n54

Stafford, T., 308n16
Starkey, L. M., 281n24
Steinmetz, D. C., 307n27
Stendahl, K., 48–49, 287n4, 287n6
Stokes, M. B., 281nn14–15, 289n4
Stone, B. P., 305n25
Stookey, L. H., 316n29
Stuckenbruck, L. T., 287n4
Sugden, E. H., 283n51, 299n21, 306n15
Suh, N.-D., 295n25

Tanner, K., 298n9, 305n28
Taylor, J., 28
Telford, J., 277n3, 278n7, 278n18, 279n29, 279n35, 279n39, 280n56, 282n37, 285n14, 285n19, 296n53, 304n13, 317n12, 317n17, 317nn20–21
Terry, B., 308n5
Thérése of Lisieux, 220
Thiselton, A. C., 297n65
Thomas à Kempis, 12, 317n26
Thomas Aquinas, 40–41, 127, 285–86n22, 286n25, 321n43, 321n46
Thompson, R., 308n4
Thompson, W. M., 320n25
Thorsen, D., 303nn3–4, 307n1, 312nn9–10
Tolbert, M. A., 294–95n21
Torrance, I., 298n9, 305n8
Traina, R. A., 298n5
Troeltsch, E., 49, 54, 287n9, 288n12
Trueman, C., 319n1
Turner, G. A., 287n1
Turner, N. E., 190, 311nn48–52
Tyacke, N., 319n6

Ursinus, J. H., 322n13

Van Kirk, N. B., 299n4, 302n33
Vanhoozer, K. J., 285n22
Vasconcelos, J., 89–90
Vickers, J. E., 76, 197, 284–85n3, 291n43, 291n57, 299n4, 301–2n28, 302n33, 303n8, 304n11,

304n14, 304n16, 306n36, 312n6, 313n18, 320n32

Wainwright, G., 252, 300–301n19, 304n15, 316–17n8, 320n24, 320n28
Walker, S., 317n17
Wall, R. W., 162–63, 166, 196, 198, 200, 212, 280n55, 285n10, 286n27, 303nn4–5, 305n33, 306n4, 306n8, 306n14, 306n19, 312nn2–4, 314n35, 315nn4–5
Walvoord, J. F., 287n1
Warburton, W., 31, 151, 317n26
Warner, L. C., 322n11, 323n36
Warner, R. S., 100, 294n14, 294n16, 295–96n33, 296n34
Watson, D. F., 303n2
Watson, F., 285n22
Watson, K. M., 315n7
Watts, I., 234, 319n4
Webster, J. B., 139, 141, 144, 148, 156, 169, 298n9, 300n13, 301n24, 302n35, 303nn5–6, 305nn28–31, 307n26
Welz, J. von, 322n13
Wesley, C., 5, 20–21, 66, 140, 144, 150, 165, 217–20, 228–31, 234–36, 242, 245, 278n9, 300–301n19, 304n16, 316n22, 317n10, 317n16, 318n29, 318n31, 318n33, 318n41
Wesley, Samuel, 21, 278n11, 279n25
Wesley, Susanna, 21

Westerfield Tucker, K. B., 319n48, 319n9
Wheatly, C., 27
Wiles, M., 303n9
Willard, F., 222
Williams, C. W., 68, 290n14
Williams, J., 279n28
Willimon, W., 297n77, 312n1
Wilson, C., 282–83n42
Wilson, J., 309n24
Wilson, J. R., 310n42
Wogaman, J. P., 307n2
Wolfe, A., 309n18, 311n53
Wolterstorff, N., 306n18
Wood, C. M., 201, 204, 313n26
Work, T., 141, 301n25, 302nn30–31, 302n36
Wright, N. T., 43, 140, 286n33, 300n16, 301n20

Ybarrola, S., 109, 296n48, 296n57, 297nn68–69
Yi, M.-Y., 293nn6–8
Yi, S.-T., 295n22
Yoder, J. H., 324n55
Yoo, D. K., 294n18, 297n66
Yoo, J. C.-H., 296n52
Young, F. M., 208, 286n23, 315n53
Yrigoyen, C., Jr., 290n14
Yung, H., 108, 296n50

Zangeneh, M., 311n48

SUBJECT INDEX

affections: *see* tempers
analogy of faith, 15, 29, 42–45, 53–55, 57, 59, 61, 70, 79, 118, 173, 202–5, 208, 248–49, 252, 284n61
Apocrypha, 8–9, 21, 162, 237–38
authority, 68–70, 79, 135–39, 199, 290n14, 300nn8–12, 300n14, 313n19; of Christ, 261, 264, 272; church, 15, 70, 86, 96, 143–44, 182, 232, 274; of God, 300n7; individual, 38–39, 86; of masters over slaves, 71, 74; of nature, 16; of Scripture, 4, 11, 16–18, 23, 33, 68–69, 77–80, 85–87, 101, 126, 133–46, 147, 151, 153, 157, 242, 251, 299n4, 302n29, 302n34

biblical criticism, 26, 33–34, 36, 40–41, 48–54, 57, 121, 200–201, 204–5, 278n20, 285n17, 286n25, 287n2, 288n12, 294n21, 304n10, 307n34; *see also* canonical criticism; historical criticism
Book of Common Prayer, 9, 164, 229, 232, 237, 255, 316n5, 316n7, 318n37, 318n40, 318n42

canon, 7–11, 37, 43, 118, 124–25, 127–29, 131, 139–41, 143, 147, 161–76, 202, 205, 212, 243, 251, 279nn25–26, 282n31, 285n10, 300n8, 302n29, 306n7, 306n9, 306n13, 306n18, 306n22, 307n39, 310n33, 314n35; *see also* canonical criticism; canonical theism
canonical criticism, 162, 166, 182, 188, 307n34, 307n37
canonical theism, 282n33, 282n36, 299n4, 301n28, 302n33, 306n23
conference, -ing, 4, 12–18, 20, 263
creeds, 15–16, 37, 43–44, 69, 143, 149, 151, 155–57, 164, 190, 202, 231–33, 239, 280n56, 306n13

figural reading, 203, 208–9, 315n54

gambling and Scripture, 180–94, 308nn5–6, 308nn12–16, 309nn18–19, 311n48, 311n53

334

hermeneutics, 26, 28, 32, 35, 38, 41, 43, 68, 77–80, 82, 84, 111–13, 118, 120, 143, 151, 154, 161, 171–73, 188, 193, 195–210, 211, 253, 284n1, 285n9, 287n1, 287n4, 291n68, 296n47, 298n5, 301n21, 308n4, 312nn1–2, 313n22, 314n37, 316n8

historical criticism, 7, 47–62, 120, 131, 149, 163, 170, 173, 195, 197–200, 205, 252, 272, 279n22, 286n25, 287nn4–7, 287n9, 288n14, 307n36; *see also* biblical criticism; history

history: of Bible, 36–37, 99; Christian/Methodist/Wesleyan, 11, 77, 79, 81, 85, 92, 102, 106, 148, 152, 167, 174, 181, 196, 225, 228, 258, 274, 277n6, 285n16, 292n2, 293n1, 294n9, 294n12, 294n18, 296n40, 299n22, 308n10, 319n2; consideration of historical context, 6–8, 28, 37, 40, 47–62, 93, 120, 130, 168, 171, 173, 206, 251, 289n25, 312n14; of early Christianity, 4, 21, 164; genre of, 65; God's actions within, 44, 78, 105, 112, 131, 149, 170, 172, 175, 203, 209, 241; historical accuracy of Scripture, 11, 41, 135, 141–42, 145, 166, 284n78; *see also* historical criticism

holiness, 10, 13, 20, 29, 34–35, 39, 41–42, 44–45, 55, 101, 109, 111, 113, 115, 146, 147–48, 151–53, 181, 186, 214, 224, 249–51, 159, 161, 173, 180–81, 183, 185–87, 192–93, 209, 213–14, 216–17, 220, 223–25, 248–49, 251, 253–54, 256, 259–62, 268, 273, 303n6, 307n1, 308n11, 309n27, 310n32, 320n14, 320n28; of the church, 44, 193, 246, 259; of "conversation," 261, 263; of God, 25, 42, 185, 207, 230, 153, 155–58, 305n28; of Scripture, 38, 66, 99, 147–59, 303n4, 305nn32–35; of the writers of Scripture, 48; *see also* Holiness Movement; Holy Spirit

Holiness Movement, 220–21, 293n3

Holy Spirit, 10, 12–13, 17, 19–20, 22–23, 25, 27, 29–35, 38–40, 45–46, 95–97, 106, 114, 121, 129, 139–40, 143, 148, 155–59, 169–70, 172, 176, 207–9, 214, 218, 221, 227, 230–32, 242, 246–48, 250–52, 254–58, 260, 262, 264–67, 272, 275, 281n24, 300n17, 302n29, 302n31, 303n6, 305n33, 306n15, 310n38, 310n43, 311n56; gifts of, 27, 39, 95–96, 190, 216, 222, 249, 252, 258, 301n28; presence of, 24, 30, 32, 156–57, 213, 301n28; *see also* illumination; inspiration

homo unius libri: *see* "a man of one book"

illumination, 23, 25, 118, 121–22, 124, 140, 143, 164–65, 212–15, 219, 224–25, 248, 250–51, 255–56, 259, 261

inspiration, 23–24, 34–35, 43–44, 53, 141–43, 145, 180, 234, 263, 265, 267, 275, 317n26

lectio divina, 22, 213, 215–17, 225, 315n14

literal sense, 8, 28–30, 33–35, 39–42, 53, 57, 59–60, 71, 74, 77, 79, 88, 118, 196, 200–204, 207–8, 231, 252–53, 285n8, 285n22, 286n25, 286n 27, 286nn30–31, 304n10, 313n23, 313n29; *see also* plain meaning; spiritual sense

"a man of one book," 3–18, 23, 33, 212, 283n57

means of grace, 3, 19–32, 35, 39, 45, 122, 134, 139, 144–46, 158, 163–64, 168, 170, 186, 188–89, 192, 208–9, 213–14, 246, 249,

253, 255–56, 258, 268, 271–72, 274, 279n38, 281n8, 281n12, 315n9, 317n15, 319n9, 324n56

ordinance of God, 19, 213–14, 231, 238, 317n15

plain meaning, 24, 28–30, 33, 40–41, 53, 59–60, 182, 201, 212, 219, 221, 231; *see also* literal sense

quadrilateral, 68–70, 147, 151, 154, 179, 197, 284n2, 285n13, 290n14, 298n17, 303n3, 307n1, 312n9

revelation, 3, 10, 16, 23–24, 27, 36–37, 42, 44, 46, 52, 59, 65–66, 76, 79, 96, 117–32, 138–40, 152, 204, 207, 211, 215–16, 218–22, 225, 227–28, 246, 249, 252, 255–56, 259–60, 288n13, 298n13, 301n23

rule of faith, 15, 23, 43–44, 134, 149, 151, 153–55, 157, 163–64, 167, 202, 242, 280n43

salvation, 10, 17–18, 23, 35, 36, 38, 40, 42, 44, 60, 66, 80, 102, 106, 109, 118–19, 122, 129, 131–32, 134, 139–43, 144–45, 149, 154–56, 162, 167, 168–75, 193, 196, 202–5, 208–9, 215, 218, 224, 235, 237, 241–42, 256, 266, 274, 290n10, 291n67, 301n25, 302n31, 303n1, 304n23, 313n23, 320n31; *see also* "way of salvation"

science and Scripture, 16–17, 26, 41, 51, 56–57, 65, 71, 77, 79, 88, 132, 149, 246, 251, 301n21, 304n10

slavery and Scripture, 66–68, 71–79, 92, 111, 171, 187, 289n5, 290n11, 291n39, 291n41, 307n28

sola Scriptura, 15, 34, 36, 65, 68, 165, 170, 307n27, 313n19; *see also* "a man of one book"

soteriology: *see* salvation; "way of salvation"

Spirit: *see* Holy Spirit

spiritual sense, 29–30, 37, 57, 118, 201, 252–53

tempers, 3, 20, 27, 45, 248, 250, 259–61

text criticism, 7, 36–37, 51–53, 212, 289n25

Three-One God: *see* Trinity

tradition, 11, 15–16, 24, 36–37, 40, 43, 49, 57, 68–70, 85, 103, 118, 125, 128, 144, 151, 163–64, 170, 175–76, 197, 199, 246–47, 252, 254, 263, 268, 274–75, 285n13, 301n22, 303n3, 306n11, 313n20; Wesleyan, 4, 27, 68, 83, 117, 121–22, 126, 129–30, 144, 146–48, 166, 175, 179–81, 183, 196–200, 206, 245–46, 249, 263–64, 307n2, 310n34, 313n19

Trinity, 16, 44, 140, 148–57, 159, 168, 171–72, 242, 255, 272, 288n17, 304n11, 304nn15–16, 304n24, 305n27, 315n52, 316n8, 320n28

unity of Scripture, 15, 29, 44, 50, 53–54, 60, 173–76, 192, 196, 200–201, 204–5, 243, 288n13, 306n18, 307n39–40, 314n34

via salutis: *see* "way of salvation"

"way of salvation," 39, 44–45, 70, 101, 118, 145, 161, 168–73, 203–4, 213, 249, 251, 254–56, 263–68, 271–75, 286n31, 306n24, 321nn5–6, 323n46; *see also* salvation

worship and Scripture, 13, 17, 34, 101, 124, 134, 144, 155, 166–67, 172, 176, 216–20, 222, 224–25, 227–43, 252, 255, 258, 272–73, 319n48, 319n9

www.ingramcontent.com/pod-product-compliance
Lightning Source LLC
Chambersburg PA
CBHW021818300426
44114CB00009BA/217